Language and Language Use

A Reader
edited by
A. K. Pugh, V. J. Lee and J. Swann
at the Open University

Heinemann Educational Books
in association with
The Open University Press

Heineman Educational Books Ltd
22 Bedford Square, London WC1B 3HH
LONDON EDINBURGH MELBOURNE AUCKLAND
HONG KONG SINGAPORE KUALA LUMPUR NEW DELHI
IBADAN NAIROBI JOHANNESBURG
EXETER (NH) KINGSTON PORT OF SPAIN

Language and language use.
1. Language and languages
I. Pugh, A K   II. Lee, V J
III. Swan, J
400 P106

ISBN 0-435-10720-8 cased
0-435-10721-6 paper

Typeset by The Castlefield Press of Northampton and printed in Great
Britain by Biddles Ltd, Guildford, Surrey

Contents

Preface

These readings are selected for students taking the Open University course *Language in Use*. The course is produced in the Faculty of Educational Studies but is intended to have a broad appeal to Open University students. Hence it is both introductory in nature and wide in scope. The course is, in fact, a multidisciplinary approach to several aspects of the study of language in use in speech and in writing.

Since the readings are primarily chosen to complement other materials — notably correspondence texts, broadcasts and cassettes* — they in no sense constitute a course in their own right. Nevertheless, we appreciate and welcome the fact that Open University Readers are used outside the University and we have, so far as other constraints permit, attempted to produce a reasonably balanced and coherent selection.

A reader, like a course, requires and represents both collaborative effort and individual hard work. The selections here are chosen and introduced, in five sections, by the members of the course team who are responsible for particular parts of the course. Suggestions for articles were obtained from authors who wrote contributions to one of these parts and the selections, like the other constituents of the course, were subject to thorough comment and discussion with colleagues. Nevertheless, the major responsibility and credit for the sections rests with the section editors.

The course is in six blocks, the last of which is an updating and revision block and is, therefore, not represented here. Other blocks have roughly equal space in this reader.

Block 1, on Language Variation, has several functions in the course; not least to introduce the course and some of the methods and concerns in the recent study of linguistics. Thus Section 1 here includes a wide range of articles, most of them of necessity short, on methods used by linguists as well as, mainly, on social, interactive and affective aspects and effects of language variation.

*Most of these materials will be made generally available in 1982. Address any enquiries to: OUEE, 12, Cofferidge Close, Stony Stratford, Milton Keynes, MK MK11 1BY.

Section 2 takes up the concern with social aspects of language, but now with an emphasis on institutional uses of language, on intra-personal as well as inter-personal functions, and on political and ideological questions.

In Section 3, 'Language Learning and Language Teaching', the articles represent two of the points of view from which native language learning has been studied and discussed. Thus there are articles on the early development of child language, the stage which has been of most concern to linguists and psychologists, as well as on what should be taught as 'English' in British schools, a question of great concern to curriculum planners but also a matter of far broader interest.

'Language and Literature', Section 4, concentrates on one parti-cular area of description of literature − the structuralist approach, or more accurately a number of approaches which have been designated structuralist. Although the selections represent, in one sense, a debate over some fundamental issues, they all tend to stress the role of the reader as well as the text in our interaction with literature.

In Section 5, 'Talk and Text', methods for analysis of conversa-tion, discourse and text are examined. Account is taken of the relatively neglected role of the participants in reading a text as well as those taking part in a conversation.

In addition to the components of the course already mentioned, Open University students are required to study four set books alongside this reader. Since these, in a way, complete the selection it may be useful to note that they are:

P. Trudgill, *Sociolinguistics*, Harmondsworth, Penguin Books, 1974;
P.A. and J.G. de Villiers, *Early Language*, London, Fontana/ Open Books, 1979;
H. G. Widdowson, *Stylistics and the Teaching of Literature*, London, Longman, 1975;
J. Aitchison, *The Articulate Mammal*, London, Hutchinson, 1976.

Finally, we hope that our students and others who use this reader will find value, as we have, in this bringing together of work from several traditions which have bearing on how we use language and, the less resolved question, as to the extent to which it moulds and limits us.

A. K. Pugh

SECTION 1

Language and Language Variation

Introduction

The articles in this section give some indication of the scope of work available on Language and Language Variation. Gordon begins by reminding us that professional linguists by no means have an exclusive interest in language and that the distinction between lay or naive conceptions ('folk-linguistics') and professional and scholarly descriptions deserves more careful scrutiny.

Linguists, we should remember, are themselves members of the speech community. This observation is similar to that made in a later article (Turner, article 5.3) with regard to a sociologist's professional relationship to his data. Linguists, too, like their fellow speakers, have intuitions and beliefs about language and will use language which betrays their own upbringing and position in the community. The article by Fischer is an early study of the way our use of language, (whether we are linguists or not) reflects our social identities and the contexts of speaking. The major insights of this paper have been substantiated by much of the more rigorous and recent work in this field, and the paper deserves to be made more widely available.

Ervin-Tripp's paper is by now a classic one. Some of the interest of this article, which discusses how we choose terms of address, lies in the way the author's discussion is couched in a manner characteristic of linguists, rather than, say, sociologists or psychologists. That is, she is neither interested in statistical correlations between address terms chosen and the contexts of their use, nor in the decision sequence which might lead a speaker to select one or another term. Ervin-Tripp gives us, rather, a logical model of an address term system which has something of the quality of a linguist's grammar.

Silcock discusses McIntosh's work on Middle English dialects. The article reminds us that language variation is by no means a modern phenomenon. Also the topological model of variation, on which McIntosh's study is based, provides a most intriguing and practical application of a theory of geographical distribution of linguistic features to the location of the origins of particular medieval manuscripts.

1

The first reading made the point that many who would not consider themselves to be linguists, nevertheless may have a legitimate, scholarly interest in language. The next paper, by Giles, gives us a glimpse of some work in social psychology which has begun to show how subtle yet powerful our responses to different accents may be. The fact that our language variety is a part of our social identity is shown even more convincingly by Milroy, who, by careful fieldwork and detailed interpretation of data discusses the mechanism by which our friends, colleagues and relations help fashion and maintain our use of language.

In the last paper, Rosen discusses the difficulties involved in an attempt to tabulate the languages or language varieties spoken by London schoolchildren. These difficulties, Rosen argues, arise precisely because the choice and use of language has such great social significance and is best not approached as a 'brute fact'. Both papers, by Milroy and by Rosen, have been prepared specially for this reader. Each, in a different way, gives a rather fuller discussion of methodological questions and their relevance to theory than is customary. It is for this, as much as for their results alone, that they are included here.

D. Graddol

1.1 Who Counts as a Linguist?
J. C. B. Gordon

If a team of investigators were to collect statements about language and language-use from a large sample of native speakers of English, their data might include such items as:

1. I don't talk proper.
2. There's an awful lot of foul language used on TV these days — things like four-letter Anglo-Saxon words, you know.
3. A word is preceded and followed by a space.
4. Speech is a debased form of the written language.
5. You mustn't split infinitives.
6. German is gutteral.

If the investigators turned their attention to printed material they might find also the following:

7. 'Many teachers in schools and in colleges of Further Education see themselves that "Educational failure is primarily *linguistic* failure" . . .'
(Doughty and Thornton 1973:5)

8. 'One indication of declining standards in recent years was contained in evidence received from the Professor of English referred to in paragraph 1.3. He told us that distrust of formal teaching and formal structures of language has had considerable influence on the low standards of English among students today. He talked of "the dilution of English teaching, and the reaction against spelling and grammar." He stated further that students coming into higher education could often be described as semi-literate and he supplied samples of deplorable work to illustrate his contention.'
(From Mr Froome's 'Note of Dissent' on the Bullock Report 1975: 556).

Finally, it would be a great pity that the investigators would have missed the following statement made by a colleague of the present author at a committee meeting about five years ago:

9. Latin is a mathematically logical language.

All the above are statements about language, but they can all be

U.E.A. Papers in Linguistics 9 (1979), pp. 11-20, University of East Anglia, Norwich.

dismissed as examples of *folk-linguistics*, namely *misconceptions about language* — sometimes pathetic, sometimes silly, often amusing and occasionally sinister. Yet the concept of folk-linguistics is, in fact, problematical; for however one defines it, the concept suggests a neat division between popular notions or folklore about language on the one hand, and professional knowledge on the other. But, as Hymes has observed (Hoenigswald 1966: 23):

> We should be very careful in this area, however, especially if we call it "folk-linguistics", not to assume that we already have the truth as a standard of comparison for other conceptions of the nature of language.

Moreover, it is *not* the case that society contains an accepted and recognized body of experts on linguistics. Of course, academic linguists (in the sense of those who teach linguistics in universities and polytechnics) may like to think of themselves as just such a body; but there are other groups in society that could reasonably advance claims to expert knowledge, at least of certain areas of the subject — and how many academic linguists can claim more than partial knowledge of their subject? These groups include:

i.   Teachers in First Schools (and equivalents).
ii.   Teachers (at all levels) of English whether as a native or foreign language.
iii.   Teachers (at all levels) of foreign languages (including dead languages).
iv.   Lecturers who train teachers of reading and English, and foreign languages.
v.   Translators and interpreters.
vi.   Speech therapists.
vii.   Anthropologists.
viii. Philosophers.

With the growth of interdisciplinary studies an increasing number of educationists, psychologists and sociologists have come to take a professional interest in language.

A few years ago Crystal (1969: 1) remarked that large sections of the population are unaware of the existence of linguistics as an academic discipline:

> 'Linguistics' is a word which seems particularly prone to misunderstanding. To begin with, when people hear the name for the first time, they usually do not ask 'What *is* Linguistics?', but 'What *are* Linguistics?' — as if the word referred to a collection of 'linguisticky' objects conveniently gathered together for examination, like pictures at an exhibition. It is not really surprising, though, that people should react in this way . . . The subject has not been in existence

long enough to be generally recognised as the name of an intellectual discipline. It has been studied in an academic context only since the turn of the century, and it has really developed in British universities only since about 1960.

The implicit claims of the academic linguists to special knowledge and expertise have not gone unchallenged; nor is the nature and scope of their work necessarily well understood. The following letter published in *The Guardian* on 21 January 1978 illustrates both these points:

Sir, — Your feature on psychobabble (January 14) and subsequent correspondence do not seem to offer an explanation for the linguistic origins of the phenomenon. Theoretically, one should be able to consult linguistic scientists on this question, but they themselves have been so bewitched by American technocratic jargon that an impartial study would be unlikely: at a recent lecture on linguistics I discovered that the ability to understand is now a matter of 'being programmed to process the speech-stream', and a recent book on the language of children (beg your pardon — child language) by Professor Crystal is subtitled: 'An Overview for the Teaching and Therapeutic Professions.'

No help from that source, but perhaps the word 'overview' itself can give us a clue. It is derived from the German *überblick* [sic] just as 'hopefully' (meaning 'one hopes that') and 'no way' ('by no means') are derived from *hoffentlich* and *keineswegs*.

Similarly, the German compound is so conveniently streamlined (and sounds so impressive) that its use has become virtually obligatory: no self-respecting academic would speak of a 'way of life,' let alone of a *modus vivendi*: it is now a 'life-style' (*Lebensstil*).

Perhaps one could derive from this the hypothesis that the postwar influx of Germans, particularly scientists, into the United States is beginning to have as profound an influence on American English as that of the Normans on Old English. Whether it need happen here is a matter for the media and schools to decide.

E. Burke

Eltham College,
London SE9.

(For an example of a gratuitously offensive challenge see Hegarty's review of Trudgill (1965) in the *Times Educational Supplement*, 30 January 1976, p. 24.)

A further difficulty arises from the fact that Chomskyan linguistics has proclaimed that the native speaker's intuition is the sole arbiter of grammaticality. This doctrine — widely accepted among academic linguists — is the equivalent, for linguistics, of the doctrine of the priesthood of all believers in Protestant theology. That some academic linguists do not accept the doctrine is of little relevance since they all rely on native speaker intuition in this area, whether they wish to acknowledge the fact or not: after all, grammatical rules do not leap up at the linguist out of a corpus of data! But why does a linguist who is only too ready to accept the native speaker's verdict that the sentence *What Ann did to the Lake District was explore it* is ungrammatical, wince if the same native speaker says that *It's me* and *He don't know nothing* are also ungrammatical? To argue that in the latter two cases the intuition is not a *bona fide* one but the result of instruction really is not good enough. How can one be absolutely sure that the intuition that leads the informant to judge the first example ungrammatical is not the result of instruction too? In fact, the very idea of academic linguists distinguishing between genuine and phoney intuition is ludicrous.

But why is the 'linguistic priesthood of all native speakers' confined to questions of grammaticality? Why is it that if a native speaker says 'My intuition tells me that *The new headmaster changed his tie and the whole system* is ungrammatical except as a joke' his intuition is accorded the status of truth, while if he says 'My intuition tells me that Standard English is more logical than regional dialects' his intuition is simply regarded as an interesting curiosity – a mere datum? A number of academic linguists have touched on this problem briefly. Labov, for example, distinguishes between speakers' *unconscious* and *overt* responses and notes that the former are 'extremely consistent and uniform' whereas 'The inadequacy of people's overt remarks about their own language is directly reflected in the fact that there are only a few words that they use to convey the subjective response that they feel. For example, nasal.' (Hoenigswald 1966: 23). These observations, though useful, do not clarify the status of native speaker intuition. Another approach is to treat all reported native speaker intuitions as mere data having no necessary inherent truth-value. This seemingly attractive solution, however, leaves out of account the academic linguist's own native speaker intuitions, which must necessarily enter into his work, especially at the stage where hypotheses are formulated. The theoretical status of the relationship between the academic linguist *qua* linguist, native speakers and the academic linguist *qua* native speaker himself is unsatisfactory and is likely to remain so for the foreseeable future.

The relationship between the academic linguist's knowledge and that of other professions concerned with language is also beset with problems. Some years ago, when the range of linguistics papers available in the final examination at the University of East Anglia was extended a working party was set up to define more closely which areas of the subject fell within the scope of each paper and to draw up specimen question papers. When the specimen paper on Applied Linguistics was

---

*The asterisk is used by linguists to indicate that a sentence is ungrammatical or anomalous in some way. [*Editor's note*]

discussed some members of the working party argued that a number of the questions could be answered without a 'specialist' knowledge of linguistics. One question in particular attracted unfavourable comment. It read: 'Discuss the case for and against the use of the i.t.a. in the infant school.' One member of the working party, whose wife is a primary school teacher, said disparagingly: 'My wife could write a perfectly good answer on that question!' After the meeting another colleague said: 'If that is really true, then his wife's a linguist even if she doesn't know all the gobbledegook.'

There is evidence of at least the makings of considerable tension between academic linguists and some of the other professions listed above (pp.3—4), in particular educationalists, educational psychologists and schoolteachers. The most contentious issue concerns the wholesale uncritical acceptance of the verbal deficit hypothesis (and Bernstein's early papers) by some educationalists, educational psychologists, and specialists in the sociology of education and the subsequent, allegedly widespread dissemination of these theories in Colleges and Departments of Education. Although the deficit hypothesis has been attacked by some educationalists (for example, Keddie (1972) and Flude (1974)), some of the fiercest criticism of both the hypothesis and Bernstein's sociolinguistics (or at least aspects of it) has come from academic linguists, for example, Labov (1969), Coulthard (1969), Trudgill (1975), Stubbs (1976b), Dittmar (1976)[1]. On one level, the attacks have been concerned with a specific set of propositions, but on a more fundamental level many of them in effect deny the claims of the educationalists concerned to be taken seriously as linguists until and unless they adopt the same basic framework as the academic linguists. The general thrust of most of the attacks is that the deficit hypothesis and most of the disseminations of both this hypothesis and of Bernstein's work — and perhaps even Bernstein's sociolinguistics itself — are deeply rooted in folk-linguistic value-judgements on non-standard dialects. Although the attacks are directed for the most part against the original proponents of the verbal deficit hypothesis (and Bernstein), popularizers are sometimes criticized as well. For example, Trudgill (1975: 92-97) takes Herriot (1971) and Wilkinson (1971) severely to task and also criticizes Creber (1972), and Rogers (1976: 22-23) attacks Sugarman (1970). Ultimately, the linguistic knowledge and conceptions of schoolteachers come in for criticism too. Stubbs (1976a: 35) writes:

> I suspect that many linguists assume that people as a whole — and teachers in particular — are now relatively familiar with standard linguistic (non-prescriptive) views of language. Unfortunately this is often not so, and in many cases confusion and misunderstanding of basic concepts reign supreme.

Rogers (1976: 20) observes:

> The almost religious fervour with which the work of Bernstein is

associated has tended to lead to a generation of newly trained teachers with a veneration of his work hardly matched by their understanding of it. I may be accused of overstating my case in the use of the words 'almost religious fervour.' However, my own researches indicate that Bernstein's work is now firmly part of the core of orthodox ideas current in much educational and teacher training thinking.

Trudgill (1975: 93) writes:

The current confusion of 'restricted code' with non-standard dialect in the minds of many teachers and educationists is particularly unfortunate. It has meant that, at a time when many people in education are beginning to recognise that non-standard dialects are in no way inferior, others have had their prejudices about non-standard speech reinforced.

Apart from Bernstein's vigorous attempts to dissociate his work from the verbal deficit hypothesis, there has been virtually no debate between the two sides, despite the fact that in some cases the academic linguists have attacked with unusual ferocity. Indeed, at least in this country, the silence on 'the other side' has been so complete as to raise doubts as to whether it is even aware that it is under fire!

What characterizes an academic linguist is not so much his specialized knowledge as a certain perspective on language. Simply to call this perspective *scientific* is facile. The linguistic perspective is essentially a framework of basic assumptions about language. Some of the more important of these include the following:

1. There is no objective support for value-judgements on the (alleged) intrinsic merits of different languages, dialects, accents, styles or (except in the case of pathological disorder) idiolects.
2. All people acquire at least one dialect of the language spoken in the immediate environment in which they grow up (except in a few, extremely rare pathological cases).
3. Neither language itself nor any variety of it have any mysterious properties that make for misinformation, deception or that pre-destine people to academic success or failure. It is always *people* who misinform, deceive, succeed, fail, and fail others.
4. That kind of concept of correctness which has preoccupied so many self-styled grammarians in the past and has produced the well known traditional lists of 'don'ts' is wholly alien to the true nature and function of language. At its worse, as epitomized by Fowler (1926), it is a form of esoteric aestheticism which seeks to pretend that 'correct English' is the preserve of a handful of *cognoscenti*, well versed in English literature (from *Beowulf* to Virginia Woolf) and the Classics.
5. With some exceptions, discussed below, there is no justification for prescriptions — for telling people how to speak.

The first four statements are straightforward, but the last raises more problems than is generally acknowledged. Few academic linguists, if indeed any, would argue that no-one should ever be told anything about how to speak or write. To deny the need for teaching reading and writing would be absurd; and since writing is something rather different from just a graphic representation of speech, children will normally need some guidance on a number of stylistic conventions. It is, of course, very much open to question whether *all* the conventions traditionally associated with the written language should be enforced, and since they are arbitrary and not rational there is an excellent case for re-examining them and rejecting some. But none of this involves teaching the *basic grammatical rule-system*. In some cases, it may be necessary to draw children's attention to the fact that in formal contexts one normally writes Standard English and that this deviates in some minor respects from their own dialect. Where this is necessary it is important that teachers and pupils should be fully conscious of the fact that they are dealing with conventions and dialect differences and not with any absolute criteria of correctness.

It is desirable that everyone should learn to communicate effectively, both in speech and writing. Most children will need some guidance on, for example, how to write to strangers, such as potential employers. Some may need advice on various sociolinguistic conventions − for example, on the likely effects of using taboo words in certain kinds of contexts and with certain kinds of people. Similarly, there is no harm in telling some adults that the use of jargon when addressing non-specialists may offend rather than impress. But all these are purely questions of etiquette, practical hints and conventions − and it is as such that they should be taught. It may even be useful to warn children and adolescents that some people positively *revel* in taking offence at regional dialect forms, spelling mistakes and curious things that they like to label *solecisms*. No-one should see any of this as teaching 'grammar' or teaching people to 'talk properly'[2].

As can be seen from this brief discussion, the rejection of prescriptivism needs some qualification, and there are still some unresolved ambiguities as to exactly what academic linguistics understand by *prescriptivism* and what kinds of prescription they are willing to accept as legitimate. Superficially, matters might be clarified by distinguishing between the case for rejecting prescriptivism in linguistics itself − the actual study of language − on the one hand, and in society in general on the other; but linguistics has no well-defined 'cut-off' point. Although this is particularly obvious with sociolinguistics, it applies to all areas of linguistics.

The problems associated with the rejection of prescriptivism serve to highlight the importance of keeping the academic linguists' basic assumptions under constant review. Not only have a number of folk-linguistic concepts − such as *word, sentence, grammar, the English language*, etc. — been taken over into linguistics, but the basic framework of assumptions requires further clarification. In the last analysis these assumptions are not only a matter of insight, but also of deliberate choice.

Notes

[1] Some academic linguists, for example Halliday, Hasan and Turner, are much more sympathetic to Bernstein's ideas, especially those to be found in his papers published in and after 1962.

[2] It is worth noting that the Bullock Report (1975: 169) suggests that many schoolteachers understand something very different by the term *grammar* from the meaning that it has in linguistics:

> In our discussions with teachers it became obvious that the term was often being used to include sentence construction, precis, paragraphing, vocabulary work, punctuation, and more besides.

References

Bullock Report (1975) *A Language for Life: Report of the Committee of Inquiry Appointed by the Secretary of State for Education and Science under the Chairmanship of Sir Alan Bullock, FBA*, HMSO; London 1975.

Coulthard, M. (1969) 'A Discussion of Restricted and Elaborated Codes', in Open University, *Language in Education: A Source Book*, prepared by the Language and Learning Team at the Open University, Routledge and Kegan Paul in association with the Open University Press; London 1972, 95-101.

Creber, J. W. P. (1972) *Lost for Words: Language and Educational Failure*, Penguin Books in association with the National Association for the Teaching of English; Harmondsworth, Middlesex 1972.

Crystal, D. (1969) *What Is Linguistics?* 2nd. ed., Edward Arnold; London 1969.

Dittmar, N. (1976) *Sociolinguistics: A Critical Survey of Theory and Application*, translated from the German by P. Sand, P. A. M. Seuren and K. Whiteley, Edward Arnold; London 1976.

Doughty, P. and Thornton, G. (1973) *Language Study, the Teacher and the Learner*, Edward Arnold; London 1973.

Flude, M. (1974) 'Sociological Accounts of Differential Educational Attainment', in M. Flude and J. Ahier (eds.), *Educability, Schools and Ideology*, Croom Helm; London 1974, 15-52.

Fowler, H. W. (1926) *A Dictionary of Modern English Usage*, Oxford University Press; London 1926.

Herriot, P. (1971) *Language and Teaching: A Psychological View*, Methuen; London 1971.

Hoenigswald, H. M. (1966) 'A Proposal for the Study of Folk-Linguistics', in W. Bright (ed.), *Sociolinguistics*, Mouton; The Hague 1966, 16-26.

Keddie, N. (1972) 'Social Differentiation II. Cultural Deprivation: A Case in Point', in *Sorting Them Out: Two Essays on Social Differentiation*, Open University Press, Milton Keynes, Buckinghamshire (Course E282, Units 9-10), 55-140.

Labov, W. (1969) 'The Logic of Nonstandard English', in J. E. Alatis (ed.), *Report of the Twentieth Annual Round Table Meeting on Linguistics and Language Studies*, Georgetown University Press, Washington, D.C. 1970 (*Georgetown Monograph Series on Languages and Linguistics*, No. 22, 1969), 1-39.

Rogers, S. (1976) 'The Language of Children and Adolescents and the Language of Schooling', in S. Rogers (ed.), *They Don't Speak Our Language: Essays on the Language World of Children and Adolescents*, Edward Arnold; London 1976, 13-32.

Stubbs, M. W. (1976a) Review of Trudgill (1975), *Nottingham Linguistic Circular*, Vol. 5 (1975-1976), No. 1, 35-38.

Stubbs, M. W. (1976b) *Language, Schools and Classrooms*, Methuen; London 1976.

Sugarman, B. (1970) 'Social Class, Values and Behaviour in School', in M. Craft (ed.), *Family, Class and Education: A Reader*, Longman; London 1970, 241-254.

Trudgill, P. (1975) *Accent, Dialect and the School*, Edward Arnold; London 1975.

Wilkinson, A. (1971) *The Foundations of Language: Talking and Reading in Primary Schools*, Oxford University Press; London 1971.

1.2 Social Influences on the Choice of a Linguistic Variant
John L. Fischer

During the year 1954-55 my wife and I were engaged in a study of child-rearing in a semi-rural New England village.[1] In the course of the study I had occasion to record two or more interviews on Audograph discs or tapes, with each of the 24 children of our sample. Previously certain inconsistencies in the children's speech had attracted my attention, especially the variation between -*in* and -*ing* for the present participle ending.[2] Accordingly, in transcribing the discs and tapes, I decided to note the choice of these two variants, and this paper is intended to summarize and discuss this information.

To begin with, all of the 24 children, except three, used both forms to some extent at least. The three exceptions used only the -*ing* form, and since they were less loquacious than most of the other children, it is possible that a larger sample of their speech would have revealed the use of the other variant as well. This may then be regarded as a case of so-called free variation of two linguistic forms within a local speech community, and within the speech of most individual members of our sample community. In general, the choice of one or the other of the variants would not affect the denotation of acts, states, or events by the word.

'Free variation' is of course a label, not an explanation. It does not tell us where the variants came from nor why the speakers use them in differing proportions, but is rather a way of excluding such questions from the scope of immediate inquiry. Historically, I presume that one could investigate the spread of one of these variants into the territory of another through contact and migration, and this would constitute one useful sort of explanation. However, another sort of explanation is possible in terms of current factors which lead a given child in given circumstances to produce one of the variants rather than another, and it is this which I wish to discuss here.

Before discussing the determinants of selection of the variants it will be helpful to understand a little of the general background of the data. The 24 children in our sample consisted of an equal number of boys and girls, both divided into two equal age groups, ages 3-6 and 7-10. By the time the recordings were made my wife and I had been observing

Word 14 (1958) pp. 47-56.
This reading is an edited version of the original article.

the children periodically for eight to ten months and most of the children were fairly well acquainted with us. Most of the children were interviewed in an office in our house, which was located in the middle of the village. Most of the children had visited our house before, some a number of times. Four younger children who had not were interviewed in their own homes. Three general types of text were obtained:

1. Protocols for all children for a verbal thematic apperception test (TAT) in which all the children were asked to make up stories starting out from short sentences given by the investigator.
2. For older children only, answers to a formal questionnaire.
3. For a few of the older children, informal interviews asking them to recount their recent activities.

I shall present first some counts of variants in the TAT protocols, since this test was administered to all the children. As is shown in Table I, a markedly greater number of girls used *-ing* more frequently, while more boys used more *-in*.

Table I. Number of children favoring *-ing* and *-in* variant suffixes in TAT protocols according to sex

	-ing > *-in*	*-ing* ≤ *-in*
Boys	5	7
Girls	10	2

Chi square: 2.84; $0.5 < P < .1$ (by two-tailed test)

This suggests that in this community (and probably others where the choice exists) *-ing* is regarded as symbolizing female speakers and *-in* as symbolizing males.

Within each sex, differences in personality are associated with the proportion of frequency of *-ing* to *-in* as illustrated in Table II.

Table II. Frequency of use of *-ing* and *-in* in TAT protocols of two boys

	-ing	*-in*
'Model' boy	38	1
'Typical' boy	10	12

Chi square: $19.67; P < .001$

The first boy was regarded by his teacher and others as a 'model' boy. He did his school work well, was popular among his peers, reputed to be thoughtful and considerate. The second boy was generally regarded as a 'typical' boy — physically strong, dominating, full of mischief, but disarmingly frank about his transgressions. The 'model' boy used almost exclusively the *-ing* ending here, while the 'typical' boy used the *-in* ending more than half the time, as shown above.

In Table III below, one may also note a slight tendency for the *-ing* variant to be associated with higher socio-economic status, although this is not statistically significant with a sample of this size. The community studied is fairly small and does not have strong class lines, which is probably why more marked results did not appear.[3]

Table III. Number of children favoring *-ing* and *-in* endings according to family status

	-ing > *-in*	*-ing* ⩽ *-in*
Above Median	8	4
Below Median	7	5

Chi square (corrected): 0; P > .9

Besides asking *who* uses which variant and how much, we may also ask whether there are situational differences in *when* a single speaker uses these variants. One variant in the situation may be described as degree of formality: in the children's terms I would think of this as degree of similarity to a formal classroom recitation. The best child to examine for this variable is the 'model' boy of Table II since he was interviewed in all three situations mentioned above and was obligingly talkative in each. As Table IV shows, the frequency of choice of variants changed from an almost exclusive use of *-ing* in the TAT situation to a predominance of *-in* in the informal interviews.

Table IV. Frequency of *-ing* and *-in* in a ten-year-old boy's speech in three situations in order of increasing informality

	TAT	Formal Interview	Informal Interview
-ing	38	33	24
-in	1	35	41

Chi square: 37.07
P < .001

Of course, these three situations should not be regarded as exhaustive of the frequency range of these variants in this boy's speech. In the interviews I myself used the *-ing* variant consistently and this probably influenced the informant's speech somewhat. Probably in casual conversation with his peers the *-in*/*-ing* ratio is even higher than in the informal interview.

Another measure similar in implication to the frequency of variants by type of interview would be differences in frequency between the beginning and later parts of a single interview. Especially in the TAT protocols, which are the most formal texts, I noticed for a number of children that the *-ing* frequency was higher in the beginning of the interview and later dropped off, presumably as the child became more relaxed and accustomed to the situation. In only one child was the reverse trend noted, and there are reasons to believe that this particular child may have become more tense during the administration of the test.

A linguist might ask whether there is any association between the suffix variant and specific verbs. The corpus is not large enough to establish stable frequency indices for the suffixes of individual words, but there is certainly a trend for markedly 'formal' verbs to have the *-ing* suffix and markedly 'informal' verbs to have the *-in* suffix. The first boy in Table II above, for instance, used *-ing* in *criticizing, correcting, reading, visiting, interesting*, and used *-in* in *punchin, flubbin, swimmin, chewin, hittin*. For some common verbs, however, such as *play, go*, and *do* he used both alternatively. Probably only a few verbs are formal or informal enough in their connotations so that the same variant would always be used with them. Of course, the choice of verb vocabulary is itself related to personality and situational factors.

In brief, then, the choice between the *-ing* and the *-in* variants appear to be related to sex, class, personality (aggressive/cooperative), and mood (tense/relaxed) of the speaker,[4] to the formality of the conversation and to the specific verb spoken. While these are 'free variants' in the standard type of description of languages in which only grammatical facts and differences in none but 'denotative' meaning are taken into account, if we widen our scope of study to include the meaning of these variants to the conversants we might call them 'socially conditioned variants,' or 'socio-symbolic variants,' on the grounds that they serve to symbolize things about the relative status of the conversants and their attitudes towards each other, rather than denoting any difference in the universe of primary discourse (the 'outer world'). [. . .]

The untrained listener will not, of course, generally be able to reproduce or identify the differences in the speech of others whom he encounters, unless he is an accomplished mimic. But he does react to these differences by making interpretations about the social situation on the basis of them and will be able to tell when a speaker is talking like a woman, like an upper class person, like a relaxed person, etc., even though he cannot specify all the variant forms on which he bases his judgment. (This is not to deny the presence or importance of other 'non-linguistic' features of speech as well as things entirely unconnected with speech such as dress, physical appearance, gestures, etc., which also serve as cues for judgments of the conversational situation.)

In analyzing socio-symbolic variants there will obviously be a certain amount of association between variant series. In many of the series at least one variant could be distinguished as 'formal', and another as 'informal.' But it is a question for empirical investigation whether this distinction applies to all variant series, and, if so, with how much force. I have suggested above a number of factors which influence the *-in/-ing* distinction. Conceivably they all bear on formality, that is, compliance, tenseness, femaleness, and high class all make for formal behaviour. But even if this is true for these factors in American culture, are they a unitary complex in all cultures, and may there not be other social factors affecting socio-symbolic variants which are independent of the formality complex? Are variants associated with being female always associated as well with formality? In three languages with which I am acquainted, English, Japanese, and Ponapean, I can think of a number of instances where this link is found, but there also appear to be exceptions. In Ponapean, for instance, a minority of women have an unusual allophone for the *r* phoneme, but this seems to have no relation to the degree of formality. Lisping in English is regarded as feminine, but would indicate little about degree of formality. [. . .]

I have been stressing here the synchronic implications of socio-symbolic variants. The diachronic implications are at least equally interesting. Obviously the threshold [of formality] for a given variant does not *necessarily* remain the same, generation after generation. If a particular variant has for whatever reason greater prestige, it will gradually be adopted in more situations by more people: its threshold will be lowered. But as its threshold is lowered and approaches universality in the speech community, its socio-symbolic load is reduced and eventually vanishes. One could hardly convey much of an air of informality, for example, by saying [ə] for the indefinite article, though saying [ey] would be quite stilted. But presumably new series of variants keep arising to replace those which achieve uniformity in this way.

Now what is meant by 'variants of greater prestige'? One could determine which of a pair of variants had the greater prestige by noting which tended to 'spread' when two conversants who in other situations differed in their choice came together. But the grounds of prestige clearly vary according to individuals and societies. A variant which one man uses because he wants to seem dignified another man would reject because he did not want to seem stiff. Societies likewise have characteristic average value preferences. Using the variable of formality, it is quite possible that one society would show a tendency, at least in some situations, to show a preference for adoption of formal forms of speech, and another in analagous situations show a preference for informal forms. These preferences could in turn be related by persons so inclined to social structure. One would end up with a statement not simply of the direction of linguistic drift, but what this drift meant psychologically and what social changes might check it. It would be very interesting, for instance, to find and examine cognate variants from some related societies with differing descent practices, and see whether the current drift is in the direction of feminization or masculinization. Such data would not only illuminate the mechanism of linguistic drift, but would provide students of social structure with extremely valuable indices of the distribution of envy and cross-segmental identification in the communities speaking the language studied.

Notes

1 This study was part of a larger cross-cultural study of socialization financed by the Ford Foundation and under the general direction of John Whiting of the Harvard Graduate School of Education and others.

2 The variation in this dialect between -in and -ing in the participle ending does not extend to words with a final -in in an unstressed syllable in standard speech. This variation is therefore probably best viewed as a case of free alternation of two allomorphs which happen to differ in respect to one phoneme, rather than as a case of phonological free variation.

3 Most previous studies of sociological factors connected with linguistic variants have been concerned with linguistic indices of class, caste, or occupational groups. Group boundaries have been regarded, implicitly or explicitly, as barriers to communication analogous to political boundaries, geographical distance, etc. The emphasis in this paper is rather on variations within a face-to-face community whose members are in frequent free communication: variations between social categories of speakers and between individual speakers, and situational variations in the speech of individual speakers, as noted below.

4 And doubtless of the person spoken to, although this was not investigated.

1.3 Sociolinguistic Rules of Address
Susan M. Ervin-Tripp

A scene on a public street in contemporary U.S.:
>   'What's your name boy?' the policeman asked . . .
>   'Dr. Poussaint. I'm a physician . . . .'
>   'What's your first name, boy? . . .'
>   'Alvin.'

Poussaint (1967; 53)

Anybody familiar with American address rules[1] can tell us the feelings reported by Dr. Poussaint: 'As my heart palpitated, I muttered in profound humiliation . . . . For the moment, my manhood had been ripped from me . . . . No amount of self-love could have salvaged my pride or preserved my integrity . . . [I felt] self-hate.' It is possible to specify quite precisely the rule employed by the policeman. Dr. Poussaint's overt, though coerced, acquiescence in a public insult through widely recognized rules of address is the source of his extreme emotion.

Brown and Ford (Hymes 1964) have done pioneering and ingenious research on forms of address in American English, using as corpora American plays, observed usage in a Boston business firm, and reported usage of business executives. They found primarily first name (FN) reciprocation or title plus last name (TLN) reciprocation. However, asymetrical exchanges were found where there was age difference or occupational rank difference. Intimacy was related to the use of multiple names.

Expanding their analysis from my own rules of address, I have found the structure expressed in the diagram in Fig. 1. The advantage of formal diagraming is that it offers precision greater than that of discursive description (Hymes 1967). The type of diagram presented here, following Geoghegan (1971), is to be read like a computer flow chart. The entrance point is on the left, and from left to right there is a series of selectors, usually binary. Each path through the diagram leads to a possible outcome, that is, one of the possible alternative forms of address.

Note that the set of paths, or the rule, is like a formal grammar in that it is a way of representing a logical model. The diagram is not

---

Ervin-Tripp, S.M. (1969) 'Sociolinguistics', in L. Berkowitz (ed.) *Advances in Experimental Social Psychology*, Vol. 4 1969 pp. 93-107.
This reading is an extract taken from the original article.

intended as a model of a process of the actual decision sequence by which a speaker chooses a form of address or a listener interprets one. The two structures may or may not correspond. In any case, the task of determining the structure implicit in people's knowledge of what forms of address are possible and appropriate is clearly distinct from the task of studying how people, in real situations and in real time, make choices. The criteria and methods of the two kinds of study are quite different. Just as two individuals who share the same grammar might not share the same performance rules, so two individuals might have different decision or interpretation procedures for sociolinguistic alternatives, but still might have an identical logical structure to their behaviour.

The person whose knowledge of address is represented in Fig. 1 (p.20) is assumed to be a competent adult member of a western American academic community. The address forms which are the 'outcomes' to be accounted for might fit in frames like 'Look, – – – –, it's time to leave.' The outcomes themselves are formal sets, with alternative realizations. For example, first names may alternate with nicknames, as will be indicated in a later section. One possible outcome is no-naming, indicated in Fig. 1 by the linguistic symbol for zero [$\emptyset$].

The diamonds indicate selectors. They are points where the social categories allow different paths. At first glance, some selectors look like simple external features, but the social determinants vary according to the system, and the specific nature of the categories must be discovered by ethnographic means. For example, 'older' implies knowledge of the range of age defined as contemporary. In some southeast Asian systems, even one day makes a person socially older.

The first selector checks whether the addressee is a child or not. In face-to-face address, if the addressee is a child, all of the other distinctions can be ignored. What is the dividing line between adult and child? In my own system, it seems to be school-leaving age, at around 18. An employed 16-year-old might be classified as an adult.

Status-marked situations are settings such as the courtroom, the large faculty meeting, or Congress, where status is clearly specified, speech style is rigidly prescribed, and the form of address of each person is derived from his social identity, for example, 'Your honour,' 'Mr Chairman.' The test for establishing the list of such settings is whether personal friendships are apparent in the address forms or whether they are neutralized (or masked) by the formal requirements of the setting. There are, of course, other channels by which personal relations might be revealed, but here we are concerned only with address alternations, not with tone of voice, connotations of lexicon, and so on.

Among nonkin, the dominant selector of first-naming is whether alter is classified as having the status of a colleague or social acquaintance. When introducing social acquaintances or new work colleagues,

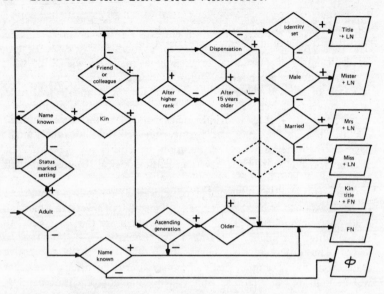

Fig. 1. An American address system.

it is necessary to employ first names so that the new acquaintances can first-name each other immediately. Familiarity is not a factor within dyads of the same age and rank, and there are no options. For an American assistant professor to call a new colleague of the same rank and age 'Professor Watkins' or 'Mr Watkins' would be considered strange, at least on the West Coast.

Rank here refers to a hierarchy within a working group, or to ranked statuses like teacher − pupil. In the American system, no distinction in address is made to equals or subordinates since both receive FN. The distinction may be made elsewhere in the linguistic system, for example, in the style of requests used. We have found that subordinates outside the family receive direct commands in the form of imperatives more often than equals, to whom requests are phrased in other ways at least in some settings (see below).

A senior alter has the option of dispensing the speaker from offering TLN by suggesting that he use a first name or by tacitly accepting first name. Brown and Ford (Hymes 1964) have discussed the ambiguity that arises because it is not clear whether the superior, for instance, a professor addressing a doctoral candidate or younger instructor, wishes to receive back the FN he gives. This problem is mentioned by Emily Post:

'It is also effrontery for a younger person to call an older by her or his first name, without being asked to do so. Only a very underbred, thick-skinned person would attempt it' (Post 1922: 54). In the American system described in Fig. 1, age difference is not significant until it is nearly the size of a generation, which suggests its origin in the family. The presence of options, or dispensation, creates a locus for the expression of individual and situational nuances. The form of address can reveal dispensation, and therefore be a matter for display or conceal-ment of third parties. No-naming or $\emptyset$ is an outcome of uncertainty among these options.[2]

The *identity* set refers to a list of occupational titles or courtesy titles accorded people in certain statuses. Examples are Judge, Doctor, and Professor. A priest, physician, dentist, or judge may be addressed by title alone, but a plain citizen or an academic person may not. In the latter cases, if the name is unknown, there is no address form (or zero, $\emptyset$) available and we simply no-name the addressee. The parentheses below refer to optional elements, the bracketed elements to social selectional categories.

[Cardinal] :	Your excellency
[U.S. President] :	Mr President
[Priest] :	Father (+ LN)
[Nun] :	Sister (+ religious name)
[Physician] :	Doctor (+ LN)
[Ph.D., Ed.D.] , etc.:	(Doctor + LN)
[Professor] :	(Professor + LN)
[Adult] , etc.;	(Mister + LN)
	(Mrs + LN)
	(Miss + LN)

Wherever the parenthetical items cannot be fully realized, as when last name (LN) is unknown, and there is no lone title, the addressee is no-named by a set of rules of the form as follows: Father + $\emptyset \rightarrow$ Father, Professor + $\emptyset \rightarrow \emptyset$, Mister + $\emptyset \rightarrow \emptyset$, etc. An older male addressee may be called 'sir' if deference is intended, as an optional extra marking.

These are my rules, and seem to apply fairly narrowly within the academic circle I know. Nonacademic university personnel can be heard saying 'Professor' or 'Doctor' without LN, as can school teachers. These delicate differences in sociolinguistic rules are sensitive indicators of the communication net.

The zero forms imply that often no address form is available to follow routines like 'yes', 'no', 'pardon me,' and 'thank you.' Speakers of languages or dialects where all such routines must contain an address form are likely in English either to use full name or to adopt forms like 'sir' and 'ma'am,' which are either not used or used only to elderly addressees in this sytem.

One might expect to be able to collapse the rule system by treating kin terms as a form of title, but it appears that the selectors are not identical for kin and nonkin. A rule which specifies that *ascending generation* only receives title implies that a first cousin would not be called 'cousin' but merely FN, whereas an aunt of the same age would receive a kin title, as would a parent's cousin. If a title is normally used in direct address and there are several members of the kin category, a first name may also be given (e.g., Aunt Louise). Frequently there are additional features marked within a given family such as patrilineal vs. matrilineal, and near vs. distant. Whenever the address forms for an individual person's relatives are studied, this proves to be the case, in my experience.

Presumably, the individual set of rules or the regional dialect of a reader of this article may differ in some details from that reported in Fig. 1. Perhaps sociolinguists will begin to use a favourite frame of linguists: 'In my dialect we say . . .' to illustrate such differences in sociolinguistic rules. For example, I have been told that in some American communities there may be a specific status of familiarity beyond first-naming, where a variant of the middle name is optional among intimates. This form then becomes the normal or unmarked address form to the addressee.

> 'What's your name, boy?'
> 'Dr. Poussaint. I'm a physician.'
> 'What's your first name, boy?'
> 'Alvin.'

The policeman insulted Dr Poussaint three times. First, he employed a social selector for race in addressing him as 'boy,' which neutralizes identity set, rank, and even adult status. If addressed to a white, 'boy' presumably would be used only for a child, youth, or menial regarded as a nonperson.

Dr Poussaint's reply supplied only TLN and its justification. He made clear that he wanted the officer to suppress the race selector, yielding a rule like that in Fig. 1. This is clearly a nondeferential reply, since it does not contain the FN required by the policemen's address rule. The officer next treated TLN as failure to answer his demand, as a non-name, and demanded FN; third, he repeated the term 'boy' which would be appropriate to unknown addressees.

According to Fig. 1, under no circumstances should a stranger address a physician by his first name. Indeed, the prestige of physicians even exempts them from first-naming (but not from 'Doc') by used-car salesmen, and physicians' wives can be heard so identifying themselves in public in order to claim more deference than 'Mrs.' brings. Thus the policeman's message is quite precise: 'Blacks are wrong to claim adult status or occupational rank. You are children.' Dr. Poussaint was stripped of all deference due his age and rank.

Communication has been perfect in this interchange. Both were familiar with an address system which contained a selector for race available to both black and white for insult, condescension, or deference, as needed. Only because they shared these norms could the policeman's act have its unequivocal impact.

Notes

[1] 'Rules' in this article are not prescriptive but descriptive. They may not be in conscious awareness. Unlike habits, they may include complex structures inferred from the occurrence of interpretable and appropriate novel behaviour.

[2] In this system in Fig. 1, it is possible to create asymmetrical address by using FN to a familar addressee who cannot reciprocate because of rank or age difference, and his unwillingness or lack of dispensation, e.g., a domestic servant. E. Hughes has noted a shift from TLN to FN by physicians whose patients move from private fees to Medicare. This usage does not fit into the rule in Fig. 1.

References

Geoghegan, W. (1971), 'Information processing systems in culture', in P. Kay (ed), *Explorations in Mathematical Anthropology*, MIT Press.

Hymes, D. (ed.) (1964), *Language in Culture and Society,* Harper & Row.

Hymes, D. (1967), 'Models of the interaction of language and social setting', *Journal of Social Issues,* vol. 23 no. 2 pp. 8-28.

Post, E. (1922), *Etiquette,* Funk and Wagnalls.

Poussaint, A. F. (1967), 'A Negro psychiatrist explains the Negro psyche', *New York Times Magazine,* August 20, p. 52.

1.4 *The Birth of your Dialect*

Bryan Silcock

Professor Higgins could place Eliza Doolittle's birthplace within a few London streets in the early minutes of Shaw's *Pygmalion*. Scholars at the University of Edinburgh have found that they can use the regional English dialects of 600 years ago to fix with equally startling accuracy the place of origin of medieval manuscripts.

After many years of painstaking research, they have almost completed a dialect atlas of English in the time of Chaucer — a work without parallel in any other language. When finished it will make it possible to say where the scribes of most manuscripts of the time learned their craft to an accuracy in some cases, of perhaps five or ten miles. It will map, with all the accuracy of a modern dialect survey, the varieties of English when our language was slowly growing to its modern form.

Oddly, they can discover far more about the equivalents of Cockney, Brummie, and Geordie in the late Middle Ages than at any other time until modern scholars started taking an interest in current dialects, and equipment became available to record them.

The reason is simple. The period between 1350 and 1450 is the only time in the history of English when documents were actually written down in dialect. Before 1350, there were virtually no documents in English as we now recognize it. In 1430 the adoption of English by the Chancery in London led to the rapid establishment of a standard written form of the language — a process later accelerated by the invention of printing, since the first presses in Britain were all in London.

The realization that manuscripts from this period could be used to study the geography of the dialects of the time came to Professor Angus McIntosh as long ago as 1952, while he was working on a study of modern Scottish dialects based on written questionnaires. He found that he could often identify the village of an un-named writer by his or her answers to the questions alone, just as Higgins was able to place Eliza by her speech.

Professor McIntosh and Professor M. L. Samuels of Glasgow have been working on their Middle English dialect atlas ever since, as funds permitted. A recent big grant from the Mellon Foundation in the United States will make it possible to complete the project in the next few years.

Sunday Times 10 July 1977, p. 13.

They have based their atlas on an analysis of some 1,100 Middle English manuscripts of all kinds — wills and other legal documents, state, ecclesiastical and family papers, and literary works. They found scribes usually modified a text to suit their local dialect even when copying something as fixed in form as verse. One obscure poem, called the Prick of Conscience, exists in 117 versions by different scribes.

The dialects of these 1,100 manuscripts are sampled with the help of about 270 key words — chosen because they are both common to as many of the manuscripts as possible, and because they show a wide range of variation.

The variations are of several different kinds. It may be that a word occurs in totally different forms, like 'bairn' and 'child.' It may be a set of different spellings — like 'uche,' 'iche,' 'ilke,' 'ilche,' 'euche,' and 'eche' for the modern 'each'. It may be a combination of the two — like 'kirk,' 'chirch,' 'cherch' and 'church,' for 'kirk,' now a mainly northern dialect word, used to extend as far south as Norfolk. Yet other variations are in how words are written — like the use of the runic letter called 'thorn' in place of 'th' or 'y.'

Among the 1100 manuscripts are over a hundred of known origin. Some are signed by the scribe and give his place of work. These 'anchor texts' make it possible to map the variations in key words dialect by dialect.

Within this network it is possible to assign relative positions to the dialects of the remaining 90 per cent of the manuscripts. They turn out to be remarkably consistent. Again and again the same pattern of variation occurs in a particular manuscript; that confirms that the differences come from where the copy was made and not the quirks of the scribe. And one variant merges into another, town by town, just as one accent merges into another today.

The results of the analysis are a series of maps for each of the key words — more complex versions of the one we show overleaf. With the help of these maps, it is possible to assign the dialect of a manuscript of of unknown origin to a particular part of the country with considerable confidence. One manuscript in the British Museum, for example, was traced to Lichfield. A closer look at the handwriting revealed that it was indeed the work of a known Lichfield scribe.

Of course there are many difficult manuscripts — a copy of a letter from London copied in Durham, for example, might show signs of both dialects. And some parts of the country, notably the North and South-West are under-represented in documents. But a big majority of the manuscripts so far examined conform to the geographical pattern of dialects. There is a total of 5,000-6,000 Middle English manuscripts in existence, so the atlas is based on about 20 per cent of the available material.

Among the available manuscripts, the many copies of the [...] *Prick of Conscience* provide an opportunity for an exceptionally detailed study — both of the mediaeval dialect and the changes undergone by a particular text as it passed from scribe to scribe. A long moralistic tract in verse, of doubtful literary merit, it was nevertheless extraordinarily popular in its time. [. . .]

There were probably more than 3,000 copies made between the early fourteenth century and the end of the fifteenth.

Its popularity may have been due to the fact that it was a kind of compendium of popular sermons, perhaps read out in churches all over the country. This would have been a particular incentive for a scribe copying it to produce a version in the local dialect.

Professor McIntosh fantasizes about putting all 117 surviving versions of the poem — a total of about 7,500,000 words — into a computer and tracing their family tree by the changes in the text. In practice he is having to make do with a sample of each — but it could make an obscure religious text the cornerstone of our understanding of language in the years when our dialects were being born.

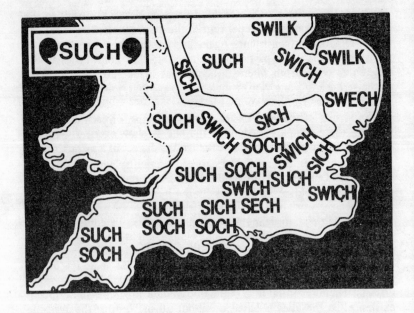

1.5 Our Reactions to Accent
Howard Giles

An English schoolboy would only ask his friend: 'Wassa time, then?' To his teacher he would be much more likely to speak in a more standard-ized accent and ask: 'Excuse me, sir, may I have the correct time please?' People are generally aware that the phrases and expressions they use are different from those of earlier generations; but they concede less that their own behaviour also varies according to the situation in which they find themselves. People have characteristic ways of talking which are relatively stable across varying situations. Neverthe-less, distinct contexts, and different listeners, demand different patterns of speech from one and the same speaker.

Not only this, but, in many cases, the way someone speaks affects the response of the person to whom he is speaking in such a way that 'modelling' is seen to occur. This is what Michael Argyle has called 'response matching.' Several studies have shown that the more one reveals about oneself in ordinary conversation, and the more intimate these details are, the more personal 'secrets' the other person will divulge.

Response matching has, in fact, been noted between two speakers in a number of ways, including how long someone speaks, the length of pauses, speech rate and voice loudness. The correspondence between the length of reporters' questions when interviewing President Kennedy, and the length of his replies, has been shown to have increased over the duration of his 1961-63 news conferences. Argyle says this process may be one of 'imitation.' Two American researchers, Jaffe and Feldstein, prefer to think of it as the speaker's need for equilibrium. Neither of these explanations seems particularly convincing. It may be that response matching can be more profitably considered as an uncon-scious reflection of speakers' needs for social integration with one another.

This process of modelling the other person's speech in a conversa-tion could also be termed speech convergence. It may only be one aspect of a much wider speech change. In other situations, speech divergence may occur when certain factors encourage a person to modify his speech away from the individual he is dealing with. For example, a retired brigadier's wife, renowned for her incessant snobbishness, may return her vehicle to the local garage because of inadequate servicing, voicing her complaint in elaborately phrased, yet mechanically unsophisticated language, with a high soft-pitched voice. These superior airs and graces may simply make the mechanic reply with a flourish of almost incomprehensible technicalities, and in a louder, more deeply-pitched voice than he would have used with a less irritating customer.

We don't know enough yet about all aspects of speech, but I have been experimenting with response matching in the use of accents, and have attempted to apply the ideas of speech convergence-divergence to cope with the phenomenon of accent change.

To begin with, it is necessary to abstract a speaker's accent repertoire. This is schematically represented in Fig. 1. Obviously, accent response matching is not of such a power as to occur between people regardless of their regional colourings. We do not order curry (or sausage and chips, for that matter) in an Indian restaurant with a Peter Sellers brogue. Response matching at this level operates with pronunciation patterns in which the speaker has had some extended experience. In its full range, the repertoire comprises a continuum of accent usage — standard variant, to the broadest local regional variant (whatever it may be). This standard accent in Britain has been called 'recieved pronunciation' (RP) by linguists. It is conventionally envisaged as the accent of a BBC newscaster.

affected
pronunciation

received
pronunciation

idiolect

broad
regional "B"
(eg South Wales)

broad
regional "A"
(eg Cardiff)

Now, the way most people's accents change are along this single continuum, from BBC to regional — but there are exceptions. It is likely that, if an individual lives in an area with two dialects (such as Cardiff, which has its own accent besides the more common south Wales lilt), then there would be at least one other regional 'branch' (as is shown opposite).

There is also the possibility of another 'branch' in the opposing direction, that is towards affected RP, more popularly thought of as the accent of the upper classes. Though most people can both standardize and broaden their most usual way of speaking (ie, their *idiolect*) at least slightly, it is also true that some people are practically immobile in this respect due to the limitation of their early vocal environments (for example, ghetto children; but, perhaps even more so, public school children).

Accent change in conversation may take either one of two directions, depending on whether the speaker wishes to be accepted by his listener — when his accent will converge — or whether he wishes to emphasize differences — in which case his accent may grow more dissimilar.

Accents can converge in two ways. To appreciate the distinction between the two, it is necessary to assume that the way that pronunciation varies in a speaker's repertoire also reflects prestige. This being the case, 'standard' patterns of pronunciation will have the highest status while the broadest regional varieties will have the lowest. So if a speaker thinks that his listener's way of speaking is higher than his is in terms of accent prestige (ie, it is more 'standard'), then, provided he wants to be accepted by the listener, he will modify his accent and *upward* accent convergence will occur. The only other direction of accent convergence is 'down', and imples that a speaker thinks his listener's pronunciation puts him in a lower prestige bracket — in other words, it's broader.

Since accent prestige often reflects social status, a move like this on the part of the speaker may be adopted so as to reduce embarrassment, due to social differences, and to prepare a common basis for the communication of ideas and feelings. This assumes, of course, that 'downward' convergence is more conscious than 'upward'.

Naturally enough, accent divergence can take on two directions also (see overleaf). Think of a woman who has bought some expensive clothing in an exclusive store which neither changes articles, nor refunds the cash after they have been bought. When the woman returns home she discovers a glaring flaw in the dress and returns it to the shop assistant demanding a replacement. The assistant has her instructions and soon finds a rather persistent customer on her hands. Of course, the floor manager is summoned to a situation he is all too familiar with and he assumes his usual authoritative and unrelenting approach, polishing his accent to a fine gilt edge (*upward* divergence). His aloof manner and his immediate dismissal of the whole affair arouses the woman's

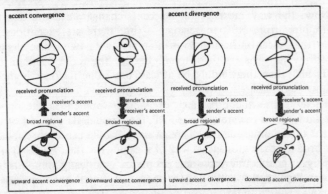

indignation and she storms off, voicing disgust in an unrefined manner (*downward* divergence).

I have been looking at just one direction of accent response matching, but, nevertheless, an important social one in Britain – 'upward convergence'.

It's unlikely that most people, when talking, achieve enough flexibility in pronunciation to be considered *similar* by their listeners – unless the gap in the prestige between their accents is very small. From the work of Wallace Lambert, and his colleagues at McGill University in Canada, on the way people evaluate various spoken languages and dialects, we know that there may be three 'rewards' for the speaker who upgrades his accent one or two notches towards his partner. These are: (i) an increase in perceived status; (ii) an increase in perceived favourability of personality; and (iii) an increase in the perceived quality and persuasiveness of the content of the message. So, if a person wishes to ingratiate himself with a person whom he is talking to, and whose accent has more prestige, it would seem reasonable for the speaker to show himself (and what he says) in the most favourable light.

Before proceeding to show that 'upward accent convergence' actually occurs in social interaction. I thought that it would be ideal at first to try to show that the range of accents does, in fact, reflect social prestige, with RP being superior in this respect. Second, I have tried to test whether or not these three potential 'rewards' work.

In order to find out whether RP really did have more prestige than regional varieties, I used the 'matched-guise' technique. This consisted of playing tape recordings of speakers with different accents, reading the same emotional-neutral passage of prose, to listeners who we asked to rate these voices on certain dimensions, including status. Actually, all the voices were produced quite realistically (after laborious practice) by the same male speaker, so that all accents were matched for timbre, speech rate, personality and so on. This procedure was necessary to stop listeners reacting to aspects of these voices other than that of accent. We found that RP and affected RP had by far the most prestige, while even certain foreign accents (French, German and northern American accents) had more social standing than our own regional ones.

Other interesting findings also emerged. For instance, we found that twelve year-olds relied heavily on aesthetic judgments of accent when allocating prestige, unlike their more objective 17 year-old counter-parts. As expected, subjects rated their own regional variety more favourably than listeners who were not from their region, although this bias did decrease with age and was more pronounced with working class and male people. Nevertheless, subjects appeared to 'repress' recognition of their own accent by rating the attitude item, 'an accent identical to your own' more favourably than the voice or name label representing their own region.

In another study, listeners had played to them the matched-guises of mild and broad variants of northern Irish, south Welsh and Birmingham accents. Listeners could easily detect these differences in accent broadness and rated the mild variants consistently superior in prestige and pleasantness, to the broader variants. Interestingly enough, 21 year-old listeners heard a greater difference between the variants than twelve year-olds, who, on the other hand, thought there was more difference in prestige between the variants than did the maturer group. Welsh listeners also tended to think there was less of a physical difference between the mild and broad Welsh voices than the Somerset listeners.

It would seem safe to conclude from these studies, therefore, that pronunciation differences between accents, and also within the same accent, are associated with prestige. This then enables the speaker at least one 'reward' for standardization, in that the milder his accent, the greater status he has.

We also investigated the second reward (concerned with personality gains and accent) by using the 'matched-guise' technique. A two minute tape-recorded prose passage was read in three accents (RP, mild south Welsh and Somerset) by two male speakers, and this was played to listeners who were asked to evaluate the voices on 18 adjective traits (for example, generous-mean, intelligent-dull). The notion of 'accent' was never introduced and listeners were told that their immediate impressions from the voice was all that we wanted. Besides certain interesting age, regional and personality differences, a distinct pattern of values emerged. We found that RP speakers were seen more favourably in terms of their competence (their ambition, intelligence, self-confidence, determination and industriousness) but less favourably in terms of personal integrity and social attractiveness (their seriousness, talkativeness, good-naturedness and sense of humour) than the regional speakers. The same was true for RP versus northern English and Scottish speakers. Although this finding was somewhat surprising it does explain, in part, the vitality of regional accents.

The third 'reward' (concerned with the importance of content and accent) we looked at, first of all, by finding out whether 17 year olds' attitudes towards capital punishment were stable over a period of seven days. As this fact was substantiated in a pilot study, the experiment proper was designed. More than 500 sixth formers' attitudes towards capital punishment were obtained, so that five groups of 50 subjects might be formed, each matched for sex, and attitude scores. Seven days after these attitudes were given, each group was provided with the same information against capital punishment, but in a different way — in typescript, or in one of the four recorded male matched-guises of RP, south Welsh, Somerset and Birmingham (that is, in decreasing order of accent prestige). After the passage had been given them, each group was asked for its attitude on the topic as it then stood, together with a rating of the quality of the argument.

Even though the argument was exactly the same, irrespective of its mode of presentation, the quality ratings, as expected, were related to the prestige of the accent. Rather surprising, however, was the finding that only the regional guises were effective in producing a significant change in attitudes; the typescript and RP guise were not. It may be that the integrity associated with regional speech (as I mentioned earlier) is a more pervasive force in persuading people, than what they see as the expertise of the argument or the speaker. Alternatively, it may have been that listeners were surprised more by the stand taken by the regional than the RP speaker, as this view is perhaps seemingly un-characteristic of the group a regional voice is thought to represent. In this case, listeners may have afforded the regional guises great integrity despite the quality of their arguments and hence their greater effective-ness. Although more research needs to be done on this, the speaker, by means of 'upward convergence,' would seem to attract a third 'reward' by what is seen as the increased quality of his message. 'Upward conver-gence' is rewarding then — but how exactly does it occur? We tested this by having nine sixth formers with Bristol accents interviewed individually by someone their own age, but with a strong Bristol accent like themselves; and separately by someone of higher social status with an RP accent.

The similar-status interviewer was a sixth former that we got from a different school. He was trained in the art of interviewing over a number of pilot trials and until he and the other interviewer achieved equivalent styles of informality; the use of slang was to be avoided wherever possible. The interviews themselves were tape recorded, unknown to the interviewees, by means of concealed microphones; and they did not know the true purpose of the study. They were, in fact, told that their personalities were being assessed in each interview (thereby assuring their cooperation), and that the hypothesis we were testing was that someone of equal station in life would be more accurate in their assessments (when compared to a more objective pencil-and-paper test of personality) than someone of a higher status, who would probably have a totally different value system. The interviewees were also told that the results of the study would be used for recommendations to industry on personnel selection and to colleges for student selection. Each interview lasted about 20 minutes and after the first 15 of these, the interviewees were posed a standard question on their attitudes towards capital punishment.

The first minute's speech, in response to the capital punishment question in each situation, was recorded into a third 'analysis' tape but edited such that the interviewer's voice did not intrude. A group of Welsh students and a matching group of Bristol students were asked to listen to each of these nine pairs of voices and, having heard them, determine whether they could detect a difference in accent and a difference in how formal the grammar was. If they could detect differences between members of a pair, they were asked to say which accent was the broader, and which was grammatically the less formal; they then had to rate how wide these differences were. It was emphasized that there were no right or wrong answers and it was up to them to determine when modifications had occurred, if at all.

The listeners claimed to see differences within all nine pairs. But, more important, the differences they saw, in accent *and* grammatical change, were in the direction we predicted. In other words, listeners (without knowledge of how these voices were obtained) identified the nine voices spoken in the presence of the RP interviewer as less broad, and also grammatically more formal, than the voices produced by the *same* speaker with the regional interviewer.

However, we found interesting differences between the two groups of listeners in their reactions to these speech changes. For instance, the Bristol listeners made significantly more 'errors' in identifying accent (but not grammatical) change than the Welsh 'aliens.' It may be that people become saturated with their own local accent so that they are less efficient at detecting variations in it. Furthermore, from the Welsh listeners' ratings, there was no relationship between the extent of a speaker's accent shift and the extent of his grammatical shift. This seems to indicate that listeners can successfully analyse speech changes in two independent ways. But, when we look at the Bristol listeners' ratings, we see that they saw a *strong* relationship between the extent that a speaker changed his accent and the extent that he changed his grammar. Because both groups rated a speaker's change of accent very similarly, it looks as though the Bristol listeners were relying more than the Welsh on grammatical cues when weighing up how much a speaker's accent had changed.

It would appear that grammatical changes were important aspects of the speakers' accent convergence, since I thought the interviewers were similar in how formal their grammar was — and they were, of course, trained to be so.

Until recently, speech was rarely seen as a dynamic, flexible process. Even now, we lack an adequate theory of what speech changes a particular person or situation will provoke in all ways — like accent and grammar. But with our attempts to produce at least a temporary framework for the study of one variable (the listener's accent) on one aspect (the speaker's accent), perhaps a more comprehensive picture will eventually emerge.

References

Howard Giles, 'Evaluative reaction to accents' (*Educational Review*, vol. 23, 211-227, 1970); 'Patterns of evaluation in reactions to RP, south Welsh and Somerset accented speech' (*British Journal of Social and Clinical Psychology*, 1971).

J. D. Matarazzo, A. N. Wiens, R. G. Matarazzo and G. Sascow, 'Speech and silence behaviour in clinical psychotherapy and its laboratory correlates,' in J. M. Schlein, H. F. Hunt, J. D. Matarazzo and C. Savage (eds), *Research in Psychotherapy*, vol. 3 (Washington DC, American Psychological Association, 1968).

W. Labov, 'Phonological correlates of social stratification' (*American Anthropologist*, vol. 66, No. 6 (2)p, p. 164-176, 1964).

J. T. Webb, 'Subject speech rates as a function of interviewer behaviour' (*Language and Speech*, vol. 12, pp. 54-67.

1.6 Social Network and Language Maintenance[1]
Lesley Milroy

Introduction

Many of those recent urban sociolinguistic studies which follow the general model provided by Labov (1966) have tried to account for patterns of variability in language and have frequently looked for evidence of ongoing linguistic change. Although the study of urban language described here makes use of a number of Labov's concepts and analytic techniques, the emphasis is not on *change* and *variability*, but rather on *stability* and *focussing*. In this respect I share with Le Page (1979) an interest in the question of how a stable set of linguistic norms emerges and maintains itself in a relatively focussed form. Although this question is seen by Le Page, a creolist, to be of fundamental importance to sociolinguistic theory, it is not one which is often asked by scholars working in the urban dialectological tradition of Labov.

The kind of linguistic norm still most commonly referred to in the literature is the publicly legitimized *prestige* norm. All fully standardized languages appear to be characterized by norms of this kind, which are codified in the form of grammars, dictionaries and elocution handbooks. The manner in which these norms emerge diachronically and are maintained in a relatively focussed form by mechanisms such as a writing system and public educational and broadcasting systems has been carefully analysed by Haugen (1972). A model of sociolinguistic structure such as that proposed by Labov depends fundamentally on the investigator's ability to identify a single set of prestige norms of this kind. Moreover, analytic procedures which link language variability to hierarchically stratified social groupings tacitly assume the speech community's awareness of a set of prestige norms which underlies regular and consistent sociolinguistic stratifications. These prestige norms may be seen as symbolizing publicly recognized values of a status-oriented kind.

However, scholars have long been aware of the existence of other, sometimes opposing, sets of norms which also have a powerful capacity to influence linguistic behaviour; these may be described as vernacular norms. Characteristically, vernacular norms are perceived as symbolizing values of solidarity and reciprocity rather than status, and are not

---

First publication.

publicly codified or recognised. Black English Vernacular is one famous example of a set of highly focussed vernacular norms; most industrial cities have associated with them low status varieties which also are overtly stigmatized.

Many bidialectal and bilingual communities maintain, in a parallel way, low status dialects or languages in their repertoires which have the capacity to persist, often over centuries, in the teeth of powerful pressures from a legitimized norm. Social psychologists have concluded that it is the capacity of these low status varieties to symbolize solidarity and group identity, values important to their users, which accounts for their persistence (Ryan 1979). From their systematic studies of patterns of codeshifting, linguists have arrived at a similar conclusion. For example, Blom and Gumperz (1972) suggest that two sets of norms, the standard and the dialectal, exist side by side in the Norwegian town of Hemnesberget because of their capacity to symbolize opposing sets of values — those of solidarity and local loyalty as opposed to the status-oriented and cosmopolitan. In many ways, Gal's recent study of a bilingual community in Austria provides a corollary to Blom and Gumperz's conclusions in showing how one of the two codes may disappear when the values it symbolizes cease to be important to its users (Gal 1978).

We therefore know in a general way *why* low status varieties persist, but are not yet in a position to answer the question posed by Labov (1972) with regard to Black English Vernacular, of *how* it manages to maintain itself in a consistent form over long periods of time. Although it is clear that low status norms are not codified and maintained by institutional means, the social mechanisms which *do* maintain them are not at all apparent.

In a recent study of the phonology of the low status urban vernacular of Belfast, this problem was considered (see Milroy, L. 1980 for a fuller account of the investigation).

The aim of the research was to produce an account, in as much detail as seemed reasonable, of patterns of variation within a single social class in three different communities in inner city Belfast. The fieldwork was carried out (during 1975-6) by means of a modified participant observation technique, and attention was focussed on pre-existing social groups in each of the three areas. The data presented here are derived from extensive analyses of the language of forty-six working class speakers. Both sexes are represented in this sample, and two age groups (18-25; 40-55) are considered.

Before describing procedures and presenting results, it is necessary to give a brief account of the general social characteristics and informal social organisation of the three communities. This is because one of the main analytic procedures discussed here depends on the notion of the individual's *personal network* structure — that is, the character of his informal social ties with those around him.

The Communities

The social structure of Belfast differs from that of many British and
North American cities in that the possibilities of upward social mobility
are very much more limited. The same group of people — the migrants,

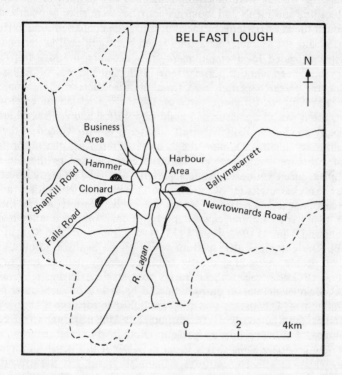

mostly Catholic, who came to the city in search of work during the
late nineteenth and early twentieth centuries — has occupied the lowest
status position for very many years, and has not been displaced by
subsequent waves of immigrants. In this respect, Belfast is quite unlike
most British industrial cities. Many investigators relate the persistent
and notorious problems of ethnic conflict in the city to this immobility
(see Boal 1978 for an influential and lucid account of the stability
and persistence of patterns of segregation and conflict). It was therefore
the language of pre-existing social groups in three *stable* poor working
class communities which was studied — Ballymacarrett (Protestant),
the Clonard (Catholic) and the Hammer (Protestant). Ballymacarrett,
arguably due to its location in the shipyard area at the centre of a
heavy industrial complex, differed from the others in suffering very
little from male unemployment. The Clonard (Catholic), and the
Hammer (Protestant) suffered male unemployment rates of around

35 per cent. This distribution of male unemployment had a considerable effect on informal social relationships in the areas, as Ballymacarrett men tended to work locally and find their entertainment in local pubs and clubs, often interacting almost exclusively within narrow territorial boundaries. Women were much more inclined to look for work outside the locality, and men's and women's activities were sharply polarized. Although the same patterns of social organization could be found in the Clonard and the Hammer at a time when the traditional Ulster linen industry provided local employment, this declining industry has for some time been almost non-existent in the inner areas of Belfast. During the research period, men from the Clonard and the Hammer were travelling to different parts of the city in search of employment, often shared domestic and child-care duties, and contrasted less markedly than their Ballymacarrett counterparts with women in their socialization habits. Despite these local differences, the informal social structure of all three communities corresponded to the dense, multiplex, often kin-based network patterns described by many investigators as characteristic of stable working-class communities, and particularly characteristic of areas like Ballymacarrett where men work together at a homogeneous and traditional form of employment (Young and Wilmott 1962; Fried 1973; Dennis, Henriques and Slaughter 1957). The communicative pattern which recurs in these accounts is one of people interacting mostly within a clearly defined territory, tending to know each others' social contacts (i.e. having relatively *dense* personal networks) and tending to be linked to each other by *multiplex* ties. This means that they are linked to each other in several capacities simultaneously – for example, as kin, neighbours and co-employees. Following Bott's arguments (Bott 1971), social anthropologists now generally agree that a social network of this dense multiplex type, which in effect constitutes a bounded group, has the capacity to impose general normative consensus on its members. This point is of general relevance to the reasoning used here. For the moment, it is worth recalling Labov's remarks on the capacity of closeknit peer groups to impose consensus on specifically *linguistic* norms upon their members (Labov 1972: 257).

Although this relatively dense, multiplex network structure could be found in all three Belfast working class communities, in very sharp contrast to middle class neighbourhoods, the extent to which *individuals* were linked to local networks varied considerably. Some people for example worked outside the area and had no local kin and no local ties of voluntary association, while others were linked to local networks in all these capacities. These differences in personal network structure, which appeared to be the result of many complex social and psychological factors, cut across categories of age, sex and locality. Predictably, much *individual* variation in language use could not be accounted for by grouping speakers into these categories, although they are certainly relevant to any account of sociolinguistic structure. The strongest vernacular speakers appeared however rather consistently to be those whose local network ties were strongest. This observation was treated as a hypothesis, and tested in the manner described in the following section.

Language/Network Correlations

An individual network score on a scale of 0-5 was calculated for each of the forty-six informants. This scale took account of the character of the individual's network ties in the sectors of work, kin, neighbourhood and voluntary association (see Cubitt 1973 for a discussion of the general importance of these particular network sectors). The score assigned to each individual provided a means of reflecting differences in muliplexity and density of personal networks without using corporate group constructs based on, for example, *status* as a means of differentiating individual speakers.

An informant's network score was calculated by assigning him one point for each of the following conditions he fulfilled:

1. Membership of a high density, territorially based cluster (i.e. any identifiable bounded group).
2. Having substantial ties of kinship in the neighbourhood. (More than one household, in addition to his own nuclear family.)
3. Working at the same place as at least *two* others from the same area.
4. The same place of work as at least two others of the same sex from the area.
5. Voluntary association with workmates in leisure hours. This applies in practice only when conditions three and four are satisfied.

Condition one is designed as an indicator of density, and reflects Cubitt's (1973) insistence on the importance of taking account of the density of specific clusters in considering networks (as we are here), as norm enforcement mechanisms. (A cluster is defined as a portion of a personal network where relationships are denser internally than externally.) The Jets, Cobras and T-Birds described by Labov (1972) form clusters; many of the young men in the Belfast communities belong to similar clusters; some of the middle-aged women belong to clusters of six or seven individuals who meet frequently to drink tea, play cards and chat. Some individuals on the other hand avoid association with any group of this kind.

Conditions two, three, four and five are all indicators of multiplexity; if they are all satisfied, the proportion of the individual's interactions which are with members of the local community is very high. Three and four are intended to reflect the particular capacity of an area of homogeneous employment to encourage the development of dense, multiplex networks; four also reflects the fact that polarization of the sexes usually occurs when there is a large number of solidary relationships in a specific neighbourhood.

It may appear at first sight that multiplex ties of the kind reflected in conditions three, four and five are usually contracted by men, and that men would, therefore, automatically score higher on the network strength scale. In fact, since both the Hammer and the Clonard are areas of high *male* unemployment, individual women frequently score as high as or higher than men.

The scale is capable of differentiating individuals quite sharply. Scores range from zero for someone who fulfills none of the conditions, (although a zero score is rare) to five for several informants who fulfil them all. Such individuals must be considered extremely closely integrated into the community in the sense that their kin, work and friendship ties are all contracted within it; additionally, they have formed particularly close ties with a corporate group (such as a football fans' club) or a less formal group based in the area. The defined territorial base associated with the kind of network structure which interests us here is reflected in conditions one and two. This is very important, for geographical mobility appears to have the capacity to destroy the structure of long established networks (Turner 1967; Young and Wilmott 1962).

It is important to emphasise that the network strength scale is designed fundamentally as a tool for measuring differences in an individual's level of integration into the local community. It is not claimed that this scale is the *only* means of doing so; for example attitudinal factors are likely also to be good indicators. However, the major advantage of the scale adopted here is that the indicators are based on an explicit set of procedures for analysing social relationships. Further, they can be observed directly and are subject to checking and verification (see Boissevain 1974 for a full account of network theory and Milroy L. 1980 for a discussion of its relevance to sociolinguistic method and theory).

Scores for each individual speaker on eight separate phonological variables were calculated (using the methods developed by Labov 1966) and a large number of rank order correlation tests carried out as a means of testing the hypothesis that network patterns were related to patterns of language use. When all subjects were considered together, significant results were obtained for five of the eight variables. This result appears to confirm the hypothesis that the strongest vernacular speakers are those whose network ties are strongest. Of those eight variables, only the five significant ones are considered here.

Before proceeding further, it is necessary to explain the relevant phonological features associated with these variables. This account is necessarily brief and partial; a fuller description of the complexities of this urban vernacular phonology can be found in Milroy J. (forthcoming) and to a more limited extent in Milroy L. (1980) and Hughes and Trudgill (1979).

1. (a) Index scores are used, measuring degrees of retraction and back—raising in items of the /a/ class (e.g. *hat, man, grass*). A five point scale is used, ranging from one for tokens with [æ] to five for tokens with [ɔə] . Scores are based on 60-80 tokens per speaker.
2. (th) Percentage scores measure deletion of intervocalic [ð] in a small lexical set (e.g. *mother, brother*). Since the lexical distribution of this variable is limited, scores are based on only 856 tokens for all speakers — approximately 16-20 tokens per speaker.
3. (ʌ) Percentage scores measure frequency of the [ʌ] variant in a small lexical set which alternates between the /ʌ/ and /ʉ/ word-classes: e.g. *pull, shook, foot.* Altogether, 1500 tokens are considered. An account of this word class and its importance for theories of lexical diffusion and linguistic change can be found in J. Milroy (1980).
4. (ε¹) Percentage scores measure frequency of a low vowel [ǣ] (as opposed to a mid-vowel [èᵉ] in items of the |ε| class (*peck, bet, went, health*). This analysis is restricted to monosyllables closed by a voiceless stop. or by a voiceless obstruent preceded by a liquid or nasal.
5. (ε²) Percentage scores measure frequency of the same low vowel in di- and polysyllables.

Table 1. Correlations between network scores, and linguistic variable scores for all subjects. N refers to the number of subjects tested for a given variable

Variable	r	t	N	level of significance
(a)	0.529	3.692	37	p < .01
(th)	0.485	3.591	44	p < .01
(ʌ²)	0.317	2.142	43	p < .05
(ε¹)	0.255	1.709	44	p < .05
(ɔ̃ʳ)	0.321	2.200	44	p < .05

The correlations between individual scores for these variables and individual network scores are presented in Table 1. This significant relationship between network structure and language use was further explored by dividing the informants into subgroups based on sex, age and area and again correlating linguistic scores with network scores. It is the results which emerged when the subgroups were divided according to area which are considered here.

Table 2*. Correlations between network scores and linguistic
variable scores calculated separately for three areas.
B = Ballymacarrett, H = Hammer, C = Clonard

Variable		r	t	N	level of significance
(a)	B	0.930	8.360	13	$p < .01$
	C	0.345	2.287	15	$p > .05$
	H	-0.344	2.286	9	$p > .05$
(th)	B	0.816	4.679	13	$p < .01$
	C	0.011	0.039	15	$p > .05$
	H	0.346	1.379	16	$p > .05$
(Λ^2)	B	0.426	1.560	13	$p > .05$
	C	-0.042	0.151	15	$p > .05$
	H	0.247	0.920	15	$p > .05$
(ε^1)	B	0.771	4.016	13	$p < .01$
	C	-0.118	-0.429	15	$p > .05$
	H	0.053	-0.199	16	$p > .05$
(ε^2)	B	0.719	3.433	13	$p < .01$
	C	0.027	0.098	15	$p > .05$
	H	0.096	0.361	16	$p > .05$

*One further variable, (I), showed a significant relationship to network scores
only in the Hammer:

$r = 0.528$, $t = 2.327$, $N = 16$, $p < .05$.

Since $N = 16$ (maximum) in this second set of tests, significant
results were less easily obtained than when $N = 46$, as previously.
Where the N is so relatively small, therefore, significant results are
likely to indicate a rather close relationship between network and
linguistic variables.

In fact, it is only in Ballymacarrett that many phonological variables
correlate significantly with personal network structure. Four of the
eight give statistically significant results in Ballymacarrett, one in the
Hammer and none in the Clonard (see Table 2 and footnote).

To interpret these results, it is necessary to refer back to the variant
network patterns in the three communities. In Ballymacarrett *male*
networks seemed more closeknit largely as a result of local employment
patterns and contrasted sharply with the relatively looseknit *female*
network pattern. This contrast between the sexes was not apparent
in other areas. A series of analysis of variance tests were carried out
to check on significant differences in the distribution of *network*
scores by age, sex and area (see Milroy L. 1980 for details). Although
many significant differences and interactions emerged, the important
result for our purposes here is that *only in Ballymacarrett* are male
and female network scores significantly different (means = 3.9583:
1.3333). These may be compared with the Hammer (2.125: 1.875)

and the Clonard (2.750: 2.875). Considered overall, network scores did not vary significantly simply according to area.

Conclusion

Pulling the threads of the argument together, we may infer from the overall correlations that personal network structure is of great importance in any attempt to describe patterns of language use. When a speaker belongs to a stable, low status community, a dense, multiplex personal network structure predicts relative closeness to vernacular norms. However, the *constraints* on the capacity of network structure to influence language use are equally important, for the relationship between language and network is not absolute. It exists in its most consistent form in the community where traditional differences between the socialization patterns of the sexes are maintained, with men contracting more closeknit localized ties than women. Thus, with regard to the social mechanisms which impel some speakers to use higher levels of the vernacular than others, we must conclude that the variables of sex and network structure work together in a complicated way. Any explanation of why there is a better correlation between language and network in Ballymacarrett than in the other areas must take into account the network structures of both sexes as well as overall areal differences in network structure.

I would interpret these results from the perspective of sociolinguistic theory by referring first to the widely accepted anthropological view that a closeknit network has the capacity to function as a norm enforcement mechanism; there is no reason to suppose that linguistic norms are exempted from this process. Moreover, a closeknit network structure appears to be very common − some would claim universal − in low status communities (Lomnitz 1977). This link between social status and personal network structure, taken together with the correlations between language and network reported here, begins to explain the complicated social mechanisms which enable low status varieties to persist over long periods of time despite counter-pressures of various kinds. The closeknit network may be seen as an important social mechanism of vernacular maintenance, capable of operating effectively in opposition to a publicly endorsed and status-oriented set of legitimized linguistic norms.

Note

[1]This paper draws its data from research projects, HR3771 and HR5777, supported by Social Science Research Council grants. The help of SSRC is gratefully acknowledged here as is that of James Milroy, Rose Maclaran, Domini O'Kane and Sue Margrain, who have worked on the Belfast projects.

References

Blom, J. P. and J. Gumperz (1972) 'Social meaning in linguistic structures: codeswitching in Norway' in Gumperz and Hymes (eds.), 407-434.

Boal, F. W. (1978) 'Territoriality on the Shankhill-Falls divide, Belfast: the perspective from 1976', in Lanegran and Palm (eds.), 58-77.

Boissevain, J. (1974) *Friends of Friends: Networks, Manipulators and Coalitions*, Oxford, Blackwell.

Boissevain, J. and Mitchell, J. C. (eds.) (1973), *Network Analysis: Studies in Human Interaction*, The Hague, Mouton.

Bott, E. (1971) *Family and Social Network* (Rev. ed.), London, Tavistock.

Cubitt, T. (1973) 'Network density among urban families', in Boissevain and Mitchell (eds.), 67-82.

Dennis, N., Henriques, F. M. and Slaughter, C. (1957) *Coal is our Life*, London, Eyre and Spottiswood.

Fried, M. (1973) *The World of the Urban Working Class*, Cambridge Mass, Harvard University Press.

Gal, S. (1978) 'Variation and change in patterns of speaking: Language shift in Austria', in Sankoff (ed.), 227-238.

Giles, H. and St. Clair, R. (eds.) *Language and Social Psychology*, Oxford, Blackwell.

Gumperz, J. and Hymes, D. (1972) *Directions in Sociolinguistics*, New York, Holt Rinehart & Winston.

Haugen, E. (1972) *The Ecology of Language*, Stanford, Stanford University Press.

Hughes, A. and Trudgill, P. (1979) *English Accents and Dialects*, London, Arnold.

Labov, W. (1966) *The Social Stratification of English in New York City*, Washington, DC, Center for Applied Linguistics.

Labov, W. (1972) *Language in the Inner City*, Philadelphia, Penn. University Press.

Lanegran, D. A. and Palm, R. (eds.) (1978) *An Invitation to Geography*, (2nd ed.), New York, McGraw Hill.

Le Page, R. B. (1979) Review of Dell Hymes' *Foundations of Sociolinguistics* and Norbert Dittmar's *Sociolinguistics, Journal of Linguistics* 15, 168-179.

Lomnitz, L. A. (1977) *Networks and Marginality*, New York, Academic Press.

Milroy, J. (1980) 'Lexical alternation and the history of English' in E. Traugott *et al* (eds.).

Milroy, J. (forthcoming) *The Pronunciation of English in Belfast*, Belfast, Blackstaff.

Milroy, L. (1980) *Language and Social Networks*, Oxford, Blackwell.

Ryan, E. B. (1979) 'Why do low prestige language varieties persist?' in Giles and St. Clair (eds.), 145-157.

Sankoff, D. (ed.) (1978) *Linguistic Variation: Models and Methods*, New York, Academic Press.

Traugott, E. *et al* (eds.), *Papers from the 4th International Conference in Historical Linguistics*, Amsterdam, Benjamins.

Turner, C. (1967) 'Conjugal roles and social networks', *Human Relations* 20, 121-130.

Young, M. and Wilmott, F. (1962) *Family and Kinship in East London*, Harmondsworth, Penguin.

1.7 Linguistic Diversity in London Schools
Harold Rosen

(The author wishes to acknowledge his debt to the collective work of all participants in the project, *Language in inner-city schools*. To keep the record straight I must single out my outsize debt to my colleague, Tony Burgess, Research Officer for the survey reported in this article. In particular, the statistical work and the questionnaire are almost entirely his.)

Introduction: Who Speaks What?

The collection of statistics in education is a well-established practice and the Department of Education has its annual multi-volume Doomsday Book (*The Statistics of Education*). Nevertheless, there remain some disconcerting gaps, among them some badly needed information about the language spoken by pupils in our schools. This article is concerned with that information. We need to know the answer to a question of apparently unambiguous simplicity: *Which languages and dialects are spoken by how many school pupils?*

Given funding and stamina the answers should not be hard to come by. However, no information-gathering survey is free from conceptual problems but some are much more straightforward than others. If you want to know the average weight of ten-year-olds in a given population you will almost certainly have fewer difficulties than if you wish to survey the athleticism of the same population. Our initial question immediately prompts several others.

i. What constitutes a distinct language? (If an informant claims to speak two African languages, are they really two separate languages or two dialects of the same language?)
ii. When can we say someone speaks an identifiable dialect? (How do we accommodate in our classification a speaker of standard who always uses some but not all of the features of Cockney? At what point do we call him a Cockney speaker or standard speaker?)
iii. What do we mean when we say someone speaks a language? (How proficient must he be? Does he speak like a native? Or fluently

First publication.
This article is based on *Language and Dialects of London Schoolchildren*: Rosen, H. and Burgess, T. (Ward Lock, 1980).

but like a foreigner? Or can he produce enough for many routine communicative purposes?)

iv. What exactly is someone's 'mother tongue'? (Is it the language of the home? Or is it the first aquired language now being ousted by another?)

v. Can we accurately or usefully say someone speaks a language without specifying which dialect of it he speaks? (If it is Italian, do we mean standard or Neapolitan or Venetian?)

Asking for information about someone's language is always personal, often political and sometimes a delicate matter. It is reasonable to ask of any survey: who wants this information? How do they propose to gather it? Will the information-gathering process distort, falsify or obscure important matters?

The interests and aims of the survey will shape its emphasis and form. A sociolinguist might be centrally concerned to discover the contexts in which different languages are used, an educational administrator with the provision of ESL teachers and a classroom teacher with why some pupils write the way they do. In addition, looming over such an enterprise, are difficult and often frustrating methodological problems. Even though the investigators may have alerted themselves to all the complexities of the operation, how is it possible to gather reasonably refined and reliable information?

This article describes how a survey was carried out, and reports its findings. It was an attempt to answer the question 'Who speaks what?' with a sample of London school pupils. In order to understand that operation, its biases, its limitations and its methods, some brief mention of its history is necessary, sufficient at least to reveal the commitment of the investigators, the kinds of resources they commanded and why it adopted one procedure rather than another.

The Context: Historical and Educational

The English Department at the University of London Institute of Education, the central concern of which is the teaching of English as a mother tongue, found itself involved in this survey chiefly because our experience in schools drove us towards it. Firstly, we were slowly obliged to acknowledge that teachers of English in schools were teaching many pupils for whom English was not a mother tongue. Secondly, the delusion could no longer be sustained that English-as-a-second-language teachers would so transform pupils that they could enter the English-as-a-mother-tongue classroom and merge comfortably with their fellow pupils. As for speakers of a Caribbean creole, it was supposed that they would soon pick up the habits of the natives. Thirdly, the stubborn fact of the possession of another language or dialect, submerged though it might be by the assimilative influences of school, asserted itself strongly to those of us who felt that the cultural experiences of all pupils needed recognition in the school curriculum. There were also some more specific reasons than these. Our research had for several years concentrated on language in inner-city schools and was based on a network of teachers in inner London schools who collaborated in our working parties and conferences. Again and again the theme of linguistic diversity was raised in our discussions. We soon realized that none of us possessed really hard information about the languages and dialects spoken by the school population. At that stage it made sense to produce a do-it-yourself instrument to enable teachers to carry out their own small-scale investigations. The central principle which informed our *Guidelines for the investigation in the language of inner-city pupils* (Institute of Education 1977) was that teacher and pupils should be active participants in the collection of data. When later that year we were given a small grant by the DES for six months to carry out a survey we then had to give our sustained attention to a much more formal operation which was not only unlike any of our previous research studies but which also required us to extend our own understanding into areas hitherto at the periphery of our concerns.

The survey would not of course be conducted in a vacuum; to get even the co-operation of schools meant that we had to recognize the force of very powerful traditions both inside and outside the educational system. The monolingual and monocultural tradition in British life is deeply entrenched. The early political unification of the country, the absence of powerful minority languages fortified by education and political power meant that by the time universal education came to be established (1870) the English language appeared to be the non-controversial and undisputed choice for schools. It could have been asserted with considerable credibility that everyone spoke English. However, the superficiality of this view is belied if we look at the treatment of linguistic minorities within the school system i.e. both minority languages and dialects. Stephens (1976) documents in some detail the repression of Welsh and Gaelic both through legal enactment and the functioning of the educational system, which countenanced the humiliating punishment of children for speaking their mother tongue. The education system has similarly been the major channel through which standard English has been steadfastly promoted and regional and social dialects discriminated against. Thus the historic legacy has been one of the establishment of English not simply as the supreme language without serious rival claimants nationally but eventually without substantial opposition regionally or locally. In England no other language available to pupils through their domestic culture was accorded an acknowledged position in the educational system. For centuries communities of speakers of such languages as French, Yiddish, Polish and Cantonese have established themselves in Britain but their acceptability has traditionally been measured by the completeness with which they could anglicize themselves. Any efforts to sustain their own culture and language had to be engaged in by the communities themselves and drew virtually no support from official agencies. A centuries-old process has been at work both through explicit policy and the might of economic and political forces to persuade us that we speak one language and that those who do not speak it are either soon going to leave or will in a generation or two be linguistically absorbed. Experience of multi-lingualism both of communities and of individuals is not a component of national consciousness as it is in vast areas of the world. Nor have most schools been obliged to come to terms with the phenomena of bilingualism, plurilingualism, bidialectalism, diglossia, interlanguage and language loyalty. In England (but not Wales) we have not had to agonize over the selection of a language for the medium of instruction, let alone wrestle with questions of standardization and the national language(s) the answers to which inevitably make a deep impact on schools. On the one hand then we have figures to show that repression of minority languages has been successful in weakening their position[1], on the other hand a monolingual outlook led to our underestimating the diversity which existed in various forms.

The Contemporary Picture

Thus it is that we have in the past thought of diversity of languages as something which happens somewhere else and we do not have distributed through our public and social life the formal and informal expertise about language diversity which is desperately needed in contemporary Britain. We now have good reason to know that the monolingualism of England both as a state of mind and as a relative linguistic truth can no longer be easily sustained, particularly in those areas where new minorities have settled. The whole linguistic configuration has changed dramatically in twenty years though the process was beginning before that. Throughout the country but above all in the great industrial centres there arrived thousands of people who spoke a language other than English or who spoke an overseas dialect of English which British English speakers found difficult to understand (the latter in the main from the Caribbean). There were many features of this wave of immigration which made it a novel and, for many, an overwhelming experience, at any rate, within living memory. Secondly, the newcomers were virtually from all over the globe bringing with them not only many more languages but also languages with which very few people in Britain had even a nodding acquaintance. Thirdly, since many of them came from Asia, Africa and the Caribbean attitudes to their language were tainted by racism and the legacies of colonialism.

Two other features of this immigration should be noted: London received the greatest numbers and the greatest diversity and, secondly, the education system was totally unprepared for this sudden change in its clientele. The history of the multiplicity of attempts to accommodate it cannot be given here since it has to be traced through the labyrinth of legislation, Select Committee Reports, financial policy, special agencies created by government (the Community Relations Commission, the Commission for Racial Equality), DES circulars and advice and varied policies of local authorities. There pervades this history a persistent concern for the new language situation in schools, but also a strong sense of people grappling with an unfamiliar problem and no reservoir of well-tried resources and strategies on which they could draw.

As the investigators became more aware of both the historical and contemporary context of the survey, the most promising strategy seemed to be one which would keep our educational motives to the forefront. We had good reason to believe that the monolingual tradition was still strong in schools. We also knew that even in those schools which were becoming hospitable to linguistic diversity, there was a lack of information about the languages and dialects of their pupils and of understanding of some of the linguistic phenomena present in their midst. We finally came to see the survey as an operation which could involve the teachers and the pupils in the schools, create a climate of concern and open up discussions on the educational implications of linguistic diversity. This is not to say that we were not concerned to elicit information which could be of wider use and significance but it does imply that our procedures were profoundly affected by these considerations. To some extent we were cutting our coat according to the cloth. Knowing that much of the information we could collect was relatively coarse and that some of the information which would come our way would not find its way into final tables, we wanted the survey to be carried out with more than a meticulous concern for filling cells on coding sheets and the act of carrying out the survey to have an independent and valued function.

The Study of Linguistic Diversity in Britain

One stark simple fact was a spur to our work — the absence of any up-to-date reliable information on the size of ethnic minority populations and the numbers of speakers of minority languages. It comes as something of a shock that a country as highly organized as the United Kingdom, possessing sophisticated data-collection resources can only provide unsatisfactory and incomplete data. The collection of statistics about ethnic minorities and their language is, of course, a sensitive political issue and this fact has inhibited official enquiry. In the attempts which have been made, the concern has been to register 'country of origin' rather than language. Beyond bare statistics of national or regional origin there exists no comprehensive study though there have been several attempts either to give a broad picture or study in detail particular communities (see Kranz 1971; Watson 1977; Khan 1979).

How limited is our knowledge is best illustrated by our dependence on the 1971 Census. A careful analysis by Campbell-Platt (1976) is preceded by the gloomy remark that, 'It is impossible to construct, from published sources, an accurate linguistic map of minorities in Britain.' This was echoed and amplified by Derrick (1977) who is commenting on the conference at which Campbell-Platt presented her paper (CILT 1976).

Not only do we know very little about how our immigrants see themselves and their future, but we know very little too about their attitudes to their mother tongue. It would seem reasonable for local authorities to want to know more about potential mother-tongue language learners themselves before embarking on any large scale new policy, especially, one might add, when there are still unresolved difficulties about the policy of teaching English as a second language in schools.

What emerges most clearly from the CILT conference report is how little is known about language and minority groups in Britain and what a need there is for reliable information if any far-reaching decisions about the curriculum are to be made. In the first place we do not have any accurate information about what vernaculars are spoken by minority groups, by what numbers and to what extent. (p. 53)

Derrick was writing of 'language and minority groups' but we should add that the dearth of information to which she refers applies to vernacular speakers of all kinds in Britain with the exception of the Welsh and Gaelic-speaking Scots.

Using Campbell-Platt as our source we can only attempt a second-best, based on the 1971 Census country of birth figures. As she points out the countries of origin are not reliable indicators of the languages for speakers and even less reliable as an indicator of the language of their children. They will tell us almost nothing of those of Caribbean origin. Campbell-Platt estimates that the most widely spoken languages in descending order of population are Punjabi, Urdu, Bengali, Gujarati, German, Polish, Italian, Greek, Spanish and Cantonese or Hakka. Her table (CILT 1976) fills out the rest of this.

We must emphasize that these figures are themselves out of date and illustrate the point made above that they do not represent *linguistic* information. For example, they cannot tell us about Yiddish or Hebrew speakers. In the London area alone in the 1970s 24 primary schools and 10 secondary schools taught modern spoken Hebrew and in one school the medium of instruction is Yiddish. The fact that Pakistan is

Table 1. Distribution of overseas-born population of Great Britain by selected countries of birth, 1971

Country of birth		Number resident in Great Britain
Total population of Great Britain		53,978,540
Total born in Great Britain		50,388,690
Total overseas-born population (UK) of which:	3,088,110	
Total Europe	*632,770*	
of which:	Germany	157,680
	Italy	108,980
	Poland	110,925
	Spain	49,470
	Malta and Gozo	33,840
Total NC* Africa	*164,205*	
of which:	Ghana	11,215
	Kenya	59,500
	Nigeria	28,565
	Tanzania	14,375
	Uganda	12,590
Total NC* Asia and Oceania	*638,285*	
of which:	Ceylon	17,040
	Cyprus	73,295
	Hong Kong	29,520
	India	321,995
	Malaysia	25,685
	Pakistan	139,935
	Singapore	27,335
Other countries		
	China**	13,495

(Census 1971, Great Britain, Country of birth tables)

*New Commonwealth countries   **mainland and Formosa

given as the country of birth cannot tell us the proportion of Bengali or other speakers. The same obscurity applies to some of the African languages since African countries are characteristically plurilingual. In any case these figures must be reinterpreted for the school population to allow for such facts as that the German-origin population is largely from an older pre-war refugee immigration, that they do not include the now numerous British-born population and that new groups of immigrants have arrived since 1971 (eg Portuguese). Certainly we can get no inkling of the degree of linguistic assimilation. For how many children is English now a first language? How many of them can also speak another?

Since we shall be concentrating on London we can also look at the Census for the GLC area comparing it with the country as a whole.

Table 2

1. Europe: Selected Countries

	Germany	Italy	Poland	Spain	Malta and Gozo
GB	157,680	108,980	110,925	49,470	33,840
GLC	34,300	32,545	32,505	25,640	8,305

2. Africa: Selected Countries

	Ghana	Kenya	Nigeria	Tanzania	Uganda
GB	11,215	59,500	28,865	14,375	12,590
GLC	6,840	24,535	18,540	5,905	5,560

3. Selected Asian and Oceanic countries

	Ceylon	Cyprus	Hong Kong	China	India	Malaysia	Pakistan	Singapore
GB	17,040	73,295	29,520	13,495	321,995	25,685	139,935	27,335
GLC	8,470	53,095	6,865	3,815	106,380	8,520	30,135	4,460

The largest concentration of new ethnic and linguistic populations are in London, and they are highly concentrated in certain London boroughs. As recently as January 1979 the GLC reported that more than half the children born in London boroughs were born to immigrant mothers, ranging from Brent with 65% to Havering and Bexley with less than 10%. Haringey, Kensington and Chelsea had over 50%, Hammersmith, Newham, Camden, Islington, Lambeth and Wandsworth over 40%.

To the figures selected from those assembled by Campbell-Platt, with bilingualism in mind, we must add those for the West Indian population. Edwards (1979) while warning that the figure is an estimate offers 543,000 for 1971. This includes all of West Indian origin whether born in Britain or the islands. Lomas (1973) suggests a growth from 15,300 in 1951 to 446,200 in 1971. Probably well over one half are Jamaican or of Jamaican origin. The language of West Indians both in the West Indies and in Britain is such a complex and important question that we shall return to it later from the point of view of its occurrence in schools.

The Bullock Report (1975), concerned with the *school* population, gives us a general picture:

It is, of course, helpful to have some idea of the number of children of families of overseas origin at school in Britain, though there is considerable difficulty in arriving at useful statistics. In 1973, by the DES definition then existing, there were 284,754 'immigrant children' in maintained primary and secondary schools in England

and Wales, comprising 3.3 per cent of the total school population. More significantly, since immigrant populations are concentrated largely upon greater London and industrial cities in the Midlands and North, individual local education authorities can have as high a proportion of immigrant children on roll as 27 per cent. Raw statistics such as these help to show why such a large measure of attention has to be paid in some areas, much more than in others, to the educational needs of the children labelled 'immigrant'. Obviously what is needed is as sharp a measure as possible of these special educational needs. An immigrant child does not present problems to a school simply because he is an immigrant child. Centrally collected figures cannot, for instance, indicate exactly the numbers of children with linguistic needs nor give any measure of these needs. The only people who can do this satisfactorily are the people on the spot, the teachers in the schools and the local education authorities. A few authorities have already had considerable practice in making such assessments. Bradford is notable in having carried out for several years an annual survey of immigrant children in its schools, distinguishing between their different ethnic origins, identifying their levels of proficiency in English, and making flexible educational arrangements accordingly. We recommend that all authorities with immigrant children should make similar surveys regularly, in order to achieve a greater refinement in their educational arrangements. (p. 284)

In discussing the language needs of immigrant children it is important to distinguish between two broad groups. The first consists of families from the Caribbean, whose mother tongue is English — even if in several respects it differs from the kind of English spoken in England. The second group is made up of those whose mother tongue is a totally different language and who speak little or no English on arrival. We will consider these in turn. The 1972 D E S statistics revealed that there were 101,898 children of West Indian origin (including Guyana) in the schools. Other evidence suggests that about half of these were from Jamaica, the remainder from the smaller islands of the group. For most of them the language of childhood and of the home is an English-based Creole, a variety or dialect of English. Jamaican Creole has been extensively studied and described over the last 20 years. (p. 287)

It was clear from the Bullock Report that its authors did not have any useful breakdown of the figures which it could present.

There are signs of a significant shift of focus in the attention given to the language of minority groups. Hitherto the concern has been to discover how many people need to be taught, and how much people need to be taught, and of what kind. There is now emerging at different levels an interest in the variety of mother tongues as a basis for some form of maintenance within the British community of those languges.[2]

It might be thought that, in conducting a survey of linguistic diversity researchers could draw on a rich experience of similar undertakings.

However, there was no indigenous model for reasons we have explained. Insofar as diversity has been a matter of interest it has focused on dialect. The methods and limitations of those studies do not make them particularly helpful since they were concerned in the main with the geographical distribution of phonological and lexical items and the population selected for study deliberately excluded those people who would have revealed diversity of speech. Bilingualism has been seen through the Welsh and Gaelic experience, but those languages have for centuries been the languages of settled communities for whom English was the incomer.

It was only to be expected that those whose interests were in societies where a multiplicity of languages coexisted would look to such areas as Africa and Asia, but the social and cultural circumstances of those countries are so different from our own as to make the work limited in its relevance. An inspection of the papers in *Language Surveys in Developing Nations* (Ohannessian, Ferguson, Polome, 1975) brings this out very clearly with its emphasis on language planning and governmental language policies and attention, quite properly, to societies which have been multilingual for centuries. Nevertheless, some of the literature raises matters of general principle and interest. Stewart (1968) proposed the development of 'a framework for describing national multilingualism' which would 'emphasize social, functional and distributional relationships within (and to some extent across) national boundaries.' Certainly the surveys reported in Ohannessian *et al* carried out by highly organized teams over a long period were of that kind. With similar resources at one's disposal some of that work could be of direct use (see for example Ansre (1975) for an individually administered questionnaire with very thoughtfully worded questions). Nothing of that kind has been done in Britain and we were in no position to do it for our sample except incidentally. What it amounts to is this. When we produce figures for the numbers of pupils speaking a given language these figures tell us nothing about the status of that language in its country of origin or about how the critical social description may have changed for the speakers of that language in this country. Typically the social and functional description of language must change when from being the dominant language of the mother country it becomes the language of a minority group of recent immigration attempting to preserve or assert its identity — Italian in Italy as against Italian in Bedford. That description remains to be done.

The languages and dialects spoken by London school pupils will in many cases be related to 'ethnicity'. Fishman (1977) has argued that language can often be the most salient symbol of ethnicity because it carries the past, expresses the present and future attitudes and aspirations. Giles (1977) has collected together recent work in this field and, linking social psychology and linguistics, explored linguistic diversity from the perspective of inter-group relations. In schools this poses questions like: When, if at all, does a pupil speak the language of his ethnic group? How do others react to this? In what ways, if any, does the school acknowledge the existence of this language? The survey was not equipped with the resources to discover how far the possession of a language (or even an accent, Bourhis and Giles 1977) was also a symbol of ethnicity. What it could do was to prepare the ground by mapping the range and scale of languages spoken by pupils. With the figures at hand it is important to bear in mind that the relationship between ethnicity and language, especially in multilinguistic communities is not a simple one. A black West Indian Londoner may not talk patois but have a strong sense of ethnic identity; on the other hand he may choose to learn patois in his teens in order to assert it very deliberately. The magnetic pull of London Jamaican is so powerful that black African pupils often choose to adopt it. The implications of an issue like ethnicity, like other social and political questions, cannot be read off sets of figures.

Linguistic Diversity in London Schools

The survey was concerned with London school pupils, youngsters growing up in a metropolis who cannot be said to be growing up in a speech community as that term has sometimes been understood, ie a linguistically homogeneous group. Halliday (1978) points out,

> A city is not a speech community in the classical sense. Its inhabitants do not all talk to each other. They do not speak alike; furthermore they do not mean alike. But a city is an environment in which meanings are exchanged. In this process conflicts arise, symbolic conflicts which are no less real than conflicts over economic interest; and these conflicts contain the mechanism of change. . . . The city dweller's picture of the universe is not, in the typical instance, one of order and constancy. But at least it has — or could have, if allowed to — a compensating quality that is of some significance; the fact that many very different groups of people have contributed to the making of it. (p. 163)

The 'classical sense' which saw a speech community in simple terms, rarely applies, and never applied to London. Certainly, large cities cannot be thought of as linguistic patchwork maps, ghetto after ghetto, not only because languages and dialects have no simple geographical distribution but also because interaction between them blurs whatever boundaries might be drawn. Both a geographical model and social class model would be false, though each could contribute to an understanding. Add to this the fact that London as a metropolis represents the extreme of all kinds of diversity and we can confidently expect that schools too will offer a complex picture, a picture moreover which will not necessarily be a mirror image of the locality which surrounds it. A few streets and shops may constitute a tightly-knit ghetto but the children from them may be dispersed in a mulit-ethnic school.

In London there are speakers of standard who live and learn side by side with all kinds of other speakers. London Black English (which as yet has no accepted name) will be found *par excellence* in Brixton where it is community-based but it might crop up anywhere else. Change, an abiding feature of language, is typical of London diversity. New languages appear and relatively settled languages change. The language X spoken in X-land becomes the language X as spoken in London. It would seem that a London Punjabi has developed which has now been acknowledged in the written language of newspapers. The Caribbean dialects change into a recognizable London variety. A speaker for whom English is a second language and who unmistakably speaks 'foreigner-English' may often be said to be speaking 'foreigner-London-English' since his speech contains features of London phonology, idioms etc. Thus dialects and languages are beginning to influence each other. Urbanization is a great eroder of linguistic frontiers. This does not mean that London is a linguistic melting pot or that we have any reason to believe that in a generation or two the languages which are newcomers will have disappeared but rather that London, in common with other large cities, is a great transformer of the languages which arrive on its doorstep. The communication system of a metropolis is so highly developed that very few can remain uninfluenced by languages different from their mother tongues. Typically these would be the oldest members of certain immigrant communities, especially women, and the very young. The more general process at work is the creation of thousands of bilingual and to a certain extent bidialectal speakers on a scale and of a diversity unprecedented in our history. Which dialect of English they learn depends in the main on their social class position in this country. It is common practice to talk of the 'target language' of a second-language learner. In London it will be a moving target, though undoubtedly most by virtue of their social position will have as their chief model London working-class speech. In schools where the acquisition of standard is usually seen as an unquestionable goal, this creates additional complexities for learners and dilemmas for parents.

This gives some notion, a cursory one, of the linguistic context of the survey. Fishman's famous question (1965) 'Who speaks what language to whom and when?' remains unanswered for London. Indeed no one has attempted to answer it comprehensively. The need to start on that process is manifest and it is to be hoped that in the near future we have the kind of studies which have been undertaken in other parts of the world and are beginning in Great Britain (see Trudgill 1978).

Sociolinguistic Issues and the Survey

The method of the survey required that the pupils themselves should be a major source of information. It was not the intention that an interviewer should confront a pupil and work his way through question after question. In the main the information was obtained in group discussions with pupils, the theme of which was their language resources. Nevertheless, however positive and non-threatening the procedure, it must be acknowledged that to ask pupils about what languages and dialects they speak can at times be a delicate business. Answers are, quite rightly, not to be had for the asking. School is a domain where certain sensitivities and attitudes will take on a special emphasis and educationally can become critical. We need to know the strength of a pupil's allegiance to his/her language(s) remembering that this allegiance is itself dynamic, changing across time and from situation to situation. What evokes pride and warmth in the family circle or at a wedding may perhaps evoke embarrassment or shame in a setting like school. Pupils who may be content or delighted to speak their minority group language in certain out-of-school situations may not wish attention drawn to it in school when it will seem to emphasize or suggest alien-ness.

The attitudes of parents often differ from those of their children. The parents may be eager for their children to learn Greek or Cantonese and press their children to attend out-of-school classes: some children accept this, others resent it both as loss of liberty and a badge of separatism.

On the other hand parents themselves may take an integrationist stance and be anxious for their children to become as English as possible as soon as possible, in particular to learn 'good English' and leave behind the culture and language of the country of origin. For dialect speakers the situation can become particularly fraught with tension and conflict. We are familiar with the fact that many speakers hold their own speech in low esteem. That is an oversimplification since speakers may feel differently about their speech in different situations. We may cite a group of girls in one school who on first being questioned said they spoke no other language than English. It emerged later that they were speakers of a French Creole which they did not see as a language in the school sense.

Thus it was that the enquiry in schools had to be conducted in an informal atmosphere in which pupils could feel they were participating in an exploration of their own language resources. Some inquiries which have attempted rapidly to gather data on, for example, first languages other than English have had as their aim discovering pupils for whom special measures might be thought necessary. Clearly they ran the risk of producing either reluctance or hostility.

We have already suggested that the familiar process of change to which all languages are subject applies to new arrivals. The old established varieties of London English change but some varieties of English are new. Amongst the new arrivals are varieties of English which also undergo processes of change which are far from predictable.

In spite of all the diversity there is a prevailing dialect (still awaiting a full description). Most people in England can identify with ease a fully London (Cockney) speaker and many would rapidly identify the origin of a speaker of standard which contains a few phonological features which are markers of London English.

A quarter of a century ago it might have been plausible (forgetting minorities) to regard London speech as a *continuum*. A similar continuum might apply in other cities but this needs investigation.

Cockney ⟶ Modified Cockney ⟶ Standard with ⟶ Standard
(full dialect) (adopting some   Cockney accent   with
                features of   Received
                standard)   Pronunciation

This continuum would represent the main categories for certain speakers but would also represent the choices in a repertoire which could be differentially drawn upon by any speaker. The more 'distant' the category the less likely is it that it would be included in a speaker's repertoire. The adjacent categories are the most readily available. We have now to accommodate new varieties of English which do not fit into that continuum. The survey had to devise categories and questions which were sensitive to these new varieties. However, London was probably never a linguistically homogeneous society. Only a most ingenious model could incorporate the relationships and distributions of dialects and languages even if we knew them. The continuum cannot be regarded as any more than a beginning in bringing some kind of order to a heterogeneous data.

Firstly there are many pupils whose English is *interlanguage,* that is it is at some stage between total ignorance of English and native-like mastery. They include those who are fluent speakers of English. They may even use English more than any other language. If however they retain in their speech a number of features which mark them out as unmistakably foreign, their English could still be called interlanguage. This may be true for the rest of their lives. We may even find communities the members of which reinforce each other's interlanguage in such a way as to create a new variety of English. The target language for most interlanguage speakers will be at the working-class end of the continuum since they are mostly amongst the poorest sections of the community and live and work amongst the working class.

It is customary in sociolinguistic literature to speak of *code-switching* when someone changes from one dialect or language in his repertoire to another. The metaphor of switching is certainly appropriate for some dialect speakers whose change from one dialect to another is marked by sharp discontinuity, as it might be in a person who has acquired standard through social and geographical mobility and revisits his childhood home. Intuitively we recognize the Cockney speaker not only by his grammar, his accent and lexicon, but also by his use of voice quality, his discourse style and the gestures integrated into the speech flow. He will also have an abundance of idioms and expressions of his own. Even among such readily recognized speakers there are differences. It is typical of urban diversity that a Cockney can adopt features of standard in certain contexts; he can be more Cockney or less. In educational circles it is often declared policy to foster bidialectalism ('the language of the playground and the language of the school'). But what we are discussing is not code-switching. There is usually no unambiguous cut-off point at which London pupils can be said to have switched from Cockney to Standard. It would be better to talk of *code-sliding* along the continuum.

> . . . to assume that each dialect has an autonomous grammar, and that bidialectal speakers shut off one grammar and switch on another, is just not credible in a case where most of the rules in the supposedly autonomous grammars would be exact duplicates of each other. (Fasold 1975, p. 214)

The most complex problem for the enquiry was the categorization of West Indian speech. The questionnaire[3] shows how it was solved in practical decision-making terms. We explore here some of the difficulties. Of course, there are Londoners of West Indian origin who are in precisely the same position as other London children somewhere on the London continuum. Once that is said the possibilities are numerous basically because there is a dynamic, highly mobile relationship between varieties of West Indian English and varieties of London English. These are the starting points:

i.   one of the Caribbean English-based Creoles;
ii.   a Caribbean standard;
iii.   anywhere between i. and ii. on the Creole continuum;[4]
iv.   London Jamaican.

The major complexity arises from the fact that a London West Indian pupil's language is influenced by the interaction of two continua thus:

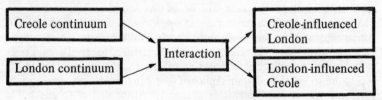

The West Indian element in his speech may derive from any part of the Creole continuum and the London element from any part of the London continuum. Thus the range of possibilities is enormous. A further complexity is added by the unpredicted emergence of London Jamaican. In general, like speakers on the London continuum, West Indians slide from one position to another but with a wider range of choices. However, it is important to bear in mind that in this intricate picture London Jamaican occupies a unique position for London school pupils which frequently differentiates them from their parents. In London all other creoles tend to disappear leaving it as the undisputed candidate for a symbolic role, the identity marker and channel for protest. There are many school pupils whose language differs in no way or very little from that of white London pupils but many, usually in their early teens, learn London Jamaican and are highly conscious of the symbolic nature of this act. Learning 'to talk black' is the more impressive since it often runs counter to the attitudes of parents who disapprove of 'bad talk'. The use of two dialects by black pupils (and a few white ones!) is more aptly described as code-switching rather than code-sliding.

Some black pupils have Creole features in their speech which remain concealed or suppressed in school unless they become deeply involved or, for some other reason, drop their guard. A single item of vocabulary or of phonology will reveal this.

If we take a mono-dialectal view of the kinds of English which we might find in a London school, then this list would be comprehensive:

Standard
London (Cockney)
Non-London British Isles dialects
Overseas dialects of English (a) English-based Creoles (b) Others
London Jamaican
Interlanguage

But that list fails to plot possible relationships between the varieties when we look at them from the point of view of the individual speaker. The table on the following page shows some of the major possibilities.

Confronted with these complexities, the compilers of the questionnaire were highly conscious of the fact that, given the limitations of time and resources and, above all, the fact that the collectors of the information were not linguists but for the most part practising teachers, they had to reach a compromise between the delicacy of the complexities within the picture of diversity and practical possibilities. The compromise insofar as the questionnaire was concerned attempted to go far beyond the bald information hitherto collected (What non-English language(s) does the pupil speak?) but did not incorporate all the discrimination indicated above.

Table 3. Code sliding

Dominant dialect or variety	Moving towards
Standard	(i)——►London
	(ii)——►London Jamaican
London	(i)——►Standard
	(ii)——►London Jamaican
	(iii)——►London Jamaican and Standard
Non-London British Isles	(i)——►London
	(ii)——►Standard
	(iii)——►London and Standard
English-based Creoles	(i)——►London Jamaican
	(ii)——►London
	(iii)——►Standard
	(iv)——►London and Standard
	(v)——►London and Standard and London Jamaican
Interlanguage	(i)——►London
	(ii)——►London and Standard
	(iii)——►Standard

In addition there is code-switching:

London Continuum ——————————————►London Jamaican

The Survey: Central Principles

We can now return to the question we posed at the outset 'Which language and dialect are spoken by how many pupils?' *The Survey of Linguistic Diversity in London Schools* to which we have been referring throughout was an attempt to provide an answer to that question for a limited school population in London. It was carried out in the period 1977-78. The grant from the Department of Education and Science made possible the employment of one Research Officer for six months. In practice without the use of volunteer labour (staff and students of the Institute of Education and teachers in the schools) the work would never have been accomplished. However, in acknowledging the limitations which have already been touched on and will emerge further as we proceed, we must also stress that it was the first study of its kind in the United Kingdom. As a pioneer study it offers itself for replication and refinement. The following features should be borne in mind when considering the whole undertaking.

i. The survey was concerned with the language of all pupils not because of some vague democratic sentiment but because that is how language diversity confronts teachers and pupils in their daily lives. There is scarcely an issue raised by the new kind of diversity which was not there before. However, in the new context they are harder to ignore. Thus the survey was not confined to ethnic minorities, bilinguals, 'immigrants' etc. The aim was to look at the overall pattern of diversity, a pattern to which all pupils in the sample would contribute.

ii. The information was to be gathered in the main by teachers using an introduction to the questionnaire and a briefing session as a guide. This together with follow-up discussion of results constituted a major in-service operation the positive consequences of which are still being felt.

iii. The survey attempted to create a positive climate in the schools. The researchers were anxious to avoid the impression that they were collecting statistics in order to measure the size of linguistic and ethnic minority problems. On the contrary they wanted the survey to be seen much more as a means of registering the rich linguistic resources now available in the schools.

iv. It follows from iii that the survey was also an attempt to do more than register the dominant language of a pupil. The aim was also to record as much as possible of his/her repertoire. Thus the survey was not asking, 'What is this pupil's mother tongue?' but 'What are the languages and dialects which this pupil has available to use, for what purposes and with what degree of competence?'

v. Given the educational intentions underlying the survey, it included some assessment of the pupils' literacy including their competence as readers and writers of English.

Teachers were asked to base their judgments on the classroom language of the pupils and supplement that by other information available from the pupils or from other sources. There are obvious hazards here. Classroom language may well constitute a shift along the continuum towards standard and the extent to which this was true would be governed by classroom climate. The view might be taken, therefore, that the survey could only yield information on a somewhat constrained variety of English. Anyone familiar with inner-London secondary schools will know that it is extremely unlikely that a teacher would not hear the spontaneous speech of pupils. The point, nevertheless, remains that there can be no certainty about this. Even less is it true that the results incorporate all the items in the repertoires of all pupils. A quite different kind of study would be called for to reduce the distortions and simplifications of this one. Firstly it would have to have the resources to check on the first responses. For example, a pupil says he speaks Pushtu. Does he? Of what kind? When? At what level of proficiency? Answering these questions calls for the protracted study of individual speakers. When all that is said, it remains true that the survey can give valuable information on such questions as the *extent* of bilingualism in a way which directs the attention of schools to the linguistic resources of their pupils and also opens up the possibility for them to undertake their own enquiries.

We have already referred to the problems of describing varieties of West Indian speech as they are encountered in London. Put briefly, they arise from the interaction of the creole continuum with the London continuum and the wide range of possibilities to which that interaction gives rise. We have also referred to the special position of London Jamaican and code-switching. We must now add yet another complexity. It has taken a long time for teachers and others to become aware of the fact that there are different Caribbean varieties spoken in different islands and parts of the mainland. The ignorance may be deplorable but it is understandable, firstly because our ears find it difficult to discriminate and secondly because we frequently encounter these varieties in already modified forms (unlike fifteen to twenty years ago). It would therefore seem paradoxical that the questionnaire asked which Caribbean variety a pupil spoke. In practice other sources of information are often available, the pupil him/herself, other pupils, other teachers etc but a safeguard was introduced, the category, 'Caribbean — loose categorization only'. No one has yet provided a basic description of the varieties of London West Indian English which would have served as a starting point for the survey. Although the findings could not be refined, what they did do was to avoid stereotypes and false homogeneity. The assumption of the survey was that many, perhaps most, London secondary school pupils of West Indian origin are fluent speakers of London English but that they incorporate in their speech to a greater or lesser degree features of Caribbean English. The extent to which they do so depends, amongst other things, partly on situation and the 'temperature' of the interaction in which they are engaged and partly on the composition of the face-to-face group.

We have attempted to show that any kind of language census calls for some analysis which takes us further than the matching of names of languages and numbers of speakers. The translation of such analysis into the realities of an investigation is another matter. We can now give a highly compressed account of the survey and a selection from its findings.

Methods and Findings of the Survey

The original intention had been to use a carefully selected sample of schools, but access to schools proved to be difficult. The survey had therefore to be limited to those schools which indicated a willingness to participate. Thus certain biases crept into the sample. The over representation of North London almost certainly led to the over-representation of Turkish and Greek speakers and the under representation of some Asian languages. The main details of the sample are given below.

No. of pupils	4600 (boys 46%; girls 54%)
No. of schools	28 (all secondary : 10 single sex 18 mixed)
Age group	11-12 yrs. (i.e. first year pupils only)
% of age group	14%

Data collectors were required to probe beneath the *lingua franca* of the classroom (English, of course) to unearth the linguistic resources of the pupils. All the detailed judgments followed from the basic allocations of a pupil one of two categories.

Category A	Speakers of Great Britain-based dialects of English
Category B	Speakers of overseas languages and dialects

Even these categories are not clear cut and the final allocation was made on the possession of an unambiguous native-like competence in a Great Britain based dialect or of some other language or dialect.

That first allocation having been made, the questionnaire elicited more precise information i.e. which dialect or which language. Finally, it gathered details of further languages and dialects spoken by the pupils i.e. data on bilingualism and bidialectalism.

The first findings to look at are those which tell us about what we may call the surface stratum of the pupil's language. Table 4 shows us a picture of diversity based on the dominant language in use in school.

Table 4. Proportions in the Main Language Groupings
(excluding considerations of bidialectalism and bilingualism)

	%	%
Great Britain based dialects of English		84
London dialect	67	
Non-London dialect	2	
Standard	15	
Overseas Dialect		10
Language other than English		6

Table 5 fills out this picture and reveals the extent of bilingualism and bidialectalism. Of pupils allocated to Section A (i.e. Great Britain-based dialects of English) 47% spoke a further language or dialect. On the other hand all but 3% of those allocated to Section B (i.e. overseas dialects of English and languages other than English) were recorded as being fluent speakers of English. Almost all of the 3% had some command of English. We can say that 30% of the sample were bidialectal or bilingual (excluding UK-based bidialectalism).

Table 5. Proportions in the Main Language Groupings
(expressed as proportions of monolingual, bidialectal
and bilingual speakers)

	%	%
Monolingual speakers with use of a Great Britain-based dialect of English only		70
London	56	
Non-London	2	
Standard	12	
Bidialectal speakers with some use both of a Great Britain and an overseas based dialect of English		14
Great Britain and Caribbean	13	
Great Britain and other overseas dialect	1	
Bilingual speakers with some use both of English and a language other than English		14
Overseas dialect dominant		1
Overseas language dominant		1

Some form of London dialect (and that label is itself open to question) dominates the sample (67%). A century of mass education has not eliminated it. It permeates London classrooms with sufficient infectious power to affect the speech of many younger, non-London teachers which itself raises doubts about the frequently used description of it as a 'non-prestige' or 'low-status' dialect. Standard speakers are scattered throughout the schools, if they crop up at all. Only nine schools contained more than twenty and some contained none at all. It is these realities which make the *de facto*, as distinct from pedagogic, target language a far from easily defined goal.

Table 6 considers speakers of overseas dialects of English (15% of the sample), 71% of them with speech deriving from Jamaican English, 17% from other regions of the Caribbean and South America and 6% from other parts of the Anglophone world. The classification in Table 6 can be studied by comparing it with our exploration earlier of the difficulties of teaching satisfactory questionnaire categories. However, the broad configurations can be discovered in Table 6 in which three simplified categories are used; speakers of:

a. full creoles, usually as their dominant speech
b. standard, either that of an overseas region or UK standard with some overseas features
c. a variety of English in which London and an overseas dialect are blended in different ways.

Table 6. Distributions for pupils speaking an overseas dialect of English by country of origin and type of dialect spoken
N = 711

	Creole (N = 100)	Standard (N = 70)	London/ overseas dialect (N = 500)
Jamaica	52	11	444
Eastern Caribbean (N = 121)			
Antigua	6		3
Barbados	9	7	10
Dominica	3		5
Grenada	8	3	6
Guyana	2	1	12
Martinique			1
Montserrat			1
Nevis		1	
St. Lucia	6	6	12
St. Vincent	1		3
Trinidad	7	4	3
Tobago	1		
Africa (N = 30)			
Nigeria		15	
Uganda		2	
Ghana		4	
Mauritius		1	
South Africa		1	
West Africa	1		
Sierra Leone	4	2	
Other Countries (N = 12)			
USA		8	
Canada		1	
Australia		2	
New Zealand		1	

Miscellaneous attributions e.g. to Caribbean general not included = 41.

Bilingual and plurilingual speakers constituted 14% of the sample. One in sixty was plurilingual. These bare facts cry out for further study.

Table 7. Languages other than English, where spoken by one or more pupils

European	African	South Asian	Mid-Eastern	Far Eastern	Other
Greek	Yoruba	Gujerati	Iranian	Cantonese	French creoles
Turkish	Hausa	Bengali	'Moroccan'	Chinese (new	(Dominican,
Italian	Ibo	Punjabi	Arabic	standard	St. Lucian,
Spanish	Gambian	Hindi		Mandarin)	Guyanese,
German	Gur	Urdu		Japanese	Mauritian)
Portuguese	Swahili	Katchi		Malay	Maori
French	Twi	Nepalese			Maltese
Dutch	Zulu	Pushtu			Romany
Finnish	Afrikaans	Sinhalese			
Gaelic		Tamil			
Hungarian					
Polish					
Swedish					
Serbo-croat					
Sloven					
Russian					
Armenian					
Latvian					
Yiddish					
Hebrew					
21	9	10	3	5	7

Total number of languages 55

We should find out, for example, what roles are now played in the London context by languages of East African Asians or West Africans. Because of the North London bias of the sample the figures given in Tables 7 and 8 cannot be read as representative either for London as a whole or for the adult community. But they do constitute something of a guide and a dramatic reminder of just how multilingual we have become. It is certain that 55 languages registered by the survey would be increased by a more extensive survey but the picture presented by Tables 7 and 8 would change only in the weighting of certain languages.

Table 8. Distribution of languages other than English, where spoken by more than 14 pupils

	N	Percentage of all bilingual pupils (N = 749)
Greek	(156)	22
Turkish	(97)	13
Italian	(46)	6
Gujerati	(41)	5
Spanish	(35)	5
Cantonese	(33)	4
French creoles	(33)	4
German	(30)	4
Portuguese	(28)	4
Bengali	(20)	3
Punjabi	(18)	2
French	(17)	2
Yoruba	(17)	2
Arabic	(16)	2
Hindi	(15)	2
Urdu	(15)	2

To the surface stratum of diversity which has been presented by Tables 4-8 we can now add what information the survey collected which begins to probe a little deeper. We have already indicated the complexities confronting the researcher when looking at dialect in general and bidialectalism in particular. Tables 9 and 10 incorporate as much as it was reasonable to ask teachers to condense from what they heard (or thought they heard) and arrived at from listening to audio-tapes and through discussion. Their sensitivity to overseas dialects, of course, varied considerably. From the broad categories with which they were asked to operate there emerged the basic characteristics of a second/third generation. For very few pupils is the overseas dialect dominant but amongst 'Jamaican' pupils a considerable number are placed as dialect speakers 'in certain contexts'. The accessibility of

Table 9. Strength of overseas dialect features in the speech of bidialectal pupils (numbers in sample)

	Jamaican	Eastern Caribbean	Non-Caribbean Countries	Miscellaneous	Total
A full overseas, dialectal speech	20	3	6		29
Basically a London (or Standard) speaker though incorporating some overseas dialectal features	487	118	36	41	682

Table 10. Extent of use of overseas dialect in the speech of bidialectal pupils (numbers in sample)

	Jamaican	Eastern Caribbean	Non-Caribbean Countries	Miscellaneous	Total
Speaks the overseas dialect regularly in certain contexts	90	8			98
Overseas dialect is pupil's dominant speech	17	4	8		29
Basically a London (or Standard) speaker, but occasionally deepens overseas dialectal features	400	109	34	41	572

London Jamaican and its meaning for them would account for this and that accords with the experience of many teachers. This is confirmed by other data which showed that the same group dominated amongst those who showed themselves interested in reading and writing in an overseas dialect.

Most bidialectals are of Caribbean origin and the survey points to the need to avoid two extreme views of their language. One view is that inevitably it is converging and will increasingly converge on some form of London speech which predated the large-scale immigration and the other that most or many of them can switch into a creole.

About half the pupils described as bilingual were fluent in English and another language ('effectively bilingual'). It is more common for speakers of South Asian languages, Arabic and Cantonese to be bilingual ('regular speakers') or to have the overseas language dominant than for speakers who have some command of a European language. Regional languages like Gujerati, Punjabi and Bengali figure more strongly in bilingualism than national languages like Hindi or Urdu. The details set out in Tables 11, 12 and 13 give rise to many other possible connections between aspects of bilingualism and the speakers of particular languages (e.g. how far do figures reflect recency of arrival, accessibility in London of a community using the language for social purposes, the accessibility of publications in the relevant language, the existence of mother tongue schools or classes, the interaction between literacy in an overseas language and literacy in English). They cannot be pursued in any detail here. Any careful inspection of these tables would give rise to many others. The figures do not resolve any of them but they do reveal some of the directions which further studies need to take. Deeper understanding need not await elaborate and lengthy investigations. Small scale studies could offer valuable insights.

We remarked at the outset that the motives for investigating linguistic diversity in Britain might vary widely and that this investigation was prompted by educational pre-occupations. The results, however, do suggest that nationally we have not come to terms with the facts of our multilingual and multidialectal community. They have implications for our whole communications network, political policies for minorities and race relations. The implications for the educational system urgently need the kind of elaboration and discussion which can lead to the forging of new policies: on mother tongue maintenance, the place of dialect in the school system, teacher education, the response of the examination and assessment system, library and text book provision, revision of the teaching of English curriculum for a multi-cultural society, the study of language in schools, resources and materials and the relation between the community and the school. It is to issues of this kind that those who worked on the survey are now addressing themselves.

Table 11. Comparison of amount of use of languages other than English, where spoken by more than 14 pupils

Percentages of sub-groups speaking each language

	Bilingual: regularly speaks language	Overseas language dominant	Other: speaks some phrases
	%	%	%
Gujerati	80	10	10
Punjabi	66	17	17
Greek	65	5	30
Turkish	61	.2	39
Cantonese	60	27	13
Bengali	60	30	10
Arabic	56	25	19
Portuguese	54	14	32
Hindi	53	–	47
Spanish	51	14	35
French creoles	39	3	57
Italian	35	2	59
French	35	–	65
Urdu	33	27	40
German	23	–	77
Yoruba	23	–	77

Table 12.   Comparison of proportions of pupils allocated as 'unambiguously speakers of English' or as 'incorporating features deriving from a language other than English' for languages, where spoken by more than 14 pupils

Percentages of sub-groups speaking each language

	Unambiguously speakers of English	*Incorporating features from overseas language*
	%	%
German	90	10
Yoruba	88	12
Italian	82	18
French	82	18
Hindi	73	27
Greek	72	28
French creoles	60	40
Turkish	60	40
Spanish	60	40
Portuguese	50	50
Punjabi	50	50
Gujerati	41	59
Urdu	40	60
Arabic	31	69
Bengali	30	70
Cantonese	18	82

Table 13. Estimates of competence as speakers of English for pupils speaking a language other than English, where spoken by more than 14 pupils

Percentages of sub-group speaking each language

	Initial	Intermediate	Fluent
	%	%	%
Cantonese	18	36	46
Bengali	15	35	50
Arabic	25	12	63
Urdu	13	13	74
Gujerati	5	15	80
Portuguese	6	14	80
Spanish	11	6	83
Hindi		13	87
Greek		12	88
Turkish	1	11	88
French		12	88
Punjabi	5	5	90
French creoles		9	91
Italian		9	91
Yoruba		6	94
German		3	97

Notes

[1] Stephens (1976) gives these figures for bilingual Gaels; 1891: 210, 677; 1971: 88, 415; and for Welsh speakers; 1911: 977, 400; 1971: 542, 402.

[2] *Linguistic Minorities Project*, funded by the DES and housed in the EFL Department of the University of London Institute of Education is the clearest indication of this shift. It is likely because of its scale and duration to produce data of a quality which has so far not been approached.

[3] The questionnaire can be found in full in Appendices 1 and 2 (pp. 145-177) of *Languages and Dialects of London Schoolchildren*, Rosen, H. and Burgess, T., Ward Lock, 1980.

[4] Edwards (1979) 'The linguistic situation in the West Indies can best be described in terms of a continuum with broad Creole at one end and standard English at the other. Each speaker will command a span on the continuum rather than simply occupying a point on it.' (p. 16)

References

Ansre, G. (1975) 'Madina: three polyglots and some implications for Ghana' in Ohannessian *et al.*

Bourhis, E. Y. and Giles, H. (1977) 'The language of intergroup distinctiveness' in Giles, H. (ed.).

Campbell-Platt, K. (1976) 'Distribution of linguistic minorities in Britain' in *Bilingualism and British Education*, CILT.

Derrick, J. (1977) *The Language Needs of Minority Group Children*, NFER.

Edwards, V. (1979) *The West Indian Language Issue in British Schools*, Routledge and Kegan Paul.

Fasold, R. W. (1975) review of J. L. Dillard, *Black English: Its History and Usage in the United States*, in *Language in Society*, Vol IV, no. 2, pp. 198-221.

Fishman, J. A. (1977) 'Language and ethnicity' in Giles, H. (ed.).

Giles, H. (ed) (1977) *Language, Ethnicity and Intergroup Relations*, Academic Press.

Halliday, M. A. K. (1978) *Language as Social Semiotic*, Arnold.

HMSO (1975) *A Language for Life* (the Bullock Report).

Institute of Education (1977) *Guidelines for the investigation of the language of inner-city pupils*, mimeo.

Khan, Verity (ed.) (1979) *Minority Families in Britain*, Macmillan.

Kranz, E. (1977) *Ethnic Minorities in Britain*, Paladin.

Lomas, G. (1974) *The Coloured Population of Great Britain*, Runnymede Trust.

Ohannessian, S., Ferguson, G. A. and Polome, E. C. (1975) *Surveys in Developing Nations*, Centre for Applied Linguistics, Arlington, Va.

Stephens, M. (1976) *Linguistic Minorities in Western Europe*, Gomer Press.

Stewart, W. A. (1968) 'A sociolinguistic typology for describing national multilingualism' in Fishman, J. (ed.) *Readings in the Sociology of Language*, Mouton.

Trudgill, P. (1978) *Sociolinguistic Patterns in British English*, Arnold.

Watson, J. L. (ed.) (1977) *Between Two Cultures*, Blackwell.

SECTION 2

Social Aspects of Language

Introduction

Section 2 opens with an article in which Halliday looks at certain aspects of the relationship between language and the social system. His framework is the distinction between language as institution, its variation into dialects and registers, and language as system, consisting of semantics, grammar and phonology. In his treatment of language as institution Halliday distinguishes several important ideas, such as the difference between geographical and social dialects. He stresses that the most significant thing about language as system is that it is structured into what he terms *functional components*. Variation theory is what Halliday sees as the factor unifying language as system and language as institution. Throughout, he emphasizes that the categories the linguist uses are idealized, and too neat to fit reality exactly.

In the second paper Hymes develops two ideas which have been of enormous influence in studies of language, Chomsky's concepts of competence, 'the speaker-hearer's knowledge of his language', and performance, 'the actual use of language in concrete situations'. Hymes adds a new dimension to these concepts, the social, as he attempts to broaden the idea of linguistic competence, for instance, to communicative competence. He argues that Chomsky's theory fails to deal with the real person because it neglects socio-cultural factors, and this is what he sets out to rectify.

The third and fourth articles examine communication and the way social reality is structured. In the third article Mueller deals with the relationship between communication and the maintenance of the *status quo*. Major areas of interest here are the role of collective beliefs, the position of the working-class and the influence of government upon communication. Mueller argues that it is very difficult for the man in the street to understand governmental policy because information is withheld, or, if it is given, the issue is clouded because ritualistic language is used. Hence, these are two ways of maintaining the *status quo*.

But not the only ways, argues Mueller. He sees a structured consensus in a similar light. This consensus is either imposed upon the public by a political elite or stems from factors in the political-economic system itself. One such factor, for instance, is the need to maintain economic growth. This leads to communication being dominated by the promise of such things as more affluence to workers to encourage economic growth.

Mueller then moves on to examine how communication is affected by language itself; i.e. he analyses how information can be lost for purely linguistic reasons. So, he argues, groups bound by a restricted code cannot cope with sophisticated messages. The final part looks at the question of ideologies and their relationship to the communication of political reality.

Emerson, in the fourth article, looks at a concrete situation, a gynaecological examination, and interprets it to show how reality is enshrined in routines. In such a situation contradictory definitions of reality exist at one and the same time, and she attempts to define the complexity of those realities — the medical definition and opposing ones. The gynaecological examination exaggerates what is found in all situations, the internally contradictory nature of definitions of reality. Emerson discusses the routine arrangements which embody the definition of reality. During the encounter threats to the definition arise, and measures have to be taken to neutralize those threats. Constructing reality depends upon such techniques as knowing when to make things explicit and when to leave them implicit.

The fifth article shows a change of direction: Fishman is dealing with Whorf's hypothesis, central to which is the idea that language influences or determines reality. Fishman sees Whorf's theory as having its heyday in the 1950s and early 1960s, part of our yesterday. Although he considers that Whorf's arguments do not provide a convincing explanation of the relationship between language and reality, he nevertheless regards Whorf as a researcher and a thinker who has radically altered man's view of himself. Fishman discusses what he sees as the important legacies of the Whorfian hypothesis: an interest in language universals, and in ethno-sciences where such fields as colour-terms have been looked at as part of 'current ways of viewing'. Although the Whorfian model of 'one society — one language' does not really portray the relationship between language and society, there has developed from the discussion of it a view of societal bilingualism and the way it affects individual behaviour. That is how Fishman sees the central concern of today. In the future, he argues, the main interest must be language planning, as a bilingual is rarely equally fluent in both languages on all topics, and his behaviour is affected differentially. To sum up his viewpoint, Fishman presents ten conclusions about language planning.

V. J. Lee

2.1 An Interpretation of the Functional Relationship between Language and Social Structure
M. A. K. Halliday

In this [essay] I shall [consider . . .] how language expresses the social system. In the course of the discussion I shall move towards the view that the relation of language to the social system is not simply one of expression, but a more complex natural dialectic in which language actively symbolizes the social system, thus creating as well as being created by it. This, it is hoped, will clarify my interpretation of language within the framework of the culture as an information system, and give some indication of what I understand by the concept of 'language as social semiotic'.

As an underlying conceptual framework, I shall distinguish between (i) *language as system* and (ii) *language as institution*. The salient facts about language as *system* are (a) that it is *stratified* (it is a three-level coding system consisting of a semantics, a lexicogrammar and a phonology) and (b) that its semantic system is organized into *functional* components (ideational, including experiential and logical; interpersonal; textual). The salient fact about language as *institution* is that it is *variable*; there are two kinds of variation, (a) *dialect* (variation according to the *user*), and (b) *register* (variation according to the *use*). This is, of course, an idealized construct; there are no such clearcut boundaries in the facts themselves.

1   Language as Institution

1.1   Dialect

Classical dialectology, as developed in Europe, rests on certain implicit assumptions about speakers and speech communities. A speech community is assumed to be a social unit whose members (i) communicate with each other, (ii) speak in a consistent way and (iii) all speak alike. This is obviously, again, an idealized picture; but in the type of settled rural community for which dialect studies were first developed, it is near enough reality to serve as a theoretical norm.

Dialectal variation, in such a model, is essentially variation *between* speech communities. We may recognize some variation also within the community — squire and parson, or landlord and priest, probably speak

Halliday, M. A. K. (1978), *Language as Social Semiotic*, London, Edward Arnold, pp. 183-192.

differently from other people — but this is at the most a minor theme; and we do not envisage variation as something that arises *within* the speech of an individual speaker.

When dialectology moved into an urban setting, with Labov's monumental New York city studies, variation took on a new meaning. Labov showed that, within a typical North American urban community, the speech varies (i) *between* the members according to social class (low to high), and (ii) *within* each member according to 'style scale' (amount of monitoring or attention paid to one's own speech, casual to formal). The effect of each of these factors is quantitative (hence probabilistic in origin), but the picture is clear: when single dialect variables are isolated for intensive investigation, some of them turn out to be socially stratified. The forms of the variable ('variants') are *ranked* in an order such that the 'high' variant is associated with higher social status *or* a more formal context of speech, and the 'low' with lower social status *or* a more casual context of speech.

1.2 Social dialect

As long as dialect variation is geographically determined, it can be explained away: one group stays on this side of the mountain, the other group moves to the other side of the mountain, and they no longer talk to each other. But there are no mountains dividing social classes; the members of different social classes do talk to each other, at least transactionally. What is the explanation of this socially determined variation? How do 'social dialects' arise?

One of the most significant of Labov's findings was the remarkable uniformity shown by people of all social groups in their attitudes towards variation in the speech of others. This uniformity of attitude means that the members are highly sensitive to the social meaning of dialectal variation, a form of sensitivity that is apparently achieved during the crucial years of adolescence, in the age range about 13-18.

We acquire this sensitivity as a part of growing up in society, because dialect variation is functional with respect to the social structure. And this is why it does not disappear. It was confidently predicted in the period after World War II that, with the steadily increasing dominance of the mass media, dialects would disappear and we should soon all be speaking alike. Sure enough, the *regionally* based dialects of rural areas are disappearing, at least in industrial societies. But with the urban dialects the opposite has happened: diversity is increasing. We can explain this by showing that the diversity is socially functional. It expresses the structure of society.

It would be a mistake to think of social structure simply in terms of some particular index of social class. The essential characteristic of social structure as we know it is that it is hierarchical; and linguistic variation is what expresses its hierarchical character, whether in terms of age, generation, sex, provenance or any other of its manifestations, including caste and class.

Let us postulate a perfectly homogeneous society, one without any of these forms of social hierarchy. The members of such a society would presumably speak a perfectly homogeneous language, one without any dialectal variation. Now consider the hypothetical antithesis of this: a society split into two conflicting groups, a society and an antisociety. Here we shall expect to find some form of matching linguistic order: two mutually opposed linguistic varieties, a language and an antilanguage. These are, once again, idealized constructs; but phenomena approximating to them have arisen at various times and places. For example, the social conditions of sixteenth-century England generated an antisociety of 'vagabonds', who lived by extorting wealth from the established society; and this society had its antilanguage, fragments of which are reported in contemporary documents. The antilanguage is a language of social conflict — of passive resistance or active opposition; but at the same time, like any other language, it is a means of expressing and maintaining the social structure — in this case, the structure of the antisociety.

Most of the time what we find in real life are dialect hierarchies, patterns of dialectal variation in which a 'standard' (representing the power base of society) is opposed by nonstandard varieties (which the members refer to as 'dialects'). The nonstandard dialects may become languages of opposition and protest; periods of explicit class conflict tend to be characterized by the development of such protest languages, sometimes in the form of 'ghetto languages', which are coming closer to the antilanguage end of the scale. Here dialect becomes a means of expression of class consciousness and political awareness. We can recognize a category of 'oppressed languages', languages of groups that are subjected to social or political oppression. It is characteristic of oppressed languages that their speakers tend to excel at verbal contest and verbal display. Meaning is often the most effective form of social action that is available to them.

1.3 Register
Dialects, in the usual sense of that term, are different ways of saying the same thing. In other words, the dialects of a language differ from each other phonologically and lexicogrammatically, but not, in principle, semantically.

In this respect, dialectal variation contrasts with variation of another kind, that of *register*. Registers are ways of saying different things.

Registers differ semantically. They also differ lexicogrammatically, because that is how meanings are *expressed*; but lexicogrammatical differences among registers are, by and large, the automatic consequence of semantic differences. In principle, registers are configurations of meanings that are typically exchanged – that are 'at risk', so to speak – under given conditions of use.

A dialect is 'what you speak' (habitually); this is determined by 'who you are', your regional and/or social place of origin and/or adoption. A register is 'what you are speaking' (at the given time), determined by 'what you are doing', the nature of the ongoing social activity. Whereas dialect variation reflects the social order in the special sense of *the hierarchy of social structure*, register variation also reflects the social order but in the special sense of *the diversity of social processes*. We are not doing the same things all the time; so we speak now in one register, now in another. But the total *range* of the social processes in which any member will typically engage is a function of the structure of society. We each have our own repertory of social actions, reflecting our place at the intersection of a whole complex of social hierarchies. There is a division of labour.

Since the division of labour is *social*, the two kinds of language variety, register and dialect, are closely interconnected. The structure of society determines who, in terms of the various social hierarchies of class, generation, age, sex, provenance and so on, will have access to which aspects of the social process – and hence, to which registers. (In most societies today there is considerable scope for individual discretion, though this has not always been the case.) This means, in turn, that a particular register tends to have a particular dialect associated with it: the registers of bureaucracy, for example, demand the 'standard' (national) dialect, whereas fishing and farming demand rural (local) varieties. Hence the dialect comes to symbolize the register; when we hear a local dialect, we unconsciously switch off a large part of our register range.

In this way, in a typical hierarchical social structure, dialect becomes the means by which a member gains, or is denied, access to certain registers.

So if we say that linguistic structure 'reflects' social structure, we are really assigning to language a role that is too passive. (I am formulating it in this way in order to keep the parallel between the two expressions 'linguistic structure' and 'social structure'. In fact, what is meant is the linguistic *system*; elsewhere I have not used 'structure' in this general sense of the organization of language, but have reserved it for the specialized sense of constituent structure.) Rather we should say that linguistic structure is *the realization of* social structure, actively symbolizing it in a process of mutual creativity. Because it stands as a metaphor for society, language has the property of not only transmitting the social order but also maintaining and potentially modifying it. (This is undoubtedly the explanation of the violent attitudes that under certain social conditions come to be held by one group towards the speech of others. A different set of *vowels* is perceived as the symbol of a different set of *values*, and hence takes on the character of a threat.) Variation in language is the symbolic expression of variation in society: it is created by society, and helps to create society in its turn. Of the two kinds of variation in language, that of dialect expresses the diversity of social structure, that of register expresses the diversity of social process. The interaction of dialect and register in language expresses the interaction of structure and process in society.

2 Language as System

2.1 Function

We have considered how variation in language is socially functional. We must now consider how the linguistic *system* is socially functional.

The most important fact about language as system is its organization *into functional components*.

It is obvious that language is used in a multitude of different ways, for a multitude of different purposes. It is not possible to enumerate them; nor is it necessary to try: there would be no way of preferring one list over another. These various ways of using languages are sometimes referred to as 'functions of language'. But to say language has many 'functions', in this sense, is to say no more than that people engage in a variety of social actions — that they do different things together.

We are considering 'functions' in a more fundamental sense, as a necessary element in the interpretation of the linguistic system. The linguistic system is orchestrated into different modes of meaning, and these represent its most general functional orientations. No doubt language has evolved in this way because of the ways in which it is used; the two concepts of function are certainly interrelated. But if we seek to explain the internal workings of language we are forced to take into consideration its external relation to the social context.

The point is a substantive one, and we can approach it from this angle. Considered in relation to the social order, language is a resource, a meaning potential. Formally, language has this property: that it is a coding system *on three levels*. Most coding systems are on two levels: a *content*, and an *expression*: for example, traffic signals, with content 'stop/go' coded into expression 'red/green'. But language has evolved a third, abstract level of *form* intermediate between the two; it consists of content, form and expression, or, in linguistic terms, of semantics, lexicogrammar and phonology. Now, when we analyse the content side, the semantic system and its representation in the grammar, we find that it has an internal organization in which the social functions of language are clearly reflected.

2.2 Functional components

The semantic system is organized into a small number of components

— three or four depending on how one looks at them — such that *within* one component there is a high degree of interdependence and mutual constraint, whereas *between* components there is very little: each one is relatively independent of the others.

The components can be identified as follows:

1. ideational (language as reflection), comprising
   (a) experiential
   (b) logical
2. interpersonal (language as action)
3. textual (language as texture, in relation to the environment)

When we say that these components are relatively independent of one another, we mean that the choices that are made within any one component, while strongly affected by other choices within the same component, have no effect, or only a very weak effect, on choices made within the others. For example, given the meaning potential of the interpersonal component, out of the innumerable choices that are available to me I might choose (i) to offer a proposition, (ii) pitched in a particular key (e.g. contradictory-defensive), (iii) with a particular intent towards you (e.g. of convincing you), (iv) with a particular assessment of its probability (e.g. certain), and (v) with indication of a particular attitude (e.g. regretful). Now, all these choices are strongly interdetermining; if we use a network mode of representation, as in systemic theory, they can be seen as complex patterns of internal constraint among the various sub-networks. But they have almost no effect on the ideational meanings, on the *content* of what you are to be convinced of, which may be that the earth is flat, that Mozart was a great musician, or that I am hungry. Similarly, the ideational meanings do not determine the interpersonal ones; but there is a high degree of interdetermination *within* the ideational component: the kind of process I choose to refer to, the participants in the process, the taxonomies of things and properties, the circumstances of time and space, and the natural logic that links all these together.

2.3 Functional components and grammatical structure
So far, I have been looking at the matter from a semantic point of view, taking as the problem the interpretation of the semantic system. Suppose now we take a second approach, from a lexicogrammatical point of view — 'from below', as it were. In the interpretation of the lexicogrammatical system we find ourselves faced with a different problem, namely that of explaining the different *kinds of structure* that are found at this level. Consideration of this problem is beyond our scope here; but when we look into it, we find that the various types of grammatical structure are related to these semantic components in a systematic way. Each kind of meaning tends to be realized as a particular kind of structure. Hence in the encoding of a text each

component of meaning makes its contribution to the structural output; but it is a contribution which has on it the stamp of that particular mode of meaning. We would summarize this as follows (see Halliday 1977):

Semantic component	Type of grammatical structure by which typically realized
1. ideational:	
(a) experiential	constituent (segmental)
(b) logical	recursive
2. interpersonal	prosodic
3. textual	culminative

2.4 Functional components and social context

Thirdly, we may approach the question 'from above', from the perspective of language and the social order — at which I have called the 'social semiotic' level. When we come to investigate the relation of language to social context we find that the functional components of the semantic system once again provide the key. We saw that they were related to the different types of grammatical structure. There is also a systematic relationship between them and the semiotic structure of the speech situation. It is this, in part, that validates the notion of a speech situation.

Let us assume that the social system (or the 'culture') can be represented as a construction of meanings — as a semiotic system. The meanings that constitute the social system are exchanged through a variety of modes or channels, of which language is one; but not, of course, the only one — there are many other semiotic modes besides. Given this social-semiotic perspective, a *social context* (or 'situation', in the terms of situation theory) is a temporary construct or instantiation of meanings from the social system. A social context is a semiotic structure which we may interpet in terms of three variables: a 'field' of social process (what is going on), a 'tenor' of social relationships (who are taking part) and a 'mode' of symbolic interaction (how are the meanings exchanged). If we are focusing on language, this last category of 'mode' refers to what part the language is playing in the situation under consideration.

As said above, these components of the context are systematically related to the components of the semantic system; and once again, given that the context is a semiotic construct, this relation can be seen as one of realization. The meanings that constitute the social context are *realized* through selections in the meaning potential of language.

To summarize:

Component of social context	Functional-semantic component through which typically realized
1. field (social process)	experiential
2. tenor (social relationship)	interpersonal
3. mode (symbolic mode)	textual

The linguistic system, in other words, is organized in such a way that the social context is predictive of the text. This is what makes it possible for a member to make the necessary predictions about the meanings that are being exchanged in any situation which he encounters. If we drop in on a gathering, we are able to tune in very quickly, because we size up the field, tenor and mode of the situation and at once form an idea of what is likely to be being meant. In this way we know what semantic configurations – what register – will probably be required if we are to take part. If we did not do this, there would be no communication, since only a part of the meanings we have to understand are explicitly realized in the wordings. The rest are unrealized; they are left out – or rather (a more satisfactory metaphor) they are out of focus. We succeed in the exchange of meanings because we have access to the semiotic structure of the situation from other sources.

3 Language as Social Semiotic

3.1 Variation and social meaning

The distinction between language as system and language as institution is an important one for the investigation of problems of language and society. But these are really two aspects of a more general set of phenomena, and in any interpretation of the 'sociolinguistic order' we need to bring them together again.

A significant step in this direction is taken by variation theory. We have said that a feature of language as *institution* is that it is variable: different groups of speakers, or the same speakers in different task-roles, use different dialects or registers. But this is not to imply that there is no variation in the *system*. Some linguists would deny this, and would explain all variation institutionally. Others (myself among them) would argue that this is to make too rigid a distinction between the system and the institution, and would contend that a major achievement of social dialectology has been to show that dialect-like variation is a normal feature of the speech of the individual, at least in some but possibly in all communities. At certain contexts in the language a speaker will select, with certain probability, one among a small set of variants all of which are equivalent in the sense that they are alternative realizations of the same higher-level configuration. The conditions determining this probability may be linguistic or social or some combination of the two. To know the probability of a particular speaker pronouncing a certain variant (say [t] , glottal stop or zero) at a certain point in the speech chain (say word-final), we take the product of the conditioning effects of a set of variables such as: is the word lexical or structural? does the following word begin with a vowel? is the phrase thematic? is the speaker angry? and is his father a member of the working class? (This is, of course, a caricature, but it gives a fair representation of the way these things are.)

So variation, which we first recognize as a property of language as institution (in the form of variation *between* speakers, of a dialectal kind), begins to appear as an extension of variation which is a property of the system. A 'dialect' is then just a sum of variants having a strong tendency to cooccur. In this perspective, dialectal variation is made out to be not so much a consequence of the social structure as an outcome of the inherent nature of language itself.

But this is one-sided. In the last analysis, the linguistic system is the product of the social system; and seen from that angle, dialect-like variation *within* an individual is a special case of variation *between* individuals, not the other way round. The significant point, however, is that there is no sharp line between this externally conditioned, so-called 'sociolinguistic', variation that is found in the speech of an individual *because* it is a property of language as institution, and the purely internally conditioned variation that occurs within a particular part of the linguistic system (e.g. morpho-phonemic alternation). Conditioning environments may be of any kind; there is ultimately no discontinuity between such apparently diverse phenomena as (i) select [ʔ] not [t] before a consonant and (ii) select [ʔ] not [t] before a king. This explains how it comes about that all variation is potentially meaningful; any set of alternants may (but need not) become the bearer of social information and social value.

3.2 Language and social reality

Above and beyond 'language as system' and 'language as institution' lies the more general, unifying concept that I have labelled 'language as social semiotic': language in the context of the culture as a semiotic system.

Consider the way a child constructs his social reality. Through language as system — its organization into levels of coding and functional components — he builds up a model of the exchange of meanings, and learns to construe the interpersonal relationships, the experiential phenomena, the forms of natural logic and the modes of symbolic interaction into coherent patterns of social context. He does this very young; this is in fact what makes it possible for him to learn the language successfully — the two processes go hand in hand.

Through language as institution — its variation into dialects and registers — he builds up a model of the social system. This follows a little way behind his learning of grammar and semantics (compare the interesting suggestion by Sankoff (1974) that some patterns at first learnt as categorical are later modified to become variable), though it is essentially part of a single unitary process of language development. In broadest terms, from dialectal variation he learns to construe the patterns of social hierarchy, and from variation of the 'register' kind he gains an insight into the structure of knowledge.

So language, while it represents reality *referentially*, through its words and structures, also represents reality *metaphorically* through its own internal and external form. (1) The functional organization of the semantics symbolizes the structure of human interaction (the semiotics of social contexts, as we expressed it earlier). (2) Dialectal and 'diatypic' (register) variation symbolize respectively the structure of society and the structure of human knowledge.

But as language becomes a metaphor of reality, so by the same process reality becomes a metaphor of language. Since reality is a social construct, it can be constructed only through an exchange of meanings. Hence meanings are seen as constitutive of reality. This, at least, is the natural conclusion for the present era, when the exchange of information tends to replace the exchange of goods-and-services as the primary mode of social action. With a sociological linguistics we should be able to stand back from this perspective, and arrive at an interpretation of language through understanding its place in the long-term evolution of the social system.

3.3 Methodological considerations

It has been customary among linguists in recent years to represent language in terms of rules.

In investigating language and the social system, it is important to transcend this limitation and to interpret language not as a set of rules but as a *resource*. I have used the term 'meaning potential' to characterize language in this way.

When we focus attention on the processes of human interaction, we are seeing this meaning potential at work. In the microsemiotic encounters of daily life, we find people making creative use of their resources of meaning, and continuously modifying these resources in the process.

Hence in the interpretation of language, the organizing concept that we need is not structure but *system*. Most recent linguistics has been structure-bound (since structure is what is described by rules). With the notion of system we can represent language as a resource, in terms of the choices that are available, the interconnection of these choices, and the conditions affecting their access. We can then relate these choices to recognizable and significant social contexts, using sociosemantic networks; and investigate questions such as the influence of various social factors on the meanings exchanged by parents and children. The data are the observed facts of 'text-in-situation': what people say in real life, not discounting what they think they might say and what they think they ought to say. (Or rather, what they *mean*, since saying is only one way of meaning.) In order to interpret what is observed, however, we have to relate it to the system: (i) to the linguistic system, which it then helps to explain, and (ii) to the social context, and through that to the social system.

After a period of intensive study of language as an idealized philosophical construct, linguists have come round to taking account of the fact that people talk to each other. In order to solve purely internal problems of its own history and structure, language has had to be taken out of its glass case, dusted, and put back in a living environment — into a 'context of situation', in Malinowski's term. But it is one thing to have a 'socio-' (that is, real life) component in the explanation of the facts of language. It is quite another thing to seek explanations that relate the linguistic system to the social system, and so work towards some general theory of language and social structure.

References

Halliday, M.A.K. 1977, 'Types of linguistic structure, and their functional origins', (Mimeo).

Labov, William 1966, *The Social Stratification of English in New York City*, Washington, DC, Centre for Applied Linguistics.

Sankoff, Gillian 1974, 'A quantitative paradigm for the study of communicative competence', in Richard Bauman and Joel Sherzer (eds.), *Explorations in the Ethnography of Speaking*, Cambridge, Cambridge University Press.

2.2 On Communicative Competence
Dell Hymes

[. . . In this reading, I am] concerned to explain how a child comes rapidly to be able to produce and understand (in principle) any and all of the grammatical sentences of a language. Consider now a child with just that ability. A child who might produce any sentence whatever — such a child would be likely to be institutionalized: even more so if not only sentences, but also speech or silence was random, unpredictable. For that matter, a person who chooses occasions and sentences suitably, but is master only of fully grammatical sentences, is at best a bit odd. Some occasions call for being appropriately ungrammatical.

We have then to account for the fact that a normal child acquires knowledge of sentences, not only as grammatical, but also as appropriate. He or she acquires competence as to when to speak, when not, and as to what to talk about with whom, when, where, in what manner. In short, a child becomes able to accomplish a repertoire of speech acts, to take part in speech events, and to evaluate their accomplishment by others. This competence, moreover, is integral with attitudes, values, and motivations concerning language, its features and uses, and integral with competence for, and attitudes toward, the interrelation of language with the other code of communicative conduct (cf. Goffman 1956: 477; 1963: 335; 1964). The internalization of attitudes towards a language and its uses is particularly important (cf. Labov 1965: 84-5, on priority of subjective evaluation in social dialect and processes of change), as is internalization of attitudes toward use of language itself (e.g. attentiveness to it) and the relative place that language comes to play in a pattern of mental abilities (cf. Cazden 1966), and in strategies — what language is considered available, reliable, suitable for, *vis-à-vis* other kinds of code.

The acquisition of such competency is of course fed by social experience, needs, and motives, and issues in action that is itself a renewed source of motives, needs, experience. We break irrevocably with the model that restricts the design of language to one face toward referential meaning, one toward sound, and that defines the organization of language as solely consisting of rules for linking the two. Such a model implies naming to be the sole use of speech, as if languages

Excerpts from Dell Hymes, *On Communicative Competence*, University of Pennsylvania Press, 1971.

were never organized to lament, rejoice, beseech, admonish, aphorize, inveigh (Burke 1966: 13), for the many varied forms of persuasion, direction, expression and symbolic play. A model of language must design it with a face toward communicative conduct and social life.

Attention to the social dimension is thus not restricted to occasions on which social factors seem to interfere with or restrict the grammatical. The engagement of language in social life has a positive, productive aspect. There are rules of use without which the rules of grammar would be useless. Just as rules of syntax can control aspects of phonology, and just as semantic rules perhaps control aspects of syntax, so rules of speech acts enter as a controlling factor for linguistic form as a whole. Linguists generally have developed a theory of levels by showing that what is the same on one level of represent-ation has in fact two different statuses, for which a further level must be posited. The seminal example is in Sapir (1925) on phonology, while the major recent examples are in the work of Chomsky and Lamb. A second aspect is that what is different at one level may have in fact the same status at the further level. (Thus the two inter-pretations of 'He decided on the floor' − the floor as what he decided on/as where he decided − point to a further level at which the same-ness of structure is shown.) Just this reasoning requires a level of speech acts. What is grammatically the same sentence may be a statement, a command, or a request; what are grammatically two different sentences may as acts both be requests. One can study the level of speech acts in terms of the conditions under which sentences can be taken as alternative types of act, and in terms of the conditions under which types of act can be realized as alternative types of sentence. And only from the further level of acts can some of the relations among communicative means be seen, e.g. the mutual substitutability of a word and a nod to realize an act of assent, the necessary co-occurrence of words and the raising of a hand to realize an oath.

The parallel interpretations of 'he decided on the floor' and 'she gave up on the floor' point to a further level at which the sameness in structure is shown.

Rules of use are not a late grafting. Data from the first years of acquisition of English grammar show children to develop rules for the use of different forms in different situations and an awareness of different acts of speech (Ervin-Tripp, personal communication). Allo-cation of whole languages to different uses is common for children in multilingual households from the beginning of their acquisition. Com-petence for use is part of the same developmental matrix as competence for grammar.

The acquisition of competence for use, indeed, can be stated in the same terms as acquisition of competence for grammar. Within the developmental matrix in which knowledge of the sentences of a language is acquired, children also acquire knowledge of a set of ways in which sentences are used. From a finite experience of speech acts and their interdependence with sociocultural features, they develop a general theory of the speaking appropriate in their community, which they employ, like other forms of tacit cultural knowledge (competence) in conducting and interpreting social life (cf. Goodenough 1957; Searle 1967). They come to be able to recognize, for example, appropriate and inappropriate interrogative behaviour (e.g. among the Araucanians of Chile, that to repeat a question is to insult; among the Tzeltal of Chiapas, Mexico, that a direct question is not properly asked (and to be answered 'nothing'); among the Cahinahua of Brazil, that a direct answer to a first question implies that the answerer has no time to talk, a vague answer that the question will be answered directly the second time, and that talk can continue).

The existence of competency for use may seem obvious, but if its study is to be established, and conducted in relation to current linguistics, then the notions of competence and performance must themselves be critically analysed, and a revised formulation provided.

The chief difficulty of present linguistic theory is that it would seem to require one to identify the study of the phenomena of concern to us here with its category of performance. The theory's category of competence, identified with the criterion of grammaticality, provides no place. Only performance is left, and its associated criterion of acceptability. Indeed, language use is equated with performance: 'the theory of language use — the theory of performance' (Chomsky 1965: 9).

The difficulty with this equation, and the reasons for the making of it, can be explained as follows. First, the clarification of the concept of performance offered by Chomsky (1965: 10-15) [. . .] omits almost everything of sociocultural significance. The focus of attention is upon questions such as which among grammatical sentences are most likely to be produced, easily understood, less clumsy, in some sense more natural; and such questions are studied initially in relation to formal tree-structures, and properties of these such as nesting, self-embedding, multiple-branching, left-branching, and right-branching. The study of such questions is of interest, but the results are results of the psychology of perception, memory, and the like, not of the domain of cultural patterning and social action. Thus, when one considers what the sociocultural analogues of performance in this sense might be, one sees that these analogues would not include major kinds of judgement and ability with which one must deal in studying the use of language (see below under appropriateness).

Second, the notion of performance, as used in discussion, seems confused between different meanings. In one sense, performance is observable behaviour, as when one speaks of determining from the data of performance the underlying system of rules (Chomsky 1965: 4), and of mentalistic linguistics as that linguistics that uses performance

as data, along with other data, e.g. those of introspection, for determination of competence (p. 193). The recurrent use of 'actual' implies
as much, as when the term is first introduced in the book in question,
'actual performance', and first characterized: 'performance (the actual
use of language in concrete situations)' (pp. 3-4). In this sense performance is 'actual', competence underlying. In another sense, performance itself also underlies data, as when one constructs a performance
model, or infers a performative device (e.g. a perceptual one) that is to
explain data and be tested against them (p. 15); or as when, in a related
sense, one even envisages the possibility of stylistic 'rules of performance'
to account for occurring word orders not accounted for by grammatical
theory (p. 127).

When one speaks of performance, then, does one mean the behavioural data of speech? or all that underlies speech beyond the grammatical? or both? If the ambiguity is intentional, it is not fruitful; it
smacks more of the residual category and marginal interest.

The difficulty can be put in terms of the two contrasts that usage
manifests:

1. (underlying) competence v. (actual) performance;
2. (underlying) grammatical competence v. (underlying) models/rules
   of performance.

The first contrast is so salient that the status of the second is left
obscure. In point of fact, I find it impossible to understand what
stylistic 'rules of performance' could be, except a further kind of
underlying competence, but the term is withheld. [. . .]

It remains that the present vision of generative grammar extends
only a little way into the realm of the use of language. To grasp the
intuitions and data pertinent to underlying competence for use requires
a sociocultural standpoint. To develop that standpoint adequately,
one must transcend the present formulation of the dichotomy of
competence: performance, as we have seen, and the associated formulation of the judgements and abilities of the users of a language as
well. To this I now turn.

There are several sectors of communicative competence, of which
the grammatical is one. Put otherwise, there is behaviour, and underlying it, there are several systems of rules reflected in the judgements
and abilities of those whose messages the behaviour manifests. (The
question of how the interrelationships among sectors might be conceived
is touched upon below.) In the linguistic theory under discussion,
judgements are said to be of two kinds: of *grammaticality*, with respect
to competence, and of *acceptability*, with respect to performance.
Each pair of terms is strictly matched; the critical analysis just given
requires analysis of the other. In particular, the analysis just given
requires that explicit distinctions be made within the notion of 'acceptability' to match the distinctions of kinds of 'performance', and at the

same time, the entire set of terms must be examined and recast with respect to the communication as a whole.

If an adequate theory of language users and language use is to be developed, it seems that judgements must be recognized to be in fact not of two kinds but of four. And if linguistic theory is to be integrated with theory of communication and culture, this fourfold distinction must be stated in a sufficiently generalized way. I would suggest, then, that for language and for other forms of communication (culture), four questions arise:

1. Whether (and to what degree) something is formally *possible*;
2. Whether (and to what degree) something is *feasible* in virtue of the means of implementation available;
3. Whether (and to what degree) something is *appropriate* (adequate, happy, successful) in relation to a context in which it is used and evaluated;
4. Whether (and to what degree) something is in fact done, actually *performed*, and what its doing entails.

A linguistic illustration: a sentence may be grammatical, awkward, tactful and rare. (One might think of the four as successive subsets; more likely they should be pictured as overlapping circles.)

These questions may be asked from the standpoint of a system *per se*, or from the standpoint of persons. An interest in competence dictates the latter standpoint here. Several observations can be made. There is an important sense in which a normal member of a community has knowledge with respect to all these aspects of the communicative systems available to him. He will interpret or assess the conduct of others and himself in ways that reflect a knowledge of each (possible, feasible, appropriate), done (if so, how often). There is an important sense in which he would be said to have a capability with regard to each. This latter sense, indeed, is one many would understand as included in what would be meant by his competence. Finally, it cannot be assumed that the formal possibilities of a system and individual knowledge are identical; a system may contain possibilities not part of the present knowledge of a user (cf. Wallace 1961b). Nor can it be assumed that the knowledge acquired by different individuals is identical, despite identity of manifestation and apparent system.

Given these considerations, I think there is not sufficient reason to maintain a terminology at variance with more general usage of 'competence' and 'performance' in the sciences of man, as is the case with the present equations of competence, knowledge, systemic possibility, on the one hand, and of performance, behaviour, implementational constraints, appropriateness, on the other. It seems necessary to distinguish these things and to reconsider their relationship, if their investigation is to be insightful and adequate.

I should take *competence* as the most general term for the capabilities of a person. (This choice is in the spirit, if at present against the letter, of the concern in linguistic theory for underlying capability.) Competence is dependent upon both (tacit) *knowledge* and (ability for) *use. Knowledge* is distinct, then, both from competence (as its part) and from systemic possibility (to which its relation is an empirical matter.) Notice that Cazden (1967), by utilizing what is in effect systemic possibility as a definition of competence is forced to separate it from what persons can do. The 'competence' underlying a person's behaviour is identified as one kind of 'performance' (performance A, actual behaviour being performance B). The logic may be inherent in the linguistic theory from which Cazden starts, once one tries to adapt its notion of competence to recognized facts of personal knowledge. The strangely misleading result shows that the original notion cannot be left unchanged.

Knowledge also is to be understood as subtending all four parameters of communication just noted. There is knowledge of each. *Ability for use* also may relate to all four parameters. Certainly it may be the case that individuals differ with regard to ability to use knowledge of each: to interpret, differentiate, etc. The specification of *ability for use* as part of competence allows for the role of noncognitive factors, such as motivation, as partly determining competence. In speaking of competence, it is especially important not to separate cognitive from affective and volitive factors, so far as the impact of theory on educational practice is concerned; but also with regard to research design and explanation (as the work of Labov indicates). Within a comprehensive view of competence, considerations of the sort identified by Goffman (1967: 218-26) must be reckoned with – capacities in interaction such as courage, gameness, gallantry, composure, presence of mind, dignity, stage confidence, capacities which are discussed in some detail by him and, explicitly in at least one case, as kinds of competency (p. 224).

Turning to judgements and intuitions of persons, the most general term for the criterion of such judgements would be acceptable. Quirk (1966) so uses it, and Chomsky himself at one point remarks that 'grammaticalness is only one of the many factors that interact to determine acceptability' (1965: 11). (The term is thus freed from its strict pairing with 'performance'.) The sources of acceptability are to be found in the four parameters just noted, and in interrelations among them that are not well understood.

Turning to actual use and actual events, the term *performance* is now free for this meaning, but with several important reminders and provisos. The 'performance models' studied in psycholinguistics are to be taken as models of aspects of ability for use, relative to means of implementation in the brain, although they could now be seen as a distinct, contributory factor in general competence. There seems, indeed, to have been some unconscious shifting between the sense in which one would speak of the performance of a motor, and that in which one would speak of the performance of a person or actor (cf. Goffman, 1959, pp. 17-76, 'Performances') or of a cultural tradition (Singer, 1955; Wolf, 1964, pp. 75-6). Here the performance of a person is not identical with a behavioural record, or with the imperfect or partial realization of individual competence. It takes into account the interaction between competence (knowledge, ability for use), the competence of others, and the cybernetic and emergent properties of events themselves. A performance, as an event, may have properties (patterns and dynamics) not reducible to terms of individual or standardized competence. Sometimes, indeed, these properties are the point (a concert, play, party.)

The concept of 'performance' will take on great importance, insofar as the study of communicative competence is seen as an aspect of what from another angle may be called the ethnography of symbolic forms — the study of the variety of genres, narration, dance, drama, song, instrumental music, visual art, that interrelate with speech in the communicative life of a society, and in terms of which the relative importance and meaning of speech and language must be assessed. The recent shift in folklore studies and much of anthropology to the study of these genres in terms of performances with underlying rules (e.g. Abrahams 1967) can be seen as a reconstruction on an ethnographic basis of the vision expressed in Cassirer's philosophy of symbolic forms. (This reconstruction has a direct application to the communicative competence of children in American cities, where identification and understanding of differences in kinds of forms, abilities, and their evaluation is essential.)

The concept 'performance' will be important also in the light of sociological work such as that of Goffman (cited above), as its concern with general interactional competence helps make precise the particular role of linguistic competence.

In both respects the interrelation of knowledge of distinct codes (verbal: non-verbal) is crucial. In some cases these interrelations will bespeak an additional level of competence (cf., e.g., Sebeok 1959: 141-2): 'Performance constitutes a concurrently ordered selection from two sets of acoustic signals — in brief, codes — language and music . . . These are integrated by special rules . . .'). In others, perhaps not, as when the separate cries of vendors and the call to prayer of a muezzin are perceived to fit by an observer of an Arabic city, but with indication of intent or plan.

The nature of research into symbolic forms and interactional competence is already influenced in important part by linguistic study of competence (for some discussion see Hymes 1968). Within the view of communicative competence taken here, the influence can be expected to be reciprocal.

Having stated these general recommendations, let me now review relations between the linguistic and other communicative systems, especially in terms of cultural anthropology. I shall consider both terminology and content, using the four questions as a framework.

1   Whether (and to what degree) something is formally possible

This formulation seems to express an essential concern of present linguistic theory for the openness, potentiality, of language, and to generalize it for cultural systems. When systemic possibility is a matter of language, the corresponding term is of course *grammaticality*. Indeed, language is so much the paradigmatic example that one uses 'grammar' and 'grammaticality' by extension for other systems of formal possibility (recurrent references to a cultural grammar, Kenneth Burke's *A Grammar of Motives*, etc.). For particular systems, such extension may well be the easiest course; it is much easier to say that something is 'grammatical' with respect to the underlying structure of a body of myth, than to say in a new sense that it is 'mythical'. As a general term, one does readily enough speak of 'cultural' in a way analogous to grammatical (Sapir once wrote of 'culturalized behaviour', and it is clear that not all behaviour is cultural). We may say, then, that something possible within a formal system is grammatical, cultural, or, on occasion, communicative (cf. Hymes 1967b). Perhaps one can also say uncultural or uncommunicative, as well as ungrammatical, for the opposite.

2   Whether (and to what degree) something is feasible

The predominant concern here, it will be recalled, has been for psycholinguistic factors such as memory limitation, perceptual device, effects of properties such as nesting, embedding, branching, and the like. Such considerations are not limited to linguistics. A parallel in cultural anthropology is Wallace's hypothesis (1961a: 462) that the brain is such that culturally institutionalized folk taxonomies will not contain more than twenty-six entities and consequently will not require more than six orthogonally related binary dimensions for the definitions of all terms. With regard to the cultural, one would take into account other features of the body and features of the material environment as well. With regard to the communicative, the general importance of the notion of means of implementation available is clear.

As we have seen, question 2 defines one portion of what is lumped together in linguistic theory under the heading of performance, and, correspondingly, acceptability. Clearly a more specific term is needed for what is in question here. No general term has been proposed for this property with regard to cultural behaviour as a whole, so far as I know, and *feasible* seems suitable and best for both. Notice, moreover, that the implementational constraints affecting grammar may be largely those that affect the culture as a whole. Certainly with regard to the brain there would seem to be substantial identity.

3. Whether (and to what degree) something is appropriate

As we have seen, appropriateness is hardly brought into view in the linguistic theory under discussion, and is lumped under the heading of performance, and, correspondingly, acceptability. With regard to cultural anthropology, the term *appropriate* has been used (Conklin, Frake, etc.), and has been extended to language (Hymes 1964: 39-41). 'Appropriateness' seems to suggest readily the required sense of relation to contextual features. (Since any judgement is made in some defining context, it may always involve a factor of appropriateness, so that this dimension must be controlled even in a study of purely grammatical competence (cf. Labov 1966). From a communicative standpoint, judgements of appropriateness may not be assignable to different spheres, as between the linguistic and the cultural; certainly, the spheres of the two will intersect. (One might think of appropriateness with regard to grammar as the context-sensitive rules of sub-categorization and selection to which the base component is subject; there would still be intersection with the cultural.)

Judgement of appropriateness employs a tacit knowledge. Chomsky himself discusses the need to specify situations in mentalistic terms, and refers to proper notions of 'what might be expected from anthropological research' (1965: 195, n. 5). Here there would seem to be recognition that an adequate approach to the relation between sentences and situations must be 'mentalistic', entailing a tacit knowledge, and, hence, competence (in the usage of both Chomsky and this paper). But the restriction of competence (knowledge) to the grammatical prevails, so far as explicit development of theory is concerned. By implication, only 'performance' is left. There is no mention of what might contribute to judgement of sentences in relation to situations, nor how such judgements might be analysed. The lack of explicitness here, and the implicit contradiction of a 'mentalistic' account of what must in terms of the theory be a part of 'performance' show again the need to place linguistic theory within a more general sociocultural theory.

4. Whether (and to what degree) something is done

The study of communicative competence cannot restrict itself to occurrences, but it cannot ignore them. Structure cannot be reduced to probabilities of occurrence, but structural change is not independent of them. The capabilities of language users do include some (perhaps unconscious) knowledge of probabilities and shifts in them as indicators of style, response, etc. Something may be possible, feasible, and appropriate and not occur. No general term is perhaps needed here, but the point is needed, especially for work that seeks to change what is done. This category is necessary also to allow for what Harold Garfinkel (in discussion in Bright 1966: 323) explicates as application of the medieval principle, *factum valet*: 'an action otherwise prohibited by rule is to be treated as correct if it happens nevertheless.'

In sum, the goal of a broad theory of competence can be said to be to show the ways in which the systemically possible, the feasible, and the appropriate are linked to produce and interpret actually occurring cultural behaviour. [. . .]

We spoke first of a child's competence as 'in principle'. Of course no child has perfect knowledge or mastery of the communicative means of his community. In particular, differential competence has itself a developmental history in one's life. The matrix formed in childhood continues to develop and change throughout life with respect both to sentence structures and their uses (Labov 1965: 77, 91-2; Chomsky 1965: 202) and recall the northeast Amazon situation mentioned earlier. Tanner (1967: 21) reports for a group of Indonesians: 'Although the childhood speech patterns . . . foreshadowed those of the adult, they did not determine them . . . For these informants it is the principle of code specialization that is the important characteristic of childhood linguistic experience, not the pattern of code specialization itself. (All are multilingual from childhood.) Not one person interviewed reported a static linguistic history in this respect.' (See now also Carroll 1968.)

Perhaps one should contrast a 'long' and a 'short' range view of competency, the short range view being interested primarily in understanding innate capacities as unfolded during the first years of life, and the long range view in understanding the continuing socialization and change of competence through life. In any case, here is one major respect in which a theory of competence must go beyond the notion of ideal fluency in a homogeneous community, if it is to be applicable to work with disadvantaged children and with children whose primary language or language variety is different from that of their school; with intent to change or add, one is presupposing the possibility that competence that has unfolded in the natural way can be altered, perhaps drastically so, by new social factors. One is assuming from the outset a confrontation of different systems of competency within the school and community, and focusing on the way in which one affects or can be made to affect the other. One encounters phenomena that pertain not only to the separate structures of languages, but also to what has come to be called *interference* (Weinreich 1953) between them: problems of the interpretation of manifestations of one system in terms of another.

Since the interference involves features of language and features of use together, one might adopt the phrase suggested by Hayes, and speak of *sociolinguistic interference*. (More generally, one would speak of *communicative interference* to allow for the role of modes of communication other than language; in this section, however, I shall focus on phenomena of language and language *per se*.)

When a child from one developmental matrix enters a situation in which the communicative expectations are defined in terms of another, misperception and misanalysis may occur at every level. As is well known, words may be misunderstood because of differences in phonological systems; sentences may be misunderstood because of difference in grammatical systems; intents, too, and innate abilities, may be misevaluated because of difference of systems for the use of language and for the import of its use (as against other modalities).

With regard to education, I put the matter some years ago in these words (Hymes 1961: 65-6):

> . . . new speech habits and verbal training must be introduced, necessarily by particular sources to particular receivers, using a particular code with messages of particular forms via particular channels, about particular topics and in particular settings – and all this from and to people for whom there already exist definite patternings of linguistic routines, of personality expression via speech, of uses of speech in social situations, of attitudes and conceptions toward speech. It seems reasonable that success in such an education venture will be enhanced by an understanding of this existing structure, because the innovators' efforts will be perceived and judged in terms of it, and innovations which mesh with it will have greater success than those which cross its grain.

The notion of sociolinguistic interference is of the greatest importance for the relationship between theory and practice. First of all, notice that a theory of sociolinguistic interference must begin with heterogeneous situations, whose dimensions are social as well as linguistic. (While a narrow theory seems to cut itself off from such situations, it must of course be utilized in dealing with them. See, for example, Labov and Cohen (1967) on relations between standard and non-standard phonological and syntactic rules in Harlem, and between receptive and productive competence of users of the non-standard vernacular.)

Second, notice that the notion of sociolinguistic interference presupposes the notion of sociolinguistic systems between which interference occurs, and thus helps one see how to draw on a variety of researches that might be overlooked or set aside. (I have in mind for example obstacles to use of research on 'second-language learning' in programs for Negro students because of the offensiveness of the term.) The notions of sociolinguistic interference and system require a conception of an *integrated theory of sociolinguistic description*. Such work as has been done to contribute to such a theory has found it necessary to start, not from the notion of a language, but from the notion of a *variety* or *code*. In particular, such a descriptive theory is forced to recognize that the historically derived status of linguistic resources as related or unrelated languages and dialects, is entirely secondary to their status in actual social relationships. Firstly, [note] the need to put language names in quotes [. . .] Secondly, the degree of linguistic similarity and distance cannot predict mutual intelligibility, let alone use. Thirdly, from the functional standpoint of a sociolinguistic description, means of quite different scope can be employed in equivalent roles. A striking example is that the marking of intimacy and respect served by shift of second person pronoun in French (*tu: vous*) may be served by shift of entire language in Paraguay (Guarani: Spanish). Conversely, what seem equivalent means from the standpoint of languages may have quite different roles, e.g., the elaborated and restricted codes of English studied by Bernstein (1965). In short, we have to break with the tradition of thought which simply equates one language, one culture, and takes a set of functions for granted. In order to deal with the problems faced by disadvantaged children, and with education in much of the world, we have to begin with the conception of the speech habits, or competencies, of a community of population, and regard the place among them of the resources of historically-derived languages as an empirical question. As functioning codes, one may find one language, three languages; dialects widely divergent or divergent by a hair; styles almost mutually incomprehensible, or barely detectable as different by the outsider; the objective linguistic differences are secondary, and do not tell the story. What must be known is the attitude toward the differences, the functional role assigned to them, the use made of them. Only on the basis of such a functionally motivated description can comparable cases be established and valid theory developed.

Now with regard to sociolinguistic interference among school children, much relevant information and theoretical insight can come from the sorts of cases variously labelled 'bilingualism', 'linguistic acculturation', 'dialectology', 'creolization', whatever. The value of an integrated theory of sociolinguistic description to the practical work would be that

1. it would attempt to place studies, diversely labelled, within a common analytical framework; and
2. by placing such information within a common framework, where one can talk about relations among codes, and types of code-switching, and types of interference as between codes, one can make use of the theory while perhaps avoiding connotations that attach to such labels as 'second-language learning', (I say perhaps because of course it is very difficult to avoid unpleasant connotations for any terms used to designate situations that are themselves intrinsically sensitive and objectionable.)

William Stewart's (1965: 11, n. 2) suggestion that some code relationships in the United States might be better understood if seen as part of a continuum of cases ranging to the Caribbean and Africa, for example, seems to be from a theoretical standpoint very promising.

It is not that most code relationships in the United States are to be taken as involving different languages, but that they do not involve relationships among different codes, and that the fuller series illuminates the part. Stewart has seen through the different labels of dialect, creole, pidgin, language, bilingualism, to a common sociolinguistic dimension. Getting through different labels to the underlying sociolinguistic dimensions is a task in which theory and practice meet.

Let me now single out three interrelated concepts, important to a theory of sociolinguistic description, which have the same property of enabling us to cut across diverse cases and modes of reporting, and to get to basic relationships. One such concept is that of *verbal repertoire*, which Gumperz (1964) has done much to develop. The heterogeneity of speech communities, and the priority of social relationships, is assumed, and the question to be investigated is that of the set of varieties, codes, or subcodes, commanded by an individual, together with the types of switching that occur among them. (More generally, one would assess communicative repertoire.)

A second concept is that of *linguistic routines*, sequential organizations beyond the sentence, either as activities of one person, or as the interaction of two or more. Literary genres provide obvious examples; the organization of other kinds of texts, and of conversation, is getting fresh attention by sociologists, such as Sacks, and sociologically oriented linguists, such as Labov. One special importance of linguistic routines is that they may have the property that the late English philosopher Austin dubbed *performative* (Searle 1967). That is, the saying does not simply stand for, refer to, some other thing; it is itself the thing in question. To say 'I solemnly vow' is to solemnly vow; it does not name something else that is the act of vowing solemnly. Indeed, in the circumstances no other way to vow solemnly is provided other than to do so by saying that one does so. From this standpoint, then, disability and ability with regard to language involve questions that are not about the relation between language and something else that language might stand for or influence; sometimes such questions are about things that are done linguistically or not at all. (More generally, one would analyse linguistic routines, comprising gesture, paralinguistics, etc. as well.)

A third concept is that of *domains of language behaviour*, which Fishman has dealt with insightfully in his impressive work on *Language Loyalty in the United States* (1966: 424-39). Again, the complexity and patterning of use is assumed, and the focus is upon 'the most parsimonious and fruitful designation of the occasions on which one language (variant, dialect, style, etc.) is habitually employed rather than (or in addition to) another' (p. 428). (More generally, one would define domains of communicative behaviour.)

Too often, to be sure, the significance of a sociolinguistic feature, such as a code, routine, or term or level of address, is sought by purely distributional means. The feature is traced through the set of contexts in which it can be used without regard to an intervening semantic structure. Such an approach neglects the fact that sociolinguistic features, like linguistic features, are 'signs' in the classical Saussurean sense, comprising both a form and meaning (*significant* and *signifié*). The difference is that one thinks of a typical linguistic sign as comprising a phonological form and a referential meaning (*chien* and the corresponding animal), whereas a sociolinguistic sign may comprise with respect to form an entire language, or some organized part of one, while meaning may have to do with an attitude, norm or interaction, or the like. (Recall the Paraguayan case of Spanish/distance: Guarani/ closeness (among other dimensions.)) Thus the relation between feature and context is mediated by a semantic paradigm. There is an analogue here to the representation of a lexical element in a language in terms of form (phonological features), meaning (semantic features), and context (features of syntactic selection), or, indeed, to the tripartite semiotic formula of Morris, syntactics, semantics, pragmatics, if these three can be interpreted here as analogous of form, meaning and context.

If the distributional approach neglects semantic structure, there is a common semantic approach that neglects context. It analyses the structure of a set of elements (say, codes, or terms of personal reference) by assuming one normal context. This approach (typical of much componential analysis) is equally unable to account for the range of functions a fluent user of language is able to accomplish (cf. Tyler 1966). It is true that the value of a feature is defined first of all in relation to a set of normal contexts (settings, participants, personal relationships, topics, or whatever). But given this 'unmarked' (pre-supposed) usage, an actor is able to insult, flatter, colour discourse as comic or elevated, etc., by 'marked' use of the feature (code, routine, level of address, whatever) in other contexts. Given their tacit knowledge of the normal values, hearers can interpret the nature and degree of markedness of the use.

Thus the differences that one may encounter within a community may have to do with:
1. presence or absence of a feature (code, routine, etc.);
2. the semantic value assigned a feature (e.g., English as having the value of distance and hostility among some American Indians);
3. the distribution of the feature among contexts; and
4. the interrelations of these with each other in unmarked and marked usages.

This discussion does not exhaust the concepts and modes of analysis relevant to the sort of theory that is needed. A number of scholars are developing relevant conceptual approaches, notably Bernstein, Fishman, Gumperz, Labov (my own present formulation is indicated in Hymes 1967a). The three concepts singled out do point up major dimensions: the capacities of persons, the organization of verbal means for socially defined purposes, and the sensitivity of rules to situations. And it is possible to use the three concepts to suggest one practical framework for use in sociolinguistic description [. . .].

Note

This paper is revised from one presented at the Research Planning Conference on Language Development Among Disadvantaged Children, held under the sponsorship of the Department of Educational Psychology and Guidance, Ferkauf Graduate School, Yeshiva University, June 7-8, 1966. The original paper is included in the report of that conference, issued by the Department of Educational Psychology and Guidance (pp. 1-16). I wish to thank Dr Beryl Bailey and Dr Edmund Gordon of Yeshiva University for inviting me to participate and Dr Courtney Cazden, Dr John Gumperz, Dr Wayne O'Neill and Dr Vera John for their comments at that time.

References

Abrahams, R.D. (1967), 'Patterns of performance in the British West Indies', mimeographed working paper.
Bernstein, B. (1965), 'A sociolinguistic approach to social learning', in J. Gould (ed.), *Social Science Survey,* Penguin.
Bright, W. (1966), *Sociolinguistics,* Mouton.
Burke, K. (1966), *Towards a Better Life, Being a Series of Epistles, or Declamations,* University of California Press (first published 1932).
Carroll, J.B. (1968), 'Development of native language skills beyond the early years', in Reed and J.B. Carroll (eds.), *Language Learning,* National Council of Teachers of English.
Cazden, C.B. (1966), 'Subcultural differences in child language: an interdisciplinary review', *Merrill-Palmer Q.,* vol. 12, pp. 185-218.
Cazden, C.B. (1967), 'On individual differences in language competence and performance,' *J. Spec. Educ.,* vol. 1, pp. 135-50.
Chomsky, N. (1965), *Aspects of the Theory of Syntax,* MIT Press.
Fishman, J.A. (1966), *Language Loyalty in the United States,* Mouton.
Goffman, E. (1956), 'The nature of deference and demeanor', *AmA,* vol. 58, pp. 473-502.
Goffman, E. (1959), *The Presentation of Self in Everyday Life,* Doubleday; Allen Lane, The Penguin Press.
Goffman, E. (1963), *Behavior in Public Places,* Free Press.
Goffman, E. (1964), 'The neglected situation', in J.J. Gumperz and D. Hymes (eds.), *The Ethnography of Communication, AmA,* vol. 66, no. 6, part 2.
Goffman, E. (1967), *Interaction Ritual,* Doubleday.
Goodenough, W.H. (1957), 'Cultural anthropology and linguistics', in P. Garvin (ed.), *Report of the Seventh Annual Round Table Meeting on Languages and Linguistics,* Georgetown University Press.
Gumperz, J.J. (1964), 'Linguistic and social interaction in two communities', in J.J. Gumperz and D. Hymes (eds.), *The Ethnography of Communication, AmA,* vol. 66, no. 6, part 2.

Hymes, D. (1961), 'Functions of speech: an evolutionary approach', in F. Gruber (ed.), *Anthropology and Education*, University of Pennsylvania.

Hymes, D. (1964), 'Directions in (ethno-) linguistic theory', in A.K. Romney and R.G. D'Andrade (eds.), *Transcultural Studies of Cognition*, American Anthropological Association.

Hymes, D. (1967a), 'Models of the interaction of language and social setting', *J. Soc. Iss.*, vol. 23, pp. 8-28.

Hymes, D. (1967b), 'The anthropology of communication', in F. Dance (ed.), *Human Communication Theory: Original Essays*, Holt, Rinehart & Winston.

Hymes, D. (1968), 'Linguistics — the field', *International Encyclopedia of the Social Sciences*, Macmillan Co.

Labov, W. (1965), 'Stages in the acquisition of standard English', in R. Shuy (ed.), *Social Dialects and Language Learning*, National Council of Teachers of English.

Labov, W. (1966), *The Social Stratification of English in New York City*, Center for Applied Linguistics.

Labov, W., and Cohen, P. (1967), 'Systematic relations of standard and non-standard rules in the grammar of Negro speakers', paper for Seventh Project Literacy Conference, Cambridge, Mass.

Quirk, R. (1966), 'Acceptability in language', *Proceedings of the University of Newcastle-upon-Tyne Philosophical Society*, vol. 1, no. 7, pp. 79-92.

Sapir, E. (1925), 'Sound patterns in language', *Language*, vol. 1, pp. 37-51.

Searle, J. (1967), 'Human communication theory and the philosophy of language: some remarks', in F. Dance (ed.), *Human Communication Theory*, Holt, Rinehart & Winston.

Sebeok, T. (1959), 'Folksong viewed as code and message', *Anthropos*, vol. 54, pp. 141-53.

Singer, M. (1955), 'The cultural pattern of Indian civilization: a preliminary report of a methodological field study', *Far East. Q.*, vol. 15, pp. 223-36.

Stewart, W. (1965), 'Urban Negro speech: sociolinguistic factors affecting English teaching', in R. Shuy (ed.), *Social Dialects and Language Learning*, National Council of Teachers of English.

Tanner, N. (1967), 'Speech and society among the Indonesian élite a case study of multilingual community', *Anthrop. Linguistics*, vol 9, no. 3, pp. 15-40.

Tyler, S. (1966), 'Context and variation in Koya kinship terminology', *AmA*, vol. 68, pp. 693-707.

Wallace, A.F.C. (1961a), 'On being just complicated enough', *Proceedings of the National Academy of Sciences*, vol. 47, pp. 438-64.

Wallace, A.F.C. (1961b), *Culture and Personality*, Random House.

Weinreich, U. (1953), *Languages in Contact*, Linguistic Circle of New York.

Wolf, E. (1964), *Anthropology*, Prentice-Hall.

2.3 The Maintenance of the Status Quo
Claus Mueller

An anomaly of Western industrial society is that social disparities persist amidst plenty while the structure of domination remains virtually unchallenged. Domination, used in this sense, is the control by a limited and relatively small number of people over the allocation of resources and the access to significant participation in the decision-making process. The following discussion will deal with several factors which permit the continuation of existing institutional arrangements and economic stratification, with particular emphasis on constraints of public communication. This analysis of the status quo will also take into account the crucial role played by collective beliefs, which provide the evaluative dimension in communication, the position of the working class *vis-à-vis* change and political communication, and the influence of both governmental structures and economic imperatives on public communication. This article [. . .] will draw largely from material dealing with the United States.

Constrained Communication

Conformity to a political system may best be described as the un-questioning acceptance of dominant institutions that determine the quality of life of the society as a whole. Both directed and arrested communication are distortions of political communication in that they prevent individuals and groups from articulating their interests. They are not, however, the only factors which prevent this articulation. Although there hardly exists absolute knowledge in the sense of ultimate political theories and concepts independent of time and space, there are at each point in societal development explanatory concepts which allow for a political understanding of society. Constrained communication, that is, communication between the government and the public and public communication regarding societal problems which are subject to the systematic bias of governmental and private interests, makes such an understanding difficult to achieve. Constrained commun-ication is, of course, either reinforced or modified by the ability to conceptualize and the language code of a group or an individual.

Chapter 3 of Mueller, C. (1973) *The Politics of Communication*, New York, Oxford University Press, pp. 86-126.
The article has been edited, and only pp. 86-112 are quoted here.

Political Communication and System Maintenance

Political interpretations are influenced by the withdrawal of information and the dissemination of rationalizations which are not meant to become apparent to the public. Policies, explanations, and data can be couched in a language which itself contains predefinitions and interpretations that serve the purpose of maintaining an undisturbed exercise of political power. If the members of a political community are not significantly involved in the decision-making process and if they do not dispose of sufficient sociopolitical knowledge as well as a language that facilitates the unscrambling of governmental jargon and expository style often designed to disguise intent, they have no counterinterpretations to offset offical ones, nor can they establish relationships among fragmented pieces of political information they may obtain through the mass media.

Basic societal problems can be camouflaged by the dominant groups* which occupy or influence positions of political authority and therefore are not subject to political debate unless they cause overt disruption of such proportions that defy concealment. It does not serve the interests of any government to propagate the ills of a society. This is a task left to those who seek election to public office, to journalists and social scientists, and to the groups which experience the social or economic consequences of societal problems.

In advanced industrial society, information has become a crucial prerequisite for both political control and opposition politics, a necessity which is due to factors such as the complexity of society, the growth of governmental bureaucracies, and the tremendous distance between those who make the decisions and the individual citizen. Even though the mass media and the growing literacy of the population create the preconditions for an informed public, it could be argued that the political information the individual possesses decreases in proportion to the total information that exists, much of which is reposited with governmental agencies. The limited knowledge of contemporary society that can be acquired through educational institutions in addition to governmental constraints on communication leave most of the public ignorant of the mechanisms of the decision-making process and the forces influencing it. Unfamiliarity with the facts and arguments considered in political decisions and policy formation results in a reluctance to evaluate governmental actions, especially if they do not seem to have a bearing on everyday life.

Probably no social scientist would dispute the contention that

---

* The term 'dominant group' will be used to denote that minority of individuals which controls the decision-making process. Beyond the group's unifying interest of preserving the structures of domination and an unchanged economic system, the policies of that group are not uniform since different segments of the group are motivated by the goal of maximizing their particular interests. These segments will be designated by the plural, 'dominant groups.'

governmental restrictions on public debate are prevalent in modern politics. These constraints became even more evident under the Nixon administration during which civil servants refused, on executive order, to testify before a congressional hearing investigating foreign policy. Further insulating the presidency from the public, Nixon invoked executive privilege to withhold information from the Senate Foreign Relations Committee and condoned the systematic obstruction of the Watergate investigation.* Inquiry into governmental policies was also restricted by the Supreme Court decisions of 1972 that removed congressional immunity to grand jury investigation and that denied journalists the right to use the first amendment in order to protect their sources of information.

The purpose and policies of constrained communication were candidly stated by Justice Lewis F. Powell, two months prior to his appointment to the Supreme Court by President Nixon, in a confidential memorandum that was circulated by the United States Chamber of Commerce among high echelons in the business community. It was recommended in this memorandum that individuals and groups with opposing or critical views of American business should be 'penalized politically,' businessmen should influence universities for reasons of 'balancing' faculties, and textbooks should be 'evaluated' as part of an all-out effort in which 'the wisdom, ingenuity and resources of American business [ought] to be marshalled against those who would destroy it.' Television programmes 'should be monitored in the same way that textbooks should be kept under constant surveillance. This applies not merely to so-called educational programmes ... but to the daily "news analysis" which so often includes the most insidious type of criticism of the enterprise system.'[2]

Grand jury proceedings against publishers and writers and the interference of the CIA into the publication of material alleging its implication in the South East Asia drug traffic are overt governmental attempts to infringe upon the public's right to know.†[3] A complete understanding of governmental policy is made difficult if not impossible if information regarding political decisions is withheld or deliberately beclouded. Nor will history necessarily be able to unravel the snare. As one official investigation into the decision-making process revealed, the manner in which important decisions are arrived at frequently cannot be reconstructed, simply because written records do

---

* In August 1971 President Nixon refused to provide the Senate Foreign Relations Committee with a copy of the Pentagon's five-year foreign military assistance plan.[1] The most notable recent case concerning a domestic issue occurred in 1973 when attempts were made to extend the executive privilege to all White House staff members who were involved in the Watergate cover up.
† According to the Veterans Administration, about 20 per cent of those that served in Vietnam experimented with hard drugs with at least 2 per cent returning to the United States as drug addicts.[4]

not exist for all stages of the process. Such was the lesson of the *Pentagon Papers*.[5] 'The Pentagon researchers generally lacked records of the oral discussions of the National Security Council or the most intimate gatherings of the Presidents with their closest advisers, where decisions were often reached.' But the leakage of this document about American involvement in Vietnam also indicates the limits of governmental constraints on communication. The total compliance of civil servants, consultants, and politicians involved in the formulation and execution of policy is critical in order to keep the public uninformed. Because civil servants have refused to remain silent, the attention of the public has been drawn during the last few years to a number of issues such as the corruption of civil servants and elected politicians and the surveillance of civilians by the army and other governmental agencies.[6] The ignorance of large segments of the public of pertinent information and paradigms excludes them from effective political communication. This limited use of communication is beneficial for the interests of dominant groups since the less people know, the easier it is to govern them and thereby achieve ends which may not have the consent of a significant portion of the population. An individual may respond to his lack of knowledge about politics with what Hannah Arendt calls the privatization of meaning. When sociopolitical reality is relentlessly obfuscated by official incantations, the individual withdraws, in surrender, from politics and ceases to participate in political communication.

The obfuscation of political reality can be achieved with the use of a highly evocative, ritualistic language.[7] Political campaigns and careers are dependent upon symbolic, rhetoric-laden statements which have little if any effect on the decision-making process. Elected and appointed officials may agree publicly with abstract demands for equality and better education for the poor and rush to microphones and cameras when an emotional issue such as the state of mental institutions has caught public attention never to be heard of again after public interest and the commerical gain of the media from the issue have been exhausted. Politicians trumpet their concern about rising prices and crime in the street, stage public hearings, and listen to the voice of the common man. The public is – and probably wants to be – reassured by political symbolism of its civic importance while the decision-making process itself runs counter to its interests. Regulatory agencies respond to that desire by engaging in public impression management while they serve the very economic interests they are meant to regulate.[8] It seems that the more often the public interest is invoked by politicians and government officials the less often such rhetoric has any consequences.

One of the functions of constrained communication is that office holders retain control over the management of public issues. Moynihan's suggestion that the government limit public statements about poverty and racism reflects the principle that nothing should be transformed into a political issue that cannot be accommodated within the existing political framework. Put differently, issues which challenge dominant private and governmental interests must become nonissues and must be kept as such. If that attempt fails, the problem is to be given token recognition.

In his critique of the pluralistic orientation in political science which systematically disregards the existence of nonissues and the structural constraints of political communication, Kenneth Dolbeare has pointed out that 'established institutions and processes permit only certain relatively congenial pressures to be aired, and they repress or label illegitimate all they cannot absorb. By the time an issue reaches the stage of public consideration within the bounds established by these institutions and processes, it has already been hammered into a form that can be accommodated without serious difficulty.'[9]

Peter Bachrach and Morton S. Baratz developed the concept 'mobilization of bias' in their analysis of the decision-making process. This phrase describes the process in which 'the dominant values and the political myths, rituals, and institutional practices' are mobilized to 'favour the vested interests of one or more groups. . .'[10] Systematic bias in political communication suspends the articulation of those issues which would require a change in the orientation of existing policies or in the present allocation of benefits and privileges. These issues are therefore 'suffocated . . . kept covert; or killed before they gain access to the relevant decision making arena.'[11] If subordinate groups do not possess the knowledge and material and organizational resources that are strategically necessary for the pursuit of their goals, they can be disregarded. The bias of the political process rarely becomes evident because the nature of public controversy is shaped in advance by the elites and because 'power utilized in this form is usually exercised covertly, far removed from the glare of the public.'[12]

Structured Consensus
Just as the suppression of public issues delimits the parameter of political communication so does a structured consensus. A structured consensus is either one which is reached by political elites and passed down to the public that responds as an acclamatory agent only, or one which is formulated according to the imperatives of the political-economic system. There is obviously a close relation between the two types of structured consensus, as the elite consensus is often influenced by the imperatives of system maintenance. Nevertheless it is necessary to separate the two types analytically because the second type that is tied to system maintenance imperatives may induce a consensus independent of group or class interests that are the core of the first type of structured consensus. Interest in economic growth is, for example, shared by trade unionists and property holders alike, even

though its benefits are distributed unequally.

There is no question that the foremost determinant of the structured consensus is the necessity to sustain economic growth, a necessity which takes precedent over all other system requirements. It is essential that economic growth be perpetuated in order to generate enough for the capital needs of the private sector and for governmental operations. Because the political compliance of the population is no longer ensured by an integrating ideology [. . .] continued mass loyalty has to be obtained through material and social compensations, that is, primarily through the fulfillment of consumer demands, the maintenance of a high standard of living, and the promise of even more affluence and leisure to consume even more enticing goods and, secondarily, through the provision of social services such as education, medical care, welfare, and social security. These topics dominate political communication in advanced industrial societies. What is significant about the economic constraint that structures consensus and distorts communication is that issues that cannot be tied to the goal of production and increased revenues will not be considered seriously. The system requirement of economic growth adumbrates all areas of decision making.

In his work *Consent and Consensus*, Percy H. Partridge wrote that 'some components of the prevailing consensus on which the system depends will be the products of pressures exerted by dominant institutions and elites: the system itself plays a part in the manufacture of attitudes and habits required for its own survival. Elements of consensus are implanted and consolidated by the downward pressures of institutional practice.'[13] If one follows that perspective, consensus is understood as descending from the top instead of ascending from the bottom. Structural mechanisms rather than the public determine the orientation and direction of political communication. This obviously does not mean that there are no areas left that are susceptible to the public will. But whatever is left to public discretion is secondary, having no long-range societal consequences. Capital punishment, abortion, or state aid to parochial schools appear insignificant as issues when compared with the initial decision of committing American forces to Vietnam.

It follows the logic of the interest in system maintenance that public debate about secondary issues is encouraged since it deflects attention from crucial issues and creates the illusion of participation in the political process. As long as important segments of the public believe in democratic principles, this illusion has to be perpetuated in order to preclude dissatisfaction and sustain loyalty. The political and economic imperatives of system stability establish a range of priorities and goals which decide the substance of a manufactured consensus. The task of governmental elites is the implementation of these goals rather than the questioning of goals or priorities.

When the above imperatives of system maintenance and the interests of the dominant groups are taken into account, it becomes apparent that constrained communication and the transformation of consensus into 'a product of, rather than a condition for, a political system of domination'[14] creates a communicative framework which structurally excludes feedback from the public and ruptures the liberal notion of the public as a countervailing force to those in power. Although structured consensus is linked to political imperatives and interests, there are, however, other constraints that are engendered by social structures which also distort political communication.

Language as Noise

Groups which share a restricted speech code unwittingly contribute to the objective of constrained communication because their linguistic patterns introduce 'noise' or distortion into communication. [. . .] Language is a distorting factor when it impedes the acquisition of information and when it introduces noise into the process of communication. In highly organized and differentiated societies, a considerable amount of sociopolitical knowledge and communicative competence is required for effective participation in political communication. Groups and individuals who have internalized and are thus bound by a restricted language code cannot cope with sophisticated messages nor effectively comprehend a complex political environment.

That language can interfere in communication can be shown in an analysis of the transmission of information through the media. As a source of information and interpretations, the media are increasingly important in political communication and form, what is for the most part, a precarious link between the individual and all the governmental, quasigovernmental, and private institutions which constitute the dominant forces in his society.

According to communication theory, there is no transmission of information without some loss of information. In most cases this loss results from the nature of the channel used for the transmission of information. But it is also due to entropy or loss of information stemming from human factors as studies of retention capacity and attention span show. The further possibility that information can be lost for linguistic reasons has not frequently been a topic of empirical research. Because language is a communicative instrument used for the transmission of thoughts, messages, and information, it can be analyzed as a source of noise in two capacities: as a channel (syntax, conceptual framework) and as a medium (vocabulary). If the channel is not intricate enough for the transmission or reception of complex messages, noise is generated and information will be lost. A language without a conditional mode or prepositional constructions, for example, is adequate to communicate only the most rudimentary thoughts. As a medium, language can be a source of noise if the lexical differentiation that is necessary for the transmission and reception of qualified messages is missing. The quality of both medium and the channel directly affects the quality of the communication.

The following simplified model may serve to illustrate potential loss of information: From a general situation (1), a specific event is chosen by a news medium (2). In the encoding process (the code being defined by the social referents and interpretation framework of the encoder), the event is translated into a message (3). The message, consisting of a definite number of bits of information, passes through a channel where it is transformed into signals (4) the form of which is determined by the type of medium chosen (television, radio, periodicals). The signals arrive at the receiver (5) who reconstitutes them as a message (6) and decodes it according to his framework of interpretation (7).

Since a loss of information can occur during each stage of the process, the net result of the transmission is in all likelihood a refracted understanding. A specific event among many possible ones is chosen, the context of which cannot always be re-established during the reception of the message. In the process of encoding, an interpretation within a given framework is imposed on the event. Technical factors cause the loss of information during the transmission. In the decoding stage, the message is filtered through the semantic and ideational code of the receiver.

The processes of encoding and decoding are influenced by sociolinguistic as well as interpretational factors. If the receiver is confronted with complex messages which are communicated in terms unknown to him, he will most likely scan the message only very superficially. If he continues to listen to the message he may apply an interpretation far different from the one used by the commentator, provided that the receiver considers the message to be relevant and disposes of an interpretational framework. A message encoded as 'students demand participation' will be decoded according to the receiver's linguistic code and interpretational framework. Those sharing the restricted code may not be able to translate participation into something meaningful and retain only those elements of the message which are secondary. If the message is transmitted against the visual background of an occupied campus building, the restricted code speaker will probably understand it in terms of student unrest *per se* instead of what the unrest is inspired by or directed toward.

A different response is likely for groups sharing the elaborated code. The message does not pose a semantic problem as far as the meaning of the term nor a syntactic one as far as the qualifications employed are concerned. Moreover, the issue of participation is closer to the dominant values of the elaborated code speaker than it is to those of restricted code speakers. It is obvious that an understanding of the message does not necessarily imply an agreement with the particular demand contained in this message, though any agreement or disagreement is contingent upon an understanding of the concept. Information can also be lost, or more precisely disregarded, if the framework of interpretation used for the message by the transmitter contradicts the interpretational rules used by the receiver.

The Influence of the Media

A number of other factors govern the transmission and reception of messages. It is clear that any medium, whether television, radio, or periodicals which generates too much noise in the transmission of information will be in perpetual search of an audience and that such a situation is the exception rather than the rule. In most cases there is a correspondence between the sophistication of a medium – with respect to language and interpretations – and that of the audience. An analysis of the *Daily News* and the *New York Times* by James Chambers showed significant differences between the two papers in the use of syntax and vocabulary.[15] The simplified wording and sentences of the *Daily News* correlated, as would be expected, with the class background of its readership which tends toward a restricted code, while the more complex vocabulary and syntax of the *New York Times* corresponded to the generally elaborated code of its middle-class readers. Research on a German mass circulation paper, the *Bildzeitung*, corroborates Chambers's analysis. Ekkehart Mittelberg found a number of stylistic elements in this German paper which are typical of the restricted code, such as concrete metaphors, dichotomized statements, simplified sentence structures, typified formulations, an undifferentiated vocabulary, and stereotypifications.[16] The use of a restricted code by these papers results in unqualified descriptions of political reality which more often than not are conservatively slanted. Because of the style utilized, the reader's language does not inhibit comprehension, but he may be manipulated through the effective application of the very stereotypes which he uses in his everyday language. As Mittelberg suggested, an appeal to emotions, strong metaphors, and superficial formulations suspend the reader's thinking.[17] The frame of reference of these papers is consistent, and it is possible to predict with a high degree of accuracy their interpretations of a given political event. Sensationalism, repetition, and a simplistic depiction of political reality contribute little to the readers' knowledge of society.

Other observers of media addressed to both lower- and middle-class groups have come up with similar findings. The French philosopher and sociologist Henri Lefebvre remarked that the 'mass media form the taste and dilute judgement. They instruct and they condition. They fascinate and they debase by saturation with images, with "news" that is not newsworthy. They proliferate communication and threaten coherence and reflection, vocabulary and verbal expression, and language itself.'*[18]

Editorial policies in the mass media cannot be detached from commericial considerations which require that the largest possible audience be reached. Interpretations which may alienate either the sponsor or the audience of a programme generally will not be transmitted. In early 1972 David W. Rintels, chairman of the Committee on Censorship of the Writers Guild of America, testified before the Senate Subcommittee on Constitutional Rights that, according to a poll of the Guild, of those who responded

> eighty-six per cent have found, from *personal* experience, that censorship exists in television. Many state, further, that they have never written a script, no matter how innocent, that has not been censored. Eighty-one per cent believe that television is presenting a distorted picture of what is happening in this country today – politically, economically and racially. Only eight per cent believe that current television programming is 'in the public interest, convenience and necessity' as required by the Federal Communications Act of 1934.[20]

This censorship is exerted prior to and during the production of a programme not only by the sponsor but also by companies that invest heavily in television advertising. This was the case in the spring of 1972 when the National Broadcasting Company removed a section from a documentary on the conditions of migrant workers employed by a Florida subsidiary of the Coca-Cola Company because of the pressures applied by the parent corporation.[21]

The 'dramatic, low taste content' of entertainment is most likely to appeal to the majority of the consumers who are little educated and who do not critically evaluate the programmes they watch or hear.[22] Programming corresponds for the most part to the tastes and preferences of the audience and serves to 'maintain the financial equilibrium of a deeply institutionalized social system [the media] which is tightly integrated with the whole of the American economic institutions.'[23] This function of the media deflects public attention from political issues and perpetuates the definition of the 'good life' in strictly materialistic terms.

Though the audience may influence the type of entertainment presented in the media, it has little control over the selection of information and quality of interpretation transmitted. The flow of information is downward as is the direction of influence.[24] Certainly, the individual can disregard a message because he deems it irrelevant or incorrect. But the validity of political messages, such as those pertaining

---

* If the receiver of a message has doubts about its content, it will be repeated since redundancy 'is the simplest way of reducing the equivocation [of] the receiver.' Persuasion calls for repetition and the reduction of complex matters into a limited number of typifications and their associated negative or positive connotations.[19]

to foreign and fiscal policies, cannot be assessed at the moment of transmission, since any evaluation presupposes an acquaintance with the relevant facts most of the audience does not have.

It is precisely in this area where the stabilizing influence of the media becomes apparent. [. . .] Individuals belonging to the lower classes are more dependent on group norms than those coming from the middle classes. Conformity and allegiance to established authority as well as resistance to change were found to be political predispositions of individuals brought up in the lower classes. Empirical research also demonstrates that class-specific factors such as conformity, reception to one-sided arguments, and the absence of scepticism correlate with the susceptibility to persuasion and manipulation.[25] Influence of interpretations and opinions disseminated by the media on large segments of the audience cannot be doubted.

Governmental constraints on political communication, the mobilization of bias by powerful interests, and the commercial character of the media create a situation where news items that would invite challenges of the status quo are either omitted or embedded in interpretations which depreciate them. If members of the audience have no counter-interpretations or alternative sources of information, they may mistake for the real world the selected messages presented by the media. In doing so they unwittingly support existing institutions and policies. Renate Mayntz has described this condition as the 'half-resigned acceptance of the *status quo* [which] may well be reinforced by a fake cultural integration and feeling of participation induced by the mass media.'[26]

The proposition that mass media contribute to the reinforcement of existing conditions has to be qualified by reiterating that such a reinforcement is possible only if the messages transmitted correspond to the communicative competence of the audience and if the audience has a framework of interpretation similar to the one used by the media. The latter qualification opens the door for an inquiry into a larger area, namely the collective beliefs and ideologies which shape the interpretation of political messages.

Collective Beliefs: Ideologies and Para-Ideologies

The expectations which guide man's political behaviour and the manner in which he interprets his condition are structured by values and collective beliefs transmitted in the socialization process. No matter how refracted and irrational these beliefs and values may be, they influence the political positions an individual may take.

Nature and Function of Ideologies
The continuity of collective beliefs, whether they take the form of ideologies, religions, or para-ideologies, is a stabilizing force in any

political system. Collective beliefs can express the interests of the dominant group which provides seemingly plausible interpretations of political reality, or they can convey or abet counterinterpretations, usually finding their adherents among groups or classes which do not participate in or benefit from the decision-making process. Ideologies are considered here as integrated belief systems which provide explanations for political reality and establish the collective goals of a class or group, and in the case of a dominant ideology, of society at large. They have an evaluative component in that they attach either negative or positive judgments to conditions in society and to political goals. The normative dimension of an ideology is an essential component without which an ideology could not function effectively. By setting standards of action and priorities, this dimension cements the believer's loyalty to the group, class or society which shares the ideology.

In order that an ideology is accepted by a class or a group, it must translate its economic needs and social aspirations into a coherent structure. An ideology posits a model of the political order which is subjectively plausible to the individual since it validates his interests and position. The success or failure of an ideology is therefore contingent upon the extent to which it makes what people experience in their daily lives comprehensible in political terms. When an ideology is accepted, those who come to adhere to it recognize themselves in that ideology; through it they can express their aspirations and define their political objectives. In such a case an ideology serves to mobilize people.

Any analysis of ideology in the twentieth century has been influenced by Marx's critique of ideologies which clearly established the political function of collective beliefs. Marx and Engels contended that man's consciousness is shaped by the material conditions of his existence. His thoughts, beliefs, and ideological predispositions, they asserted, are not independent of the individual's position in the production process. True, 'men are the producers of their conceptions ... [but] consciousness can never be anything else than conscious existence, and the existence of men is their actual life process. ... Life is not determined by consciousness but consciousness by life.'[27] Man's consciousness is thus a product of his ongoing activities pursued within the confines of his socioeconomic conditions.

According to this Marxian definition, the division of society into social classes set apart by differing material conditions and life styles gives rise to class-specific beliefs based upon the respective economic interests of these classes. Marx held that all forms of political thought (though not including his own theories) and all ideologies distorted reality since they originated – in the ultimate analysis – in the material interests of one class or another and not in the interests of society as a whole. For Marx, ideologies are understood as systems of misleading ideas based on illusions. Ideology is equated to a consciousness of reality wherein 'men and their circumstances appear upside down as in a *camera obscura*.'[28] This false consciousness is the erroneous belief that political conceptions are independent of material reality, that is, economic conditions and interests. Claims of independence from class-specific interests are alone proof that ideologies distort political reality.

The dominant ideology of a society reflects, in the Marxian analysis, the interests of the ruling class, whether this ideology is expressed in political theories such as pluralism or conservatism, in the legal frame-work, or in religious beliefs such as those of feudal Europe or theocratic Geneva. An ideology is 'representative of determinate limited interests' which the dominant class pursues. From this perspective the claim of the right to private property is not understood as a natural right but as a right linked to the interests of those who hold property. A dominant ideology is transmitted through educational institutions; if subordinate groups accept it, they will develop a false consciousness since they come to adhere to political conceptions which do not express their own interests. The consciousness of groups and classes is thus shaped by the dominant political belief system and the socioeconomic context in which they are living.*

In Marx's interpretation, a dominant ideology serves to provide interpretations of social reality. It mobilizes groups and classes around the goals and values of society and legitimates the exercise of political domination by suggesting that the existing political structures, and thus the status quo, are the only possible ones. The political perception of the individual is predefined and distorted by a dominant ideology that makes the repression of primary and secondary needs acceptable.

The concept ideology will be used here to designate all politically mobilizing beliefs no matter which group or class adheres to them. All ideologies reflect class- or group-specific interests and differ only in the degrees of distortion of political reality. Dominant ideologies form conceptual foundations which uphold a political system and its institutions. Counterideologies serve to mobilize oppressed groups or classes to oppose the political system. The obvious question is whether in advanced industrial societies dominant ideologies or counterideologies still perform the function they did in the industrial society observed by Marx. Is it possible to understand contemporary political commun-ication using the concept 'ideology' and if so, is a dominant ideology generally shared by the population?

If ideologies are understood as belief systems that explain socio-political reality and contribute to the cohesion of a society, then it appears unlikely that the majority of the population has a coherent ideological understanding of social and political processes. Today the

---

* Marx held that no social group or class is able to formulate nonideological conceptions. According to Karl Mannheim, this task is left to those individuals he called the 'unattached intellectuals.'

dominant group invokes less and less frequently traditional ideologies to justify its policies. Nor does it attempt to propagate a new ideology which could function as a dominant one. More significantly, since interpretations offered by an ideology have to correspond to the life experience of the individual, they must be able to integrate and explain new information and new conditions. The rapid change in advanced industrial society would require a constant updating of a dominant ideology, a revision which would in itself alienate the old believers and limit its claim to absolute veracity.

Instead of placing the cause for the decline of ideologies in the attenuation of social conflicts — which could be the expression of a generalized false consciousness — this analysis suggests that the decline is due to the loss of plausibility of traditional ideologies and their interpretations of the political order. Advanced industrial society and newly emerging needs can no longer be grasped within the framework of traditional ideologies. In the liberal ideology, politics is understood as a market place where demands can be fulfilled by means of the purchasing power of the ballot and where laws and legal procedures guarantee equal participation of all. These notions run counter to the political experience of a large proportion of the population. The simultaneous emphasis on social equality and the right to private property, particularly in view of the forms and proportions private property has taken in advanced industrial societies, is contradictory. The goals of liberalism, such as the reduction of inequality, may be acceptable to much of the population, but the liberal explanations of the political process and how these goals can be attained are less easily accepted.

The conservative ideology confronts similar difficulties. Less prevalent than the liberal ideology and less often explicit in public policy and legal decisions, the goals and interpretations offered by conservative spokesmen are rarely in harmony with the aspirations or experiences of most of the population. The proposed reduction by the 'individualist-conservative' of governmental responsibilities in the economic and social sectors of society and the concomitant emphasis on freedom of choice, individual action, and self-interest are simply contrary to the factual dependency of all groups and classes on the state.[29] 'Organic conservatism' which places a greater emphasis on society and authority than on the individual's free choice, postulates that governmental authority should be based on moral principles independent of any group or class interests and considers men as inherently unequal, irrational, and incapable of self-government. In fact, moral principles are rarely applied to political questions. Rather there is the widespread sentiment that those 'who have the power are out to take advantage of the population . . . and don't really care what happens to the people.'[30] The assumed inherent inequality among men, on the other hand, cannot be reconciled with the quest for social equality by large segments of the population and the democratic ideal of the political equality of all people.

Unlike conservatism and liberalism, socialism (that is, Marxist socialism) claims to have an objective historical basis which can be proven by subjecting social development to scientific examination. However, a number of its predictive statements, like the inevitability of severe economic crises or the absolute pauperization of the working class, have been proven erroneous. Several theoretical and practical problems of socialist ideology are readily apparent. Socialist societies have not been able to reconcile the democratic ideals of their ideology with the demands of a centrally planned economy or to overcome the obstacles to realizing social equality while achieving economic equality. Furthermore, axioms such as the proposition that human labour is the sole source of surplus are questionable in light of the role of science and technology as forces of production. To a great extent, however, the declining plausibility of socialism is due to the experience of totalitarian and bureaucratic communism rather than to problems inherent in the ideology.

If liberalism, conservatism, and socialism are not plausible today, it is in part because the socioeconomic foundations of advanced industrial society are radically different from those of nineteenth century market capitalism during which time these ideologies gained prominence. The nineteenth century saw the birth of the proletariat and the maturation of the bourgeoisie, two classes which provided the social basis for new ideologies. With the possible exception of the ascendence of the upper-middle class over the last decades [. . .], advanced industrial society has not experienced the emergence of a new class on a similar scale. But it would be too facile to explain the declining plausibility of traditional political ideologies as due to simply the development of new economic structures. Mostafa Rejai has enumerated a number of changes within capitalist society that have led to a decline in the intensity of ideological debate. Among these changes are: 'an increasing general affluence; an increasing exposure to education and the media of communication; an increasing reliance on science and expertise; an increasing attenuation of class and party conflict; a gradual attainment of political and economic citizenship by the lower classes; a gradual emergence of a vast, homogeneous, professional-managerial middle class; a gradual transformation of *laissez-faire* capitalism into the welfare state; and a gradual institutionalization of stable political processes for [the] resolution of political issues.'[31] In his over-all view of society, Rejai seems to underestimate socioeconomic disparity among social classes and the changes in political configurations proceeding from the economic developments that he notes. Nevertheless, the factors which he singles out, have, by and large, undermined the plausibility of traditional ideologies. [. . .]

The Emergence of a Para-ideology

As noted above one of the functions of ideologies is the legitimation of domination. Ideologies justify the use of force to maintain the status quo, to initiate social change, and to suppress revolutionary activities. An ideology, if successfully propagated, stabilizes a political system. But when ideology is seen as an integrated system of meaning providing sociopolitical interpretations, the concept has lost much of its usefulness for political analysis. In twentieth-century advanced industrial society, an ideology which defends the exercise of political power by a select minority can claim very little adherence either among the dominant group, institutional elites, or the population at large. It therefore is difficult to explain the integration of large segments of the population and specifically of the working class in terms of a false consciousness induced by a dominant ideology. The absence of an integrating ideology poses two questions: First, what substitutes for such an ideology in advanced industrial society; and, second, to what extent is legitimacy and the exercise of authority impaired by the absence of an integrating ideology? [. . .]

What is possible to chart in contemporary society that resembles a collective belief system is a generalized acceptance of consumer patterns and a diffuse, abstracted agreement about political institutions. Collective imagery rooted in material and social compensations and slogans of a para-ideological nature have taken over some of the functions of traditional ideologies. Collective images like 'the great society,' 'defense of democracy,' 'power to the people,' 'law and order,' and 'the silent majority' act as substitutes, however pallid, for traditional ideologies.

Historically, the decline of religious value systems was accompanied by a secularization of political ideologies. In advanced industrial society, a justification for the exercise of political power which can embrace both the populace and leaders is not propagated by the ruling group. Instead, one notices the crystallization of para-ideology which can be understood within the framework of functional rationality. On the surface this para-ideology, which Jürgen Habermas analyzed, though not designating it as such, in his seminal essay, *Technology and Science as 'Ideology,'* appears to be independent of class-specific interests and is rooted in the presumed rational administration of a political system.[32] The difference between this para-ideology and traditional ideologies is that it 'disconnects legitimating principles from the organization of social life and therefore from social norms of interaction, thus depoliticizing these criteria. Instead they are embedded in the functions of a presumed system of purposive-rational action.'[33] Questions of efficiency (or principles of purposive-rational action) rather than of morality dominate decisions. By definition, science and technology, which are part of the system of purposive-rational action, do not provide ethical standards of conduct. For these reasons science and technologies cannot fulfil the spiritual and moral needs of advanced industrial society. Nor do they offer transcendent goals unifying the worker, businessman, and professor. Any 'ideology' based on science and technology lacks the normative basis which is an integral part of an ideology; it is a para-ideology only.

The rational administration of society is, according to the para-ideology of science and technology, detached from phenomena such as class conflict or group-specific interests. Habermas argues that 'the system justifies itself by achievements which may not, in principle, be interpreted politically. Rather [these achievements] are interpreted directly according to the allocation of money and leisure and indirectly according to the technocratic rationale for excluding practical* [i.e., normative] questions.' This allocation is neutral (*verwendungsneutral*) since there are no political norms regarding the use of money and leisure.[34] Habermas suggests that this system of purposive-rational action increasingly governs the institutions of society, the political framework of which is subverted by purposive-rational thinking that does not take into account the possibility of alternatives either to the existing structure of domination or its policies. Technical rules replace societal norms as guidelines for political action, and rationalization is understood as a process which leads to 'the growth of productive forces [and] the expansion of technical-administrative power' instead of 'emancipation, individuation, [and] the expansion of domination-free communication.'[35]

In the logic of the structured consensus, political debate is shifted from a discussion of ends to one of means, or to put it in Weber's terms, from substantive rationality to functional rationality. Contrary to its claim, this para-ideology cannot be disconnected from class-specific interests. By presenting the given political system as the only possible one, it serves the interests of those groups who profit most from the system. The rationality behind the para-ideology, however, seems to cut across class lines since efficiency, rational administration, and technical rules appear to be at first glance disassociated from any class interest. In fact, a growing importance is being accorded to the role of the expert and scientist. The governmental decision-making process appears depoliticized as technical competence and administrative expertise become key criteria. According to Habermas, the impression is created by this para-ideology that the allocation of resources is independent of values which, however, are always at the base of political decisions. When scientific and technological knowledge are

---

* Praktisch in Habermas' writing can be understood as a synonym for 'normative' or 'ethical' and usually refers to questions pertaining to society. The terms 'norm' and 'normative value' denote a standard of social behaviour which the members of a community are expected to adhere to and which can be enforced by sanctions, both positive and negative. Since norms specify how men ought to act, they have moral and evaluative connotations.

invoked in formulating policies, it becomes more difficult for the population to examine the merits of a decision or to perceive alternatives.

Seymour M. Lipset has made a similar, though less abstract, analysis. He links the declining ideological debate to,

> the acceptance of scientific thought in matters which have been at the centre of political controversy. Insofar as most organized participants [thus the active minority] in the political struggle accept the authority of experts in economics, military affairs, interpretations of the behaviour of foreign nations, and the like, it becomes increasingly difficult to challenge the views of opponents on moralistic 'either/or' terms. Where there is some consensus among the scientific experts on specific issues, these tend to be removed as possible sources of intense controversy. As the ideology of 'scientism' becomes accepted, the ideologies of the extreme left and right lose much of their impact.[36]

The selection of a problem as well as its solution cannot be disconnected from political and social norms.[37] Solicited advice of experts can be disregarded if it does not conform to the political values of the office holders, as Presidential commission reports readily demonstrate, their destiny not infrequently being a library shelf or a locked filing cabinet. And if scientists were in positions of authority, their research and consensus would be influenced as much by normative predispositions as the politicians' are.

To recapitulate, the para-ideology of science and technology makes the exercise of governmental power acceptable by seemingly depoliticizing politics. Scientific and technological knowledge conceal class-specific interests, value systems, and the nature of domination. Because scientific methodologies do indeed develop independently from group or class interests, it is easy to convey implicitly the idea that an ideology based on science and technology is just as detached from special interests. This invocation of scientific methods seriously and deleteriously obscures the political process. The extent to which the para-ideology of science and technology is accepted by the population is unknown, but traces of it can be found in the refracted belief that solutions to social problems can and will eventually be found through scientific research and the application of technological knowledge. Such a belief cements the status quo by de-emphasizing political solutions to society's problems. Compared to traditional ideologies, this para-ideology has little normative power since it provides no ethical criteria. The rationale of efficiency which it embodies is precarious since the efficiency of a policy or an institution can be readily evaluated by the citizen in light of his everyday experience, though it is often documented evaluations of this kind which are the targets of political constraints on communication. [. . .]

Notes

[1] *The New Republic* (September 18, 1971), p.7.

[2] As quoted by Jack Anderson, *New York Post* (September 29, 1972), p.30.

[3] Alfred McCoy, "A Correspondence with the CIA," *The New York Review of Books* (September 21, 1972).

[4] *New York Times* (July 2, 1972), Sec. 4, p. 9. *New York Times* (April 29, 1973), Sec. 4, p. 7 and personal communication from Seymour Fiddle. It is virtually impossible to get precise data on the rate of addiction among Vietnam Veterans, because of the political nature of that issue.

[5] The Pentagon account notes that at times the highest Administration officials not only kept information about their real intentions from the press and Congress but also kept secret from the government bureaucracy the real motives for their written recommendations or actions. *The Pentagon Papers*, Hedrick Smith, (ed.) New York, Bantam Books, 1971, pp. xxiii, xxiv.

[6] Charles Peters and Taylor Branch, *Blowing the Whistle: Dissent in the Public Service*, New York, Praeger, 1972.

[7] Murray J. Edelman, *The Symbolic Uses of Politics*, Urbana, Ill., University of Illinois Press, 1967.

[8] Murray J. Edelman, 'Symbols and Political Quiescence,' in Kenneth M. Dolbeare, ed., *Power and Change in the United States*, New York, Wiley, 1969.

[9] Kenneth M. Dolbeare, 'Political Change in the United States,' in Dolbeare, *Power and Change in the United States*, p.263.

[10] Peter Bachrach and Morton S. Baratz, *Power and Poverty: Theory and Practice*. New York, Oxford University Press, 1970, p. 11.

[11] Ibid., p. 44.

[12] Peter Bachrach, ed., *Political Elites in a Democracy*, New York, Atherton, 1971, p.7.

[13] Percy H. Partridge, *Consent and Consensus*, New York, Praeger, 1971, p.118.

[14] Claus Offe, 'Massenloyalität'. Stranberg, Max Planck Institute, 1971, typescript, p. 9.

[15] James Chambers, 'The Content Analysis of Two Newspapers to Determine the Existence of Class-Specificity,' master's thesis, Hunter College, 1972.

[16] Ekkehart Mittelberg, *Wortschatz und Syntax der Bildzeitung*, Marburg, Ewart Verlag, 1967.

[17] Ibid., p. 46.

[18] Henri Lefebvre, *Critique de la Vie Quotidienne*, Tôme II, Paris, Arche Éditeur, 1961, p. 226.

[19] Colin Cherry, *On Human Communication*, Cambridge, Mass., M.I.T. Press, 1966, p. 210.

[20] *New York Times,* March 5, 1972, Sec. 2, p. 1.

[21] *New York Times,* June 4, 1972, p. 14.

[22] See, for instance, the collection of essays, 'Mass Culture and Mass Media,' *Daedalus*, Spring 1960.

[23] Melvin L. Defleur, *Theories of Mass Communication*, New York, McKay, 1970, pp. 169, 171. Distortions in 'high brow' media are reported in several comparative studies. See, for example, G. S. Turnbull, 'Reporting of the War in Indochina,' *Journalism Quarterly*, Vol. 34, No. 1 (1957); E. J. Rossi, 'How 50 Periodicals and the *New York Times* Interpreted the Test Ban Controversy,' *Journalism Quarterly*, Vol. 41, No. 4 (1964); G. Lichtheim, 'All the News that's Fit to Print,' *Commentary*, No. 3 (1965); C. C. Conway, 'A Comparative Analysis of the Reporting of News from China by *Le Monde* and the New York Times, September 1967–September 1968,' manuscript.

[24] See Elihu Katz and Paul F. Lazarsfeld, *Personal Influence*, Glencoe, The Free Press, 1955. For evidence from small group research, see O. R. Larsen and T. Hill, 'Social Structure and Interpersonal Communication,' *American Journal of*

Sociology, Vol. 63, March 1958.
[25] I. L. Janis, 'Personality as a Factor in Susceptibility to Persuasion,' Wilbur Schramm, (ed.), *The Science of Human Communication*, New York, Basic Books, 1963, pp. 62ff, 58ff; N. Z. Medalia and N. L. Otto, 'Diffusion and Belief in a Collective Delusion,' *American Sociological Review*, Vol. 23, No. 2 (1958); see also H. Cantril, 'The Invasion from Mars,' G. W. Swanson, ed., *Readings in Social Psychology*, New York, Holt, 1952.
[26] Renate Mayntz, 'Leisure, Social Participation, and Political Activity,' *International Social Science Journal*, Vol. 12, No. 4 (1960), p. 574. For a similar argument, see W. Breed, 'Mass Communication and Socio-Cultural Integration,' *Social Forces*, Vol. 37, No. 2 (1958).
[27] Karl Marx and Friedrich Engels, *The German Ideology*, New York, International Publishers, 1963, pp. 14, 15.
[28] Ibid., p. 14.
[29] Kenneth M. Dolbeare and Patricia Dolbeare, *American Ideologies*, Chicago, Markham, 1971, pp. 207-27. The terms 'individualistic-conservative' and 'organic' conservatism are suggested by Dolbeare.
[30] Harris Poll, as quoted in the *New York Post* (June 19, 1972), p. 6.
[31] Mostafa Rejai, ed., *Decline of Ideology?* New York, Atherton Press, 1971, pp. 18, 19.
[32] Jürgen Habermas, *Technik und Wissenschaft als Ideologie,* Frankfurt, Suhrkamp, 1968, pp. 48–104. This essay is included in a collection of essays, Jeremy Shapiro, (translator), *Toward A Rational Society*, Beacon Press, 1971. Our pagination refers to the German edition.
[33] Ibid., p. 90.
[34] Ibid., p. 90.
[35] Ibid., p. 64.
[36] Seymour M. Lipset, 'The Changing Class Structure and Contemporary European Politics,' *Daedalus*, Vol. 93 (Winter 1964), pp. 272-73, as quoted by Rejai, *Decline of Ideology?*, pp. 19, 20.
[37] Cf. Habermas, 'The Scientization of Politics and Public Opinion,' *Toward A Rational Society*.

2.4 Behaviour in Private Places: Sustaining Definitions of Reality in Gynaecological Examinations
Joan P. Emerson

1 Introduction

In *The Social Construction of Reality*, Berger and Luckmann discuss how people construct social order and yet construe the reality of everyday life to exist independently of themselves.[1] Berger and Luckmann's work succeeds in synthesizing some existing answers with new insights. Many sociologists have pointed to the importance of social consensus in what people believe; if everyone else seems to believe in something, a person tends to accept the common belief without question. Other sociologists have discussed the concept of legitimacy, an acknowledgement that what exists has the right to exist, and delineated various lines of argument which can be taken to justify a state of affairs. Berger and Luckmann emphasize three additional processes that provide persons with evidence that things have an objective existence apart from themselves. Perhaps most important is the experience that reality seems to be out there before we arrive on the scene. This notion is fostered by the nature of language, which contains an all-inclusive scheme of categories, is shared by a community, and must be learned laboriously by each new member. Further, definitions of reality are continuously validated by apparently trivial features of the social scene, such as details of the setting, persons' appearance and demeanour, and 'inconsequential' talk. Finally, each part of a systematic world view serves as evidence for all the other parts, so that reality is solidified by a process of intervalidation of supposedly independent events.

Because Berger and Luckmann's contribution is theoretical, their units of analysis are abstract processes. But they take those processes to be grounded in social encounters. Thus, Berger and Luckmann's theory provides a framework for making sense of social interaction. In this paper observations of a concrete situation will be interpreted to show how reality is embodied in routines and reaffirmed in social interaction [. . . .]

A reality can hardly seem self-evident if a person is simultaneously aware of a counter-reality. Berger and Luckmann write as though

Patterns of Communicative Behaviour ed. by Hans Peter Dreitzel, *Recent Sociology* no. 2, Collier-MacMillan, New York, 1970, pp. 74-97. The article has been edited, and only pages 74-84 are quoted here.

definitions of reality were internally congruent. However, the ordinary reality may contain not only a dominant definition, but in addition counterthemes opposing or qualifying the dominant definition. Thus, several contradictory definitions must be sustained at the same time. Because each element tends to challenge the other elements, such composite definitions of reality are inherently precarious even if the probability of disconfirming events is low.

A situation where the definition of reality is relatively precarious has advantages for the analysis proposed here, for processes of sustaining reality should be more obvious where that reality is problematic. The situation chosen, the gynaecological examination, [2] is precarious for both reasons discussed above. First, it is an excellent example of multiple contradictory definitions of reality, as described in the next section. Second, while intrusive and deliberate threats are not important, there is a substantial threat from participants' incapacity to perform.

Dramaturgical abilities are taxed in gynaecological examinations because the less convincing reality internalized by secondary socialization is unusually discrepant with rival perspectives taken for granted in primary socialization. [3] Gynaecological examinations share similar problems of reality-maintenance with any medical procedure, but the issues are more prominent because the site of the medical task is a woman's genitals. Because touching usually connotes personal intimacy, persons may have to work at accepting the physician's privileged access to the patient's genitals. [4] Participants are not entirely convinced that modesty is out of place. Since a woman's genitals are commonly accessible only in a sexual context, sexual connotations come readily to mind. Although most people realize that sexual responses are inappropriate, they may be unable to dismiss the sexual reaction privately and it may interfere with the conviction with which they undertake their impersonal performance. The structure of a gynaecological examination highlights the very features which the participants are supposed to disattend. So the more attentive the participants are to the social situation, the more the unmentionable is forced on their attention.

The next section will characterize the complex composition of the definition of reality routinely sustained in gynaecological examinations. Then some of the routine arrangements and interactional manoeuvres which embody and express this definition will be described. A later section will discuss threats to the definition which arise in the course of the encounter. Measures that serve to neutralize the threats and reaffirm the definition will be analysed. The concluding section will turn to the theoretical issues of precariousness, multiple contradictory definitions of reality, and implicit communication.

2 The Medical Definition and its Counterthemes

Sometimes people are in each other's presence in what they take to be a 'gynaecological examination'. What happens in a gynaecological examination is part of the common stock of knowledge. Most people know that a gynecological examination is when a doctor examines a woman's genitals in a medical setting. Women who have undergone this experience know that the examination takes place in a special examining room where the patient lies with her buttocks down to the edge of the table and her feet in stirrups, that usually a nurse is present as a chaperone, that the actual examining lasts only a few minutes, and so forth. Besides knowing what equipment to provide for the doctor, the nurse has in mind a typology of responses patients have to this situation, and a typology of doctors' styles of performance. The doctor has technical knowledge about the examining procedures, what observations may be taken to indicate, ways of getting patients to relax, and so on.

Immersed in the medical world where the scene constitutes a routine, the staff assume the responsibility for a credible performance. The staff take part in gynaecological examinations many times a day, while the patient is a fleeting visitor. More deeply convinced of the reality themselves, the staff are willing to convince sceptical patients. The physician guides the patient through the precarious scene in a contained manner: taking the initiative, controlling the encounter, keeping the patient in line, defining the situation by his reaction, and giving cues that 'this is done' and 'other people go through this all the time'.

Not only must people continue to believe that 'this is a gynaecological examination' but also that 'this is a gynaecological examination going right'. The major definition to be sustained for this purpose is 'this is a medical situation' (not a party, sexual assault, psychological experiment, or anything else). If it is a medical situation, then it follows that 'no one is embarrassed'[5] and 'no one is thinking in sexual terms'.[6] Anyone who indicates the contrary must be swayed by some non-medical definition.

The medical definition calls for a matter-of-fact stance. One of the most striking observations about a gynaecological examination is the marked implication underlying the staff's demeanour towards the patient: 'Of course, you take this as matter-of-factly as we do'. The staff implicitly contend: 'In the medical world the pelvic area is like any other part of the body; its private and sexual connotations are left behind when you enter the hospital'. The staff want it understood that their gazes take in only medically pertinent facts, so they are concerned not with an aesthetic inspection of a patient's body. Their nonchalant pose attempts to put a gynaecological examination in the same light as an internal examination of the ear.

Another implication of the medical definition is that the patient is a technical object to the staff. It is as if the staff work on an assembly line for repairing bodies; similar body parts continually roll by and the staff have a particular job to do on them. The staff are concerned with the typical features of the body part and its pathology rather than with the unique features used to define a person's identity. The staff disattend the connection between a part of the body and some intangible self that is supposed to inhabit that body.

The scene is credible precisely because the staff act as if they have every right to do what they are doing. Any hint of doubt from the staff would compromise the medical definition. Since the patient's nonchalance merely serves to validate the staff's right, it may be dispensed with without the same threat. Furthermore, the staff claim to be merely agents of the medical system, which is intent on providing good health care to patients. This medical system imposes procedures and standards which the staff are merely following in this particular instance. That is, what the staff do derives from external coercion — 'We have to do it this way' — rather than from personal choices which they would be free to revise in order to accommodate the patient.

The medical definition grants the staff the right to carry out their task. If not for the medical definition the staff's routine activities could be defined as unconscionable assaults on the dignity of individuals. The topics of talk, particularly inquiries about bodily functioning, sexual experience, and death of relatives might be taken as offences against propriety. As for exposure and manipulation of the patient's body, it would be a shocking and degrading invasion of privacy were the patient not defined as a technical object. The infliction of pain would be mere cruelty. The medical definition justifies the request that a presumably competent adult give up most of his autonomy to persons often subordinate in age, sex, and social class. The patient needs the medical definition to minimize the threat to his dignity; the staff need it in order to inveigle the patient into cooperating.

Yet definitions that appear to contradict the medical definition are routinely expressed in the course of gynaecological examinations. Some gestures acknowledge the pelvic area as special; other gestures acknowledge the patient as a person. These counterdefinitions are as essential to the encounter as the medical definition. We have already discussed how an actor's lack of conviction may interfere with his performance. Implicit acknowledgements of the special meaning of the pelvic area help those players hampered by lack of conviction to perform adequately. If a player's sense of 'how things really are' is implicitly acknowledged, he often finds it easier to adhere outwardly to a contrary definition.

A physician may gain a patient's cooperation by acknowledging her as a person. The physician wants the patient to acknowledge the medical definition, cooperate with the procedures of the examination, and acknowledge his professional competence. The physician is in a position to bargain with the patient in order to obtain this cooperation. He can offer her attention and acknowledgement as a person. At times he does so.

Although defining a person as a technical object is necessary in order for medical activities to proceed, it constitutes an indignity in itself. This indignity can be cancelled or at least qualified by simultaneously acknowledging the patient as a person.

The medical world contains special activities and special perspectives. Yet the inhabitants of the medical world travel back and forth to the general community where modesty, death, and other medically relevant matters are regarded quite differently. It is not so easy to dismiss general community meanings for the time one finds oneself in a medical setting. The counterthemes that the pelvic area is special and that patients are persons provide an opportunity to show deference to general community meanings at the same time that one is disregarding them.

Sustaining the reality of a gynaecological examination does not mean sustaining the medical definition, then. What is to be sustained is a shifting balance between medical definition and counterthemes.[7] Too much emphasis on the medical definition alone would undermine the reality, as would a flamboyant manifestation of the counterthemes apart from the medical definition. The next section will suggest how this balance is achieved.

3 Sustaining the Reality

The appropriate balance between medical definition and counterthemes has to be created anew at every moment. However, some routinized procedures and demeanour are available to participants in gynaecological examinations. Persons recognize that if certain limits are exceeded, the situation would be irremediably shattered. Some arrangements have been found useful because they simultaneously express medical definition and countertheme. Routine ways of meeting the task requirements and also dealing with 'normal trouble' are available. This section will describe how themes and counterthemes are embodied in routinized procedures and demeanour.

The pervasiveness of the medical definition is expressed by indicators that the scene is enacted under medical auspices.[8] The action is located in 'medical space' (hospital or doctor's office). Features of the setting such as divisions of space, decor, and equipment are constant reminders that it is indeed 'medical space.' Even background details such as the loudspeaker calling, 'Dr Morris, Dr Armand Morris' serve as evidence for medical reality (suppose the loudspeaker were to announce instead, 'Five minutes until post time'). The staff wear medical uniforms, don medical gloves, use medical instruments. The exclusion of lay persons, particularly visitors of the patient who may be accustomed to the patient's nudity at home, helps to preclude confusion between the contact of medicine and the contact of intimacy.[9]

Some routine practices simultaneously acknowledge the medical definition and qualify it by making special provision for the pelvic area. For instance, rituals of respect express dignity for the patient. The patient's body is draped so as to expose only that part which is to receive the technical attention of the doctor. The presence of a nurse acting as 'chaperone' cancels any residual suggestiveness of male and female alone in a room.[10]

Medical talk stands for and continually expresses allegiance to the medical definition. Yet certain features of medical talk acknowledge a nonmedical delicacy. Despite the fact that persons present on a gynaecological ward must attend to many topics connected with the pelvic area and various bodily functions, these topics are generally not discussed. Strict conventions dictate what unmentionables are to be acknowledged under what circumstances. However, persons are exceptionally free to refer to the genitals and related matters on the obstetrics-gynaecology service. If technical matters in regard to the pelvic area come up, they are to be discussed nonchalantly.

The special language found in staff-patient contacts contributes to depersonalization and desexualization of the encounter. Scientific-sounding medical terms facilitate such communication. Substituting dictionary terms for everyday words add formality. The definite article replaces the pronoun adjectives in reference to body parts so that for example, the doctor refers to 'the vagina' and never 'your vagina'. Instructions to the patient in the course of the examination are couched in language which bypasses sexual imagery; the vulgar connotation of 'spread your legs' is generally metamorphosed into the innocuous 'let your knees fall apart'.

While among themselves the staff generally use explicit technical terms, explicit terminology is often avoided in staff-patient contacts.[11] The reference to the pelvic area may be merely understood, as when a patient says: 'I feel so uncomfortable there right now' or 'They didn't go near to this area, so why did they have to shave it?' In speaking with patients the staff frequently uses euphemisms. A doctor asks: 'When did you first notice difficulty down below?' and a nurse inquires: 'Did you wash between your legs?' Persons characteristically refer to pelvic examinations euphemistically in staff-patient encounters. 'The doctor wants to take a peek at you,' a nurse tells a patient. Or 'Dr Ryan wants to see you in the examining room'.

In one pelvic examination there was a striking contast between the language of staff and patient. The patient was graphic; she used action words connoting physical contact to refer to the examination procedure: feeling, poking, touching, and punching. Yet she never located this action in regard to her body, always omitting to state where the physical contact occurred. The staff used impersonal medical language and euphemisms: 'I'm going to examine you'; 'I'm just cleaning out some blood clots'; 'He's just trying to fix you up a bit'.

Sometimes the staff introduce explicit terminology to clarify a patient's remark. A patient tells the doctor, 'It's bleeding now' and the doctor answers, 'You? From the vagina?' Such a response indicates the appropriate vocabulary, the degree of freedom permitted in technically oriented conversation, and the proper detachment. Yet the common avoidance of explicit terminology in staff-patient contacts suggests that despite all the precautions to assure that the medical definition prevails, many patients remain somewhat embarrassed by the whole subject. To avoid provoking this embarrassment, euphemisms and understood references are used when possible.

Highly specific requirements for everybody's behaviour during a gynaecological examination curtail the leeway for the introduction of discordant notes. Routine technical procedures organize the event from beginning to end, indicating what action each person should take at each moment. Verbal exchanges are also constrained by the technical task, in that the doctor uses routine phrases of direction and reassurance to the patient. There is little margin for ad-libbing during a gynaecological examination.

The specifications for demeanour are elaborate. Foremost is that both staff and patient should be nonchalant about what is happening. According to the staff, the exemplary patient should be 'in play': showing she is attentive to the situation by her bodily tautness, facial expression, direction of glance, tone of voice, tempo of speech and bodily movements, timing and appropriateness of responses. The patient's voice should be controlled, mildly pleasant, self-confident, and impersonal. Her facial expression should be attentive and neutral, leaning towards the mildly pleasant and friendly side, as if she were talking to the doctor in his office, fully dressed and seated in a chair. The patient is to have an attentive glance upward, at the ceiling or at other persons in the room, eyes open, not dreamy or 'away', but ready at a second's notice to revert to the doctor's face for a specific verbal exchange. Except for such a verbal exchange, however, the patient is supposed to avoid looking into the doctor's eyes during the actual examination because direct eye contact between the two at this time is provocative. Her role calls for passivity and self-effacement. The patient should show willingness to relinquish control to the doctor. She should refrain from speaking at length and from making inquiries which would require the doctor to reply at length. So as not to point up her undignified position, she should not project her personality profusely. The self must be eclipsed in order to sustain the definition that the doctor is working on a technical object and not a person.

The physician's demeanour is highly stylized. He intersperses his examination with remarks to the patient in a soothing tone of voice:

'Now relax as much as you can'; 'I'll be as gentle as I can'; 'Is that tender right there?' Most of the phrases with which he encourages the patient to relax are routine even though his delivery may suggest a unique relationship. He demonstrates that he is the detached professional and the patient demonstrates that it never enters her mind that he could be anything except detached. Since intimacy can be introduced into instrumental physical contact by a 'loving' demeanour (lingering, caressing motions and contact beyond what the task requires), a doctor must take special pains to insure that his demeanour remains a brisk no-nonsense show of efficiency.[12]

Once I witnessed a gynaecological examination of a forty-year-old woman who played the charming and scatterbrained Southern belle. The attending physician stood near the patient's head and carried on a flippant conversation with her while a resident and medical student actually performed the examination. The patient completely ignored the examination, except for brief answers to the examining doctor's inquiries. Under these somewhat trying circumstances she attempted to carry off a gay, attractive pose and the attending physician cooperated with her by making a series of bantering remarks.

Most physicians are not so lucky as to have a colleague conversing in cocktail-hour style with the patient while they are probing her vagina. Ordinarily the physician must play both parts at once, treating the patient as an object with his hands while simultaneously acknowledging her as a person with his voice. In this incident, where two physicians simultaneously deal with the patient in two distinct ways, the dual approach to the patient usually maintained by the examining physician becomes more obvious.[13]

The doctor needs to communicate with the patient as a person for technical reasons. Should he want to know when the patient feels pain in the course of examination or information about other medical matters, he must address her as a person. Also the doctor may want to instruct the patient on how to facilitate the examination. The most reiterated instruction refers to relaxation. Most patients are not sufficiently relaxed when the doctor is ready to begin. He then reverts to a primitive level of communication and treats the patient almost like a young child. He speaks in a soft, soothing voice, probably calling the patient by her first name, and it is not so much the words as his manner which is significant. This caressing voice is routinely used by hospital staff members to patients in critical situations, as when the patient is overtly frightened or disoriented. By using it here the doctor heightens his interpersonal relation with the patient, trying to reassure her as a person in order to get her to relax.

Moreover even during a gynaecological examination, failing to acknowledge another as a person is an insult. It is insulting to be entirely instrumental about instrumental contacts. Some acknowledgement of the intimate connotations of touching must occur. Therefore, a measure of 'loving' demeanour is subtly injected. A doctor cannot employ the full gamut of loving insinuations that a lover might infuse into instrumental touching. So he indirectly implies a hint of intimacy which is intended to counter the insult and make the procedure acceptable to the woman. The doctor conveys this loving demeanour not by lingering or superfluous contact, but by radiating concern in his general manner, offering extra assistance, and occasionally by sacrificing the task requirements to 'gentleness'.

In short, the doctor must convey an optimal combination of impersonality and hints of intimacy that simultaneously avoid the insult of sexual familiarity and the insult of unacknowledged identity. The doctor must manage this even though the behaviour emanating from each definition is contradictory. If the doctor can achieve this feat, it will contribute to keeping the patient in line. [. . .]

Notes

[1] Peter Berger and Thomas Luckmann, *The Social Construction of Reality*, Garden City, NY, Doubleday & Company, Inc., 1966.

[2] The data in this article are based on observations of approximately 75 gynaecological examinations conducted by male physicians on an obstetrics-gynaecology ward and some observations from a medical ward for comparison. For a full account of this study, see Joan P. Emerson, 'Social Functions of Humour in a Hospital Setting,' unpublished doctoral dissertation, University of California at Berkeley, 1963. For a sociological discussion of a similar setting, see William P. Rosengren and Spencer DeVault, 'The Sociology of Time and Space in an Obstetrical Hospital' in *The Hospital in Modern Society*, Eliot Freidson, (ed.), New York. The Free Press of Glencoe, 1963, pp. 266-292.

[3] 'It takes severe biographical shocks to disintegrate the massive reality internalized in early childhood; much less to destroy the realities internalized later. Beyond this, it is relatively easy to set aside the reality of the secondary internalizations.' Berger and Luckmann, *op. cit.*, p. 142.

[4] As stated by Lief and Fox: 'The amounts and occasions of bodily contact are carefully regulated in all societies, and very much so in ours. Thus, the kind of access to the body of the patient that a physician in our society has is a uniquely privileged one. Even in the course of a so-called routine physical examination, the physician is permitted to handle the patient's body in ways otherwise permitted only to special intimates, and in the case of procedures such as rectal and vaginal examinations in ways normally not even permitted to a sexual partner.' Harold I. Lief and Renee C. Fox, 'Training for "Detached Concern" in Medical Students' in Harold I. Lief, *et al.,* (eds.), *The Psychological Basis of Medical Practice,* New York, Harper & Row, Inc., 1963, p. 32. As Edward Hall remarks, North Americans have an inarticulated convention that discourages touching except in moments of intimacy. Edward T. Hall, *The Silent Language,* Garden City, N.Y., Doubleday & Company, 1959, p. 149.

[5] For comments on embarrassment in the doctor-patient relation, see Michael Balint, *The Doctor, His Patient, and the Illness,* New York, International Universities Press, Inc., 1957, p. 57.

[6] Physicians are aware of the possibility that their routine technical behaviour may be interpreted as sexual by the patient. The following quotation states a view held by some physicians: 'It is not unusual for a suspicious hysterical woman with fantasies of being seduced to misinterpret an ordinary movement in the physical examination as an amorous advance.' E. Weiss and O. S. English, *Psychosomatic*

Medicine, Philadelphia, W. B. Saunders Co., 1949. Quoted in Marc Hollender, *The Psychology of Medical Practice*, Philadelphia, W. B. Saunders Co., 1958, p. 22. An extreme case suggests that pelvic examinations are not without their hazards for physicians, particularly during training: 'A third-year student who had prided himself on his excellent adjustment to the stresses of medical school developed acute anxiety when about to perform, for the first time, a pelvic examination on a gynaecological patient. Prominent in his fantasies were memories of a punishing father who would unquestionably forbid any such explicitly sexual behaviour.' Samuel Bojar, 'Psychiatric Problems of Medical Students' *Emotional Problems of the Student* in Graham B. Glaine, Jr., *et al* (eds.) Garden City, N.Y. Doubleday & Company, 1961, p. 248.

[7] Many other claims and assumptions are being negotiated or sustained in addition to this basic definition of the situation. Efforts in regard to some of these other claims and assumptions have important consequences for the fate of the basic definition. That is, in the actual situation any one gesture usually has relevance for a number of realities, so that the fates of the various realities are intertwined with each other. For example, each participant is putting forth a version of himself which he wants validated. A doctor's jockeying about claims about competence may reinforce the medical definition and so may a patient's interest in appearing poised. But a patient's ambition to 'understand what is really happening' may lead to undermining of the medical definition. Understanding that sustaining the basic definition of the situation is intertwined with numerous other projects, however, we will proceed to focus on that reality alone.

[8] Compare Donald Ball's account of how the medical definition is conveyed in an abortion clinic, where it serves to counter the definition of the situation as deviant. Donald W. Ball, 'An Abortion Clinic Ethnography,' *Social Problems*, 14, pp. 293-301, Winter, 1967.

[9] Glaser and Strauss discuss the hospital prohibition against examinations and exposure of the body in the presence of intimates of the patient. Barney Glaser and Anselm Strauss, *Awareness of Dying*, Chicago, Aldine Publishing Co., 1965, p. 162.

[10] Sudnow reports that at the county hospital he studied, male physicians routinely did pelvic examinations without nurses being present, except in the emergency ward. David Sudnow, *Passing On: The Social Organization of Dying*, Englewood Cliffs, N.J., Prentice-Hall, Inc., 1967, p. 78.

[11] The following quotation suggests that euphemisms and understood references may be used because the staff often has the choice of using 'lewd words' or not being understood. 'Our popular vocabulary for describing sexual behaviour has been compounded of about equal parts of euphemism and obscenity, and popular attitude and sentiment have followed the same duality. Among both his male and female subjects, the interviewers found many who knew only the lewd words for features of their own anatomy and physiology.' Nelson N. Foote, 'Sex as Play' in Jerome Himelhock and Sylvia F. Fava, *Sexual Behaviour in American Society*, New York, W. W. Norton and Co., Inc., 1955, p. 239.

[12] The doctor's demeanour typically varies with his experience. In his early contacts with patients the young medical student may use an extreme degree of impersonality generated by his own discomfort in his role. By the time he has become accustomed to doctor-patient encounters, the fourth-year student and intern may use a newcomer's gentleness, treating the scene almost as an intimate situation by relying on elements of the 'loving' demeanour previously learned in non-professional situations. By the time he is a resident and focusing primarily on the technical details of the medical task, the physician may be substituting a competent impersonality, although he never reverts to the extreme impersonality of the very beginning. The senior doctor, having mastered not only the technical details but an attitude of detached concern as well, reintroduces a mild gentleness, without the involved intimacy of the intern.

[13] The management of closeness and detachment in professional-client relations is discussed in Charles Kadushin, 'Social Distance between Client and Professional,' *American Journal of Sociology,* 67, pp. 517-531, March 1962. Wilensky and Lebeaux discuss how intimacy with strangers in the social worker-client relation is handled by accenting the technical aspects of the situation, limiting the relationship to the task at hand, and observing the norms of emotional neutrality, impartiality and altruistic service. Harold L. Wilensky and Charles N. Lebeaux, *Industrial Society and Social Welfare,* New York, Russell Sage Foundation, 1958, pp. 299-303.

2.5 The Sociology of Language: Yesterday, Today, and Tomorrow
Joshua A. Fishman

During the summer of 1964 I was one of a group of ten sociologists, anthropologists, and linguists who were given visiting-faculty status at the Linguistic Institute then being held at Indiana University. Our task was to define the area of sociolinguistic endeavour, to explore its methods, and to formulate the future research and course work necessary for its growth and development. Almost all that has transpired in American sociolinguistics in the following decade can be traced back to the individuals and the concerns that interacted in Bloomington, Indiana, during that formative summer. Today, when I am once again a visiting faculty member at a Linguistic Institute, and when I have been asked to review some of the past, present, and future sociolinguistic efforts, it seems reasonable for me to begin by returning to one of the topics that had been of major interest prior to Bloomington: the Whorfian hypothesis. As one of the major pre-sociolinguistic prods requiring us to look beyond the structure of language *per se* and to examine the behavioural implications and concomitants of that structure, the Whorfian hypothesis is a good way of reviewing yesterday, or even the day before yesterday, *en route* to our more major concern with the today and tomorrow of the sociolinguistic enterprise.

The Whorfian Hypothesis: Part of Our Yesterday

It may come somewhat as a surprise today, but there is no doubt in my mind that the Whorfian hypothesis and its stress on the linguistic relativism of cognitive processes was one of the 'cutting edges' of the language sciences in the 1950s and early 60s. Even in the early 60s, when the birth (or rebirth) of sociolinguistic concerns was becoming apparent to those at the forefront of theory and research in the language sciences, it did not strike me as surprising to hear the prediction that 'one of the major topics of sociolinguistic attention will doubtlessly be the Whorfian hypothesis.' I did not agree with the view at all (my 1960 paper on the Whorfian hypothesis having convinced me otherwise), but it did not surprise me still to encounter it even among the most highly informed.

Current Issues in Linguistic Theory, ed. by Roger Cole, Harvester Press, London, 1977, pp. 51-75. The article has been edited to some extent: in particular, the last few pages of the original have been cut.

Today, more than a decade later, I am even more convinced of the limited validity of the Whorfian hypothesis than I was initially. Nevertheless, paradoxically, I now see it much more clearly in relation to four other major shocks to the *amour propre* of modern man. Like Copernicus, Darwin, Marx, and Freud before him, Whorf must be viewed as a prophet of sad tidings, as a bearer of the message that man is far less free and far more insignificant than he would like to be or than he believes himself to be.

The Copernican thunderbolt brought home the message that, far from being the apple of God's eye, our planet is a mere speck in a system the centre of which is occupied by a third-rate star. Three centuries later, Darwin heaped insult upon injury by demonstrating that man himself is merely a part of the entire animal kingdom, many of whose members did not escape extinction notwithstanding their various and considerable assets and distinctions. Almost simultaneously, Marx came forward to claim that human behaviour was merely part of the system of economic resources and that human culture and values were really by-products of material circumstances. Finally, Freud began the twentieth century with his similarly debunking and dethroning views that make men the prisoners of their unconscious instinctual needs and of the structures into which these are systematically organized.

All four of these men powerfully changed (and dampened) our views of ourselves. Whorf, the least successful of the great detractors, must nevertheless be seen as one of their company. His ultimate message is like theirs: Man is not free. Man is not great. He is bound. He is trapped. He does not necessarily see what is there. He does not necessarily say what he thinks. He does not even think freely. Cognitively he is a prisoner of the structure of his particular language.[1] No matter how limited the validity of this claim, and several decades of sympathetic research have produced almost no convincing confirmatory evidence, Whorf deserves to be seen in the illustrious company of the other great detractors, among whom the other social and behavioural scientists (Marx and Freud) may have been no more correct, even though they became much more famous than Whorf.

The tenacity with which the Whorfian hypothesis is subscribed to must be a matter of considerable fascination for anyone interested in the sociology of science or in the sociology of knowledge. Certainly, it is an indication of the extent to which academicians, cursed as we are with 'the talking disease,' are ourselves fascinated by the thought that we are not fully responsible for what we are saying and thinking. Be that as it may, it is clear to me that two or more decades of research have not been particularly kind to Whorf. Even when viewed most charitably, they have revealed that the phenomenon to which he referred is, at best, a remediable or transitory one and, again at best, only a partial reflection of the truly complex embeddedness of cognitive behaviour.

It may be claimed that Marx and Freud too were concerned with diseases that are both remediable and transitory. However, in their cases, they were at least as much concerned with documenting the necessary cures as with the diseases themselves. Whorf, on the other hand, was primarily a diagnostician. He left the ways and means of struggling with language relativity to others (Korzybski, Hayakawa, etc.), who made the struggle into a pseudoscience (general semantics) and recommended various types of pseudotherapy in connection with it. It seems clear to me that the pan-human struggle with linguistic relativity is generally not all that complicated, that many of us can and do overcome or counteract whatever biases our particular grammars and lexicons (and their respective ethno-typological consequences) impose upon us. All in all, we handle linguistic relativity much better than we do linguistic determinism *per se* (a much more pernicious and inescapable disease). Certainly, none of the attempts to confirm or refine the Whorfian hypothesis empirically, whether via research on memory, problem solving, classifying, or attributing (most recently see, e.g., Niyakawa-Howard 1968), has succeeded in demonstrating that linguistic relativity is even a dependable phenomenon, let alone a powerful one, when and if encountered.

More provocatively — and this is where the sociology of language enters the picture — there is much research and ample theory to imply that the contextualization of cognition is far greater and more complex than Whorf imagined. Whorf simply makes the point that how one thinks may be influenced by *the* language in which the thinking is done. However, the sociology of language leads us away from one person– one language models. So much of mankind is bi- and multilingual and the languages utilized are so often so syntactically different that we must recognize a fundamental human capacity to escape from any one grammar and any one lexicon. Basically we all learn to work with linguistic and behavioural repertoires, even those of us who are nominally monolingual. We are not so much troubled by the differing structures of the various languages and varieties that we use as we are by the demands of communicative appropriateness across a wide variety of interlocutors, topics, and purposes. We ponder how to say (write) something the *right way* to a *particular person* because of a *particular role relationship* and *situation* impinging on our *purpose* (or cross-purpose), and we try to select adeptly and appropriately between the language and varieties we control accordingly. Far from being locked in, we are constantly weighing and choosing between grammars and lexicons in our quest to advance ourselves and our purposes more adequately (Fishman 1972).

The sociology of language also helps us realize that whether or not language structure helps create sociocognitive reality (as Whorf would claim), this latter reality both creates and preserves language characteristics, including those of a highly systematic kind. As a result of this more complete causal system (rather than the one-way 'half system' that Whorf conceived of), those planning for change need to alter not only the linguistic system (in order to foster societal change) but also – and much more basically – the social system (in order to foster linguistic change and social change *per se*). The entire system is not only far more complete but also more open and manipulable than Whorf anticipated. It can be entered at any point, but, optimally, at several points, in order to produce and consolidate the kinds of change that are desired. Further evidence of the two-way relationship that exists between the organization of language and the organization of social behaviour comes from the field of 'language birth.' New languages or new varieties come into being simultaneously with new social facts (new interactions between preexisting language groups, new power constellations between such groups, etc.). There is simply no reason to focus only on language organization as the causal force or factor in sociocognitive behaviour, as Whorf implied. The total process is of a circular or feedback nature, and the causal impact of societal organization on language organization is every bit as powerful (if not more so) as the causal impact of lingual organization on the organization of social behaviour (Fishman 1972).

Notwithstanding the above qualms and criticisms, the Whorfian hypothesis seems to be eternally capable of fascinating successive generations of students in successive disciplines. Like Marxism and Freudianism, it functions as a quasi-religious experience for some in that the enormity and the clarity of its discovery (biased though it be) is indeed breathtaking and, apparently, integratingly clarifying at a level more meaningful and more compelling than the strictly intellectual alone.

There have been mistaken scientific theories and *Weltanschauungen* that have embroiled generations of scholars and students in conflicts to no greater end than to discredit thoroughly the views advanced. The Whorfian hypothesis, or, more accurately, efforts to test, refine, or revise the Whorfian hypothesis, have done much more than that for the language sciences. It has left us at least three very vibrant legacies in the form of productive research traditions and topical concentrations that we might not have otherwise come by. These three robust by-products more than justify the time that has been invested in clarifying and delimiting the Whorfian hypothesis.

Language universals

Whorf's stress on the endless and fargoing differences between languages ultimately prepared us to face the questions 'What differences are really different?' and 'Aren't there more similarities than differences?' Whorf himself realized that certain differences were not differences at all, or that they might as well be overlooked in the face of even more fargoing similarities. Thus, Whorf set up the catchall category Standard Average European (SAE) to take in all of the well-known Indo-European family whose members were viewed as differing in only unimportant ways. Whorf delighted in contrasting the basically similar SAE languages with the 'really different' North and South American Indian languages. But, obviously, these too are often members of large families and, therefore, classifiable into various Standard Average groupings of their own. Ultimately, the various Standard Average groupings must doubtlessly differ in some respects but be similar in others. Thus, the question of language universals arises, and for some at least (foremost among them: Greenberg) it arose out of the phoenixlike ashes of the Whorfian hypothesis. Linguists and anthropologists long carried the burden of saving (or at least recording) all the world's languages on the strength of the view that each was a thoroughly unique reflection of the infinite, many-splendoured variety of mankind. The counterbalancing view, which emphasized the pervasive underlying similarities across language, could not but make their disciplines broader and more balanced than they had hitherto been. We have the struggle with Whorfianism to thank for a good bit of this healthy development.

Ethnolinguistics
Another such development, which is even more fully derivable from Whorf-inspired directions and counterreactions, is the one that has blossomed into the various *ethno*-sciences (ethnolinguistics, ethno-semantics, ethnorecognition, etc.). This fruitful field of inquiry has explored the seemingly complete and tight typological systems within languages that are hardest to escape and hardest to avoid. Initially, these systems (colour nomenclatures, kinship nomenclatures, status or politeness indicators, certainty indicators, shape indicators) were studied in order to test the Whorfian hypothesis, but subsequently they came to be studied in their own right, as 'current ways of viewing' rather than as inescapable traps or blinders. Even if we grant, as I believe we should, that ethno-categories are far more malleable and far less tenacious sociocognitive guides than Whorf believed, they are still well worth identifying, if only in order to know (whether for purposes of intercultural or intra-cultural analyses) the predispositions or presuppositions that require escaping from or working on. Stripped of its Whorfian confirmatory or disconfirmatory role, this is an important contribution in its own right.

Transmitting social structure
Whorf held that the structured characteristics of particular languages bring about particular sociocognitive behaviours. Whatever support for this view we may find today is likely to be tied to the counterbalancing view that the structured characteristics of particular social systems elicit and preserve linguistic structures that are consonant with them and, therefore, supportive of them. Nevertheless, the directional sequence

that Whorf stressed is accepted (even if its directional exclusivity is not) and is in the influential work of Basil Bernstein, among others. Certainly Bernstein believes that lower-class speech is a highly structured (restricted) code that perpetuates a way of life (of thinking and acting) as a result of its early socialization role and its subsequent function in important role relations. Unfortunately, Bernstein's work has consistently been misinterpreted as having inherent or racial or genetic implications *vis-à-vis* the disadvantaged (as does Whorf's work, on occasion), but that is a problem in its own right. Here it is merely appropriate to stress that there are important researchers (including recent ones who are exploring 'female talk') who accept the notion that linguistic features can and do serve to freeze their speakers into normatively expected and ritualized social behaviours. Although these researchers often hold no brief at all for any deep-freeze view, nor are they unmindful of the contribution of social structure for freezing language usage, they are, at least to some degree, following in the footsteps of Whorf himself.

The Yiddish proverb 'a good question begets a good answer' is applicable to the Whorfian hypothesis. Basically, Whorf asked a good question and, although the answers to his question have generally cast doubt on his own preferred answer, they have themselves been good answers and have sparked their own independent and productive research traditions – as witnessed by the three healthy offspring fields mentioned above. [. . .]

Finally, the Whorfian hypothesis helped pave the way for three important sociolinguistic principles of today and tomorrow:

a. Language and society are associated in a two-way relationship, i.e., one of constant interdependence and feedback. It is this fact that makes the formulation 'language in society' (or 'language in its social setting')[2] a misnomer or, at least, a gross simplication of the true complexity of the sociology of language.

b. The relationship between language and society is not adequately represented by the Whorfian model of 'one society – one language.' On the contrary, a universal fact of social life is that speakers control a repertoire of varieties and/or languages that may be structurally very diverse. Their ability to use this repertoire nimbly is itself testimony to the human ability to escape from or to control the bonds of linguistic relativity.

c. The relationship between language and society is not so tightly structured that it cannot be altered via social planning and via language planning, not to mention the unplanned change to which this relationship and its component parts are amenable.

The remaining sections of this review will deal largely with points *b* and *c*. Let us remember that although we may now conclude that Whorf was substantially mistaken, he was undeniably a man of great vision. A truly great vision is always worth the price it exacts, even if it is in large part mistaken, for it stimulates worthwhile correctives and counter-visions. If only more of us in the sociology of language could be wrong like Marx, wrong like Freud, or wrong like Whorf, ultimately the sociology of language would certainly be stronger rather than weaker for our 'mistakes.'

Societal Bilingualism: The Bulk of Our Today and a Good Bit of Our Tomorrow

Although Whorf himself may have been bilingual[3] he unconsciously assumed, as have others before and since, that the normal model for language in society implied that each society had one language and one alone. The sociology of language, which so clearly proclaims the opposite view (and in also doing so for societies usually considered monolingual even calls into question such reifications as 'the *x* language'), must, as a result, adopt others as its grandfathers. Indeed, two grandfathers come to mind in connection with the interest in societal bilingualism, Uriel Weinreich and Einar Haugen. Since they both undertook their most seminal work on this topic roughly a quarter century ago (see Weinreich's *Languages in Contact*, 1953, and Haugen's *Bilingualism in the Americas*, 1956) enough time has passed for us to ask: How far have we come and what remains to be done in this essentially post-Whorfian (if not contra-Whorfian) topic area?

As much as Weinreich and Haugen appreciated the frequency of bilingualism, it is not clear that they really understood its normality. For both of them it was a special, somewhat heightened, state of affairs associated somehow with immigrational trauma, intergroup conflict, and other expressions of man *in extremis*. Haugen wrote poignantly of the 'pains and pleasures' of bilingualism precisely because it was assumed to be something special and not nearly as usual and ubiquitous as talking, breathing, and thinking. Underlying all their work is an innocence (or is it a scepticism?) with respect to societal bilingualism, i.e., that normal societies exist and function on a bilingual basis. Our view today stresses not only the normality of societal multi-lingualism but also its complexity and, indeed, its normal complexity across time (the centuries of recorded history) and across space (the entire world). Certainly we view it as a phenomenon infinitely more amenable to objective and quantitative analysis, as well as to integrate conceptualization, than was formerly thought to be the case.

Societal bilingualism as a worldwide phenomenon

If the frequency of an event can be cited as an indication of its 'normalcy,' then societal bilingualism is obviously a normal phenomenon. It is *present* in almost all countries and is *dominant* in a goodly number.

It is also evidenced by the spread of *lingua francas* such as English into non-English mother-tongue countries throughout the world.

In previous centuries *lingua francas* spread without official record keeping, data collecting, and professional direction of analysis. Not so today. The spread of English (and, to a lesser degree, French, Russian, Chinese, and even Arabic) is now accompanied by the search for 'hard data' as to its *relative* penetration into different countries and segments of society. The volumes being published by the International Centre for Research on Bilingualism on *The Linguistic Composition of the Nations of the World* (see Kloss 1975) are replete with information on the worldwide spread of a relatively few languages of wider communication (LWC), English in particular. My own *Bilingual Education: An International Sociological Perspective* (1976) not only documents the occurrence of such education in some 110 countries (with 5,000 secondary education units and 100,000 elementary education units being involved) but also indicates the magnitude of the co-occurrence of English plus a local language as the predominant pattern of bilingual education today. This is expressly the message conveyed by Gage and Ohannessian (1974) in their very useful recent summary of ESOL enrollments throughout the world. Finally, from my work with Cooper on the 'Sociology of English as an Additional Language' (MS), it is clear that the governmental, quasi-governmental, and nongovernmental use of English in non-English mother-tongue countries today is very great and still growing rapidly (particularly in the areas of technology, business, and mass media), but that the forces and factors leading to increased knowledge of English, use of English, and liking for English are usually quite different and unrelated to one another.

A host of factors have come together to foster the spread of *lingua francas* today, when the number of independent countries is larger than it has ever been in recorded history. Notwithstanding the proliferation of polities the number of 'internationals' keeps growing, as a result of the spread of United Nations enterprises, foreign technological experts and indigenous elites, business representatives, expatriate residents, and the vastly increased tide of tourism. In city after city throughout the world these 'internationals' constitute a speech community (composed of innumerable smaller networks that are often based on divergent mother tongues) and, much more often than not, English is their *lingua franca*, as revealed in shops, restaurants, theatres, and concerts and by parties and publications the world over. Indeed, probably not since the days of the Roman Empire has so much of the known world been so accessible via 'a single language.'[4]

National bilingualism and language planning

The above development is not always viewed with unmitigated pleasure. International bilingualism may be well and good 'in its place,' but it can and may have rather unexpected and undesired intranational consequences. Since nations are currently our largest units of effectively organized consciousness it should come as no surprise that many nations have responded at a policy level to the spread of English, to define both its desired and its undesired functions and domains. [. . .]

We now have several fine studies of such managed or controlled or planned national bilingualism, none of which was available to Weinreich or Haugen a quarter century ago. Glyn Lewis's volume on multilingualism in the Soviet Union (1972), Carol Scotton's on choosing a *lingua franca* in an African capital (1972), the various reports of the Survey of Language Teaching and Language Usage in East Africa (e.g., Ladefoged 1968; Whiteley 1975; Bender, Ferguson, and Cooper 1976; Polome *et al.*, forthcoming; Ohannessian *et al.*, forthcoming), the recent volume by Harrison *et al.* (1975) on Jordan, all include examples of research on the national level on policy and practice with respect to national bilingualism. The concern for one or more local/national languages faced by powerful *lingua francas* is everywhere patently clear, even if consensus has not yet always been reached (or imposed) on the societal allocation of languages to functions. The resolutions that are sought are increasingly nonsimplistic and nontotalistic. The functions of the *lingua francas*, vital though they may be, are restricted so as not to erode the status of local/national languages for most speech networks in the most basic and integrative functions. Certainly no massive language shifts are being avowedly engineered with respect to nonimmigrant populations, although some may occur as *lingua francas* spill over the dikes and dams with which they are surrounded. It is certainly clear that a functional allocation such as that currently envisaged by the new Philippine bilingual education policy (Filipino for ethnically encumbered fields such as national literature, history, and civics, and English for ethnically unencumbered subjects such as mathematics and the sciences) is an expression of the all-too-human quest for the best of all possible worlds. Certainly it is valuable to have one or more local/national language(s) for purposes of national integration and for mass mobilization along the road to modernity. The fact that some of the decisions have yet to be made as to which internal language(s) should discharge this function merely adds poignancy to the issue that *local/national languages are desired*.

As Americans and as purportedly rational and objective scholars many of us cannot help expressing some impatience (if not outright opposition) with the recurring need to protect mother tongues. I have defended and studied this need many times over the past score of years (see particularly Fishman 1968, 1973a, 1976), and, therefore, I merely want to point out here that with respect to planned national bilingualism an area in which further study is badly needed is the sociology of ethnicity. Only recently our ignorance of ethnicity was at least matched by a lack of interest in it. Today we are obviously more interested in ethnicity but almost as ignorant as before. This ignorance is not really primarily an American disease, although it does have some rather peculiarly American provincialisms masquerading as sophistication associated with it as secondary symptoms. The truth is that in three thousand years of social and sociological theory, spanning the period from the ancient Hebrew, Greek, and Roman thinkers, through the Church fathers, to the modern sociological schools, no full-fledged sociological theory of ethnicity has been elaborated, neither with respect to ethnicity as a recurring basis of human organization nor with respect to its developmental transformations *pari-passu* to more general societal development.[5] We are desperately in need of an un-hurried and unharried review of ethnicity as a societal parameter, and of why it has so consistently received such brief and such negative attention from the great social theoreticians. All the social sciences will gain thereby, not least the study of planned national bilingualism with its recurring struggle to protect ethnicity and the ethnic mother tongue at the same time that the benefits of LWC's accrue to those classes and networks considered worthy of such a blessing. It is to just such a study that I propose to dedicate myself during the years ahead (Nahirny and Fishman MS).

The bilingual community and its networks

National bilingual policy is a serious and very conscious (even self-conscious) affair. Operating at a far less conscious level is the socio-linguistic heartland of societal bilingualism: the bilingual community and its social networks. It is in this connection that the lion's share of empirical and theoretical progress has been made, particularly during the past decade, bringing us to a stage of sophistication far beyond that available when Weinreich and Haugen were reviewing and conceptualizing the field. The studies of bilingualism in the barrio (Fishman, Cooper, and Ma 1971), of Guarani-Spanish alternation in the Paraguayan countryside (Rubin 1968), of diglossia in Franco-phone Montreal (Lieberson 1970), of diglossia as well as its dissolution in various regions of France (Tabouret-Keller 1972) have all provided ample evidence of the sociodynamics and sociostasis of bilingual communities. We now have rather refined accounts (and rather powerful statistical treatments yielding multiple correlations in the 90s!) of the normative societal allocation of language functions that define and predict communicative competence with respect to a bilingual reper-toire. Certainly the relatively uniform and consistent individual inter-pretations and realizations of community norms — as well as of when and to what degree it is permitted to depart from the societal alloca-tion of functions for metaphorical purposes — has, in recent years, been rather well represented. Students should find it progressively easier to go back and forth between individual bilingualism and the absence or presence of societal diglossia. Soon such demonstrations will become old hat.

If there is still a new frontier in the study of societal bilingualism at the community and network level it is probably in connection with the more refined explication of the change potential and change processes that may be there. As yet no one has really traced through the implications that exist for change in community bilingualism in the Labovian displacement model. We know there are consistent inter-network differences. We know that these differences imply a lack of full consensus as to the societal allocation of functions. We know that these differences are relatable to occupational, role, and attitudinal differences between networks. We know that these differences imply not merely the *potential* for change in the societal allocation of functions but that they are actually an indication of *ongoing change*, of change incarnate. Nevertheless, no one has quite put these pieces together this way in a study of community and network bilingualism. It is an exciting prospect that remains to be realized.

The bilingual individual in societal perspective

Like all societal research, the phenomenon of societal bilingualism cannot be endlessly pursued without the use of measures and observations of individuals. Just as societal bilingualism is a consolidation or compositing of individual data, so must individual bilingualism be viewed as a reflection of societal norms. Bilinguals who are equally fluent in both languages (as measured by their facility and correctness overall) are rarely equally fluent in both languages about *all possible topics*; this phenomenon is invariably a reflection of the fact that the societal allocation of functions is normally imbalanced and in complementary distribution rather than redundant. If we find an unbalanced but fluent bilingual, we can be sure that this result is due to his or her social experiences. If we find a balanced fluent bilingual we can be equally sure that the balancing is due to special schooling and studied practice rather than to the variety of social institutions (home, friendship clique, school, church, work sphere, government) upon which normal (and, therefore, unbalanced) societal bilingualism depends (Fishman, Cooper, and Ma 1971).

Because societal multilingualism is reflected in individual behaviour, sociolinguistic researchers must carefully monitor the psycholinguistic research on bilingualism as well. Every new psycholinguistic theory or measure pertaining to individual bilingualism needs to be examined for its societal implications. All motive states, personality patterns, and cognitive styles that are related to individual bilingualism must be examined for possible translatability into societal dimensions. Psychological research on bilingualism continues to stimulate the sociolinguistic imagination and to further the refinement of theory, methods, and empirical data. Our multiple correlations are already encouragingly high but there is still sufficient unexplained variance in societally based bilingual behaviour, and sufficient alternative (perhaps more manipulable) variables to be sought to make all of us extremely attentive to the bilingualism research and theory that colleagues are hammering out in departments of psychology and/or in institutes of psychoeducational orientation.

I have tried to imply that the intellectual future of work on societal bilingualism is rather good because the field is coherent, important, and challenging. It only remains to be said that the future also seems bright for a less-thrilling but equally vital reason, namely, that many other basic issues in the sociology of language (and even in the language sciences more broadly) are best and most easily handled (studied, conceptualized) in societal bilingualism settings. The study of language planning is one such topic. The study of language and ethnicity is another. This is no little thing. Indeed, it is a great asset for the intellectual future of societal bilingualism. Since current data are now much better than Weinreich's and Haugen's, our methods are much better, and our theories are (though still formative) far more powerful. I am extremely confident that the study of societal bilingualism will be with us tomorrow and will be a strong central theme in the sociology of language as a whole.

Language Planning: The Tomorrow of the Sociology of Language

If there was little awareness of language planning among language scientists as recently as a decade ago, then obviously Whorf must have been largely unaware of it thirty and forty years ago. His focus on the causal link between language structure and sociocognitive structure was too exclusive, and his estimate of the power of that link was so exaggerated that he could not have had much sympathy for attempts to alter both of these structures as well as the link between them via planned intervention. Certainly, he could not have foreseen the very recent mushrooming of interest in language planning with more and more courses, conferences, and research grants being devoted to it.[6] It may be premature to attempt to integrate what is known in this area at such an early period in its development; nevertheless, there may be a certain benefit in doing so and thereby leaving a bench mark with which subsequent integrative efforts can be compared.[7]

The ten conclusions or generalizations that follow are clustered into two groups. The first pertains to *corpus planning* (CP), that is, to efforts to alter linguistic codes. CP efforts are normally entrusted by political and cultural authorities to academies or institutes whose responsibility it is to modernize, purify, elaborate, and/or codify the language and, at times, to disseminate the products of their efforts: nomenclatures, grammars, spellers, style manuals, textbooks, teachers guides, etc. The second grouping pertains to *status planning* (SP), i.e., to efforts by political and cultural authorities to obtain (if necessary, force) acceptance of the planned corpus for particular functions: governmental, educational, technological, etc. These two aspects of language planning often go on simultaneously, attention normally beginning with printed governmental usage and branching out from there, with either CP or SP receiving greater stress as needed by successive phases of the overall plan. Obviously, without SP success, CP can become a trivial "academic") exercise. Similarly, without CP success, SP becomes an empty declaration of intent, a language programme without linguistic shape or substance. Unfortunately, at this time, much more is known (or suspected) about CP than about SP. This is a reflection of the more delimited and the more organized nature of language, with which CP deals, than of the sum total of society, with which SP deals. Ultimately, in the tomorrow of the sociology of language, the current imbalance between these two will be evened out.

Corpus planning

1. Authorities (and not only authoritarian authorities) *can* organize effectively for CP and, indeed, can do so by some of the same methods of marshalling resources, expertise, and public opinion that are involved in agricultural planning, industrial planning, educational planning, family planning, etc. (Fishman 1973b). The view of 'language as a resource,' to be shaped, augmented, and utilized productively under competent management, is, within limits, a useful metaphor for language planning. A rational society, particularly one that is faced by integrative lag, may be well advised to attend to CP (and, of course, to its counterpart SP) in conjunction with desires to make one or more local/national languages suitable instruments for modern ethnic integration and for other modern functions.

2. CP has been focused upon every aspect of language: nomenclature, phonology, morpho-syntax (including gender, tense, honorifics), writing system, number system, colour system, etc. The fact that even the purportedly tight systems of language have been changed by concerted intervention must lead to the conclusion that there is practically no limit to what society can do to language structure (within the limits of available power to conceptualize and power to implement). The view that only relatively limited, peripheral, 'surfacy' aspects of language can be subjected to planning (for linguists this often means minor semantic systems) is certainly no longer tenable.

3. The model(s) of 'the good language,' i.e., the substantive direction that CP takes (as well as the directions that it avoids or rejects), largely derives from political, historical, and cultural considerations of considerable ideological significance rather than from objective efficiency considerations, such as those proposed by Tauli (1974). Nevertheless,

innovations are most successful when they have no pre-CP rival(s) or when no strong outside (international lingua franca) influences are at play. Ultimately, disparate parts of the code, even those originally characterized by foreign markedness, come to be widely regarded as equally authentic and indigenous.

4. In view of the foregoing, three reasonable criteria of CP 'success' are learning, using, and liking (as opposed to Taulian criteria, such as regularity, purity, and brevity, etc.). That is, CP must be judged by extracode rather than by intracode considerations in view of the non-linguistic pressures upon models of the good language. These criteria are neither highly nor even positively interrelated, and measures of all of them are needed, together with a large number of other social and attitudinal indicators, in order to predict any one of them.

5. At this time, the competence, performance, and attitudinal goals of CP (knowing, using, and liking) are highly predictable via cumulative multiple correlation methods that yield coefficients in the high 80s. Better attitudinal measurement would clearly boost the predictions to a much higher level (see Cooper, Fishman *et al.*, MS), but would not automatically result in more manipulable (practical) findings. The search for manipulable alternative or counterpart measures is an important task for the tomorrow of language planning research.

Status planning

6. Whenever CP and SP are set in motion a large segment (indeed, the bulk) of the total target population may well be beyond its principal period of language acquisition facility. These 'predates' are, nevertheless, mobilizable attitudinally and, to a lesser extent, cognitively, even though their usage patterns are only susceptible to minimal change. Attitudinal mobilization of the population over twenty years old on behalf of SP also becomes a powerful contextual factor on behalf of continued CP.

7. Those populations that have not yet passed beyond their principal period of language acquisition facility ('postdates') are most manipulable with respect to the usage goals of language planning. However, younger populations often do not have the attitudinal conflict or the language conflict experiences of their elders and, as a result, more easily lose the emotional fervour in which all early SP is conducted. As a result, a generation later the typical 'successful' language planning setting is one in which the most consistent 'users' and best 'knowers' of CP products are younger populations, who are least likely to be conscious 'likers' of these products, i.e., to have any heightened emotional attachment to them or to their functional appropriateness. Conversely, older populations are most characterizable as 'likers' but least characterizable as 'users.' This routinization process has its counterpart in other planning areas as well.

8. The implementational manipulation of rewards and punishments on behalf of language planning must also differentiate between learning, using, and liking. Because of the meagre relationship between these three criteria each of them is most fully predictable on the basis of quite different primary predictors. Learning is most predictable on a socio-demographic basis; using, along occupational lines; and liking, on related ideological-attitudinal grounds pertaining to language consciousness and national consciousness more generally (Fishman MS).

9. In the absence of sufficient power[e] to implement SP goals fully and quickly, realistic *gradual functional goals* are a useful device in the pursuit of long-term functional success. Initially modest functions are more easily expanded if they have been successfully implemented initially on pragmatic rather than on moral, ethical, ethnic, or ideological grounds.

10. In the absence of sufficient power to implement SP goals fully and quickly realistic *nontotalistic rationales* or ideologies are a useful device in the pursuit of long-term functional success. Initially modest functions are more easily expanded if no ideological downgrading of indigenous competitor languages and their speakers has taken place. Languages of wider communication also spread effectively when a low ideological and a high pragmatic profile are maintained.

What is most needed tomorrow, in order to advance language planning significantly beyond the above skeletal decalogue, is considerably more comparative research, both at the micro and macro levels and with both CP and SP concerns. The brunt of the recent language planning research and theory derives from experiences with Hebrew, Hindi, Indonesian, Norwegian, and Turkish. Future research and theory would benefit greatly from giving similar attention to Amharic, Hausa, Khmer, Filipino, Swahili, and Vietnamese.[e] All in all, however, it will benefit most from being used. Language planning is the (or at least a) major feature field for the sociology of language precisely because it encompasses theoretical, applied, and comparative dimensions. I expect that we will hear a lot about it and learn a lot more in connection with it during the decade ahead. [. . .]

Notes

[1] I have indicated extensively before (1960, 1972) that this line of thinking was by no means original to Whorf and that it stems very directly from at least a century of prior Herderian, Humboldtian, and Boazian influences in social philosophy, folkloristics, linguistics, and anthropology. Certainly, it can also be traced back far earlier in the West (to Classical Greek and Hebrew sources) as well as in the East (to Indian and Chinese sources). In Whorf's day linguistic relativism was certainly also subscribed to and articulated by Sapir and Benedict, and it fitted in harmoniously with then current emphases on cultural relativism. Nevertheless, to dub the stress on causal linguistic relativism as the *Whorfian* hypothesis is no more incorrect than to acknowledge that 'Columbus discovered America.' Regardless of the significant contemporaries who aided and abetted him in his views and formulations and who simultaneously advanced such ideas themselves, and regardless of very substantial earlier intellectual tradition out

of which these views and formulations doubtlessly grew, it was primarily Whorf, rather than others, who articulated, developed, organized, and presented these views in sufficiently telling fashion during the 1930s and 40s so as to leave an intellectual legacy with which the language sciences of the 50s and 60s (including their nascent sociolinguistic component) had to deal.

[2] The view that language structure must be investigated more broadly, as is implied by 'language in society' and similar figures of speech, may also be considered a healthy by-product of Whorfianism. Certainly there are exciting efforts within linguistics proper, in the study of both syntax and semantics, that seek to view aspects of the social setting as part of the linguistic structure requiring explanation. Admirable and welcome as these efforts are, they must be viewed as only part of the total sociolinguistic enterprise rather than its sum and substance.

[3] Here and elsewhere, I follow the American usage in accord with which *bilingualism* and *bilingual* subsume *multilingualism* and *multilingual*.

[4] The work of Kachru (1975 and earlier) and several others is informative and extremely sensitive in pointing out the ways in which English is undergoing local variation as a result of its widespread use among large populations for (almost) none of whom it is the native language and (almost) all of whom share another language as a mother tongue. Further evidence on the continued development of varieties of nonstandard (or weakly monitored) English is available 'in bulk' from the studies of pidginization and creolization. Although both these trends may be expected to continue, the value and the volume of reasonably standard English is sufficiently great and sufficiently organized to obviate any danger of the falling apart of standard English into a variety of separately normified and mutually unintelligible new languages.

[5] Anthropological theory with respect to ethnicity is certainly in a better state of repair than is its sociological counterpart. Nevertheless, what is sorely needed cannot be derived from anthropological perspective alone since that perspective is so firmly and fully embedded in ethnicity as a constant concern and context that it is difficult to conceptualize it separately from (and, therefore, to study it both when related to and when independent of) other bases of human aggregation. Anthropology at least recognizes that ethnicity is an open system and that all other bases of human aggregation (e.g., social class, occupational group, religious group membership) can become ethnicized, just as ethnic groups can become de-ethnicized and transmuted into less 'heritable', less-ascribed, and more-attained bases of human aggregation (see the work by Barth and by Depres). When, why, and how such transformations occur are things I would not expect anthropological theory alone to indicate, if for no other reason than anthropology's continued concentration on the small, pre-modern society. Certainly, we lack in the West the 'institutes of applied ethnicity' that exist in the Soviet Union and in mainland China, which are engaged not only in monitoring changes in ethnic behaviours (including ethnic sentiments, beliefs, and overt behaviours) in a wide variety of populations, but also in recommending the 'making' and 'unmaking' of ethnic groups, at least partially on the basis of the evidence that has been gathered. While I do not regret the absence of such ethnographic institutes in the West, I do regret our relative impoverished data and theory in this area.

[6] The best way of keeping abreast of this still small but rapidly growing field is to obtain the *Language Planning Newsletter* (Joan Rubin, ed.) published by the Culture Learning Institute, East-West Centre, Honolulu, Hawaii. Other good introductions to this field are Rubin and Jernudd (1971) and Fishman (1974).

[7] The conclusions enumerated in this section flow primarily from the International Study of Language Planning Process, sponsored by the International Division of the Ford Foundation and directed by Charles A. Ferguson and me (with the participation of Joan Rubin, Bjorn Jernudd, and Jyotirindra Das Gupta) from 1968 to 1972.

[8] The absence or presence of force in conjunction with SP is entirely continuous within any society with its absence or presence in connection with the implementation of other central governmental or authoritative planning. Responsiveness to popular opinion, or its absence, and the utilization or disregard of genuine expertise are also very much the same in status planning as they are with respect to other important decisions and operations. Language planning in general and status planning in particular should not, therefore, be confused with thought control or totalitarianism any more than is educational planning or family planning. Each society engages in planning, implementation, and evaluation in ways that are concordant with its own sociopolitical traditions, and language planning does not differ from other types of planning in this respect.

[9] We are also still abysmally ignorant of recent Soviet and Chinese experiences with language planning. Not only is there a wealth of such experience, but also knowledge of successes and failures within totalitarian contexts are absolutely vital if truly general theory and practice of language planning are to come into being.

References

Bender, M., Ferguson, Charles A., and Cooper, Robert, (1976) *Language in Ethiopia*, London; Oxford University Press.

Cooper, Robert A., Fishman, Joshua A., *et al.* MS, 'The sociology of English as an additional language.'

Fishman, Joshua A. (1960) 'The systematization of the Whorfian hypothesis,' *Behavioral Science* 5 pp. 323-79.

(1968) *Language Loyalty in the United States*, The Hague, Mouton.

(1972) 'Sociocultural organization: language constraints and language reflections', in *The Sociology of Language*, pp. 155-71, Rowley, Mass., Newbury House.

(1973a) *Language and Nationalism*, Rowley, Mass., Newbury House.

(1973b) 'Language modernization and planning in comparison with other types of national modernization and planning,' *Language in Society*, 2 pp. 23-44.

(1973c) The International Research Project on Language Planning Processes (IRPLPP), in Joan Rubin and Roger Shuy, (eds.) *Language Planning: Current Issues and Research*, pp. 83-85, Washington, D.C., Georgetown University Press.

(1975) 'Some implications of "The International Research Project on Language Planning Processes (IRPLPP)" for sociolinguistic surveys', in Sirarpi Ohannessian, *et al.*, (eds.) *Language Surveys in Developing Nations*, pp. 209-20, Arlington, Center for Applied Linguistics.

(1976) *Bilingual Education: An International Sociological Perspective*, Rowley, Mass., Newbury House.

MS. 'Knowing, using, and liking English as an additional language,' in R. L. Cooper, J. A. Fishman, *et al.. The Sociology of English as an Additional Language.*

(ed.) (1974) *Advances in Language Planning*, The Hague, Mouton.

Fishman, Joshua A., Cooper, R. C., and Ma, R. (1971) *Bilingualism in the Barrio*, Bloomington, Ind., Language Sciences.

Gage, William, and Ohannessian, Sirarpi. (1974) 'ESOL enrollments throughout the world,' *Linguistic Reporter* 16, no. 9, pp. 13-16.

Harrison, William, *et al.* (1975) *English Language Policy Survey of Jordan: A Case Study in Language Planning*, Arlington, Centre for Applied Linguistics.

Haugen, Einar, (1956) *Bilingualism in the Americas: Bibliography and Research Guide*, University, Ala., American Dialect Society.

Kachru, Braj, (1975) 'English in South Asia' in J. A. Fishman, (ed.) *Advances in the Study of Societal Multilingualism*, vol. I, The Hague, Mouton.

Kloss, Heinz, (1975) *The Linguistic Composition of the Nations of the World, Vol. I: Western, Central and South Asia*, Quebec, International Research Center on Bilingualism.

Ladefoged, Peter, *et al.* (1968) *Language in Uganda*, London, Oxford University Press.

Lewis, Glyn, (1972) *Multilingualism in the Soviet Union*, The Hague, Mouton.

Lieberson, Stanley, (1970) *Language and Ethnic Relations in Canada*, New York, Wiley.

Nahirny, Vladimir, and Fishman, Joshua A. MS, 'The Sociology of Ethnicity'.

Niykawa-Howard, Agnes, (1968) 'A psycholinguistic study of the Whorfian Hypothesis based on the Japanese passive,' Honolulu, Educational Research and Development Center, University of Hawaii (RP: OE-3260-2-68).

Ohannessian, Sirarpi, *et al.*, forthcoming, *Language in Zambia*, London, Oxford University Press.

Polome, Edgar, *et al.*, forthcoming, *Language in Tanzania*, London, Oxford University Press.

Rubin, Joan (1968) *National Bilingualism in Paraguay*, The Hague, Mouton.

Rubin, Joan, and Jernudd, Bjorn, (eds.) (1971) *Can Language Be Planned?* Honolulu, East-West Center Press.

Scotton, Carol (1972) *Choosing a Lingua Franca in an African Capital*, Edmonton and Champaign, Linguistic Research.

Tabouret-Keller, Andree, (1972) 'A contribution to the sociological study of language maintenance and language shift' in J. A. Fishman, (ed.), *Advances in the Sociology of Language*, vol. II, pp. 365-76, The Hague, Mouton.

Tauli, Valter, (1974) 'The theory of language planning,' in J. A. Fishman, (Ed.), *Advances in Language Planning*, pp. 48-67, The Hague, Mouton.

Weinreich, Uriel, (1953) *Language in Contact, Findings and Problems*, New York, Linguistic Circle of New York.

Whiteley, W. H., *et al.*, (1975) *Language in Kenya*, London, Oxford University Press.

SECTION 3

Language Learning and Language Teaching

Introduction

The readings in this third section of the Reader are divided into two parts: *first* those concerned with research into the development of language use in children; *second*; those preoccupied with how that development has been conceived, influenced and regulated by specific policies in the schools.

The first paper by B. Anderson is a review of research into early communicative interactions between parents and infants. These take on a 'conversational' or 'dialogue-like' quality, even from the first weeks of life. Anderson is particularly concerned with the role of vocalizations in this development, and how through vocalisations, as well as other postures and gestures, the child becomes 'incorporated' into a pre-existing social world.

The second paper, by Eve Clark, is important because it stresses the great flexibility with which children use their earliest language resources. It is important to stress this because of the way in which researchers have frequently been puzzled by aspects of child language use as seen through the eyes (or heard through the ears) of an adult, or mature language user. The use of overextensions and other aspects of semantic development are cases in point. Thus Clark illustrates how infants 'stretch' the functions of what little resources they have – improvisations which often throw researchers 'off the scent', so to speak, of how the child is developing language use.

The final article in this first part is a short research paper by Sharon James which both illustrates an important aspect of the development of language use, *and* how at least one researcher has gone about investigating it. The results show how children of above five years of age are already capable of adjusting politeness of speech to the age-status of the listener, and thus of managing relations with others through the use of language.

The readings in the second part of this section all treat English as a subject in British education. Hollingworth, in looking particularly at the subject in the public schools of a century ago, nevertheless, as he indicates, raises issues which are still current. The extract, actually the first chapter, from *The Newbolt Report* (1921) demonstrates the wide range of topics which had, by that time, come to constitute English as a school subject. English Literature, which by this report, gained firm recognition, represented only one strand. Others included a concern for the needs of industry and commerce, or what we might now call functional literacy; an (optimistic) hope that, with the aftermath of war, English studies could somehow unify the nation, and lead to a broadening of the English curriculum; and a realization that it is hard to discuss English as a subject at secondary level without also reconsidering its role in the school curriculum as a whole.

The theme of English as a medium of instruction, and of the consequently broad responsibilities which the English Department can be given, is taken up in our next extract, again a first chapter, from *The Bullock Report* (1974). There is here a much more functional bias, with less discussion of the role of literature, not only reflecting the membership of the committee (many academic literary critics on the Newbolt Committee, mostly educationists on the Bullock Committee), but also because the battle for a place in the school for English Literature had been long won. But had it? The extract from the paper which Her Majesty's Inspectorate prepared in response to *The Bullock Report*, with the aim of ensuring debate about the role of language in secondary education, seems to indicate that literature study is not at all well integrated into English.

Indeed, all the extracts in this part can be taken to suggest that the unity in variety of English which the official reports seem obliged to assert, can also be seen as a confusion as to what constitute the aims and content of the subject. If this view is justified (and it can certainly be argued, as the main texts for the *Language in Use* course show) then one can discern in these readings something of the social and ideological pressures which operate on a school subject trying to define itself.

Ken Richardson
A. K. Pugh

3.1 The Emergence of Conversational Behaviour

Barbara J. Anderson

> *"No human has ever learned to speak except in a dialogic context, so to this extent the ability to speak presupposes a prior conversation."*
> Jaffe and Feldstein (19)

Recently both psychologists and linguists have emphasized the need to provide a framework for an analysis of the communicative skills a child acquires in the early years of life (13, 26). Research on early vocal behaviour is now addressing the question posed by Bateson: 'What part of behaviour was conversation before it was linguistically differentiated?' (3). The infant's earliest linguistic environment, provided primarily by the mother, and their vocal partnership in the early months of life are now recognized as fundamental for understanding the acquisition of 'communicative competence' (34).

The first form of vocal expression is the infant's cry.

Parents quickly learn to recognize and interpret hungry, mad, or pain cries (43). Spectographic recordings have confirmed that an infant produces quite different cry patterns from the neonatal period and that noncry vocalizations which develop somewhat later are morphologically similar to early fretting sounds (44). From the first month of life the adult voice is more effective in quieting a crying infant than inanimate auditory stimulation, although the human face and inanimate visual stimuli similar in size and shape have comparable effects on crying (44). Also, it is significant that cry sounds are differentiated by parents and convey information about the infant's need states, providing the infant with the earliest experiences of interpersonal communication and regulation (4).

The infant's noncry or positive vocalizations are most commonly considered 'social responses'. Yet observations of infants in their everyday routines at home have revealed that young infants vocalize more frequently when they are alone than in an interactive context (21, 30, 38). It has been suggested that during these solitary vocal episodes the infant invents new sounds and enjoys the repetition of practising familiar sounds (28, 44). Infant noncry vocalizations are frequently

Journal of Communication, U.S.A. Spring 1977, pp. 85-91.

behavioural manifestations of physiologic cycles or states of arousal (7) or indices of differential attention to inanimate auditory and/or visual stimulation.

The infant is uniquely prepared biologically
for auditory processing of human speech sounds (14).

Experimental studies have demonstrated that infants can discriminate certain adult speech sounds from the first few days of life (9). Synchronization between the infant's body movements and articulated phrases of normal adult speech has been demonstrated as early as the neonatal period (12). Infants respond to the characteristic intonation of many verbal phrases long before they are responsive to specific phonetic forms (23). In addition, both live and audiotaped segments of normal and distorted adult speech have been shown to have differential effects on the vocal and motor activity of young infants (39, 41). Investigators have interpreted this behavioural sensitivity as evidence for the adaptive capacity of the infant to process linguistic stimulation.

There is evidence that the infant's prespeech sounds reflect phonemic features of the speech environment (34) and that infants modify the intonation of their early babbling sound to approximate the tone of their partner's voice (25). Infant positive vocalization has been called a 'social releaser' (6) which predictably elicits verbal responses, smiles, and visual attention from the parent (31). In a cyclical fashion, rates of infant vocalization increase in response to these elicited parental behaviours. Systematic naturalistic research has demonstrated that caretakers who verbalize in a distinct, face-to-face interactional style have young infants who vocalize at high rates (11, 22, 24). When the sequence of maternal and infant vocal behaviours has been taken into account, it has been reported that maternal verbalization contingent upon vocalizations of three- to six-month-old infants correlates positively with the overall rate of infant vocal activity, while total maternal verbalization shows no relationship to infant vocal production (21, 45). This relationship between increased frequency of infant vocalization to contingent vocal-social feedback has been consistently demonstrated in laboratory operant conditioning studies (29, 32, 33, 35). Comparable effects have not been reported for contingent nonsocial feedback (42). A greater increase in infant vocal activity has been demonstrated when adult visual attention accompanies verbalization to the baby either on a contingent (20) or noncontingent (5) basis.

From the neonatal period, the infant is able to process and respond selectively to the acoustic information present in adult speech and to modulate his or her social participation. Infant visual and vocal behaviour and level of arousal become coordinated very early with vocal signals from a participating adult, laying foundations for a regulated system of feedback between infant and parent in which vocalizations become a prominent form of communication. While preverbal infants do not provide their parents with 'meaningful' speech feedback, their early sensitivity to and selective reproduction of adult speech sounds and intonation patterns enhance the infant's sociability and strengthen the developing vocal partnership.

Adults, especially parents, use a modified speech model when talking to the preverbal infant.

Until the infant can produce meaningful words or behaviourally indicate receptive language capacities, there are at least two broad sources of influence on adult speech to very young infants. First, the infant provides feedback to the adult in the form of sensitivity to and production of sounds which influences the extent and quality of adult speech. A second source of influence arises from the adult's knowledge of the conventionalized subsystem of language known as 'baby talk,' a knowledge which all adult speakers of the culture share.

Playful sing-song words, stylized imaginative names, and repetitive clusters of sounds interspersed with clicking, humming, and whistling mark the everyday speech of adults to young infants. Ferguson's report of adult speech to young children in six different language groups concluded that 'baby talk' does not originate in the linguistic approximations of young children learning to speak nor in the imitation by adult caregivers of early infant sounds (15). Rather, much of what we consider appropriate speech to infants and young children is a stable, conventionalized component of language which is learned through mechanisms similar to those by which we acquire language in general. In all six languages, 'baby talk' represented deviations of intonation, simplication of consonant clusters, a small selection of vowel sounds, use of diminutive forms, and a simplified grammar, Reduplication, or the repetition of words or parts of words, characterized 'baby talk' in all cultures. It was noted that 'baby talk' was used by adults in all six language groups to convey a nurturant, affectionate, and protective relationship with the infant.

Many of the behaviours which characteristically accompany the speech of mothers to babies deviate markedly from the conventional adult conversational model.

It has been frequently observed that mothers prolong their visual attention to the infant while interacting verbally, providing what has been called a 'gaze frame' (16). In addition, while maintaining visual contact during vocal exchanges mothers often quickly change the face-to-face distance with their infants, moving in very close and then quickly away as well as bobbing up and down. Facial expressions which combine both the continual gazing and close head movements with arching eyebrows and exaggerated mouth formulations are used to communicate a mother's pretended surprise or intense interest in the infant's on-going activity (36). These paralinguistic features of maternal speech contribute to the infant's learning the rules of reciprocal participation. The mother's almost continual visual attention allows the infant to cycle in and out, satisfying needs for interaction as well as withdrawal, while the mother can adjust the intensity of her responses to maintain a mutually satisfying level of social contact (16).

From the neonatal period both the physical status and the level of social responsiveness of the infant affect the quality of adult verbal behaviour.

A mother modifies the quality of her speech to optimize the infant's state of arousal during interaction, quieting the facial-vocal activity to elicit infant attention and increasing tempo, pitch, and loudness to maintain or intensify dyadic interaction when appropriate (7). In contrast to the multiple functions which vocal responses serve for the young infant, maternal speech is more predictably adapted to communication goals, primarily to controlling the mutual affect of the interaction (7). Her vocal responses are used to regulate attention to her and to stimulate infant vocalizations which gratify and confirm her relationship with the infant, creating what have been called 'play-dialogues.' (8).

Two distinct patterns of vocal communication in the mother-infant dyad have been reported. First, investigations have confirmed the remarkably early occurrence of an alternating vocal style between mothers and infants similar to that of conversing adults (3, 37). In addition to turn-taking, lengthy periods of *simultaneous* vocalization by mother and infant have also been found to characterize their everyday vocal interactions (2, 10, 37). It is significant that this vocalization-in-unison between mothers and infants has been reported to occur most often when both partners were also expressing high levels of arousal or positive affect (37).

Vocalizations of three-month-old infants are reported to occur twice as often when the mother is talking simultaneously with the infant as when the mother is silent (2). Research indicates that periods of simultaneous vocalization most often terminate with the infant shifting to a listener's role while the mother continues to talk (2, 37). One explanation for this interactional style is that a mother learns that chatting to her infant while the baby is vocalizing increases the overall amount of infant vocal activity (10). In addition, because the mother constantly relies on her facial and vocal responses to encourage a mutually pleasant interaction experience (36), she is much more likely to try to prolong periods of vocal synchrony when they do occur than to cease talking to her baby. Unlike everyday verbal conversations which will occur from the second year of life onwards, periods of simultaneous vocalization definitely dominate early vocal interactive experiences. This suggests that the turn-system model tends to oversimplify the patterning of early interactions in which vocal responses have a major role in communicating intense, positive affect within the dyad.

In addition to episodes of 'baby talk' and simultaneous vocalization, it has also been observed that mothers of very young infants often engage in serious, continuous monologues with the baby, asking the infant a question, pausing, then answering for the infant (3, 37). Because a mother often begins to imitate her infant's sounds before the baby has developed the capacity for vocal imitation (34), she must infer or 'imagine' participation on the part of the infant (3).

Parents are frequently motivated to attribute meaning
or an intent to communicate to any sound or mouth
movement which the infant produces.

This almost instinctual maternal strategy of attributing intention, interpreting and questioning provides close, repetitive verbal and visual stimulation and encourages sequenced participation from the infant. More importantly, by repeating and giving meaning to preverbal sounds the mother is highlighting the social significance and communicative function of vocal behaviour. In early vocal interactions the infant is, in effect, 'recruited' as a partner more developmentally advanced than he or she actually is (18). Vocal responses from the infant are expected and interpreted as a cue of social participation. The infant consequently learns that vocal responses are messages which affect the partner to meet needs or to continue the exchange.

The early vocal partnership between mother and infant has developmental significance for both. Subject to physiologic limits and state of arousal, infants in the first six months of life are consistently responsive to maternal facial-vocal stimulation (1). This repetitive aspect of infant responsiveness strengthens the developing mother-infant bond (17) and gives incentive for her to continue cycles of vocal-facial behaviour (16). In turn, mothers use a linguistic style with preverbal infants which is marked by repetition: reduplication in 'baby talk,' imitation and interpretation occurring with near-constant visual attention on the infant's face, as well as the consistent pattern of 'joining in' when the infant vocalizes. In the early months of life this redundancy, especially when contingent upon the infant's own behaviours, enables the infant with a relatively immature information processing system to discover that regular and predictable stimulation exists within an otherwise continuously changing environment (27, 40). A dialogue has begun in which mother and infant together are creating the foundations of reciprocity upon which more complex interactional games, sequences of imitation, and eventually verbal conversations are built.

References

1. Appleton, T., R. Clifton, and S. Goldberg, 'The Development of Behavioural Competence in Infancy.' In F. D. Horowitz (ed.) *Review of Child Development Research*, Vol. 4 Chicago, University of Chicago Press, 1975, pp. 101-186.
2. Anderson, B. J. and P. Vietze, 'Early Dialogues: The Structure of Reciprocal Infant-Mother Vocalization.' In S. Cohen and T. J. Comiskey (eds.) *Child Development: A Study of Growth Processes* (second edition), Itasca, Ill., Peacock, in press.
3. Bateson, M. C. 'Mother-Infant Exchanges. The Epigenesis of Conversational Interaction,' *Annals of the New York Academy of Sciences* 263, 1975, pp. 101-113.
4. Bell, S. M. and M. D. S. Ainsworth 'Infant Crying and Maternal Responsiveness', *Child Development* 43, 1972, pp. 1171-1190.
5. Bloom, K., A. Esposito, and M. Lounsbury 'The Control of Infant Vocalizations by Response-Independent Social Stimulation' Paper presented at the meeting of the Southeastern Society for Research in Child Development, Chapel Hill, North Carolina, March 1974.
6. Bowlby, J., *Attachment and Loss*, Vol. 1, New York, Basic Books, 1969.
7. Brazelton, T. B., B. Koslowski, and M. Main, 'The Origins of Reciprocity: The Early Mother-Infant Interaction', in M. Lewis and L. A. Rosenblum (eds.) *The Effect of the Infant on its Caregiver*, New York, Wiley, 1974, pp. 49-76.
8. Brazelton, T. B., E. Tronick, L. Adamson, H. Als, and S. Wise, 'Early Mother-Infant Reciprocity'. In *Parent-Infant Interaction*, Ciba Foundation Symposium 33. New York, Associated Scientific Publishers, 1975, pp. 137-149.
9. Cairnes, G. F. and E. C. Butterfield, 'Assessing Infants' Auditory Functioning'. In B. Z. Friedlander (Ed.) *Exceptional Infant*, Vol. 3. New York: Brunner/Mazel, 1975, pp. 84-108.
10. Caudill, W., 'Tiny Dramas: Vocal Communication Between Mother and Infant in Japanese and American Families'. Paper presented at the Conference on Culture and Mental Health, Honolulu, March 1969.
11. Caudill, W. and H. Weinstein, 'Maternal Care and Infant Behavior in Japan and America'. *Psychiatry* 32, 1969, pp. 12-43.
12. Condon, W. S. and L. S. Sander, 'Neonate Movement is Synchronized with Adult Speech: Interactional Participation and Language Acquisition'. *Science* 183, 1974, pp. 99-101.
13. Dale, P. S., *Language Development: Structure and Function*. Hinsdale, Ill.: Dryden, 1972.
14. Eisenberg, R. B., *Auditory Competence in Early Life: The Roots of Communicative Behavior*. Baltimore, Md.: University Park Press, 1976.
15. Ferguson, C. A., 'Baby Talk in Six Languages', *American Anthropologist* 66, 1964, pp. 103-114.
16. Fogel, A., 'Temporal Organization in Mother-Infant Face-to-Face Interaction'. Paper presented at the Loch Lomond Symposium on the Microanalysis of Mother-infant Interaction, September 1975.

17. Hartup, W. W. and J. Lempers, 'A Problem in Life-Span Development: The Interactional Analysis of Family Attachments.' In P. B. Baltes and K. W. Scaie (Eds.) *Life-Span Developmental Psychology: Personality and Socialization.* New York Academic Press, 1973, pp. 235-252.

18. Hinde, R. A., 'On Describing Relationships', *Journal of Child Psychology and Psychiatry* 17, 1976, pp. 1-19.

19. Jaffe, J. and S. Feldstein, *Rhythms of Dialogue*, New York Academic Press, 1970.

20. Jones, S. J., 'An Analysis of the Infant Response System During Vocal Conditioning'. Unpublished manuscript, Child Research Branch, National Institute of Mental Health, Bethesda, Md. 1971.

21. Jones, S. J. and H. A. Moss, 'Age, State, and Maternal Behavior Associated with Infant Vocalizations', *Child Development* 42, 1971, pp. 1039-1051.

22. Kagan, J., *Change and Continuity in Infancy*, New York: Wiley, 1971.

23. Lewis, M. M., *Infant Speech*, New York: Harcourt, Brace, 1936.

24. Lewis, M. and R. Freedle, 'Mother-Infant dyad: The Cradle of Meaning.' Paper presented at the Symposium on Language and Thought: Communication and Affect, Toronto, March 1972.

25. Lieberman, P. *Intonation, Perception, and Language.* Cambridge, Ma.: M. I. T. Press, 1967.

26. Menyuk, P. *The Acquisition and Development of Language.* Englewood Cliffs, N. J.: Prentice Hall, 1971.

27. Papousek, H. and M. Papousek, 'Cognitive Aspects of Preverbal Social Interaction Between Human Infants and Adults'. In *Parent-Infant Interaction*, Ciba Foundation Symposium 33. New York: Associated Scientific Publishers, 1975, pp. 241-260.

28. Piaget, J., *The Origins of Intelligence in Children.* New York: International Universities Press, 1952.

29. Ramey, C. T. and L. L. Ourth, 'Delayed Reinforcement and Vocalization Rates of Infants.' *Child Development* 42, 1971, pp. 291-297.

30. Rebelsky, F. and G. Abeles, 'Infancy in Holland and the United States. Paper presented at the meeting of the Society for Research in Child Development, Santa Monica, California, March 1969.

31. Rheingold, H. I., 'The Social and Socializing Infant.' In D. A. Goslin (ed.) *Handbook of Socialization Theory and Research*, Chicago, Ill.: Rand McNally, 1969, pp. 779-790.

32. Rheingold, H. L., J. I. Gewirtz, and H. W. Ross, 'Social Conditioning of Vocalizations in the Infant,' *Journal of Comparative and Physiological Psychology* 52, 1959, pp. 68-73.

33. Routh, D. K., 'Conditioning of Vocal Response Differentiation in Infants', *Developmental Psychology* I, 1969, pp. 216-226.

34. Ryan J. 'Early Language Development: Towards a Communicational Analysis'. In M. P. M. Richards (ed.) *The Integration of a Child into a Social World.* London: Cambridge University Press, 1974, pp. 185-213.

35. Schwartz, A., D. Rosenberg, and Y. Brackbill. 'An Analysis of the

Components of Social Reinforcement of Infant Vocalization'. Paper presented at the meeting of the Society for Research in Child Development, Santa Monica, California, March 1969.

36. Stern, D. N., 'Mother and Infant at Play: The Dyadic Interaction Involving Facial, Vocal and Gaze Behavior'. In M. Lewis and L. A. Rosenblum (eds.) *The Effect of the Infant on its Caregiver*, New York: Wiley, 1974, pp. 187-213.

37. Stern, D. N., J. Jaffe, B. Beebe, and S. L. Bennett, 'Vocalizing in Unison and in Alternation: Two Modes of Communication Within the Mother-Infant Dyad.' *Annals of the New York Academy of Sciences* 263, 1975, pp. 89-100.

38. Strain, B. A., 'Early Dialogues: A Naturalistic Study of Vocal Behavior in Mothers and Three-Month-Old Infants'. Unpublished doctoral dissertation, Peabody College, Nashville, Tenn., 1975.

39. Turnure, C., 'Reponse to Voice of Mother and Stranger by Babies in the First Year.' *Developmental Psychology* 4, 1971, pp. 182-190.

40. Watson, J. S., "Smiling, Cooing, and 'The Game'." *Merrill-Palmer Quarterly of Behavior and Development* 18, 1972, pp. 323-339.

41. Webster, R. L., M. H. Stenhardt, and M. G. Senter, 'Changes in Infants' Vocalizations as a Function of Differential Acoustic Stimulation'. *Developmental Psychology* 7, 1971, pp. 39-43.

42. Weisberg, P., 'Social and Nonsocial Conditioning of Infant Vocalization'. *Child Development* 34, 1963, pp. 377-388.

43. Wertheim, E. S., 'Person-Environment Interaction: The Epigenesis of Autonomy and Competence III'. *British Journal of Medical Psychology* 48, 1975, pp. 237-256.

44. Wolff, P., 'The Natural History of Crying and Other Vocalizations in Early Infancy'. In B. M. Foss (ed.) *Determinants of Infant Behavior*, Vol. 4. London: Methuen, 1969, pp. 81-109.

45. Yarrow, L. J., J. L. Rubenstein, and F. A. Pedersen, *Infant and Environment: Early Cognitive and Motivational Development*, New York: Wiley, 1975.

3.2 Strategies for Communicating
Eve V. Clark

Summary

Children stretch their language in order to communicate when they lack the adult words. With object categories they often overextend terms to inappropriate instances. They may do so with certain terms in production but not in comprehension. With spatial relations they may opt for one general purpose locative term to talk about many different configurations, and with actions they often rely on general purpose verbs. What children mean on any one occasion, therefore, is bound up with their strategies for communicating.

Introduction

Language is a tool for communication. While this point has often been lost sight of in the study of language acquisition, children clearly make the most of their resources for communicating from the start. They supplement gestures with words, and they stretch their words to talk about many different situations. Their efforts to communicate even result in systematic misuses of language – both in how they use words and in which words they choose to convey particular ideas. In this paper I outline some of the strategies children seem to rely on for communicating, and, in doing so, I hope to show why it is important to keep the communicative function of language in mind as we study what children say.

The processes of language comprehension and language production make different demands on the language user. In comprehension, listeners try to interpret what they have heard from other speakers. This process, in children, is supported by the actual physical setting of the utterance combined with the children's general knowledge about the objects, events, or relations present. In contrast, in production, speakers try to convey particular meanings to others. This process, unlike comprehension, receives no direct support from the setting, since what is said depends on the speaker's intentions. Instead, it is supported by the child's ability to retrieve from memory the appropriate linguistic or nonlinguistic devices for conveying what he wants to convey (see also Clark and Clark 1977). My focus here will be on

'Strategies for Communicating', *Child Development, Vol* 49, pp. 953-959.

young children's strategies in language production — how they go about conveying particular meanings to others.

By *strategy* I mean the choice of a device to communicate a particular meaning. Children might choose a single word, a two-word combination, or a fully grammatical utterance, depending on what they want to convey and how much they know of their first language. Alternatively, they might rely on a gesture or combination of gestures in lieu of words. In illustrating some of the production strategies children rely on during the early stages of language acquisition, I will take examples from how children talk about objects, about spatial relations, and about actions and examine the extent to which they rely on general purpose terms in all three domains.

Talking about Objects

In picking out objects for a listener, young children typically rely at first on deictic gestures: they gaze intently and point at whatever interests them. In the absence of words, this strategy seems to work well enough (e.g., Bates 1976; Carter 1978). Next, these gestures are combined with words, either deictic words or category names. And from this point on, whenever they do not have names available for what they want to talk about, children seem to rely on two general production strategies. The first is to use a general purpose deictic word like *here, that*, or *look* (accompanied by pointing) to pick out specific objects or events (Clark 1978; Clark and Sengul 1978). The second is to 'stretch' words already known or partly known to cover other things that appear sufficiently similar to the originals to justify use of the same name (Clark 1974).

Children seem to rely freely on both these options as they gradually build up more extensive vocabularies. They frequently depend on deictic words combined with gestures when they do not know what something is called (e.g., Bohn 1914; Kenyeres 1927). And they just as frequently seem to stretch certain words in their vocabularies. For instance, many investigators have noted that 1- and 2-year-olds will apply a word like *doggie* not only to dogs but also to cats, sheep, horses, cows, bears, and so on — all objects that are, roughly speaking, mammal shaped, with a head and four legs. Or they will use a word like *ball* first for a ball and then stretch or overextend it to oranges, cookies, light switches, doorknobs, a cake of soap — all objects that are spherical or round. Overextensions like these have been widely documented: they appear very common in the speech of children 1-2½ years old, learning quite unrelated languages. And, in general, they seem to be governed by the perceptual similarities children notice among the different referents for the overextended word (Bowerman 1976; Clark 1973a).

With the second strategy, children produce a word already in their vocabulary (presumably whichever one they think 'fits' best or one that is readily retrievable from memory) and rely on that to guide their listeners. But whenever they overextend a word, they apply it in a way that is incompatible with adult usage. And this, one could argue, shows that they have yet to work out its full adult meaning. By working back from a child's overextensions, then, it is possible to make inferences about what meaning the child may have attached to the word so far. For example, his overextensions might show that for child A the word *doggie* picked out objects that were mammal shaped, while for child B it picked out a furry texture. These two children presumably had different hypotheses about the meaning of *doggie*, hypotheses that were revealed by the kinds of overextensions made. A third child, C, might include both shape and texture in his meaning for *doggie* and, as a result, overextend the word when needed to objects meeting both criteria – shape and texture – or to those meeting either one or the other – shape or texture. The kinds of overextensions that children produce, then, provide a good deal of information about children's meanings and about the process of acquiring meaning (Clark 1975).[1]

Overextensions in production, however, may provide us with an underestimate of how much children know about meanings. For example, children might sometimes overextend a word deliberately because they have no other word in their repertoire or because they cannot retrieve precisely the right word. But if children do overextend words deliberately after they have worked out the adult meanings, this should be detectable in an asymmetry between the production of a word (overextended) and its comprehension (correct). And, on occasion, just this type of asymmetry has been observed. Moore (1896), for instance, noticed that at one point her child overextended the word *bird* to any moving animal, yet on hearing *bird* would look around for a bird and not, for example, be satisfied on seeing a cat. In another study, Thomson and Chapman (1977) tested children's comprehension of words they had overextended in both production and comprehension, but others were always understood correctly. One child, for example, given the instructions 'Show me the dog,' only selected pictures of dogs, although in production he applied the word *dog* to all sorts of four-legged animals.

The production strategies of using general purpose deictic words or stretching words already known allow children to talk about many things for which they have not yet acquired the appropriate vocabulary. Moreover, when their production strategies result in overextensions or

---

[1]Although children also underextend some words, using them to pick out only a subset of the adult category denoted, underextensions themselves, like correct usage, reveal comparatively little about children's strategies for communicating with limited resources.

other misuses of words, they indirectly provide us with ways of finding out what meanings children have attached to particular words. Because children are intent on communicating, they choose whatever word seems to fit best on that occasion, and what fits best will depend largely on what they already know about particular words and word meanings. As they learn more about meanings, and acquire more words as well, their production strategies gradually come to match the adult's. This may take many years, though, since choosing the right words (from the adult point of view) requires a much more extensive knowledge of language than is available to the 2- or 3-year-old.

Talking about Spatial Relations

When children first talk about the location of one object with respect to another, they name the object located and use a deictic term like *here* or *there* for the location ('flower here,' 'there car'), or they name both the object located and its location ('baby chair,' 'towel bed') – in neither case specifying the exact spatial relation between the two objects. Very shortly, though, many children begin to use a general purpose locative marker. This marker is linked in some way – as a preposition, a postposition, or a suffix, depending on the language being acquired – to the word for the location. Initially, it seems to be used for a variety of different spatial relations, then it is gradually ousted from certain contexts as children begin to use other spatial terms in its place. The strategy of using one general purpose element for talking about spatial relations is closely akin to the production strategy of using general purpose deictic words in talking about objects. In both instances, children start out by applying only a few terms where adults normally apply many.

Children acquiring English often pick a schwa sound [ə] or a syllabic *n* [n] as their general purpose locative marker and simply insert it before any noun phrase denoting a location – for example, 'Ball [n] table' for 'The ball's on/under the table.' Other children choose one particular preposition and let it serve, just as a schwa or syllabic *n* does, for every spatial relation. If they choose a preposition like *in*, they will appear to use it quite appropriately as long as they talk about containment ('in the box,' 'in the house'), but when they stretch it to talk about something being 'on' the table, 'under' the bed, or 'next to' the door, its general purpose status becomes very apparent (Clark, unpublished data).

Interestingly, children acquiring English as their second language appear to rely on a very similar production strategy. Hakuta (Note 1), for instance, reported that a Japanese-speaking child he followed used *in* at first for containment and then for a variety of other spatial relations, including 'at', 'off', 'out,' and 'around.' Cancino (Note 2) reported a similar phenomenon in a Spanish-speaking child who also chose *in* as her all-purpose locative. In both cases, it is possible that the children were influenced by their first languages. Japanese has a general locative postposition, *ni*, that is attached to the location noun. This general locative marker can then be further specified by the addition of words like *side, top*, or *front*. While Spanish does not have a general locative marker like Japanese, it does use one preposition, *en*, to cover a number of spatial relations that have to be distinguished in English — for example: *en la mesa* ('on the table'), *en casa* ('at home'), *en el cuarto* ('in the room'), and so on. However, since children acquiring English as their first language follow the same strategy, it seems likely that, regardless of the language being learned, use of a general purpose locative results more generally from the kind of communicative strategy children rely on when their resources are limited.

The generality of this production strategy shows up in other languages too. In French, children tend to start out by using the preposition that means 'at' or 'to' (à) as a general purpose spatial preposition (e.g., Grégoire 1947; Guillaume 1927). Much the same happens in Danish. Rasmussen (1922) reported that his daughter Sonia, aged 2-6, overused the preposition meaning 'to' for several different spatial relations, including 'on'. In German, Stern (1924) reported similar overuse of a spatial preposition, this time one meaning 'of' or 'from' (*von*). Children acquiring Turkish and Serbo-Croatian opt for a similar production strategy and start out using one locative form as a general purpose locative marker (Slobin, Note 3). And in Russian, Museyibova (1964) observed several children use a single preposition as a general purpose locative for talking about a variety of spatial relations.

Lastly, children whose language acquisition is retarded also seem to rely on this type of production strategy. One 6-year-old acquiring English, for example, used *on* for all spatial relations. However, he would only use this locative marker when under communicative pressure to talk about how different objects were related to each other in space (Hecht, Note 4).

For spatial relations, then, just as for objects, children rely on certain production strategies to extend the range of what they can talk about. These production strategies, of course, reveal only part of what children know about the meanings they use. When they make mistakes in production, using *on* for *under* or *in* for *beside*, it becomes clear that their words cannot be taken at face value. Children may mean what they say, but they do not always mean what adults mean with the same words. Nonetheless, what they say does tell us something about their word meanings — for instance, that they realize that some spatial term is required for talking about any relation in space (e.g. Kenyeres 1927). Once this information is combined with what we can infer from their comprehension strategies (Clark 1973b; Clark and Clark 1977), it should become possible to paint a much more detailed picture of the steps children go through in working out new word meanings.

Talking about Actions

Children's earliest words for actions tend to encode the action and its result together or just the result. A particle like *up,* for example, is commonly used for the result of lifting or raising and may be produced when the child talks about any upward or downward displacement of himself — being lifted into his high chair, being put down on the floor, asking to climb into someone's lap, going up or down stairs, or requesting objects that are too high to reach. Other verb particles like *off, out,* or *on* seem to be used in a very similar way (e.g., Farwell 1975; Leopold 1949; Gruendel, Note 5). *Up,* then, is applied to a great many different situations. The same is true of words like *open* or *door,* which may be stretched from talking about a door being open or shut to getting a lid off a box or a jar, to peeling fruit, to turning a light or a tap on or off, to unlacing shoes and unbuttoning coats (e.g., Farwell 1977; Griffiths and Atkinson 1978; Guillaume 1927a). From the adult point of view, the earliest action words, like *up* and *open* (or *door),* are clear being overextended. This very limited set of terms for resultant states, though, is soon supplemented by a growing number of words that, at least for adults, pick out just the actions themselves.

When the children start to talk about actions, they face the same problem they have in naming objects. Their resources are too limited at first to cover all they want to talk about. The solution many children adopt is to use a small number of general purpose verbs for a large variety of different actions. The commonest general purpose verbs in my data are *do* and *make.* They are used for talking about building, writing, opening, knocking over, putting on, cutting out, putting away, picking up, rolling, and so on, actions for which the children at first lacked more specific terms. However, what children are talking about with general purpose *do* or *make* is usually opaque without contextual information. The precise actions being talked about in "I do it again," "The clown do!" and "Make [ə] this" cannot be understood from the utterances alone. *Make,* unlike *do,* is also used in the sense of producing or causing a resultant state, as in "Make it big" or "Make it up" (put it up) (see also Bowerman 1974; Leopold 1949).

In my own research, the youngest children recorded were just over 2, but some diary studies, as well as personal observations, suggest that *do* may be used even earlier with a general purpose function. Pollock (1878), for instance, reported a child aged 1-10 saying "Baby do't" as he watched someone spinning an ivory ring. The child then tried to spin the ring himself, failed, and asked his mother: "More 'gain/Mama 'gain/ Mama do't." Grégoire (1947) reported similar uses of French *faire* ("do", "make"); for example, Edmond, aged 2-0, asked his father to right his fallen chair by saying: *'Papa fais"* ("papa do"). Another child, aged 1-9, used *do* whenever he came across some new object to manipulate or play with and would sit playing and say: "Rodi do." Actions covered by such uses of *do* included throwing toys down the stairs, twanging a spring doorstop, and opening boxes or jars (Clark, unpublished data).

Table 1 lists some typical uses of *do* and *make* from one 2-year-old. The general purpose verbs are on the left and the context of use on each occasion is on the right. Notice that the specific actions picked out by the general purpose verbs seem very obvious with the context supplied, unlike the utterances given earlier, on their own. In addition, to *do* and *make,* children seem to use two other general purpose verbs very commonly from age 2 or so onward. The first of these is *go,* with the general meaning of "move" or "travel," and the second is *put,* used a little less frequently, with the meaning of motion of an object to a location. Both *go* and *do* are also used for talking about all sorts of noises from animals, cars, and trains, as well as noises produced as the result of some action. Bloom, Miller, and Hood (1975), not surprisingly, found these verbs were the most frequently used by far for talking about actions and locative actions.

Children acquiring English as their second language appear to use the same production strategy as native speakers for talking about actions: they rely on a small number of general purpose verbs. Spanish-speaking children, for example, commonly opt for *do, make,* and *put* for talking about all sorts of actions (Fillmore, Note 6) — for example: "How do you do dese?" "How do you do these little tortillas?" (= "make," "cook"); "How do you do dese in English?" (= "say"); "How do you make the flower?" (talking about Play-Doh); "How I put the number?" (= "dial"). Similar examples were recorded by Hakuta (Note 1) for a Japanese-speaking child acquiring English who opted for *do* as her general purpose verb. Not all children, though, identify an appropriate general purpose verb. One child Fillmore (Note 6) studied, for instance, chose *sweep,* which he then used for taking about a variety of actions — sweeping with a broom, wheeling a supermarket cart, making pastry, playing ball, and building with blocks. This persisted for several months before the child began to use more specific — and more appropriate — verbs for these different actions. His strategy, however, seems to have been the same as that of those who used the more usual *do* or *make.*

Although the commonest strategy for talking about actions seems to be to use general purpose verbs like *do, make,* or *go,* it is not the only one. At times, some children opt for another one: they use the word for an object or for a resultant state to pick out the particular action in question. Instead of a general purpose verb, therefore, they use a highly specific one. They may choose a word for the instrument used in the action (e.g., "The man is keying the door" [opening with a key]; "I want to button it" [turn off by pressing a button), a word for the

Table I
Some Typical Examples of 'Do,' 'Make,' and 'Go' in the Speech of S, Aged 2-2

Verb	Utterance	Context
Do	I do it again	Said as knocks over blocks
	You . . . do . . . doing that.	Said as watches O build blocks into a tower
	You do do it, OK?	Asking O to unroll some computer tape, after trying unsuccessfully to do it himself
	You do [ə] that!	Indicating which toy O should take out of a box
	Uh oh. I did.	Said as he turned off the tape recorder by pushing a knob
	The clown do!	Asking O to make the toy clown do what clowns do
Make	Make name!	Telling O to write his name
	I make a little doggie.	Said as cut a dog shape out of Play-Doh
	Make a dog.	Telling O what to draw next
	Make it go in there.	Asking O to get a crayon back into its box
	Make [ə] that.	Said as pointed to the hand moving on a clock; seemed to be request for O to move the hand on
Go	It go there.	Talking about a block lying on the floor
	Red went boom.	Talking about a red block that fell on the floor
	They go in the car.	Talking about two storybook characters
	'N turn [ə] go up.	Said as turned a puzzle piece the right way up
	'N go like that.	Said as dropped puzzle pieces on the floor.

Note: Examples cited come from the first month of recordings from S, a child taped at weekly intervals for 1 year from age 2-0. The utterances cited occurred without any immediately preceding use of the particular general purpose verb by either the observer (O) or the child's parents.

object affected by the action (e.g., "I'm souping" [eating soup]; "They're teaing" [having tea]; "Pillow me!" [throw a pillow at me]), a word for the end state resulting from the action (e.g., "I'm darking the letters" [scribbling over them to make them dark]; "She's rounding it" [making the jump rope into a half circle]; "Can you higher that?" [make it higher], and so on. Uses like these serve just as clear a communicative purpose as a general purpose verb: they pick out the specific action associated with the object, instrument, or end state in a particular context.

In summary, most children pick up a small number of general purpose verbs fairly early on and use these for talking about a large number of different actions. General purpose verbs are similar in function, then, to the deictic terms *this* and *that* used for talking about objects. Both play an important communicative role in the early stages of language acquisition. Both constitute devices whereby children can stretch their resources to the utmost. While many children rely primarily on the production strategy of using a general purpose verb, others may produce highly specific verbs by naming a role or state connected with an action. These forms are usually transitory in nature, serving to communicate what the child wants to convey on that occasion only. Both these production strategies seem to be put to use by young children after an initial period when they simply overextend whatever primitive action words they have (e.g., *up, off, open*) to a limited number of situations.

Conclusion

One ingredient that is all too often omitted in discussions of language acquisition is communication. But the strategies children rely on in production are motivated by communicative concerns. In the early stages of acquisition, children have only a very small vocabulary at their disposal, and, while they freely supplement this with gestures and demonstrations, it is only adequate for talking about a limited number of events. They are often faced, therefore, with wanting to talk about things for which they have no words. Their solution is to stretch their resources as far as possible: they rely on one or two general purpose deictic terms to pick out objects (and they also overextend nondeictic words), they make use of general purpose locative markers for talking about locative relations in space, and they rely on a small number of general purpose verbs for talking about actions.

Learning a language is not simply a matter of learning a system of rules for linking sounds and meanings: it is learning how to use such a system for communication. Working out new meanings, then, goes hand in hand with trying to communicate as clearly and as effectively as possible. From the investigator's point of view, what children say is doubly important: first, it reveals what options children usually take in making the most of whatever language they already have; and second, it reveals, through their special uses of certain words, what systems of meanings children are working out as they acquire language.[2]

In this paper, I have concentrated on the first point — the kinds of communicative strategies children rely on in production during the early stages of acquisition when their linguistic resources are limited.

[2]Despite this optimism, notice that apparently adultlike word usage can provide no direct information about children's lexical meanings. It is where their usage diverges from the adult's that we are most likely to be able to use production data fruitfully.

But my ultimate interest in such strategies lies with the second point — the fact that children's misuses and errors in speech are potentially revealing of what they know about their language and, in particular, about the meanings it can be used to express.

Reference Notes

1. Hakuta, K. 'Becoming bilingual at age five; the story of Uguisu,' Unpublished honours thesis, Harvard University, 1975.
2. Cancino, H. 'Grammatical morphemes in second language acquisition: Marta'. Unpublished manuscript, Harvard University, 1976.
3. Slobin Dan I., *Personal Communication,* 1977.
4. Hecht, Barbara, *Personal Communication,* 1977.
5. Gruendel, J. M. 'Locative production in the SWU period: a study of *up-down, on-off,* and *in-out'.* Paper presented at the biennial meeting of the Society for Research in Child Development, New Orleans, March 1977.
6. Fillmore, L. W. 'The second time around: cognitive and social strategies in second language acquisition.' Unpublished doctoral dissertation, Stanford University, 1976.

References

Bates, E. *Language and context: the acquisition of pragmatics,* New York, Academic Press, 1976.
Bloom, L.; Miller, P.; & Hood, L.,'Variation and reduction as aspects of competence in language development'. In A. Pick (ed.), *Minnesota symposia on child psychology,* Vol. 9. Minnesapolis, University of Minnesota Press, 1975.
Bohn, W. E. 'First steps in verbal expression', *Pedagogical Seminary,* 1914, 21, 578-595.
Bowerman, M. 'Learning the structure of causative verbs: a study in the relationship of cognitive, semantic and syntactic development', *Papers and Reports on Child Language Development,* (Stanford University), 1974, 8, 142-178.
Bowerman, M. 'Semantic factors in the acquisition of rules for word use and sentence construction'. In D. M. Morehead & A. E. Morehead (eds.), *Normal and deficient child language,* Baltimore, University Park Press, 1976.
Carter, A. L. 'Learning to point with words: the structural evolution of attention-directing communication in the second year.' In A. Lock (ed.), *Action, gesture, and symbol: the emergence of language,* London, Academic Press, 1978.
Clark, E. V. 'What's in a word? On the child's acquisition of semantics in his first language.' In T. E. Moore (ed.), *Cognitive development and the acquisition of language,* New York, Academic Press, 1973, (a).
Clark, E. V. 'Non-linguistic strategies and the acquisition of word meanings,' *Cognition,* 1973, 2, 161-182 (b).

Clark, E. V. 'Some aspects of the conceptual basis for first language acquisition.' In R. L. Schiefelbusch & L. L. Lloyd (eds.), *Language perspectives; acquisition, retardation, and intervention*, Baltimore, University Park Press, 1974.

Clark, E. V. 'Knowledge, context, and strategy in the acquisition of meaning.' In D. P. Dato (Ed.), *Georgetown University round table on languages and linguistics*, Washington, D.C., Georgetown University Press, 1975.

Clark, E. V. 'From gesture to word: on the natural history of deixis in language acquisition.' In J. S. Bruner & A. Garton (eds.), *Human growth and development: Wolfson College lectures, 1976*, Oxford, Oxford University Press, 1978.

Clark, E. V., & Sengul, C. J. 'Strategies in the acquisition of deixis,' *Journal of Child Language*, 1978, 5, 457-475.

Clark, H. H., & Clark, E. V. *'Psychology and language: an introduction to psycholinguistics,'* New York, Harcourt Brace Jovanovich, 1977.

Farwell, C. B. 'Aspects of early verb semantics — precausative development,' *Papers and Reports on Child Language Development (Stanford University)*, 1975, 10, 48-58.

Farwell, C. B. 'The primacy of *goal* in the child's description of motion and location,' *Papers and Reports on Child Language Development* (Stanford University), 1977, 13, 126-133.

Grégoire, A. *L'Apprentissage du langage* (2 vols.), Paris, Droz, 1947.

Griffiths, P. D., & Atkinson, M. 'A door to verbs'. In N. Waterson & C. E. Snow (eds.), *The development of communication: social and pragmatic factors in language acquisition*, New York, Wiley, 1978.

Guillaume, P. 'Les Débuts de la phrase dans le langage de l'enfant,' *Journal de Psychologie*, 1927, 24, 1-25. (a)

Guillaume, P. 'Le Développement des éléments formels dans le langage de l'enfant,' *Journal de Psychologie*, 1927, 24, 203-229. (b)

Kenyeres, E. 'Les Premiers Mots de l'enfant et l'apparition des espèces de mots dans son langage', *Archives de Psychologie*, 1927, 20, 191-218.

Leopold, W. F. *Speech development of a bilingual child: a linguist's record* (4 vols.), Evanston, Ill., Northwestern University Press, 1949.

Moore, K. C. 'The mental development of a child,' *Psychological Review, Monograph Supplements*, 1896, 1 (3).

Museyibova, T. A. 'The development of an understanding of spatial relations and their reflection in the language of children of pre-school age.' In B. G. Anan'yev & B. F. Lomov (eds.), *Problems of spatial perception and spatial concepts*, Washington, D.C., NASA, 1964.

Pollock, F. 'An infant's progress in language,' *Mind*, 1878, 3, 392-401.

Rasmussen, V. *Et barns dagbog*, Copenhagen, Gyldendal, 1922.

Stern, W. *Psychology of early childhood* (3d ed.; A. Barwell, Trans.), New York, Holt, 1924.

Thomson, J. R., & Chapman, R. S. 'Who is "daddy" revisited: the status of two-year-olds' overextended words in use and comprehension,' *Journal of Child Language*, 1977, 4, 359-375.

3.3 Effect of Listener Age and Situation on the Politeness of Children's Directives
Sharon L. James

Abstract

Twenty-one children between the ages of 4:6 and 5:2 years made a speaker doll address other dolls that represented an adult, a peer, and a younger listener in command and request situations. Analyses of the politeness of the elicited directives revealed that the effect of the listener's age was greatest in the command situations, with the adult listener receiving the politest directives, followed by the peer and the younger child, respectively. The listener age effect diminished in the request situations, where the child had to ask a favour of the listener. In these situations, the children were very polite to all three listeners. The results are discussed in terms of status relationships between the speaker and the listener.

Introduction

Little is known about children's knowledge and use of the pragmatic rules that govern what a speaker says and how he says it in different communicative situations (Bates 1974; Cazden 1970). The child, in order to use pragmatic rules, first must be able to notice the relevant characteristics of his listener and of the situation. He must then be able to adjust what he says and how he says it on the basis of this information. There is growing evidence that even young children adjust the speech they address to different listeners (Shatz and Gelman 1973; Ervin-Tripp 1974) and seem, therefore, to be using pragmatic rules in their communicative interactions. The specific listener characteristics and other situational characteristics to which they respond are unclear, however. This lack of information suggests the need for studies in which listener and situational characteristics are either carefully noted or experimentally manipulated as independent variables. In the present study, the effect of the listener's age on the politeness of children's directives was studied in situations designed to evoke either commands or requests.

Politeness was chosen as a reflection of pragmatic knowledge because the principle *Be polite* has been proposed as a part of adult

Journal of Psycholinguistic Research, Vol. 7, 1978, pp. 307-317.

pragmatic competence (Lakoff 1973). Lakoff argues that dolls adhere to the rules of politeness, *Don't impose, Give options,* and *Make the addressee feel good,* in their communicative interactions. If Lakoff's proposal is correct, then the rules of politeness are part of the pragmatic knowledge the child will acquire on his way to adult competence. Support for this assumption is found in the results of a study by Bayes (1974) which indicates that children as young as 3 years seem to have some notion of relative politeness in speech. Directives were studied for three reasons: they can be realized in several different syntactic forms, such as statements, interrogatives, and imperatives, which seem to reflect different degrees of politeness (Ervin-Tripp 1973); they appear very frequently in the speech of young children (Bates 1974; Ervin-Tripp 1977); and they are relatively easy to elicit from children (Alvy 1973; Bates 1974);

The politeness of the directives used by a speaker appears to be affected directly by the status relationship between the speaker and the listener. Studies with adults have shown that polite request forms such as 'May I please use your phone?' are more likely to be addressed to a listener whose age or professional position places him in a superior role (Pfuderer 1968; Dikeman and Parker 1964). For children, age tends to be one of the most potent factors in assigning status (Emmerich 1959). It seems reasonable to assume, therefore, that preschool children would assign superior status to an adult listener, equal status to a peer-aged listener, and subordinate status to a younger child. Results of work by Sachs and Devin (1976) indicate that the listener's age affected the kind of speech young children used. In addition, Ervin-Tripp (1977) has suggested, based on her observations of young children in natural communication situations, that the listener's age is one of the major variables influencing the form of children's directives.

The nature of the communicative situation also might be expected to affect the politeness of a speaker's directives. There are at least two distinctly different types of situations which will evoke directives. In one type, the request situation, the speaker wants or needs something from the listener, and he imposes on the listener by asking him to do a favour. In the other type, the command situation, the listener infringes on the speaker's rights in some way, and the speaker orders him to stop the imposition.

It was hypothesized for the present study that preschool children would adjust the politeness of their directives on the basis of the listener's age status, with the most polite directives being addressed to the adult listener and the least polite to the younger child. It also was hypothesized that the nature of the situation would affect politeness, with the directives produced in the request situations being more polite than those produced in the command situations.

Method

Subjects

Subjects were 21 monolingual English-speaking children, nine boys and 12 girls, who ranged in age from 4:6 to 5:2 years, with a mean age of 4:9. All were enrolled in either a private nursery school or a 4-year-old kindergarten which served a middle- to upper-middle-class community. With the exception of four of the children, all subjects had younger siblings.

Materials

The stimulus materials consisted of six bendable plastic dolls and several other toy objects. The six dolls included a 12-inch "Ken" doll, which represented an adult listener; two 7-inch boy dolls and two 7-inch girl dolls, one of each sex to represent the speaker in all situations and the other to represent a same-aged listener in the peer-as-listener situations; and a 5-inch female toddler-type doll, to represent a 2-year-old listener. Other toy objects used were a dog, some wooden steps, a watering can, a ball, a carton of paraffin bottles representing soda pop, a TV set, and an ice cream cone. All objects were sized appropriate in relation to the dolls.

Experimental task

Directive utterances were elicited from the subjects in various role-playing situations with dolls. Precedence for using a role-playing procedure involving dolls can be found in Sachs and Devin's (1976) study in which they required preschool children to role-play dolls representing different speakers. In the present study, the child was asked to role-play himself as a speaker addressing three other dolls which represented three different-aged listeners (adult, peer, and younger child). The use of this role-playing procedure had two obvious advantages over the communicative interaction situation used in other studies of children's speech modifications (Ervin-Tripp 1974; Shatz and Gelman 1973): it ensured that the types of utterances of interest were evoked and it allowed for control of confounding factors such as speaker-listener familiarity and differential feedback from the listeners. Therefore, the effect of only one listener characteristic and one situational factor was investigated.

There were eight role-playing situations used; four were designed to elicit commands and four to elicit requests. These eight situations were used for each of the three listeners. The following are examples of a command and a request situation.

Requestion Situation 1:
    Your dog, [dog's name], has run away and is lost. You look everywhere for him. You would like for this [man/boy/girl/little

child] to help you find your dog, wouldn't you? What would you
say to [him/her]?

Command Situation 1:
   Your ball is over here. This [man/boy/girl/little child] picks your
   ball up and is taking it away. Hey, you don't want [him/her] to
   do that, do you? What would you say to [him/her]?

Procedures
Each child was involved in three different experimental sessions, one
session for each of the three listeners. Each session consisted of the
same eight experimental situations; therefore, it was necessary to allow
some time between the three experimental sessions in order to diminish
possible carryover effects. The least amount of time allowed between
sessions was 5 days and the most was 9 days.

All experimental sessions were conducted in a quiet, private room
located in the school facilities. Each subject was tested individually by
the same white female experimenter. All experimental sessions were
tape-recorded on a Wollensak tape recorder (model No. 1500 SS).

In the first experimental session, each subject was told that he/she
was going to play a game with dolls and that one doll was going to be
him/her. The child then was shown either the two girl or the two boy
dolls, whichever was appropriate, and asked to choose the one he/she
thought looked the most like him/her. Once the child had chosen a
doll, that doll was called by the subject's name and was used as the
speaker throughout all the experimental situations. Next the child was
introduced to the dolls representing each of the listeners. For each of
the dolls, he was told what age person was represented. For example,
for the adult doll, he was told, "This is a big grownup man. See how
much bigger he is than you are?" For the peer doll, the subject was
told that "This [boy/girl] is the very same age you are, so he is
[appropriate age]. Look, he's just the same size as you are, too." The
younger doll was assigned an age of 2 years, and the size difference
between the dolls was pointed out again. The child was reminded again
of the supposed age of each doll at the beginning of the session in
which that doll was the listener.

The order in which the child spoke to the different-aged listeners
was counterbalanced so that seven subjects spoke to the adult doll first,
seven spoke to the peer first, and seven spoke to the younger child first.
Following two practice trials to ensure that the child understood the
task, the eight experimental situations were presented. The order of
presentation for the experimental situations was randomized by
shuffling the cards on which the situations were written. No two
subjects received exactly the same order of presentation for the
same listener.

The tape recordings of all experimental situations were transcribed
by the experimenter. Reliability of the transcriptions was established

by having an independent judge transcribe 25 randomly chosen responses from each of the eight audio tapes (200 out of 504 total responses). Agreement between the independent judge's and the experimenter's transcription of the 200 randomly chosen responses was 99%.

Scoring

Each of the children's transcribed responses was assigned a scale value representing the degree of politenesss. The numerical scale of politeness was empirically derived by having 40 adults perform paired comparison ratings on 14 sentences which represented the types of directives produced by the children. Scale values were derived for each of the 14 representative sentences according to the method of transformation described in Edwards (1957, pp. 33-34). The 14 sentences, the type of directive represented by each, and the scale value derived for each sentence are shown in Table I.

The children's responses were classified as one of the 14 types of directives described in Table I, or they were placed in a fifteenth category labelled "unscorable." Out of 504 responses, only three were judged unscorable. Those responses which could have been placed in more than one category were placed in the category with the highest politeness value. For example, a response which was an imperative containing both *please* and an explanation was placed in the category *Imperative – Do something + please* rather than in the *Imperative – Do something + explanation* category because the former had the higher scale value. Reliability of classification was established by having an independent judge place half of the 504 responses, randomly chosen, into the 15 categories. Agreement between the experimenter's and the judge's classifications was 94%. When a response was placed in a particular category, it was assigned the scale value belonging to that type of directive. The three responses placed in the unscorable category were not included in the analyses of the data. For each subject, the four commands per listener were averaged and the four requests per listener were averaged together; each subject then had six mean politeness values to be analyzed statistically.

Results

In order to determine if sex of the subjects and/or the listener which they addressed first were factors affecting the politeness of the responses, a two-factor analysis of variance for unequal N's (Bruning and Kintz 1968) was computed. No significant differences were found for either sex ($F < 1.00$) or listener addressed first ($F = 1.120$) or for the sex $\times$ listener interaction. Since neither factor affected the politeness of the children's directives, the data were collapsed across these factors.

Table I.   Paired Comparisons Stimuli and Derived Scale Values

Sentence	Type of directive	Scale value
May I have that magazine, please?	Interrog. — May I + please	4.070
May I have that magazine?	Interrog. — May I	3.134
Would you give me that magazine, please?	Interrog. — Would/Could/Will you + please	3,113
Can you give me that magazine, please?	Interrog. — Can you + please	2.742
Can I have that magazine, please?	Interrog. — Can/Could I + please	2.728
Would you give me that magazine?	Interrog. — Would/Could/Will you	2.459
Can you give me that magazine?	Interrog. — Can you	1.886
Can I have that magazine?	Interrog. — Can/Could I	1.755
Give me that magazine, please.	Imper. — Do something + please	1.688
Don't take that magazine, please.	Imper. — Don't do something + please	1.562
Give me that magazine because I have to read an article in it.	Imper. — Do something + explanation	1.206
Don't take that magazine because I have to read an article in it.	Imper. — Don't do something + explanation	1.081
Don't take that magazine.	Imper. — Don't do something	0.161
Give me that magazine.	Imper. — Do something	0.000

Figure 1 shows the mean politeness of the directives addressed to the different listeners in both the command and the request situations. Note that, generally, the mean politeness values for directives increased according to the listener's age in both types of situations. Note, also, that the mean politeness values for the request situations were higher than those for the command situations. The politeness values assigned to the children's responses were subjected to a treatments X treatments X subjects (listener age X situation X subjects) analysis of variance (Lindquist 1953). Significant effects were found for the listener age, F (2, 40) = 53.445, p < 0.001; the situation, $F(1,20)$ = 218.25, p <0.001; and the listener age X situation interaction, $F(2, 40)$ = 6.232, p <0.005.

In order to evaluate the significant interaction between listener age and situation, components analyses (Hays 1963) were computed. In the command situations, a significant difference (p < 0.001) was found between the politeness of the directives addressed to all three listeners, with the adult receiving the most polite speech, the peer next, and the younger child the least polite see Fig. 1). In the request situations, there was no significant difference (p>0.05) between the politeness of the directives spoken to the adult and the peer or between those addressed to the peer and the younger child. However, there was a significant

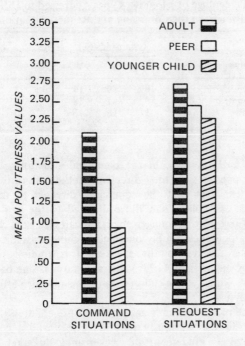

Fig. 1   Mean politeness values for directives addressed to
different-aged listeners in command and request situations.

difference ($p < 0.05$) in the request situations between the politeness of
the directives addressed to the adult and the younger child. The
requests spoken to the adult were more polite (see Fig. 1). Thus there
were differences in the politeness of the directives addressed to all three
listeners in the command situations, but differences only between the
directives addressed to the adult and the younger listener in the request
situations.

An analysis of the form and content of the directives was done to
provide a description of the kinds of changes the children made in
adjusting politeness. The percentages for each type of directive are
shown in Table II. The children used interrogative forms almost
exclusively in the request situations, regardless of listener, and most
frequently in the command situations when they were addressing the
adult listener. They used the direct inoperative most often with the
younger child, while the peer listener received modified imperatives
most frequently. The lexical item which showed the most consistent
pattern of differential use was *please*. Across both types of situations,
please was used about 84% of the time with adult listeners and only
37% with the younger listeners.

Table II   Percentage of Directive Types Addressed to Different-Aged Listeners in the Command and Request Situations

Type of directive	Commands (%)			Requests %		
	A	P	YC	A	P	YC
Interrogative	49	20	14	93	92	87
Modified Imperative	50	61	38	7	8	12
Direct imperative	1	19	48	0	9	1

Discussion

The results indicate that, in the command situations, the children adjusted the politeness of their directives on the basis of their listener's age status. The fact that the commands directed to the peer-aged listener were less polite than those directed to the adult, but more polite than those to the younger child, indicates that the children were not adjusting politeness simply on an adult-child basis, but on the basis of age status relative to the speaker. This finding supports the suggestion by Ervin-Tripp (1977) that age status is one of the listener characteristics which young children perceive and which affects the kind of speech they use.

The effect of the listener's age status on the children's directives is very similar to the previously reported effect of listener status on adults' directives (Pfuderer 1968; Dikeman and Parker 1964). The preschoolers in the present study were most polite to the adult listener, who had superior age status, and least polite to the younger child, who was subordinate in age status, in both the command and request situations.

The children's adjustments in the politeness of the directives addressed to the different listeners were affected by the nature of the situation as well as by the age status of the listener. The directives produced in the request situations were more polite than those produced in the command situations. Thus, in those situations where the children had to ask a favour of the listener, they became more polite.

The results indicate, however, that the children did not simply increase the politeness of their directives additively in the request situations; rather, they increased politeness differentially for the three listeners (see Fig. 1). In the command situations where the children had to assert their own rights and tell the speaker what to do, the age status of the listener seemed to determine how polite the directives were. However, in the request situations where the children had to ask a favour of the listener, they became very polite to all three listeners. The effect of age status diminished so that the only difference in politeness was between directives addressed to the adult and directives addressed to the younger child.

One explanation for the interaction between the situation and the listener is that the status of the peer and the younger child increased in the request situations where the children had to ask a favour. The children placed themselves in an inferior position and their listeners in a superior position in the status relationship by giving the listener the power to grant or deny a favour. The status relationship resulting from the request situations evidently took precedence over the status relationship based on age differences. Although age is a listener characteristic which affects children's perceptions of listener status, it appears that situational factors have a direct influence also.

The high percentage of interrogatives addressed to the adult listener and imperatives to the younger listener is consistent with the pattern of directive use that Ervin-Tripp (1974) found in natural communicative situations. She reported that 3-year-old children addressed imperatives more often to children than to adults and that when 3-year-olds used interrogative requests they usually were adult directed. By 4 years of age, she found that nurseryschool children were addressing embedded imperatives and interrogative requests to adults fairly frequently.

It could be argued that the children's differential use of imperative and interrogative directives reflects their reliance on at least one of the rules of politeness proposed by Lakoff (1973). One could argue that the children were adhering to the rule *Don't impose* when they used interrogative forms almost exclusively in the request situations. Since the nature of the request situations involved imposing on the listener by asking a favour, the children's use of the more polite forms could be interpreted as an attempt to lessen that imposition. In the command situations, the children were not imposing on the listener when they used a direct or modified imperative, because the listener had violated the children's rights in some way. On the other hand, the use of an imperative in the request situation would seem to constitute an even greater imposition on the listener. Thus adherence to the rule *Don't impose* could explain the low incidence of imperatives and high incidence of interrogative forms across listeners in the request situations. Such an explanation, however, involved the assumption that preschool children rely on rules which have been suggested as part of adult pragmatic competence (Lakoff 1973). It is not clear from this study that the kinds of speech modifications the children produced would have required knowledge of such sophisticated pragmatic rules as those proposed by Lakoff. Future research should seek to determine to what degree, if any, children are aware of and use these politeness rules.

Acknowledgements

The author wishes to thank Robin Chapman and John Saxman for their helpful comments during the preparation of the manuscript and to express her appreciation to the teachers and children at St. Andrews nursery school and at Edgewood kindergarten for their invaluable cooperation.

References

Alvy, K. (1973), 'The development of listener adapted communications in grade-school children from different social-class backgrounds.' *Genetic Psychology Monographs* 84: 34-104.

Baytes, E. (1974), 'Language and context: Studies in the acquisition of pragmatics.' Unpublished doctoral dissertation, University of Chicago.

Bruning, J., and Kintz, B. (1968), *Computational Handbook of Statistics,* Scott, Foresman, Glenville, Ill.

Cazden, C. (1970), 'The neglected situation in child language research and education.' In Williams, F. (ed.), *Language and Poverty,* Markham, Chicago.

Dikeman, B., and Parker, P. (1964). 'Request forms.' Term paper for Speech 160B, University of California, Berkeley. Cited by Ervin-Tripp, S. (1973), *Language Acquisition and Communicative Choice,* Stanford University Press, Stanford, Calif.

Edwards, A. (1957), *Techniques of Attitude Scale Construction,* Appleton-Century-Crofts, New York.

Emmerich, W. (1959), 'Young children's discrimination of parent and child roles.' *Child Development,* 30: 403-419.

Ervin-Tripp, S. (1973), *Language Acquisition and Communicative Choice,* Stanford University Press, Stanford, Calif.

Ervin-Tripp, S. (1974), 'The comprehension and production of requests by children.' In *Papers and Reports in Child Language Development,* Stanford University Press, Stanford, Calif.

Ervin-Tripp, S. (1977), 'Wait for me, Roller Skate.' In Ervin-Tripp, S. and Mitchell-Kernan, C. (eds.), *Child Discourse,* Academic Press, New York.

Hayes, W. (1963), *Statistics,* Holt, Rinehart and Winston, New York.

Lakoff, R. (1973), 'The logic of politeness or minding your p's and q's.' In *Papers from the Ninth Regional Meeting of the Chicago Linguistic Society,* Chicago Linguistic Society, Chicago.

Lindquist, E. (1953), *Design and Analysis of Experiments in Psychology and Education,* Houghton Mifflin, Boston.

Pfuderer, C. (1968), 'A scale of politeness of request forms in English.' Term paper for Speech 164A, University of California, Berkeley. Cited by Ervin-Tripp, S. (1973). *Language Acquisition and Communicative Choice,* Stanford University Press, Stanford, Calif.

Sachs, J. and Devin, J. (1976), 'Young children's use of age-appropriate speech styles in social interaction and role-playing.' *Journal of Child Language,* 3:81-98.

Shatz, M., and Gelman, R. (1973), 'The development of communication skills: Modifications in the speech of young children as a function of the listener.' *Monographs of the Society for Research in Child Development,* 38, 1-38.

3.4 The Mother Tongue and the Public Schools in the 1860s

Brian Hollingworth

In the uncertain sixties when the educational system of England and Wales was reviewed at all levels by a series of Government Commissions, the public schools attracted a good deal of comment and criticism. The basic attack was indeed upon their structure and government but, closely connected with this, and attracting a good deal of attention from would-be reformers, were palpable inadequacies in the curriculum wh:ch the public schools offered.

In general critics found the curriculum of the public schools inadequate in two ways. In the first place it was too narrow. In the second place it was irrelevant to the new industrial society which had established itself.

It was inevitable therefore that much of the debate should concern itself with the importance of expanding the curriculum through the development of the Sciences and the so-called Modern subjects such as History and Geography. And it was likewise inevitable that considerable attention should be paid to the role of the mother tongue as a necessary field of study within a reformed curriculum.

Now, looking back, two things seem striking about this great debate — a debate which took place through Commission, through pamphlet, through speech, through editorial, with great vigour over a whole decade — where it especially concerns the mother tongue. The first is the clarity and insistence with which the failure to teach the mother tongue was picked out as a major deficiency of the school curriculum. The second is the obscurity and half-heartedness of any practical proposals to remedy the deficiency.

To look at the Commissioners first. There is no doubt that members of the Clarendon Commission, working in the first half of the decade, recognized and by their questions elicited information concerning the completely inadequate state of English studies in the nine schools surveyed. At Eton, for instance, on the evidence, perhaps not unbiased, of the Reverend E. Coleridge, opportunities for the study of English literature were deteriorating rather than improving. Speaking of his young days he says:

> As to English books, we had them in abundance. The old English dramatists, a great deal of Dryden, a great deal of Pope, and an

British Journal of Educational Studies 22, (3) pp. 312-324.

immense deal of other English poetry were then read at Eton, besides most of the modern poems, but now I doubt whether you would find many boys out of the whole 800 that Eton contains who have read ten plays of Shakespeare.[1]

The only activity which might justifiably be called English studies to gain favourable mention throughout the report is the custom at Winchester of learning and reciting speeches 'extracted from the works of the chief English poets'[2] over a six-week period at Easter time.

Yet the Commissioners become extremely vague when it comes to making concrete proposals for instituting or improving the teaching of the mother tongue. There is merely a kind of addendum to their more zealous proposals in other fields, where the convoluted syntax seems to echo the uncertainty.

In addition to the study of the classics and to religious teaching, every boy who passes through the school should receive instruction in arithmetic and mathematics; in one modern language at least, which should be either French or German; in some one branch at least of natural science, and in either drawing or music. Care should also be taken to ensure that the boys acquire a good general knowledge of geography and of ancient history, some acquaintance with modern history, and a command of pure grammatical English.[3]

This discrepancy did not pass unnoticed by contemporary observers. The *Quarterly Review*, a sceptical, waspish but careful commentator upon the educational debates of the decade put the matter quite clearly:

The Commissioners once or twice insist on the necessity of attention to 'pure English' including spelling (Report p. 245): but this seems a mere protest, without practical effect, for though they have been at the trouble of making a new programme of school studies, in order to show how music and drawing may be introduced, they nowhere give a hint by what agency or in what manner this all-essential subject should be taught.[4]

But the Taunton Commission of 1868, looking at endowed schools and the education of the middle classes in general, proved little more constructive. The earlier section of the report makes a thorough comparison between the educational system in England and Wales and the system in other countries. They could not fail to miss one obvious point.

England is quite alone in requiring no systematic study of the mother tongue.[5]

Later they called witnesses who were acknowledged advocates of teaching the mother tongue. In addition to the views of J. R. Seeley, Professor of Latin at University College, which strongly favoured English 'well-taught',[6] there is an interesting exchange of views between Commissioner Acland and Edward Thring, the new Headmaster of Uppingham. Both these men were interested in promoting the study of English. Acland had been involved in setting up the New Oxford Examinations for the title of Associate in Arts, which included an examination in English Literature. Thring had himself produced several progressive grammar books during the 1850s. Acland plainly encouraged Thring to make his views about English known, and Thring did not fail his opportunity.

9985: Do you think that the present influences acting on classical education are thoroughly satisfactory, or would you wish in any degree to modify the ordinary mode of teaching Latin in our public schools? — No; far from it, for one thing, as far as my recollection goes, I think much more English is required to be worked into the public schools. I have found it so throughout. We teach English throughout the school in various forms, and I hold that the very highest results have been attained in a great degree by it, and that the average performance has been immensely bettered.

9986: You attach a great deal of importance (*sic*) to English composition throughout your school? — I do.[7]

This exchange was considered so significant as to be quoted fifty-five years later in the *Report on the Differentiation Of the Curriculum*,[8] yet no concrete proposals for the teaching of English come from this Commission either. Though the extension of English studies may well be implied by their suggestions for three grades of school of which only the first should be completely 'classical', the word English is not to be found at all in the recommended course of secular instruction.[9]

It was just the same where individual educators were concerned. Matthew Arnold, for instance, was plainly interested in the teaching of the mother tongue. An established poet and critic, Professor of Poetry at Oxford, then an elementary school inspector, son of a public school headmaster, during the 1860s he contributed significantly to the ongoing debate by his books on the educational systems in other countries. Indeed the confidence of the Taunton Commissioners in their statement about England's isolation where teaching the mother tongue was concerned stemmed largely from Arnold's writings and reports.

Frequently Arnold refers to the topic of the mother tongue. In *A French Eton*, written immediately after the Clarendon Report, and in direct reference to its exposures of the inadequacies of public school education, his comparison is clearly made. Commenting on the programme of studies in the French Lyceum Arnold says:

It has the scientific instruction and the study of the mother-tongue which our school course is without, and is often blamed for being without . . . . In the study of the mother-tongue the French schoolboy has a more real advantage over ours; he does certainly learn something of the French language and literature, and of the English our schoolboy learns nothing.[10]

But *A French Eton* is largely a polemic for the 'public establishment' of middle-class education, and the curriculum was not a major part of his argument. It is in his *Schools and Universities of the Continent*, his longest book, originally written as a report for the Taunton Commission, that his more significant comments are made. Perhaps the clearest comes in his discussion of French secondary schools, which he much admired.

From the bottom of the French schools to the top one finds recitation, reading and exercises in the mother tongue. Writing French is as considerable a part of a boy's work as writing Latin . . . the reading, and reciting from the classics of the mother tongue and the getting some knowledge of its literary history, is clear gain; and if the French attempt to teach too much, and of what cannot be taught, in style and the art of writing, we do not, or at least did not, when I knew our schools attempt to teach enough, and of what can.[11]

His General Conclusion on School Studies is, however, most bland. Where the study of the mother tongue is concerned it is hardly a rallying cry to reform. Merely it represents a parenthesis to his discussion of foreign languages.

We have still to make the mother tongue and its literature a part of the school course; foreign nations have done this, and we shall do it; but neither foreign nations nor we have quite learnt how to deal, for school purposes, with modern foreign languages.[12]

Such a sanguine attitude becomes even more strange when we remember how earnest was his advocacy of the mother tongue in the elementary schools. Fitch, for instance, records:

He regarded any system of popular education incomplete which did not provide for instruction in the right use of the mother-tongue, as a condition precedent to the acquisition of all else . . . some insight into the grammar and literature of the English language was in his view indispensable, and should, in the higher classes at least, be invariably insisted on.[13]

Another interesting example of such ability to recognize the deficiency, yet disinclination to provide an adequate remedy is to be found in the work of F. W. Farrar. Farrar, like Arnold, was well qualified to appreciate the weaknesses of the public school curriculum. An assistant master at Harrow during most of the 1860s he had already shown his concern with education in his novels, *Eric* (1858), *Julian Home* (1860) and *St. Winifred's* (1862). But he was deeply interested in the subject of language too, publishing 'Chapters on Language' in 1865, and lecturing on 'Families of Speech' to the Royal Institution in 1869.

His main contributions to the debate came by his editing *Essays on a Liberal Education* in 1867 and two addresses to the Royal Institution in 1868. In the Essays, indeed, are to be found the best arguments for teaching English in the public schools to appear throughout the decade. There is a separate essay devoted to 'The Teaching of English' by J. W. Hales, but this in fact is rather disappointing. It provides only a rather simplistic historical survey of the failure of English studies, and rather unconvincing suggestions for developing them through the study of 'the sentence'. Better arguments are found elsewhere and in particular in the first two essays, 'On the History of Classical Education' by Charles Stuart Parker and 'The Theory Of Classical Education' by Henry Sidgwick.

Parker points out in his essay how thoroughly the mother tongue had been taught on the continent and draws a rhetorical comparison with the state of affairs in England.

> Are learning Greek and Latin Grammar and no English Grammar, reading Greek and Latin authors and no English authors, and writing Greek and Latin exercises and no English exercises, the best means to form an English style? Are the French and Germans wrong in teaching French and German otherwise, or are their mother-tongues less nearly related to Greek and Latin? Or are our languages and literature less worthy to receive attention than theirs?[14]

Sidgwick in a closely argued and brilliant paper on the nature of liberal education, speaks strongly for the study of modern literature and quotes with approval an article in the *Quarterly Review* (Vol. cxvii p. 418) which had compared English with French education.

> Much more is it a thing to wonder at and be ashamed of, that, with such a literature as ours, the English lesson is still a desideratum in nearly all our great places of education, and that the future gentry of the country are left to pick up their mother tongue from the periodical works of fiction which are the bane of our youth and the dread of every conscientious schoolmaster.[15]

He argues specifically for the 'careful and independent teaching of English composition' and puts a very high value on the nature of English studies. We should aim, he says, to impart 'a complete grasp of what is probably the completest instrument of thought in the world'.[16]

Then, in contradistinction to the Commissioners, he *does* put forward a curriculum in which English as an independent study plays a significant part. And in his final summary he reiterates its importance.

> I think that a course of instruction in our own language and litera-
> ture, and a course of instruction in natural science, ought to form
> recognized and substantive parts of our school system. I do not
> venture to estimate the amount of time that ought to be apportioned
> to these subjects, but I think that they ought to be taught to all,
> and taught with as much serious effort as anything else.[17]

Farrar's own direct contribution to this series of essays is a paper on Greek and Latin verse-composition as a General Branch of Education in which he advocates much needed reforms in Classics teaching rather than dealing with the mother tongue specifically.

But in the first of the two lectures delivered to the Royal Institution on 31 January 1868, while talking particularly about Science teaching, he has much to say on behalf of English as a school study. Farrar was often criticized for his florid style, and certainly this address is particularly outspoken, emotional and untactful in its attack upon traditional classical education. He refers to it as a 'complete and disastrous failure' and demands no 'idle fingering at this social knot'.

> It is indeed an absurdity to say that a literary education necessarily
> means an education in Latin and Greek. . . . I should say deliberately,
> and with the most entire conviction, that if there were at this
> moment any school in England where, other advantages being equal,
> Science in its richest and broadest sense was intelligently and sys-
> tematically taught as the principal study, and where a thoughtful
> training in English Literature and in Modern Languages was substi-
> tuted for Greek and Latin, I should not indeed hold that such a
> school had elaborated a perfect theory, but I should hold that for
> all except a very few it would be furnishing a better, a more fruitful,
> and a more successful education than any at present attainable at
> our public schools.[18]

Before turning to discuss science teaching in greater detail, he betrays his own deeply emotional commitment to English literature, and in particular to the work of his heroes, John Milton and Jeremy Taylor.

> Strange that hundreds have been drilled for years into a power to
> struggle through a play of Euripides who never read a line of Keats
> or of Browning, and that for five hundred who have got up scraps
> of Demosthenes and Cicero, there are not five who know anything
> of the prose of John Milton or Jeremy Taylor. And yet, if it were
> to be a choice between Demosthenes and Cicero, or Milton and
> Jeremy Taylor, I for one should not long be hesitating.[19]

Here then was a man deeply convinced of the importance of English studies, and a man who had helped to campaign for them throughout the 1860s. Yet, when he became Headmaster of Marlborough in 1871, although he established Science teaching in the school, he does not seem to have established English as an autonomous subject. Like Thring at Uppingham, he was content to keep his English teaching within the broader context of the much maligned Classics.[20]

This peculiar ambivalence, this mote and beam situation, may suggest several reasons why English studies developed so surprisingly slowly in the public sector of education. After all, with the deficiency in English teaching so clearly pinpointed in the 1860s, with the salutary comparisons drawn to the educational systems of our economic and political rivals on the Continent, it is quite astonishing that English had scarcely established itself as an autonomous subject over wide areas of secondary education even by 1900, and that even today the last vestiges of its subservience to Classics remain.

In the first place, the ambivalence suggests that an institutional explanation for the tardy development of English studies in the later nineteenth century is unsatisfactory. At the time the argument was frequently heard that no curriculum change could be expected in the public schools while the universities so rigidly provided a classical course of study. The Athenæum's hostile review of *Essays on a Liberal Education*, for instance, suggests that the writers have not taken the conservatism of institutions into sufficient account.

> Schoolmasters are as much under the influence of Cambridge and Oxford as every trainer of thoroughbred horses is under the influence of the Jockey Club . . . what the Universities choose to examine in and prescribe, that the schools must teach, or they must fall behind in the estimation of the public.[21]

And, in similar terms, in 1900, the preparatory schools were still blaming their big brothers for the lack of English in their curriculum.[22]

But the evidence of the 1860s suggests that the outdated curriculum of the institution was an effect, and not a cause, of educators' reluctance to initiate reforms. The lukewarmness of positive suggestions for improvement in teaching the mother tongue, even from those who most clearly saw its value, suggests that the educational climate was not yet adapted to the necessary changes, and that institutional conservatism merely reflected this unreadiness.

It is therefore more profitable to conjecture why the public schools and their critics were so unready for reform at this time.

A plausible, but incomplete, explanation would be the intense hold which the Classics had over the *affections* of all the participators in the educational debate, even reformers like Arnold, Thring and, despite his diatribes, Farrar. Nobody seemed able to release himself from his classical training, nor to plan for the release of the classical stranglehold on the humanities, even when they clearly appreciated what distortions it was making to the educational process. In this respect Trollope's famous essay in the *Fortnightly Review* at the time of the Clarendon Commission's report seems exemplary. While giving a most unflattering description of his education at Harrow and admitting the iniquity of a curriculum where throughout his whole school life he was only taught two subjects — Latin and Greek — his affection conquers his zeal for reform. 'We love our public schools — loving even their faults dearly.'[23] We might also remember that Edward Thring, who has, as we have seen, some reputation as an advocate of the mother tongue, published his *Education and School* in 1864 without one single reference to English language teaching. Indeed, of the rather small early portion of the book devoted to curriculum, almost all is concerned with a spirited but, by modern standards, decidedly wrong-headed defence of the Classics.

We must, however, to find adequate reasons for the inertia, go further than this, I think, and look also at attitudes to society and attitudes to language and literature which extend far beyond individuals and their accidents of schooling and of interest. The clues to the snail pace development of English studies in public schools may lie, I believe, in two major areas. Firstly, in the largely symbolic nature of education in the later nineteenth century. Secondly, in the unsatisfactory and tentative nature of the development of aesthetic and linguistic theories concerning the native language at that time.

In considering social attitudes to education in England over the past hundred years, and even today, it is arguable that the symbolic role of education has always been pre-eminent. Education, even under the 1944 Act, seems to have been concerned with the demarcation of social classes, with establishing a differential curriculum 'suitable' for a social group, and with the development of an image of separateness by a divided (even when ostensibly unitary) system.

This symbolic function was naturally a good deal more blatant during the later nineteenth century than it would dare to be today,[24] and one of its consequences may well have been to maintain the Classics in their pre-eminent position in the public schools: The Classics were a symbol of difference between such schools and the elementary and lower grade secondary schools which were emerging to cater for the working and lower middle classes.

Matthew Arnold's attitudes provide a good example of this. As I have mentioned, *A French Eton* is a book largely devoted to seeking state help for middle-class education. One of his basic arguments, which does not seem to have been seriously questioned by liberal thinkers of the time, is as follows:

We have to regard the condition of classes, in dealing with education, but it is right to take into account not their immediate condition only, but their wants, their destination − above all, their evident pressing wants, their evident proximate destination.[25]

Leading from this hypothesis, in a fashion plainly heralding his bold generalizations in *Culture and Anarchy*, Arnold decides in three sentences the education appropriate to each social class.

It seems to me that, for the class frequenting Eton, the grand aim of education should be to give them those good things which their birth and rearing are least likely to give them: to give them (besides mere book-learning) the notion of a sort of republican fellowship, the practice of a plain life in common, the habit of self-help. To the middle class, the grand aim of education should be to give largeness of soul and personal dignity; to the lower class, feeling, gentleness, humanity.[26]

Such statements are remarkable for two reasons. Firstly, in general, because they divide so completely (though vaguely) the aims of education according to accidents of birth. There is no overlap at all. Secondly, in particular to Arnold, because it is only for the lower class that he advocates a formal education of the feelings.

Arnold's view of education, in which he is typical of the time, is therefore hierarchical. Feelings first, and this is as far as the lower classes can be expected to reach. Personal dignity second. This is the pinnacle for the middle-class child who, apparently, has been educated in feeling by birth. Republican fellowship third for the Etonian who has inherited feeling and personal dignity. With such a view, curriculum subjects plainly take on a symbolic role, and the alleged moral quality of a subject is likely to be more highly regarded that its utility or popularity.

This goes far to explain the distinction we have already noticed between Arnold's enthusiasm for English as a compulsory subject in the elementary school, and his marked lack of zeal for English in the public school. For Arnold English, or at least English literature was above all an education of the feelings:

Good poetry does undoubtedly tend to form the soul and character, it tends to beget a love of beauty and of truth in alliance together; it suggests, however indirectly, high and noble principles of action, and it inspires the emotion so helpful in making principles operative. Hence its extreme importance to all of us; but in our elementary schools its importance seems to me to be at present extraordinary.[27]

English literature, particularly necessary for the lower classes, in Arnold's symbolism, becomes somewhat less essential for the Etonian.

The second important point is the status and development of English studies themselves, apart from the schools and in the community at large. The Report on *The Teaching of English in England* of 1921 fixes the matter exactly:

It is only quite lately that we in England have begun to have the definite consciousness which the French gained in the age of Louis XIV, that we have a great and independent literature of our own, which need not lower its flag in the presence of the greatest on the earth.[28]

The reasons for this lack of self-confidence in the native literature (and the native language) would require careful analysis to discover, but the situation which it produced can be observed quite clearly in the later nineteenth century.

Where language was concerned, for instance, all descriptions of English were based on Latin models, inadequate as these were. Such improvements as were suggested by Thring in particular were improvements of method and not of description. In a true sense, therefore, English grammar was but a poor relation of the Latin, and little was to be gained by subsituting the one for the other.

More significantly the kind of scholarship in language which was most influential at the time — the historical excavation, the evolutionary approach to language studies, as exemplified in the massive work of Max Mueller, could have no relevance for the schools. Max Mueller was himself greatly interested in educational reform and in retrospect his work is fascinating for its parallels with the scientific theories of Darwin and its relationship to the political development of Imperialism. Yet, from the school point of view, Thring was surely right in his judgement:

Philology I look on as a scientific toy totally unfitted for school training, and unless pursued in a very vast and original way as one of the vanity traps of the day.[29]

But literature provided an even weaker support for school study, since its advocates remained so unsure of themselves. In the 1860s, and for a good deal later — as exemplified in the philological bias of some university studies even down to our own day — an adequate and convincing apologia for the autonomous study of English literature which could match the impressive science of philology, had yet to be made. In particular two weaknesses can be distinguished, even in the most sophisticated theorists, which encouraged inertia where curriculum reform was concerned.

Firstly there was a lack of conviction about the *independent* value of English literature. Secondly there was a failure to comprehend what were the most significant contemporary developments in that literature.

The first weakness can be seen very clearly in the writings of Farrar and Thring. Both men talk enthusiastically about literature in general and English literature in particular, yet their failure in this regard was their reluctance to distinguish the English from the Classical. Thring, for example, in the letter previously quoted goes on to talk of 'literary training' and sees his task as 'to join together the ages'.

> . . . and show how thought in heathen times worshipped form and beautiful shape, and how thought in Christian times worships expression and beautiful life, and to show the proper proportions, the true sources, the right use, and enable a right judgment to judge correctly of each.[30]

This developmental approach, admirable as it may be, has the weakness, in our context, of making English literature a derivative of the Classical, the source literature, in much the same way that the language was considered as flowing from the Latin. It did not establish English literature in its own right. In the same way the evidence seems to be that Farrar in his teaching linked the English with the Classical, but did not question the basic assumption of a tradition flowing from the Latin downwards into secondary English.

There is an interesting example of this limitation also in Arnold's writings. In *A French Eton* immediately after making the comparisons between the teaching of the mother tongue in England and France noted earlier, he makes the following surprising qualification:

> French grammar, however, is a better instrument of instruction for boys than English Grammar, and the French literature possesses prose works, perhaps even poetical works, more fitted to be used as classics for schoolboys than any which English literature possesses. I need not say that the fitness of works for this purpose depends on other considerations than those of the genius alone, and of the creative force, which they exhibit.[31]

This is quite a striking statement from a man so prominent both as a creator and a critic in his native literature. It betrays a most unexpected Augustan tone – the popular theory that English literature was at its best when most spontaneous and untrammelled by conventions, as in the work of Chaucer, Shakespeare, or the Romantic poets, a theory which Arnold enthusiastically espoused in his own lectures on poetry, is here used to cast doubt on the value of such literature in secondary education. Presumably here the restraint and order of the Classical tradition were the most important factors to be considered, and the French, more confident of their classical heritage, as their syllabuses suggest, proved more confident in their teaching of the native tongue.

In other words, developmental assumptions about literature, viewing the modern as the child of the ancient, inevitably proved inhibiting to the teaching of a literature whose parentage might be regarded as doubtful.

By the same token, of course, the educators of the age, in general, failed to acknowledge, let alone introduce to their pupils, the most significant contemporary development in English literature — the great novels of the middle years of the nineteenth century. Despite the work of such contemporary giants as George Eliot and Charles Dickens, educated society as a whole still regarded the novel as a frivolous art form, and the reading of novels as a light and not always respectable pastime. It was common enough in essays advocating the study of the mother tongue then, as now, to betray horror over the chosen reading matter of young people in their native language — but the suggested remedy was always poetry or moralistic prose, rather than better fiction.

In this situation, then, it is perhaps not surprising that English studies developed so slowly in the public schools, despite the arguments of the 1860s. To describe the situation is not, I think, necessarily to criticize men such as Arnold, Farrar, or Thring, who were so enthusiastic for English, nor indeed necessarily to criticize the public school system itself. Rather, it may be, there is an interesting illustration here of factors in curriculum development which in any age are likely to be overlooked or underestimated. Curriculum change depends upon far more than the mere identification of a deficiency in current practice. Many people in the 1860s were aware that the native language was scandalously neglected in the public schools. But one might speculate that effective change was unlikely for two good reasons which may still operate today. Firstly, in any free society, such deficiencies of curriculum, however blatant, are likely to be tolerated and condoned, if they appear to allow wider social objectives to be realized; if, that is, they assist an achieved or intended social order. Secondly, effective change depends upon a serious and adequate theory of the positive values which the new development has to offer; it is not always sufficient to justify the new in terms of the old.

The stillbirth of English studies in the 1860s may therefore have some significance for the curriculum planners of the 1970s.

Notes

1. Report of H.M. Commissioners (1864), iii, 123.
2. *Ibid.*, i, 144.
3. *Ibid.*, i, 53.
4. *Quarterly Review*, 116, 1864, 200.
5. Schools Inquiry Commission, i, 1868, 77.
6. *Ibid.*, ii, 793.
7. *Ibid.*, V, 103.
8. Report on the Differentiation in the Curriculum for Boys and Girls respectively in Secondary Schools: Board of Education, 1923, Note p. 12.
9. *Op cit.*, i, 576-85.
10. M. Arnold, *A French Eton*, London, 1892, 17-18.
11. M. Arnold, *Schools and Universities on the Continent*, Ann Arbor 1964, 115-6.
12. *Ibid.*, 299.
13. Sir J. Fitch, *Thomas and Matthew Arnold*, London 1897, 178
14. Rev. F. W. Farrar (Ed.), *Essays on a Liberal Education*, London, 1867, 73.

[15] *Ibid.*, 110 footnote.
[16] *Ibid.*, 123.
[17] *Ibid.*, 140-1.
[18] *Fortnightly Review*, No. XV, March 1868, 238.
[19] *Ibid.*, 239.
[20] Cf. R. Farrar, *Life of Frederick William Farrar*, London 1905, Ch. VII.
[21] *The Athenaum*, July-Dec. 1867, 238.
[22] Cf. *Special Reports on Educational Subjects No. 6*, London 1900, 61-79.
[23] *Fortnightly Review*, ii, 1865, 476.
[24] Cf. P. W. Musgrave (ed.): *Sociology, History and Education*, London, 1970, F. Campbell, *Latin and the Elite Tradition in Education*, 249-64.
[25] *Op. cit.*, 61.
[26] *Ibid.*, 62-3.
[27] *What Her Majesty's Inspectors Say: 1880-81*, Darlington, 36.
[28] *The Teaching of English in England*, Board of Education, 1921, 198.
[29] Letter to R. L. Nettleship, 1869; cf. *Edward Thring, Headmaster of Uppingham School*, by G. R. Parkin, London 1904, 293.
[30] *Ibid.*, 294.
[31] *Op. cit.*, 18.

3.5 The Teaching of English in England

Introduction

1. We are instructed by the terms of our reference to consider and report upon the position of English in the educational system of the country, that is to say, the position of a part in relation to the whole in which it is included. If the instruction had gone no further, it might have been reasonable to suppose that the present educational system of the country was to be accepted as a fixed framework and that our concern with English was limited to the manner in which it is fitted, or should be fitted, into its place in that framework. But the terms of reference continue as follows: — 'regard being had to be require- ments of a liberal education, the needs of business, the professions, and public services, and the relation of English to other studies.' Not only are these words significant in themselves, as giving a wide scope to our consideration of English, but we have found almost from the outset that they have imposed upon us a task at once more extensive and more complex than we had foreseen. As we considered the grow- ing mass of evidence before us, it became more and more impossible to take a narrow view of the inquiry, to regard it as concerned only with one subordinate part of an already existing structure. A declara- tion that in our present system English holds but an unsatisfactory position would have been, we saw, valueless; for however elaborately set forth it would not have taken account of the most significant part of the facts and judgments laid before us. The inadequate conception of the teaching of English in this country is not a separate defect which can be separately remedied. It is due to a more far-reaching failure — the failure to conceive the full meaning and possibilities of national education as a whole, and that failure again is due to a misunderstanding of the educational values to be found in the different regions of mental activity, and especially to an underestimate of the importance of the English language and literature. It is not required of us that we should propose in detail a complete scheme of national education, but we are compelled to indicate certain principles which must form the basis of

Board of Education (1921) *The Teaching of English in England*, (The Newbolt Report) London HMSO, Chapter 1, pp 1-26 any such scheme; because the recognition of these principles is an indispensable condition of success in providing for the best use of English as a means of intercourse and of education. Our position may be compared to that of an architect called in to advise upon what can be done with a stone which the builders have hitherto rejected. We find that the stone is invaluable; but also that the arch is too faulty to admit it. We propose to meet not one but two imperative needs by rebuilding the arch and using our stone as keystone of the whole — the use for which it, and no other, is available.

2. Before we go further we must give a brief indication of the converging lines of thought along which we have been forced to this conclusion. First, we have been struck by the fact that, although much labour and thought have been expended and many changes made, almost all in the right direction, it is still true that in this country we have no general or national scheme of education. It is understood to be the duty of the State to see that every child shall during a certain number of years, receive an education, but the meaning of this is not generally understood. Neither by tradition nor by effective instruction has the general body of citizens any clear idea of the benefit to be conferred. To some the word education means reading, writing, and arithmetic; to others, almost any kind of information. Of those who understand it to imply instruction by skilled teachers, the great majority still identify it with the imparting of information, though some consider this largely useless, while others value it as a possible means to obtaining increased wages or some other vocational advantage. In general, it may not unfairly be said that education is regarded as a suitable occupation for the years of childhood, with the further object of equipping the young in some vague and little understood way for the struggle of adult existence in a world of material interests. The existence of other ideals does not diminish the confusion. Sections of the community, for social and intellectual reasons, have persisted in maintaining schools and universities for the special treatment of their own sons and daughters. The education which they have thus provided has, in general, been superior to that provided by the State, but it has been the privilege of a minority only, and has widened the mental distance between classes in England. Matthew Arnold, using the word in its true sense, claimed that 'Culture unites classes.' He might have added that a system of education which disunites classes cannot be held worthy of the name of a national culture. In this respect we have even fallen away from an earlier and better tradition. Many of our great Public Schools, as the Natural Science Committee have pointed out,[1] though founded originally in the interest of poor scholars, are not open to poor scholars today because the scholarships and exhibitions which they offer are not, as a matter of fact, within the reach of boys from the elementary schools. The age at which they are competed for, and the subjects which they require, make them available only for those who have

received an expensive special preparation. We may recognise that it is at present more difficult than it was some centuries ago to educate the children of rich and poor side by side in the same schools, but this makes it only the more to be regretted that there is no source of unity to be found in the teaching provided by the different types of school. If there were any common fundamental idea of education, any great common divisions of the curriculum, which would stand out in such a way as to obliterate, or even to soften, the lines of separation between the young of different classes, we might hope to find more easily the way to bridge the social chasms which divide us. For this purpose it must be remembered that classical studies are not available; however effective they may have proved in one type of school, they cannot be made use of universally. Actually, by an unfortunate irony of circumstance, they have been regarded as the possession of a privileged class, and not as a pathway open to all possessed of literary ability or scholarship.

3. A second fact which has impressed us is this. Though there has been a common failure in this country to realise the true nature and effect of education, there has been at the same time a common instinctive perception of one aspect of our ill success. The English are a nation with a genius for practical life, and the chief criticism directed, whether by parents or pupils, against our present system, is a practical one; it amounts, when coherently stated, to a charge that our education has for a long time past been too remote from life. We have come to the conclusion that this charge is supported by the evidence. However men may differ as to the relative importance of different objects in life, the majority are right in feeling that education should directly bear upon life, that no part of the process should be without a purpose intelligible to everyone concerned. At a later stage we shall endeavour to trace the historical process by which the present divorce between education and reality has come about; in the meantime we note the results. A quasi-scientific theory has long been accepted that the process of education is the performance of compulsory hard labour, a 'grind' or 'stiffening process', a 'gritting of the teeth' upon hard substances with the primary object not of acquiring a particular form of skill or knowledge but of giving the mind a general training and strengthening. This theory has now been critically examined and declared to be of less wide application than was thought. Its abandonment would do much to smooth the road of education, it would make it possible to secure for the child a living interest and a sense of purpose in his work, and it would replace the old wasteful system of compulsion and mere obedience by a community of interest between pupil and teacher.

4. This community of interest would be felt instinctively and immediately by the pupil, but it is very necessary that it should be consciously understood by all those responsible for the education of the young. It must be realised that education is not the same thing as

information, nor does it deal with human knowledge as divided into so-called subjects. It is not the storing of compartments in the mind, but the development and training of faculties already existing. It proceeds, not by the presentation of lifeless facts, but by teaching the student to follow the different lines on which life may be explored and proficiency in living may be obtained. It is, in a word, guidance in the acquiring of experience. Under this general term are included experiences of different kinds; those which are obtained, for example, by manual work, or by the orderly investigation of matter and its qualities. The most valuable for all purposes are those experiences of human relations which are gained by contact with human beings. This contact may take place in the intercourse of the classroom, the playground, the home, and the outer world, or solely in the inner world of thought and feeling, through the personal records of action and experience known to us under the form of literature. The intercourse of the classroom should be for the student, especially in the earlier stages of development, the most valuable of all, since it is there that he will come under the influence of not one but two personal forces, namely, the creative power of the author whose record he is studying, and the appreciative judgment of the teacher who is introducing him to the intimacy of a greater intellect.

5. Not only must the true nature of education be clearly understood, but it will be a matter of equal importance that the teacher, at any rate, and the student, as soon as may be, should have clear and well founded ideas about morals, science and art. They must feel and, as far as possible, understand the direct interest of these as bearing upon practical life and the equipment for it. It has long been accepted, and at the present day it has been reiterated with great force by such teachers as the Dean of St. Paul's and Mr Clutton Brock, that the three main motives which actuate the human spirit are the love of goodness, the love of truth and the love of beauty. It is certainly under heads corresponding to these that education must be divided into the training of the will (morals), the training of the intellect (science) and the training of the emotions (expression or creative art). In school, therefore, science must be, for teacher and for student, the methodical pursuit of truth and the conquest of the physical world by human intelligence and skill. Literature, the form of art most readily available, must be handled from the first as the most direct and lasting communication of experience by man to men. It must never be thought of or represented as an ornament, an excrescence, a mere pastime or an accomplishment; above all, it must never be treated as a field of mental exercise remote from ordinary life. The sphere of morals in school life is limited by practical considerations with which we cannot here deal, but it is evident that if science and literature can be ably and enthusiastically taught, the child's natural love of goodness will be strongly encouraged and great progress may be made in the strengthening of the

will. The vast importance to a nation of moral training would alone make it imperative that education shall be regarded as experience and shall be kept in the closest contact with life and personal relations.

6. The facts and needs of the situation as briefly outlined above did not form the starting point of our inquiry, but they forced themselves irresistibly upon our attention from the moment when we first began to consider the present position of English in the educational system of country. From the evidence laid before us it became speedily clear that in many schools of all kinds and grades that part of the teaching which dealt directly with English was often regarded as being inferior in importance, hardly worthy of any substantial place in the curriculum, and a suitable matter to be entrusted to any member of the staff who had some free time at his disposal. It would be natural to suppose that there must be some good reason for this neglect, but on the other hand one of the most obvious facts of which we have to take account is that education in English is, for all Englishmen, a matter of the most vital concern, and one which must, by its very nature, take precedence of all other branches of learning. It is self-evident that until a child has acquired a certain command of the native language, no other educational development is even possible. If progress is not made at one time in the region of arithmetic or history or geography, the child merely remains backward in that respect, and the deficiency can be made up later. But a lack of language is a lack of the means of communication and of thought itself. Moreover, among the vast mass of the population, it is certain that if a child is not learning good English he is learning bad English, and probably bad habits of thought; and some of the mischief done may never afterwards be undone. Merely from this point of view English is plainly no matter of inferior importance, nor even one among the other branches of education, but the one indispensable preliminary and foundation of all the rest.

7. It is probable that no one would be found to dissent from this proposition, in which the meaning of the word English is limited to the language itself as a means of communication. The word, however, in our present inquiry has other and wider meanings, and these must now be brought into consideration. Even as a means of communication a language may be treated in two ways, as practical speech and as a scientific study. With regard to the first of these, the position is clear. With regard to the second, it can be made clear at once. It has been the custom in the past to attempt the teaching of the Classics from two points of view simultaneously. The student has been required during one and the same lesson to treat the work of a classical author from the point of view of science and of art; in a passage of the *Aeneid,* for example, to study simultaneously the structure and idiom of the Latin language and the personal expression of Virgil's mind in his poetry. This made the task a severe and distracting one for both teacher and pupil; success was only achieved in a small minority of cases. In the rest

failure was made almost inevitable by the fact that the scientific study of the language, though to the student far less interesting than the poetical narrative, appears to the teacher in general to be an easier task, involving less personal effort on his own part. To give out information and insist on its being accurately registered is an almost mechanical matter; to convey anything of the feeling and thought which are the life of literature the teacher must have been touched by them himself and be moved afresh by the act of communicating the touch to others. Thus not only are two different studies confused, but the less important receives the more attention. No doubt the connection between language and thought is a very intimate one, but we are strongly of opinion that in dealing with literature the voyage of the mind should be broken as little as possible by the examination of obstacles and the analysis of the element on which the explorer is floating. This last is a purely scientific study and can be to a greater extent separated from the study of the literary art, as the chemical analysis of water can be separated from the observation of the sounds and colours conveyed by it. It would be a grave misfortune if a defect of method which has proved so injurious in the case of Latin and Greek were to appear also in the teaching of English literature. We believe, therefore, that formal grammar and philology should be recognised as scientific studies, and kept apart (so far as that is possible) from the lessons in which English is treated as an art, a means of creative expression, a record of human experience.

8. We have now set apart the preliminary training of the child in the language which is to be his means of communication for all the common purposes of life, and the scientific study of language, which has a value of its own and should hold a high place among the other sciences. It remains for us to consider the actual and the possible position of English in the highest sense, that is as the channel of formative culture for all English people, and the medium of the creative art by which all English writers of distinction, whether poets, historians, philosophers or men of science, have secured for us the power of realising some part of their own experience of life. Education of the kind here implied has, for some time past, been one of the objects held in view by the Board of Education; and we have found with pleasure that there are now a number of elementary schools in which a considerable degree of success is being obtained on these lines. We must repeat, however, that in this region, as in others, there is not at present in existence any national plan. It is not the absence of a universal curriculum, an educational drill or uniform, that we are here regretting; it is the lack of a general appreciation of the true value of education and the best means of obtaining it. Even in secondary schools we find this lack of understanding evident, and it is widely spread among parents of all classes. The idea of a liberal education is either altogether ignored or struggles feebly for the right of existence; and even where it still lives, there is a singular depreciation of the value of English

literature for such a purpose. By the tradition of the public schools the Latin and Greek classics are far more highly estimated. This tradition, however, dates from a time very different in many ways from our own, a time when Latin was the common language of the educated and official world, and Greek the main source of history, philosophy and natural science; when, moreover, the literatures of Greece and Rome were beyond all comparison the greatest available for study. The modern world has a much wider outlook and more numerous and more direct roads by which to explore life, whether on the material or the spiritual side. In one respect Classics do retain their importance for the world. A knowledge of Latin civilisation is still indispensable for the full understanding of the languages, law and society of a great part of Europe, including the British Isles: and Greek literature is still the most life-giving and abundant source to which we trace our highest poetical and philosophical ideas and our feeling for artistic form. The Classics then remain, and will always remain, among the best of our inherited possessions, and for all truly civilised people they will always be not only a possession but a vital and enduring influence. Nevertheless, it is now, and will probably be for as long a time as we can foresee, impossible to make use of the Classics as a fundamental part of a national system of education. They are a great watershed of humanistic culture, but one to which the general mass of any modern nation can, at present, have no direct access. We are driven, then, in our search for the experience to be found in great art, to inquire whether there is available any similar and sufficient channel of supply which is within the reach of all without distinction. We feel that, for an Englishman, to ask this question is at the same time to answer it. To every child in this country, there is one language with which he must necessarily be familiar and by that, and by that alone, he has the power of drawing directly from one of the great literatures of the world. Moreover, if we explore the course of English literature, if we consider from what sources its stream has sprung, by what tributaries it has been fed, and with how rich and full a current it has come down to us, we shall see that it has other advantages not to be found elsewhere. There are mingled in it, as only in the greatest of rivers there could be mingled, the fertilising influences flowing down from many countries and from many ages of history. Yet all these have been subdued to form a stream native to our own soil. The flood of diverse human experience which it brings down to our own life and time is in no sense or degree foreign to us, but has become the native experience of men of our own race and culture.

9. We have now come to the point where the evidence forces our lines of thought to converge. On the one hand, our national education needs to be perfected by being scientifically refounded as a universal, reasonable and liberal process of development; on the other hand, we find coincidentally that for this purpose, of all the means available,

there is only one which fulfills all the conditions of our problem. Education is complete in proportion as it includes within its scope a measure of knowledge in the principal sciences and a measure of skill in literature, the drama, music, song and the plastic arts; but not all of these are equally useful for the training of the young. We recognise fully, on the one side, the moral, practical, educational value of natural science, on the other side the moral, practical, educational value of the arts and of all great literatures ancient or modern. But what we are looking for now is not merely a means of education, one chamber in the structure which we are hoping to rebuild, but the true starting-point and foundation from which all the rest must spring. For this special purpose there is but one material. We make no comparison, we state what appears to us to be an incontrovertible primary fact, that for English children no form of knowledge can take precedence of a know-ledge of English, no form of literature can take precedence of English literature: and that the two are so inextricably connected as to form the only basis possible for a national education.

10. It will be clearly seen that by this statement we have declared the necessity of what must be, in however elementary a form, a liberal education for all English children whatever their position or occupation in life. We are glad to record not only our own strong conviction that such a scheme is, from every point of view, just, reasonable and for the national advantage, but also the fact that in the mass of opinions sub-mitted to us we nowhere find any evidence to the contrary. The judgments and experience laid before us by those who have a large experience and every right to express a judgment, support us in our belief that an education of this kind is the greatest benefit which could be conferred upon any citizen of a great state, and that the common right to it, the common discipline and enjoyment of it, the common possession of the tastes and associations connected with it, would form a new element of national unity, linking together the mental life of all classes by experiences which have hitherto been the privilege of a limited section. From the same evidence and opinions, we have derived the further belief that to initiate all English children into such a fellow-ship, to set the feet of all upon that road of endless and unlimited advance, is an undertaking in no way impossible or visionary. The difficulties are undoubtedly great, the means available are at present very inadequate, but the difficulties and the inadequacy are largely those which are already troubling us, and would hamper any conceivable scheme of education at the present moment. On the other hand, we have the advantages given us by the necessity of a new departure among rapidly changing conditions, and by the opportunity of avoiding some causes of past failure.

11. We have already spoken of some of these causes of past failure, but there is one of them upon which we must lay stress again. We believe that in English literature we have a means of education not less

valuable than the Classics and decidedly more suited to the necessities of a general or national education, but we see also that in the future, as in the past, success or failure will depend upon our perception of the true purpose of the instrument and the right method of handling it. If we use English literature as a means of contact with great minds, a channel by which to draw upon their experience with profit and delight, and a bond of sympathy between the members of a human society, we shall succeed, as the best teachers of the Classics have often succeeded in their more limited field. If, on the contrary, we cannot obtain a competent body of teachers, if we have to commit the guidance of youth to teachers who, in default of the necessary insight and enthusiasm, will fall back upon conventional appreciations, historical details and the minute examination of words and phrases, we shall repeat the failure of the past upon a wider and more ruinous scale. For a clear view of what we must avoid we may cite the evidence of a very eminent witness. Wordsworth's criticism of the method of dealing with the Classics prevalent in his own time, and still a danger in our own, is set out in a long and remarkable passage in *The Prelude*.[2] It may be summarized as follows:—

He thought that the Classics, as taught in his time, were worthless for education: that books in general came under the same condemnation, because they did not record or foster true feelings or knowledge of human nature: that human nature could be best studied in the largest and least sophisticated masses of men: that the lessons to be learned from it could best be gathered in and delivered to the young by poets and romancers: that the poet especially has this gift because he can create by the power of words, a "great Nature," a new world in which things are presented as objects recognised, but in flashes and with a significance or glory not otherwise seen to be their own. Lastly, it is noteworthy that the poets whom he had in mind were not ancient poets but modern ones; even, it would appear, poets of the same age and country as those whom they are to teach.

It will be seen that this is not in reality a destructive, but a constructive criticism. Wordsworth is not bent on differentiating between one literature and another. He is differentiating between two different methods of using literature in education, the practical and the pedantic, the real and the unreal. He advocates the transmission, not of book learning, but of the influence of personality and the experience of human life. The distinction here made between book learning and true education is of the first importance. Books are not things in themselves, they are merely the instruments through which we hear the voices of those who have known life better than ourselves. Wordsworth had perceived what has since been repeatedly demonstrated by great men of science, that the common, unaided senses of man are not equal to the realisation of the world. Just as the physicist or the mathematician show us deeper aspects of matter or of space, which in the life of every day we should never have discovered for ourselves, so poets, philosphers, and historians have the power of revealing new values, relations of thought, feeling, and act, by which the dull and superficial sight of the multitude is illuminated and helped to penetrate in the direction of reality. It is here that Wordsworth and the literature he loves are on the side of life against book learning. The antithesis has been more recently expressed in its simplest and most extreme form by Mr. P. B. Clayton, Chaplain at Poperinghe during the late war. He is speaking with very sympathetic appreciation of the ordinary soldiers in the line. "The only trouble is that their standard of general education is so low. Put the product of the old elementary schools side by side with the man from overseas, and his mental equipment is pitiful . . . The overseas man, with his freedom from tradition, his wide outlook on life, his intolerance of vested interests and his contempt for distinction based on birth rather than on worth, has stirred in the minds of many a comparison between the son of the bondwoman and the son of the free." Some of the values here may be disputable, but the round sums will be accepted. Among the best things which education can give are certainly freedom and independence of thought, a wide outlook on life, and a strong sense of the difference between convention and reality. A less trammelled life has given these in some degree to our men overseas. Literature, which is still more untrammelled, as well as wider and more penetrating, will given them to the children of this country in a still greater degree and from an earlier age. But if it is to do this the teacher must keep it close to life: in no case must the real or practical bearing of the experience be neglected or avoided. And, as Wordsworth saw, though all great literatures will present deep and universal truths, in education that will be the more intelligible and powerful which presents the student with experience of time and circumstances more nearly related to his own.

12. In citing this opinion, which we accept and put forward with entire conviction, we are aware that we are opposing ourselves to those for whom the idea of a liberal education is inseparable from a knowledge of the Classics, and we desire to clear the ground of possible misunderstandings. In the course of our inquiry we have not found either among ourselves or the witnesses whom we have heard, any trace of hostility to the Classics. We recognise that for some minds the study of man's life and thought in a setting so far removed from modern conditions as was the ancient world may have special advantages. We recognize, also, that since many of our great writers have been influenced directly or indirectly by classical studies, the reader who approaches them with the same equipment will, in some ways, find it easier to understand them intimately and without loss of time. Further, we do not despair of the Classics or regard them as having no future in this country. We see in them sources, which can never be forgotten, of our own language, our own art, our own

experience, and we hold that no student of English will have completed his exploration, or gained all its advantages, until he has ascended the stream of literature and discovered these perennial sources for himself. Nevertheless, we are convinced, both by necessity and by reason, that we must look elsewhere for our present purpose. The time is past for holding, as the Renaissance teachers held, that the Classics alone can furnish a liberal education. We do not believe that those who have not studied the Classics or any foreign literature must necessarily fail to win from their native English a full measure of culture and humane training. To hold such an opinion seems to us to involve an obstinate belittling of our national inheritance.

13. In any case, and whatever studies may be added to it, English, we are convinced, must form the essential basis of a liberal education for all English people, and in the earlier stages of education it should be the principal function of all schools of whatever type to provide this basis.

Of this provision the component parts will be, first, systematic training in the sounded speech of standard English, to secure correct pronunciation and clear articulation: second, systematic training in the use of standard English, to secure clearness and correctness both in oral expression and in writing: third, training in reading. Under this last head will be included reading aloud with feeling and expression, the use of books as sources of information and means of study, and finally, the use of literature as we have already described it, that is, as a possession and a source of delight, a personal intimacy and the gaining of personal experience, an end in itself and, at the same time, an equipment for the understanding of life.

14. Here, again, it may be well to deal at once with possible criticisms. It may be objected that while English is indeed a necessary condition of our education, it is one which may be taken for granted, like the air we breathe or the land on which we live. We do not need, it may be said, to be taught English; to write and read, in Dogberry's opinion, comes by nature. This view is, perhaps, not likely to be now so crudely stated, but it has long been acted upon by many who are engaged in education, and is acquiesced in by many who control it. We must, therefore, state clearly that in our judgment it is an entirely unpractical view. It is repudiated not merely by literary experts but by the numerous practical men of business whom we have consulted. It is an instance of that divorce of education from reality which we have already found to be a main cause of failure in the past. English may come by nature up to a certain point; but that point is soon reached, and thenceforward the possibility of mental development, in whatever direction, is seriously diminished for those who have not achieved some mastery of their mother tongue. What a man cannot clearly state he does not perfectly know, and, conversely, the inability to put his thought into words sets a boundary to his thought. Impressions may

anticipate words, but unless expression seizes and recreates them they soon fade away, or remain but vague and indefinite to the mind which received them, and incommunicable to others. "A haziness of intellectual vision," said Cardinal Newman, "is the malady of all classes of men by nature . . . of all who have not had a really good education." It is a common experience that to find fit language for our impressions not only renders them clear and definite to ourselves and to others, but in the process leads to deeper insight and fresh discoveries, at once explaining and extending our knowledge. English is not merely the medium of our thought, it is the very stuff and process of it. It is itself the English mind, the element in which we live and work. In its full sense it connotes not merely acquaintance with a certain number of terms, or the power of spelling these terms correctly and arranging them without gross mistakes. It connotes the discovery of the world by the first and most direct way open to us, and the discovery of ourselves in our native environment. And as our discoveries become successively wider, deeper, and subtler, so should our control of the instrument which shapes our thought become more complete and exquisite, up to the limit of artistic skill. For the writing of English is essentially an art, and the effect of English literature in education is the effect of an art upon the development of human character.

Here again we desire to guard against any possible misunderstanding. We find that the nature of art and its relation to human life and welfare is not sufficiently understood or appreciated in this country. The prevalence of a low view of art, and especially of the art of literature, has been a main cause of our defective conception of national education. Hitherto literature has, even more than science, suffered in the public mind both misunderstanding and degradation. Science has too often been regarded as a kind of skilled labour, a mere handling of materials for profit. Literature has first been confused with the science of language, and then valued for its commercial uses, from the writing of business letters up to the production of saleable books. The word art has been reserved for the more highly coloured or the less seriously valued examples of the latter. We must repeat that a much higher view may be taken of both science and art, and that this higher view is the only one consistent with a true theory of education. Commercial enterprise may have a legitimate and desirable object in view, but that object cannot claim to be the satisfaction of any of the three great natural affections of the human spirit — the love of truth, the love of beauty, and the love of righteousness. Man loves all these by nature and for their own sake only. Taken altogether, they are, in the highest sense, his life, and no system of education can claim to be adequate if it does not help him to develop these natural and disinterested loves. But if it is to do this effectively we must discard or unlearn all mean views of art, and especially of the art of literature. We must treat literature, not as language merely, not as an ingenious set of symbols, a superficial and superfluous kind of decoration, or a graceful set of traditional gestures, but as the self-expression of great natures, the record and rekindling of spiritual experiences, and in daily life for every one of us the means by which we may, if we will, realise our own impressions and communicate them to our fellows. We reiterate, then, the two points which we desire to build upon; first, the fundamental necessity of English for the full development of the mind and character of English children, and second, the fundamental truth that the use of English does not come to all by nature, but is a fine art, and must be taught as a fine art.

15. We believe that such an education based upon the English language and literature would have important social, as well as personal, results; it would have a unifying tendency. Two causes, both accidental and conventional rather than national, at present distinguish and divide one class from another in England. The first of these is a marked difference in their modes of speech. If the teaching of the language were properly and universally provided for, the difference between educated and uneducated speech,[3] which at present causes so much prejudice and difficulty of intercourse on both sides, would gradually disappear. Good speech and great literature would not be regarded as too fine for use by the majority, nor, on the other hand, would natural gifts for self-expression be rendered ineffective by embarrassing faults of diction or composition. The second cause of division amongst us is the undue narrowness of the ground on which we meet for the true purposes of social life. The associations of sport and games are widely shared by all classes in England, but with mental pleasures and mental exercises the case is very different. The old education was not similar for all, but diverse. It went far to make of us not one nation, but two, neither of which shared the associations or tastes of the other. An education fundamentally English would, we believe, at any rate bridge, if not close, this chasm of separation. The English people might learn as a whole to regard their own language, first with respect, and then with a genuine feeling of pride and affection. More than any mere symbol it is actually a part of England: to maltreat it or deliberately to debase it would be seen to be an outrage; to become sensible of its significance and splendour would be to step upon a higher level. In France, we are told, this pride in the national language is strong and universal; the French artisan will often use his right to object that an expression "is not French." Such a feeling for our own native language would be a bond of union between classes, and would beget the right kind of national pride. Even more certainly should pride and joy in the national literature serve as such a bond. This feeling, if fostered in all our schools without exception, would disclose itself far more often and furnish a common meeting ground for great numbers of men and women who might otherwise never come into touch with one another. We know from the evidence of those who are familiar with schools of every type

that the love of fine style and the appreciation of what is great in human thought and feeling is already no monopoly of a single class in England, that it is a natural and not an exceptional gift, and that though easily discouraged by unfavourable circumstances it can also, by sympathetic treatment, be easily drawn out and developed. Within the school itself all scholars, though specialising perhaps on different lines, will be able to find a common interest in the literature class and the debating or dramatic society. And this common interest will be likely to persist when other less vital things have been abandoned. The purely technical or aesthetic appeal of any art will, perhaps, always be limited to a smaller number but, as experience of life, literature will influence all who are capable of finding recreation in something beyond mere sensation. These it will unite by a common interest in life at its best, and by the perpetual reminder that through all social differences human nature and its strongest affections are fundamentally the same.

16. Our inquiry cannot end here. When we have decided upon the nature and method of the education to be recommended we have still to consider as a necessary corollary the provision of an adequate teaching staff. This is a matter of great moment, for whatever kind of education is recommended, its success or failure will depend chiefly upon the intelligence and sympathy with which it is conducted. This will be even more true of an education in English than of any other; for two reasons. In the first place the teaching of English as the instrument of thought and the means of communication will necessarily affect the teaching of every other subject. Whatever view is taken of specialisation in schools, it is evidently desirable that the general education of every teacher shall be sufficiently good to ensure unceasing instruction in the English language. The teachers of all special subjects must be responsible for the quality of the English spoken or written during their lessons. In every department of school work confused and slovenly English must be regarded as the result of a failure on the part of the teacher. Secondly, since the literature lesson is no mechanical matter and is to consist not in the imparting of information but in the introduction of the student to great minds and new forms of experience, it is evidently necessary that the teacher should himself be already in touch with such minds and such experience. In other words, he must himself have received an education of the kind towards which he is to lead his class. It is no doubt true, as the Board of Education have pointed out in a circular on the teaching of English,[4] that the real teachers of Literature are the great writers themselves – the greater the work the more clearly it speaks for itself; but this only leads to the conclusion that for teachers we must have those who will not come between their pupils and the author they are reading, but will stand by them sympathetically, directing or moderating the impact of the new experience upon their minds.

17. We desire to express our strong conviction that for the purposes of such an education as we have outlined no teacher can, in his own grade, be too highly gifted or too highly trained, and that this is at least as true in the earlier as in the later stages. It is sometimes assumed that a first-rate teacher is wasted in an elementary school. This is, in our judgment, a complete misunderstanding. If any stage in education is to be considered more important than another, it must be that early stage in which the child at an elementary or preparatory school is first introduced to the great influences which are to invigorate and direct his mental life. For these schools, no teaching can be too good, and we have to consider, in the very first place, what means are available for the provision of a competent staff. Our difficulty would be infintely lessened if the general population of this country had already for years past been receiving such an education as we now advocate, but in the natural order of things, this could never be; the teacher must exist before the pupil. He is our lever, and we must first apply our whole force to him if we are to raise the mass. This has not been sufficiently recognised hitherto. Teachers have not only been inadequately paid, but care has not been taken to see that they are sufficiently supplied with the libraries and other intellectual opportunities which alone can keep them in the mental health and strength necessary for their task. A still more serious defect has been the inadequacy of their training. They have neither been grounded nor confirmed in the idea of a liberal education. They are a class for whom a university course is most desirable and yet, for the greater number, such a course is still beyond reach. In our judgment, it is a vital necessity for the nation that in its universities adequate room should always be available for those who are to be engaged in the work of education. In the meantime, until the changes necessary for this purpose can be effected, we believe that something might be done to help the existing staff of teachers by voluntary effort on the part of men and women who have themselves received a university education and have time to spare for lecturing in schools or training colleges. The enrolment of a fraternity of itinerant preachers on English Literature — a panel of men and women who are recognised authorities on their own subjects and are willing to lecture upon them occasionally — would be a step in accord with other movements of the time and with our national tradition of unpaid public service. It would not only reinforce the regular army of teachers but would have an important social effect by counteracting the influences which tend to bitterness and disintegration. Many of the differences between the lot of one class and another are of little importance: but the present advantage of rich over poor in our schools — the difficulty of the attempt to pass up the intellectual ladder and to attain the spiritual freedom conferred by a real education — is keenly and rightly felt as an unnecessary and unjust inequality. Nothing would, in our belief, conduce more to the unity and harmony of the nation than a

public policy directed to the provision of equal intellectual opportunities for all, and service to this end would be doubly effective if it came voluntarily as from those who have already received their inheritance, and desire to share with the rest of their countrymen that in which their life and freedom most truly consist.

Notes

[1] Report of the Prime Minister's Committee on the Teaching of Natural Sciences, p. 23.
[2] Book XIII, lines 160-179, 206-220, 232-249; and *see* Book V, lines 492-534, 594-607.
[3] This does not refer to dialect [which is treated elsewhere — editor].
[4] The Teaching of English in Secondary Schools, 1910, p. 21.

3.6 Attitudes to the Teaching of English

1.1 In any anxiety over a contemporary situation there is likely to be a wistful look back to the past, with a conviction, often illusory, that times were better then than now. And the times people claim to have been better are generally within the span of their own lives. Nowadays few would consider the Code and Schedules of 1880 as a model from which we have fallen; so was there a point in time between then and now when we had arrived at the optimal? Was there a standard which we can regard, if not as ideal, at least as a criterion by which to judge other times and conditions? These are not trivial questions and certainly not contentious ones. If we are to decide what kind of English is right for our pupils they are the kind of questions that need to be asked.

1.2 Many allegations about lower standards today come from employers, who maintain that young people joining them from school cannot write grammatically, are poor spellers, and generally express themselves badly. The employers sometimes draw upon past experience for comparisons, but even where they do not there is a strong implication that at one time levels of performance were superior. It is therefore interesting to find in the Newbolt Report[1] of 1921 observations of a very similar kind. There Messrs. Vickers Ltd., reported "great difficulty in obtaining junior clerks who can speak and write English clearly and correctly, especially those aged from 15 to 16 years". Messrs. Lever Bros. Ltd. said: "it is a great surprise and disappointment to us to find that our young employees are so hopelessly deficient in their command of English". Boots Pure Drug Co. remarked "teaching of English in the present day schools produces a very limited command of the English language. . . Our candidates do not appreciate the value of shades of meaning, and while able to do imaginative composition, show weakness in work which requires accurate description, or careful arrangement of detail". The last is very close to some of the observations made today, half a century later, and might almost have been taken from evidence submitted to us. We do not reproduce these to imply that things were never any better and that everything is therefore as it should be. To seek perspective is not to be

DES (1975) *A Language for Life* (The Bullock Report) London, HMSO Chapter 1, pp. 3 - 9.

complacent. But perspective *is* important, and a realistic assessment is the best point from which to move towards improvement. The issue is a complicated one. It is evident that the employers of 50 years ago were no less dissatisfied; but in any case we must ask with whom today's young employees are being compared. The situation is very much different from that before the war or for some time after it. Further and higher education has expanded enormously. More young people are staying on at school or going on to college, many of whom would at one time have gone into commerce and industry. Moreover, as the Central Statistical Office points out, there have been marked changes in the structure of employment in recent years. Agriculture and mining have employed a sharply declining proportion of the working population, manufacturing industry has remained at about the same level, and the service industries now absorb over half the total work force. The changing pattern of employment is making more widespread demands on reading and writing skills and therefore exposing deficiencies that may have escaped attention in the past. What is more, the expansion in junior management has been considerable, and one dimension of competence at this level is the ability to produce a written report.

1.3 Factors such as these should be taken into account when observations are made about the standards of school leavers. However, they do not alter the fact that these standards are not satisfying present day requirements. Furthermore, it has to be remembered that it is not only employers who express dissatisfaction. Further and higher education institutions often remark on the inability of their entrants to write correct and coherent English. The Committee was furnished with examples of essays by college of education students, with comments by the Professor of English who had submitted them. These essays contained numerous errors of spelling, punctuation, and construction, and were a disturbing indication that the students who wrote them were ill-equipped to cope with the language demands they would meet in schools. Observations to the same effect have been made to us by heads, who have complained of the poor standard of written expression of some of the young teachers who have joined their schools. These remarks by experienced educationists deserve to be taken seriously, the more so since they are not comparing the students with those of the past but measuring them against the demands of a professional function. It may be true that in commerce, industry, and higher education like comparisons with past standards are misleading, but the clear implication is that standards need to be raised to fulfil the demands that are being made upon them.

1.4 In this chapter we shall be considering briefly the different approaches to English in schools today. Generalisations are commonly made to the effect that one or another set of attitudes has virtually swept the board. In fact, as our questionnaire results showed, and as our visits to schools confirmed, the variety of practice is wide. Some teachers see English as an instrument of personal growth, going so far as to declare that "English is about growing up". They believe that the activities which it involves give it a special opportunity to develop the pupil's sensibility and help him to adjust to the various pressures of life. Others feel that the emphasis should be placed on direct instruction in the skills of reading and writing and that a concern for the pupil's personal development should not obscure this priority. There are those who would prefer English to be an instrument of social change. For them the ideal of 'bridging the social gap' by sharing a common culture is unacceptable, not simply as having failed to work but as implying the superiority of 'middle class culture'. Of course, even where a teacher subscribes to a particular approach he does not necessarily pursue it exclusively, neglecting all else. Nevertheless, these emphases do exist and in considering our own recommendations we must examine them, since we believe that in their extreme form they over-simplify what is in fact a very complex matter.

1.5 Nor is the debate on purpose and method exclusive to this country. The historical determinants in the United States of America are different from those in Britain, and this must be remembered when parallels are drawn. However, the same unease has expressed itself there. It gathered into a national head after 1957 when the Russians launched Sputnik, an event which caused the U.S.A. to look critically at many aspects of its education system. English was not identified with the national interest to the extent that the sciences and modern languages were. Nonetheless, its theorists and practitioners felt the same sense of urgency, and their self-examination emerged in "The National Interest and the Teaching of English" (N.C.T.E. 1961), a publication which expressed the deep concern of the time. In the previous year the College Entrance Examination Board had issued a short description of the proper divisions of the secondary school English curriculum: English consisted of language, literature and composition, a view summed up by the label 'The Tripod Curriculum'. Looked at in this light the study of English could be reduced to manageable proportions, and each unit invited a view of itself as a discipline capable of being structured. According to Muller[2], English in the U.S.A. was, until the structuring started, an amalgam of journalism, play-production, business letters, research techniques, use of the library, career counselling, use of the telephone, and advice on dating. He quotes Kitzhaber's remark that 'An English teacher can teach almost anything without anyone, including the teacher, realising that it is no longer English that is being taught'. Not surprisingly, the pressures we have noted issued in a definition of English which was as concerned with excluding the irrelevant as identifying the essential.

1.6 It is a characteristic of English that it does not hold together as a body of knowledge which can be identified, quantified, then transmitted. Literary studies lead constantly outside themselves, as

Leavis put it; so, for that matter, does every other aspect of English. There are two possible responses for the teacher of English, at whatever level. One is to attempt to draw in the boundaries, to impose shape on what seems amorphous, rigour on what seems undisciplined. The other is to regard English as process, not content, and take the all-inclusiveness as an opportunity rather than as a handicap. The first response can lead to a concept of the subject as divisible into compartments, each of which answers to certain formal requirements. Thus there are many teachers, in both primary and secondary schools, who feel that English language should be extracted from context and studied as a separate entity. The weekly composition on a set title, comprehension, spelling, language exercises; this pattern is still common. The language work may take the form of a class activity or it may occur in a group or individual learning situation. If the latter, the nature of the experience can be governed by the assignment card. In either case the principle is that the child is engaging with the basic skills through the medium of controllable tasks. The second response can lead to a readiness to exploit the subject's vagueness of definition, to let it flow where the child's interest will take it. Its exponents feel that the complex of activities that go to make up English cannot be circumscribed, still less quantified; the variables are too numerous and the objects too subtle.

1.7 It would be absurdly oversimplifying to say that English teaching has, without light or shade, separated itself into factions with these ideas as the manifestos. For one thing few British teachers would subscribe to the notion of the 'Tripod Curriculum', mentioned above, still less to some of the practices that separate development gave rise to, e.g. the attention to rhetoric and analysis in the teaching of composition. (Indeed, it was by no means universally embraced in the U.S.A. One American educationist said that, like Caesar, they had divided the area into three parts and then found the division so convenient they had assumed God must have made them.) It is safe to assume that no-one would any longer see English in terms of the L.C.C. official Time-Table Form of 1920, which required the time allocation to be shown for each of the following 'subjects': (*a*) Composition, Written, (*b*) Composition, Oral, (*c*) Dictation, (*d*) Grammar, (*e*) Reading, (*f*) Recitation, (*g*) Word-building, (*h*) Hand writing, (*i*) Literature. Equally, not everyone would express a contemptuous disregard for standards and say that English was merely a free-wheeling vehicle for the child's emotional and social development. Thus, although there are certainly opposed emphases there is also an area of common occupation.

1.8 It is extremely difficult to say whether or not standards of written and spoken English have fallen. There is no convincing evidence available, and most opinions depend very largely upon subjective impressions. These are not to be dismissed out of hand, but we have already shown how difficult it is to make valid comparisons with the past. We have also remarked that any speculation about standards all too frequently relates them to a particular kind of teaching. We received many letters which suggested that 'creativity' is now reverenced and that 'formal' work has virtually been banished. This is a particular area of contention where personal impression clearly counts heavily, especially since 'creativity' and 'formality' are hazy concepts. Exact or even approximate comparability of standards may be elusive, but parents and teachers alike know there have been new approaches and that some schools have operated them with remarkable success, some have adopted them uncritically, and some have set their face against them. Moreover, these approaches have frequently been discussed in the press, and they have featured prominently in publications of one kind or another and in teachers' courses. What is far from certain is how widespread is this change of emphasis. It is commonly believed that English in most primary schools today consists largely of creative writing, free reading, topic or project work, and improvised drama, and that spelling and formal language work have no place. When certain teaching methods attract a good deal of attention it is understandable that people should assume them to have become the norm. But what *is* the situation in schools? How general has been the shift of emphasis away from the formal to the 'permissive'? We decided at the outset that we would find out by enquiring of the schools themselves by way of detailed questionnaires. This survey is described in detail elsewhere in the Report, and from the tables of results it will be seen that a good deal of time is allocated to formal practice in English. The answers we received certainly did not reveal a picture of the decay of such work in the midst of a climate of unchecked creativity. Sceptics may say that the schools told us what they thought we wanted to hear, or what they surmised would present them in a respectable light. We do not believe this for one moment, but even if it were true, one is still left with a picture of what primary schools feel is the *acceptable* way to be teaching. Our survey gives no evidence of a large body of teachers committed to the rejection of basic skills and not caring who knows it. It is facile to assume that all manner of weaknesses can be ascribed simply to the wholesale spread of a permissive philosophy. One has to look more deeply. This we hope to do in the course of the Report, when we shall develop some of the points made here.

1.9   We have in effect been discussing the first of the two responses described in paragraph 1.6, and we believe that the diagnosis and remedy it offers is an over-simplification. We take the same view of the second when it regards standards of performance as of slight consequence compared with the personal growth or social orientation of the pupil. Every good teacher is concerned with the social and psychological development of his pupil. But we refer here in particular to the notion of English in the secondary school as almost exclusively a source of material for personal response to social issues. Literature is experienced largely in the form of extracts and is filleted for its social yield. Talk is shepherded into the area of publicised questions, of acute issues of the day. The writing that emerges from both is to a large extent judged for its success by the measure of commitment it seems to reveal. Genuine personal response in such circumstances is not easy to express. These public issues have been dwelt upon at length by television and the press, and the cliché responses generated inevitably find their way into the children's writing and talk. We must make it clear that we are not contesting the place of social concern in the curriculum of the secondary school. But we are questioning the philosophy of those teachers for whom it has become the core and essence of the English programme. *Of course* it is part of the English teacher's task to develop social awareness and responsibility. By its very nature this subject involves the contemplation of immediate and vicarious experience into which such sensibility enters. Indeed, English is rooted in the processing of experience through language. The pupil uses language to represent the experience to himself, to come to terms with it, to possess it more completely. It is a major part of the teacher's skill to extend the range of that experience, at first hand and through literature, in such a way that new demands are made on language. It is our contention that for some pupils that range of experience has been narrowed. We know that some very sensitive writing and lively talk have emerged from encounters with contemporary social issues. We have read and heard it. But we have read and heard as much which has reflected the child's inability to produce a genuine felt response, where he has had to fall back on the ready-made cliché reaction.

1.10 Is it possible, then, to make some kind of provisional generalisation about standards? There may be little profit in attempting to compare today's standards with those of the past, but we underline our conviction that standards of writing, speaking, and reading can and should be raised. The first thing that is required is a redefinition of what is involved. These three abilities are usually described as 'the basic skills', but like the terms 'formal' and 'progressive' this is a phrase which merits more precise definition than it tends to receive. It is often read to mean that language abilities can somehow be extracted from context, taught in the abstract, and fed back in. The evidence is that one acquires language as a pattern, not as an inert collection of units added serially, a mechanical accumulation of abstracted parts of speech. So we are not suggesting that the answer to improved standards is to be found in some such simple formula as: more grammar exercises, more formal speech training, more comprehension extracts. We believe that language competence grows incrementally, through an interaction of writing, talk, reading, and experience, the body of resulting work forming an organic whole. But this does not mean that it can be taken for granted, that the teacher does not exercise a conscious influence on the nature and quality of this growth. The teacher's first concern should be to create the conditions necessary for fluency, but he then has a responsibility to help the child improve the technical control of his work. What is the quality of the child's verbalisation of his experience? With what fidelity and coherence does he communicate it to his readers? The child should be brought up to see this technical control not as an abstraction imposed from without but as the means of communicating with his audience in the most satisfying and appropriate manner. His development of this ability can be expressed in terms of increasing differentiation. He learns to carry his use of English into a much broader range of social situations, to differing kinds of audience. The purposes to which he puts language grow more complex, so that he moves from a narrative level of organising experience to one where he is capable of sustained generalisation. Considered in these terms the handling of language is a complex ability, and one that will not be developed simply by working through a series of text-book exercises. If we regard this approach as inadequate we have equal lack of sympathy with the notion that the forms of language can be left to look after themselves. On the contrary, we believe that the teacher should intervene, should constantly be looking for opportunties to improve the quality of utterance. In schools where the principles of modern primary school education have been misinterpreted this often does not happen. We have talked to young teachers who have so misunderstood them as to believe they should never directly teach the children.

1.11   If a teacher is to control the growth of competence he must be able to examine the verbal interaction of a class or group in terms of an explicit understanding of the operation of language. We believe that because of the nature of their training this is precisely what many teachers lack, and this has implications for initial and in-service training. In succeeding chapters we discuss language and its relation to learning, and in the course of the Report we emphasise that if standards of achievement are to be improved all teachers will have to be helped to acquire a deeper understanding of language in education. This includes teachers of other subjects than English, since it is one of our contentions that secondary schools should adopt a language policy across the curriculum. Many teachers lack an adequate understanding of the complexities of language development, and they often hold the English teacher responsible for language performance in contexts outside his control. A great deal of work remains to be done to help teachers learn more about the nature of children's language development, its application to their particular subject, and their own role in the process. There is also the important question of the deployment of staff in the teaching of English itself. The English in a secondary school is sometimes in the hands of as many as 15 teachers, only four or five of whom are specialists in the subject. Almost a third of the 12 year olds in our sample had their English with more than one teacher. In the survey the replies from heads suggested that no fewer than a third of all secondary teachers engaged in the teaching of English have no qualification in the subject (see table 72).* It also revealed (table 70)* that only 37 per cent of those teaching English spend all their time on it, while 38 per cent spend less than half. In some cases a shortage of qualified English teachers forces a head to assign a non-specialist to the subject. On the other hand there are schools where no strenuous efforts are made to acquire English specialists precisely because it is thought possible to make up English time from other members of staff. Similarly, if timetable construction is presenting a difficulty it is not unknown for the recalcitrant single period to be labelled English and given to whichever teacher is not already engaged. There are, of course, many examples of schools which go to great lengths to avoid any such disadvantages to English. Moreover, we are aware that some schools adopt as a deliberate policy the kind of integrated humanities work in which a teacher of another subject becomes responsible for the pupils' English. In the best of such schemes there is strong support from the English specialists, sound planning, and good resources. However, it remains true that large numbers of pupils are taught English in circumstances which would be considered unacceptable in many other subjects. The attitude still prevails that most teachers can turn their hand to it without appropriate initial qualifications or additional training. In our view such an attitude is based on an ignorance of the demands of English teaching and the knowledge required of its practitioners. In the course of the Report we shall attempt to illustrate these, since we believe that only if they are fully recognised can an advanced in the teaching of English be achieved.

References

[1]*The Teaching of English in England* (The Newbolt Report): HMSO: 1921.
[2]H. Muller: *The Uses of English*: Holt, Rinehart, and Winston Inc: 1967.

Editors Note: These appear later in the report and are not given in this volume.

3.7 Language

The English subject specialists in Her Majesty's Inspectorate of Schools, whose thinking is summarised here, were contributors to, and have been influenced by, the arguments and suggestions in the Report of the Bullock Committee of Inquiry, published in 1975. Many of the points presented briefly here are treated in that Report with the completeness they need.

The range of this paper will necessarily be broader than that of the language of pupils and teachers in the course of the 'English' lesson. It will be broader than many current ideas about 'language across the curriculum'. It will argue the case for a 'linguistic education', much of the responsibility for which lies in the school as a community. The argument implies that we shall need teachers of all subjects who have a sure understanding of the ways in which language is used in effective learning, and that English teaching demands a more specialist understanding of language and literature. It implies also that we should develop the skill of all teachers in organising their work so that appropriate individual opportunity for language use is consistently offered to pupils. Some radical changes in examinations in all subjects, not just in English, will have to be made if they are to play their part in permitting and even encouraging real learning through effective language use.

Every teacher – indeed, every person in a relationship with other people in which language plays a part – conveys attitudes to language by his use of it, and by the uses of language that he asks or expects from others. Teachers contribute to a number of the ways in which language makes young people what they are, and what they are to become. It is an essential instrument in their understanding of themselves; it is an important factor in the views that other people have of them. It is one of the ways in which they relate to people and to experience. It is a means by which they organise their experience into conscious thought and it is therefore closely related to learning. They can be enabled to learn through language if they are allowed to use it for the purpose, and they can be prevented from learning if they are not.

A school sets out to make possible its pupils' effective language behaviour within it, and to equip them for their needs beyond it. The second of these objects is the more difficult in two ways; the

DES (1977) *Curriculum 11-16*, London, DES Section entitled *Language*, pp. 20-23.

demands will often be unpredictable, and the people who make them may have particular view of language which will influence the ways in which the demands will have to be met. Their views may be about usage and custom in language, most obviously about spelling, punctuation and certain grammatical forms, but also about features of language standardised by use in occupational, social and regional groups. In common with other forms of behaviour, language behaviour depends on an appreciation of the constraints that are operating at the time, and of the ways in which an individual can move within them. Paradoxically the deeper his understanding of the way conventions work, the more free the individual is to achieve his own purpose, to use the language appropriately as an individual but also with reference to the whole context. The best scientific and historical writing illustrates both the confident use of the conventions and the ability to bend them to make new meanings.

In much of the controversy about literacy, and in discussions about the role of the English department, it has frequently been implied that it is for 'English' to ensure that young people can use linguistic conventions (described inadequately as 'the basic skills'), but that English teachers neglect them in the promotion of 'self-expression'. The two are not, of their nature, opposites; they are opposites only in the minds of those who put them in opposition and take one side or the other. Moreover, the practice of schools as described in reports of HMI visits and in the survey of the Bullock Report[1] 'gives no evidence of a large body of teachers committed to the rejection of the basic skills and not caring who knows it'. It is important that children can use and understand the need for conventions, broadly interpreted and clearly defined in relation to contexts and groups of people. But the language they use needs to have become their own, and it is also important that they encounter the complexity of language behaviour, so that they may be more knowledgeable, critical and realistic about it.

When the school begins to feel the increasing influence of the world outside it, whether in the form of external examinations, the demands of employment or social acceptability, it is likely to lay more emphasis on the language's constraints. In doing so, it may neglect the central argument of Chapter 12 of the Bullock Report that 'learning and the acquisition of language are interlocked'. Language — spoken as well as written — is directly involved in the activity of learning, whatever the subject, and it is also used for communicating what has been learned. In children's learning, the two forms of language will often be different, since they have different purposes. We need to understand, and to tell pupils more explicitly than we have usually done, what are the opportunities and the constraints in the language of our teaching and their learning. Teachers of every subject must balance, at different stages and dependent on the work in hand, the need for such flexibility in spoken and written languages as can make the learning more effective, and for understanding and following the appropriate conventions. If all teachers are to play their part in educating all pupils in language, then we shall all need to know about language and to question our opinions and attitudes. The understanding we gain should lead us to the conviction that language matters, but people as language-users matter especially.

Anyone, by following a group of pupils through a day in a secondary school, can prove that their language experiences are largely a matter of chance. The dominant modes are exposition by teachers, questions and answers[2], the writing of notes and of answers to work sheets. On any one day, any one of these modes might be dominant. The pupils' own use of language may be subject to spasmodic correction of superficial features. All of us, to some extent, have a view of language as a mine-field when we have to use it in unfamiliar circumstances. For many pupils, this is especially true; the language of school subjects becomes more and more alien during the years of their secondary education, and they participate less and less in its processes. When they do not understand the characteristics of language in the context of learning, they may fail to develop the confidence and incentive to participate that are vital if learning is to take place.

We cannot be satisfied with the preparation we give to young people for the language needs of their lives. Nor can we be satisfied with the level of the debate that is taking place about that preparation and those needs, marked as it is by inadequate evidence, partial views and aggressive and defensive postures. We should take more account of the first three paragraphs of the Bullock Report, and especially of its point that our expectations 'need to be raised to fulfil the demands that are being made upon them [the pupils]'. In an increasingly complex society, language too becomes more complex, and for full adequate participation in that society, people need to assimilate roles and uses of language that did not exist a few generations ago. Yet they still need to be able to express ideas and feelings very simply, and to feel that their ability to do so will be valued.

It is possible now to define more clearly that part of pupils' education in language which is the responsibility of English teachers. Their objectives need to be seen in language terms. 'English' is a service agent, but not in the limited sense that it alone is responsible for pupils' spelling, punctuation and sentence construction. These features of pupils' language are a shared concern, and part of the whole school's language policy. The English department must help pupils to investigate language explicitly in its various forms, and with support from other departments, to keep alive pupils' interests in and response to language. It is from such an interest and response that the ability to use language develops in range and becomes more effective. And one of the most important ways of understanding what language does is to focus on significant contexts and situations in which it occurs. Pupils aged

11-16 need help in understanding the relevant features of many kinds of language that touch people's lives — their grammars, certainly, but also the reasons for their grammars which lie in the contexts of their use — in the nature and purpose of the task, the nature of the 'audience', the relationship of the speaker and writer with the audience, and the 'match' between language and context. The subject-matter of 'English' will be the study and production of languages in variety, and the discovery of similarity, difference and pattern. The English teacher will so contrive matters that his pupils will extend their understanding and control of varieties of language while reading and writing about experiences and subjects which interest them[3].

The field from which this subject-matter can be drawn is a vast one. It can include anything in the form of language, and anything to which a response in language is possible. But language is inseparable from almost every human activity; there is a strong verbal element in the aesthetic, the ethical, the spiritual and the social aspects of school life, and mathematics and science are also dependent on language. For other areas of the curriculum, the English department may need to be a tactful consultant and support, though there will be times when it will be offering a linguistic view, in its own right, of experience in one of these other areas.

'Literature', although part of the aesthetic and the ethical experience, must remain largely within the responsibility of English departments. Whatever else it is and does, it is one of the most important uses of language, and there is a close relationship between the response to the creation of 'literary' forms of language. Poetry, prose and drama, whether on the page or in any other of the expressive media, must play their part in developing an understanding of and a response to language. One of the purposes of looking at examples of language is that pupils should develop appropriate sensitivities to it. 'Literature' is valuable in that it is one of the most significant, memorable and deliberated kinds of language, and that it extends our experience of language and of people as 'language-makers'. Literature is patterned experience; it enables us to see the familiar in a different light, and to extend imaginatively beyond the familiar. It uses language in order to refine and make more intense our response to experience. Reading a work of literature can evoke a more complex range of responses than any other form of reading, among which is that relating the vision and intention of the writer to the language he uses. Through his encounters with literature, the pupil should appreciate the rich possibilities of choice in language, and some of the most important purposes which language choice can service.

Out of the literature and the other forms of language that surround us every day, we need to select examples that tell pupils, appropriately to their age and experience, what use man makes of words. He tells in different ways what he has seen and done, he gives orders, he formulates opinions and gives reasons, he enters the thoughts and feelings of others, he hurts and assuages, he creates understanding and misunderstanding. These are some of the uses of language that pupils will encounter themselves. In asking pupils to use language, again in ways appropriate to their age and experience, a teacher has a particular function. He needs to specify the kind of use, for whom it is intended and its purpose. He may need to tolerate, and to expect tolerance of, degrees of hesitancy and uncertainty in language, and to encourage cooperative work with it. At the same time, he needs to prepare for linguistic intolerance, and for attitudes to language which may conflict with those which he is encouraging. One of the most important things underlying the English teacher's work is that it is he, more than anyone else, who is trying to help pupils to meet the unforeseen as well as the foreseen demands on their languages. It will therefore be important to give them a broad foundation of experience in language and of man as a language-user rather than to train them to perform in restricted language modes such as the essay, the summary or the comprehension exercise in isolation.

If this broader concern with language is accepted, there may be a case for including in the curriculum some enquiry into how human beings acquire and develop language. In recent years, there has been an increased interest in this complex activity, its importance to the individual and to society, and we may ask whether the subject could be explored sensitively enough to be justifiable. We have abundant examples of young children acquiring language all around us. The subject could be interesting in its own right; older pupils would be making their own investigations and formulating their own investigations and formulating their conclusions, from their own and others' experience of developing language. They would also be equipping themselves for the role, which people need to take from adolescence onwards, of promoting the language development of children. They would be able to focus on the use and development of language in cases, where, for once, their own language resources would be superior. This should not be a matter of learning theories of language acquisition; it should enable pupils to understand how complex, subtle and elusive is the process in practice. There are few schools in which a study of children's language and literature is taken seriously, and fewer still in which it is the English department's responsibility. 'English' is concerned with man as a user of language and man is a language-user from his earliest years. More and more English teachers, it is hoped, will equip themselves with an understanding of language acquisition.

Subject 'English', we have argued, cannot be the scapegoat for all the real or imagined deficiencies in the language of school-leavers. It occupies no more than one-eighth of school time, and less than one-fortieth of the child's waking life. It is taught to groups, often of thirty or more. It needs to trim its objectives to these hard facts. It is likely that the main emphasis will continue to be on writing and reading, but practice in these modes will need to be informed by more enlightened attitudes to talking and listening.

That does not mean we cannot expect a usable understanding of and an achievement in language to result from all the hours devoted to it during the statutory years of schooling. The danger is that, if we frame our expectations in any mode too narrowly, we shall be back with exercises and tests, based upon limited and often erroneous attitudes to language from which we have been trying to escape. It does not follow that a 16-year-old who can manage certain routine functions of language can transfer his ability into non-routine uses, and so any attempts at precise measurement may produce misleading results.

This argument is well illustrated if we look at reading. It is more important that pupils are in fact reading than that they have obtained appropriate results on reading tests. Reading tests are important as a gauge of reading skills against national norms, but it is vital that the reader's own satisfaction should grow with his skill. It is the ability to read for a variety of purposes and an understanding of the importance and the uses of adult reading that are crucial. We should expect that pupils will have read books of some length and requiring some persistence during their last school year, that they find reading satisfying, and that they will have responded to their reading in a variety of ways. The response needs to be more flexible than we usually imply by 'comprehension' as a standard form of assessment. Experience of a writer's perception of his audience should enable pupils to recognise intentions other than the one of simply transmitting information in print, and they should be able to assent to or dissent from these intentions. We need individuals who are responsive to the printed works, but not gullible — who have 'reading minds of their own'. What is true of reading is also true of the other receptive mode of language — listening. Just as reading is the interrogation of print, so listening is the interrogation of spoken language. A similar range of qualities is therefore needed by the listener — the ability to hear not only the words but also their associations, their deeper implications and the purposes for which they are being used.

In addition to the two 'receptive' modes, there are two 'productive' modes, writing and talking. It is reasonable to expect that a 16-year-old should show understanding of the general principles of the English writing system, and should want to use language in accordance with that system. That is to say he should be able to follow conventions for appropriate purposes that are specified, and not merely to satisfy some criterion of performance in a test deprived of context, for example a test of spelling, punctuation or grammatical usage. He should be able to write in narrative, descriptive and explanatory forms, to respond personally to an aesthetic experience and to present a point of view or a line of thought on a topic about which he feels he has something of his own to say — all these for a known audience. His success in these kinds of writing needs to be judged from evidence that he has appreciated the nature of the written task and that he has genuinely become engaged in it. It may be misleading to ask for too precise a 'terminal' achievement in one's native language at 16; the most important feature of that 'terminal' achievement will lie in its possibilities for the future.

Subject to the same reservations, the target, in spoken language, might be that a 16-year-old should be able to meet social and linguistic demands in the ways suggested by the Bullock Report (p. 152). He should be able to shape a narrative, to argue a subject with some reference to other points of view and to range over a topic with some understanding of how its parts are related to each other and to the whole discussion. Because spoken language is usually a face-to-face activity, he should be sensitive to the language of others, and be able to accommodate himself to it when some cooperative activity using language is required. These oral uses of language are the 'informal' ones and they are needed by everyone as a participant in a community's affairs. The more formal uses, speech-making and debate, have weaker claims, and it would be inappropriate to expect achievement in formal speaking from many 16-year-olds. Yet they will all encounter the formal uses as listeners, and they will need to understand what part such uses play in the whole language activity of men. From that understanding, and with more experience, there will come the confidence to meet a wider range of demands in their oral language resources, both the informal and the formal.

If young people are to be better equipped for the linguistic ways of the world, we must all understand that a richer language environment brings two interrelated benefits — better language resources for the learner, and better learning. We need to examine our practices in order to discard those attitudes to language which limit pupils' achievement and confidence. We need to make children aware of the conventional aspects, but not to bind them tightly with the conventions. To understand how language works for individuals in society is not to neglect the grammatical and formal qualities; it is to put these qualities into a fuller understanding of the context, the 'audience' and the specific task. Children need to remain confident and adventurous in language, so that they do not become victims of the linguistic designs of others upon them. They need to add to the quality of linguistic tolerance in our society, but at the same time to be equipped to deal appropriately with the linguistic intolerance that they will encounter. A 16-year old at the end of his education can be expected to talk, listen, read and write effectively in a range of situations, and not merely to pass some formal tests in a limited range of language skills. His linguistic education cannot end at 16, however, and the most important expectation is that he should be equipped to continue it therefore, creating for himself, if need be, the opportunities for doing so.

Notes

[1] *A language for life*: HMSO 1975, pp. 434-439.

[2] See *Towards an analysis of discourse: the English used by teachers and pupils*, J. McH Sinclair and R. M. Coulthard, Oxford University Press, 1975.

[3] Throughout most of this paper, the references to 'English' are intended to include those parts of work in 'Drama' which share the aims of the teaching of English. Drama will supply, often vividly and memorably, some of the contexts and situations in which language does occur. It is capable of increasing an understanding of language which is claimed as important for English. But 'Drama' is not merely a part of 'English', and its role in the curriculum is more fully explored later in the report.

SECTION 4
Language and Literature

Introduction

The 'Language in Use' course looks at literature as a specific instance of language usage, and attempts to see to what degree the modes of description offered in that course are indeed applicable to literature. Conversely, the course examines the extent to which descriptions of literature can be generalized to apply to other examples of language in use.

The first reading (Lévi-Strauss) has by now attained the status of a classic. Written as a contribution to social anthropology, it illustrates the way in which a structuralist analysis of a corpus of myth can produce a codification of the material which a simple linear account of the narrative content would be incapable of producing. This codification is then submitted to a set of transformational procedures which, it is argued, reveal the true meaning of the texts.

The second reading (Barthes) was written as a contribution to this structural tradition of analysis. Its approach is somewhat different, however, in that it attempts to provide a grammar of narrative consisting of elements at several constitutive levels, together with a set of transformational procedures that provides linkages between them. It is not just the multiplicity of levels that distinguishes this presentation from that of Lévi-Strauss, but also the fact that, as a method, it is specifically designed to deal with all forms of narrative.

The third reading (Goldmann), although it too is described by its author as structuralist in approach, is in fact markedly different, and its affiliations are with sociology rather than anthropology or linguistics. Its main argument is that there exists a similarity of form between the structure of a given work of literature and that of the social grouping whose world-view it represents. Thus, it is claimed, a study of the structure of a work of literature can provide us with a uniquely privileged access to an understanding of the society in which it originated.

The final reading in this section (Macherey and Balibar) takes issue with most of these claims. It emphasizes the role of the reader as a part of the process of production. and, in its stress on text as something produced and worked upon, rather than pre-existent or transcendent, it constitutes a deliberately materialist approach to the debate. Seeing 'literature' as a text scarred and fissured by conflicts of ideology rather than as something transcending them, it points to absences and silences within the text as being equally as revealing as anything that is present within it.

This final reading, therefore, returns us to a consideration of issues discussed elsewhere in the 'Language in Use' course; the functioning of language as a mediator of ideology, the extent to which our perceptions of the world are limited or constrained by the language available to us, and the way in which we continuously construct our picture of reality by, through, or even in opposition to, the language uses we encounter.

P. H. Griffith

4.1 The Structural Study of Myth
Claude Lévi-Strauss

> It would seem that mythological worlds
> have been built up only to be shattered
> again, and that new worlds were built
> from the fragments.

Franz Boas[1]

[. . .] Of all the chapters of religious anthropology probably none has tarried to the same extent as studies in the field of mythology. From a theoretical point of view the situation remains very much the same as it was fifty years ago, namely, chaotic. Myths are still widely interpreted in conflicting ways: as collective dreams, as the outcome of a kind of aesthetic play, or as the basis of ritual. Mythological figures are considered as personified abstractions, divinized heroes, or fallen gods. Whatever the hypothesis, the choice amounts to reducing mythology either to idle play or to a crude kind of philosophic speculation.

In order to understand what a myth really is, must we choose between platitude and sophism? Some claim that human societies merely express, through their mythology, fundamental feelings common to the whole of mankind, such as love, hate, or revenge or that they try to provide some kind of explanations for phenomena which they cannot otherwise understand — astronomical, meteorological, and the like. But why should these societies do it in such elaborate and devious ways, when all of them are also acquainted with empirical explanations? On the other hand, psychoanalysts and many anthropologists have shifted the problems away from the natural or cosmological toward the sociological and psychological fields. But then the interpretation becomes too easy: If a given mythology confers prominence on a certain figure, let us say an evil grandmother, it will be claimed that in such a society grandmothers are actually evil and that mythology reflects the social structure and the social relations; but should the actual data be conflicting, it would be as readily claimed that the

Claude Lévi-Strauss, (1955) 'The Structural Study of Myth', originally in *Journal of American Folklore*, Vol. CXXVIII, No. 270, Oct-Dec. 1955, pp. 428-44.

The article has been edited, and only the first part appears in this reader.

purpose of mythology is to provide an outlet for repressed feelings. Whatever the situation, a clever dialectic will always find a way to pretend that a meaning has been found.

Mythology confronts the student with a situation which at first sight appears contradictory. On the one hand it would seem that in the course of a myth anything is likely to happen. There is no logic, no continuity. Any characteristic can be attributed to any subject; every conceivable relation can be found. With myth, everything becomes possible. But on the other hand, this apparent arbitrariness is belied by the astounding similarity between myths collected in widely different regions. Therefore the problem: If the content of a myth is contingent, how are we going to explain the fact that myths throughout the world are so similar?

It is precisely this awareness of a basic antinomy pertaining to the nature of myth that may lead us toward its solution. For the contradiction which we face is very similar to that which in earlier times brought considerable worry to the first philosophers concerned with linguistic problems; linguistics could only begin to evolve as a science after this contradiction had been overcome. Ancient philosophers reasoned about language the way we do about mythology. On the one hand, they did notice that in a given language certain sequences of sounds were associated with definite meanings, and they earnestly aimed at discovering a reason for the linkage between those *sounds* and that *meaning*. Their attempt, however, was thwarted from the very beginning by the fact that the same sounds were equally present in other languages although the meaning they conveyed was entirely different. The contradiction was surmounted only by the discovery that it is the combination of sounds, not the sounds themselves, which provides the significant data.

It is easy to see, moreover, that some of the more recent interpretations of mythological thought originated from the same kind of misconception under which those early linguists were labouring. Let us consider, for instance, Jung's idea that a given mythological pattern — the so-called archetype — possesses a certain meaning. This is comparable to the long-supported error that a sound may possess a certain affinity with a meaning: for instance, the 'liquid' semi-vowels with water, the open vowels with things that are big, large, loud, or heavy, etc., a theory which still has its supporters.[2] Whatever emendations the original formulation may now call for,[3] everybody will agree that the Saussurean principle of the *arbitrary character of linguistic signs* was a prerequisite for the accession of linguistics to the scientific level.

To invite the mythologist to compare his precarious situation with that of the linguist in the prescientific stage is not enough. As a matter of fact we may thus be led only from one difficulty to another. There is a very good reason why myth cannot simply be treated as language if its specific problems are to be solved; myth *is* language: to be known, myth has to be told; it is a part of human speech. In order to preserve its specificity we must be able to show that it is both the same thing as language, and also something different from it. Here, too, the past experience of linguists may help us. For language itself can be analysed into things which are at the same time similar and yet different. This is precisely what is expressed in Saussure's distinction between *langue* and *parole*, one being the structural side of language, the other the statistical aspect of it, *langue* belonging to a reversible time, *parole* being non-reversible. If those two levels already exist in language, then a third one can conceivably be isolated.

We have distinguished *langue* and *parole* by the different time referents which they use. Keeping this in mind, we may notice that myth uses a third referent which combines the properties of the first two. On the one hand, a myth always refers to events alleged to have taken place long ago. But what gives the myth an operational value is that the specific pattern described is timeless; it explains the present and the past as well as the future. This can be made clear through a comparison between myth and what appears to have largely replaced it in modern societies, namely, politics. When the historian refers to the French Revolution, it is always as a sequence of past happenings, a non-reversible series of events the remote consequences of which may still be felt at present. But to the French politician, as well as to his followers, the French Revolution is both a sequence belonging to the past — as to the historian — and a timeless pattern which can be detected in the contemporary French social structure and which provides a clue for its interpretation, a lead from which to infer future developments. Michelet, for instance, was a politically minded historian. He describes the French Revolution thus: 'That day . . . everything was possible . . . Future became present . . . that is, no more time, a glimpse of eternity.'[4] It is that double structure, altogether historical and ahistorical, which explains how myth, while pertaining to the realm of *parole* and calling for an explanation as such, as well as to that of *langue* in which it is expressed, can also be an absolute entity on a third level which, though it remains linguistic by nature, is nevertheless distinct from the other two.

A remark can be introduced at this point which will help to show the originality of myth in relation to other linguistic phenomena. Myth is the part of language where the formula *traduttore, tradittore* reaches its lowest truth value. From that point of view it should be placed in the gamut of linguistic expressions at the end opposite to that of poetry, in spite of all the claims which have been made to prove the contrary. Poetry is a kind of speech which cannot be translated except at the cost of serious distortions; whereas the mythical value of the myth is preserved even through the worst translation. Whatever our ignorance of the language and the culture of the people where it originated, a myth is still felt as a myth by any reader anywhere in the world. Its substance does not lie in its style, its original music, or its syntax, but in the *story* which it tells. Myth is language, functioning on an especially high level where meaning succeeds practically at 'taking off' from the linguistic ground on which it keeps on rolling.

To sum up the discussion at this point, we have so far made the following claims: (1) If there is a meaning to be found in mythology, it cannot reside in the isolated elements which enter into the composition of a myth, but only in the way those elements are combined. (2) Although myth belongs to the same category as language, being, as a matter of fact, only part of it, language in myth exhibits specific properties. (3) Those properties are only to be found *above* the ordinary linguistic level, that is, they exhibit more complex features than those which are to be found in any other kind of linguistic expression.

If the above three points are granted, at least as a working hypothesis, two consequences will follow: (1) Myth, like the rest of language, is made up of constituent units. (2) These constituent units presuppose the constituent units present in language when analysed on other levels — namely, phonemes, morphemes, and sememes — but they, nevertheless, differ from the latter in the same way as the latter differ among themselves; they belong to a higher and more complex order. For this reason, we shall call them *gross constituent units*.

How shall we proceed in order to identify and isolate these gross constituent units or mythemes? We know that they cannot be found among phonemes, morphemes, or sememes, but only on a higher level; otherwise myth would become confused with any other kind of speech. Therefore, we should look for them on the sentence level. The only method we can suggest at this stage is to proceed tentatively, by trial and error, using as a check the principles which serve as a basis for any kind of structural analysis: economy of explanation; unity of solution; and ability to reconstruct the whole from a fragment, as well as later stages from previous ones.

The technique which has been applied so far by this writer consists in analysing each myth individually, breaking down its story into the shortest possible sentences, and writing each sentence on an index card bearing a number corresponding to the unfolding of the story.

Practically each card will thus show that a certain function is, at a given time, linked to a given subject. Or, to put it otherwise, each gross constituent unit will consist of a *relation*.

However, the above definition remains highly unsatisfactory for two different reasons. First, it is well known to structural linguists that constituent units on all levels are made up of relations, and the true difference between our *gross* units and the others remains unexplained; second, we still find ourselves in the realm of a non-reversible time, since the numbers of the cards correspond to the unfolding of the narrative. Thus the specific character of mythological time, which as we have seen is both reversible and non-reversible, synchronic and diachronic, remains unaccounted for. From this springs a new hypothesis, which constitutes the very core of our argument: The true constituent units of a myth are not the isolated relations but *bundles of such relations*, and it is only as bundles that these relations can be put to use and combined so as to produce a meaning. Relations pertaining to the same bundle may appear diachronically at remote intervals, but when we have succeeded in grouping them together we have reorganized our myth according to a time referent of a new nature, corresponding to the prerequisite of the initial hypothesis, namely a two-dimensional time referent which is simultaneously diachronic and synchronic, and which accordingly integrates the characteristics of *langue* on the one hand, and those of *parole* on the other. To put it in even more linguistic terms, it is as though a phoneme were always made up of all its variants.

Two comparisons may help to explain what we have in mind.

Let us first suppose that archaeologists of the future coming from another planet would one day, when all human life had disappeared from the earth, excavate one of our libraries. Even if they were at first ignorant of our writing, they might succeed in deciphering it — an undertaking which would require, at some early stage, the discovery that the alphabet, as we are in the habit of printing it, should be read from left to right and from top to bottom. However, they would soon discover that a whole category of books did not fit the usual pattern — these would be the orchestra scores on the shelves of the music division. But after trying, without success, to decipher staffs one after the other, from the upper down to the lower, they would probably notice that the same patterns of notes recurred at intervals, either in full or in part, or that some patterns were strongly reminiscent of earlier ones. Hence the hypothesis: What if patterns showing affinity, instead of being considered in succession, were to be treated as one complex pattern and read as a whole? By getting at what we call *harmony*, they would then see that an orchestra score, to be meaningful, must be read diachronically along one axis — that is, page after page, and from left to right — and synchronically along the other axis, all the notes written vertically making up one gross constituent unit, that is, one bundle of relations.

The other comparison is somewhat different. Let us take an observer ignorant of our playing cards, sitting for a long time with a fortune-teller. He would know something of the visitors: sex, age, physical appearance, social situation, etc., in the same way as we know something of the different cultures whose myths we try to study. He would also listen to the seances and record them so as to be able to go over them and make comparisons — as we do when we listen to myth-telling and record it. Mathematicians to whom I have put the problem agree that if the man is bright and if the material available to him is sufficient, he may be able to reconstruct the nature of the deck of cards being used, that is, fifty-two or thirty-two cards according to the case, made up of four homologous sets consisting of the same units (the individual cards) with only one varying feature, the suit.

Now for a concrete example of the method we propose. We shall use the Oedipus myth, which is well known to everyone. I am well aware that the Oedipus myth has only reached us under late forms and through literary transmutations concerned more with aesthetic and moral preoccupations than with religious or ritual ones, whatever these may have been. But we shall not interpret the Oedipus myth in literal terms, much less offer an explanation acceptable to the specialist. We simply wish to illustrate — and without reaching any conclusions with respect to it — a certain technique, whose use is probably not legitimate in this particular instance, owing to the problematic elements indicated above. The 'demonstration' should therefore be conceived, not in terms of what the scientist means by this term, but at best in terms of what is meant by the street peddler, whose aim is not to achieve a concrete result, but to explain, as succinctly as possible, the functioning of the mechanical toy which he is trying to sell to the onlookers.

The myth will be treated as an orchestra score would be if it were unwittingly considered as a unilinear series; our task is to reestablish the correct arrangement. Say, for instance, we were confronted with a sequence of the type: 1, 2, 4, 7, 8, 2, 3, 4, 6, 8, 1, 4, 5, 7, 8, 1, 2, 5, 7, 3, 4, 5, 6, 8 . . ., the assignment being to put all the 1's together, all the 2's, the 3's, etc.; the result is a chart:

1	2		4			7	8
	2	3	4		6		8
1			4	5		7	8
1	2			5		7	
		3	4	5	6		8

We shall attempt to perform the same kind of operation on the Oedipus myth, trying out several arrangements of the mythemes until we find one which is in harmony with the principles enumerated above. Let us suppose, for the sake of argument, that the best arrangement is the one on the top of the following page (although it might certainly be improved with the help of a specialist in Greek mythology).

We thus find ourselves confronted with four vertical columns, each of which includes several relations belonging to the same bundle. Were we to *tell* the myth, we would disregard the columns and read the rows from left to right and from top to bottom. But if we want to *understand* the myth, then we will have to disregard one half of the diachronic dimension (top to bottom) and read from left to right, column after column, each one being considered as a unit.

Cadmos seeks his sister Europa, ravished by Zeus		
		Cadmos kills the dragon
	The Spartoi kill one another	
		Labdacos (Laios' father) = *lame (?)*
	Oedipus kills his father, Laios	Laios (Oedipus' father) = *left-sided (?)*
		Oedipus kills the Sphinx
		Oedipus = *swollen-foot (?)*
Oedipus marries his mother, Jocasta		
	Eteocles kills his brother, Polynices	
Antigone buries her brother, Polynices, despite prohibition		

All the relations belonging to the same column exhibit one common feature which it is our task to discover. For instance, all the events grouped in the first column on the left have something to do with blood relations which are overemphasized, that is, are more intimate than they should be. Let us say, then, that the first column has as its common feature the *overrating of blood relations*. It is obvious that the second column expresses the same thing, but inverted: *underrating of blood relations*. The third column refers to monsters being slain. As to the fourth, a few words of clarification are needed. The remarkable connotation of the surnames in Oedipus' father-line has often been noticed. However, linguists usually disregard it, since to them the only way to define the meaning of a term is to investigate all the contexts in which it appears, and personal names, precisely because they are used as such, are not accompanied by any context. With the method we propose to follow the objection disappears, since the myth itself provides its own context. The significance is no longer to be sought in the eventual meaning of each name, but in the fact that all the names have a common feature: All the hypothetical meanings (which may well remain hypothetical) refer to *difficulties in walking straight and standing upright*.

What then is the relationship between the two columns on the right? Column three refers to monsters. The dragon is a chthonian being which has to be killed in order that mankind be born from the Earth; the Sphinx is a monster unwilling to permit men to live. The last unit reproduces the first one, which has to do with the *autochthonous origin* of mankind. Since the monsters are overcome by men, we may thus say that the common feature of the third column is *denial of the auto-chthonous origin of man.* [5]

This immediately helps us to understand the meaning of the fourth column. In mythology it is a universal characteristic of men born from the Earth that at the moment they emerge from the depth they either cannot walk or they walk clumsily. [. . .]

Thus the common feature of the fourth column is *the persistence of the autochthonous origin of man.* It follows that column four is to column three as column one is to column two. The inability to connect two kinds of relationships is overcome (or rather replaced) by the assertion that contradictory relationships are identical inasmuch as they are both self-contradictory in a similar way. Although this is still a provisional formulation of the structure of mythical thought, it is sufficient at this stage.

Turning back to the Oedipus myth, we may now see what it means. The myth has to do with the inability, for a culture which holds the belief that mankind is autochthonous, [. . .] to find a satisfactory transition between this theory and the knowledge that human beings are actually born from the union of man and woman. Although the problem obviously cannot be solved, the Oedipus myth provides a kind of logical tool which relates the original problem — born from one or born from two? — to the derivative problem: born from different or born from same? By a correlation of this type, the overrating of blood relations is to the underrating of blood relations as the attempt to escape autochthony is to the impossibility to succeed in it. Although experience contradicts theory, social life validates cosmology by its similarity of structure. Hence cosmology is true.

Two remarks should be made at this stage.

In order to interpret the myth, we left aside a point which has worried the specialists until now, namely, that in the earlier (Homeric) versions of the Oedipus myth, some basic elements are lacking, such as Jocasta killing herself and Oedipus piercing his own eyes. These events do not alter the substance of the myth although they can easily be integrated, the first one as a new case of autodestruction (column three) and the second as another case of crippledness (column four). At the same time there is something significant in these additions, since the shift from foot to head is to be correlated with the shift from autochthonous origin to self-destruction.

Our method thus eliminates a problem which has, so far, been one of the main obstacles to the progress of mythological studies, namely, the quest for the *true* version, or the *earlier* one. On the contrary, we define the myth as consisting of all its versions; or to put it otherwise, a myth remains the same as long as it is felt as such. A striking example is offered by the fact that our interpretation may take into account the Freudian use of the Oedipus myth and is certainly applicable to it. Although the Freudian problem has ceased to be that of autochthony *versus* bisexual reproduction, it is still the problem of understanding how *one* can be born from *two*. How is it that we do not have only one procreator, but a mother plus a father? Therefore, not only Sophocles, but Freud himself, should be included among the recorded versions of the Oedipus myth on a par with earlier or seemingly more 'authentic' versions.

An important consequence follows. If a myth is made up of all its variants, structural analysis should take all of them into account. After analysing all the known variants of the Theban version, we should thus treat the others in the same way: first, the tales about Labdacos' collateral line including Agave, Pentheus, and Jocasta herself; the Theban variant about Lycos with Amphion and Zetos as the city founders; more remote variants concerning Dionysus (Oedipus' matrilateral cousin); and Athenian legends where Cecrops takes the place of Cadmos, etc. For each of them a similar chart should be drawn and then compared and reorganized according to the findings: Cecrops killing the serpent with the parallel episode of Cadmos; abandonment of Dionysus with abandonment of Oedipus; 'Swollen Foot' with Dionysus' *loxias*, that is. walking obliquely; Europa's quest with Antiope's; the founding of Thebes by the Spartoi or by the brothers Amphion and Zetos; Zeus kidnapping Europa and Antiope and the same with Semele; the Theban Oedipus and the Argian Perseus, etc. We shall then have several two-dimensional charts, each dealing with a variant, to be organized in a three-dimensional order, as shown in Figure 1, so that three different readings become possible: left to right, top to bottom, front to back (or vice versa). All of these charts cannot be expected to be identical; but experience shows that any difference to be observed may be correlated with other differences, so that a logical treatment of the whole will allow simplications, the final outcome being the structural law of the myth.

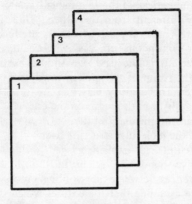

Figure 1

At this point the objection may be raised that the task is impossible to perform, since we can only work with known versions. Is it not possible that a new version might alter the picture? This is true enough if only one or two versions are available, but the objection becomes theoretical as soon as a reasonably large number have been recorded. Let us make this point clear by a comparison. If the furniture of a room and its arrangement were known to us only through its reflection in two mirrors placed on opposite walls, we should theoretically dispose of an almost infinite number of mirror images which would provide us with a complete knowledge. However, should the two mirrors be obliquely set, the number of mirror images would become very small; nevertheless, four or five such images would very likely give us, if not complete informa⁺ion, at least a sufficient coverage so that we would feel sure that no large piece of furniture is missing in our description.

On the other hand, it cannot be too strongly emphasized that all available variants should be taken into account. [. . .]

Three final remarks may serve as conclusion.

First, the question has often been raised why myths, and more generally oral literature, are so much addicted to duplication, triplication, or quadruplication of the same sequence. If our hypotheses are accepted, the answer is obvious: The function of repetition is to render the structure of the myth apparent. For we have seen that the synchronic-diachronic structure of the myth permits us to organize it into diachronic sequences (the rows in our table) which should be read synchronically (the columns). Thus, a myth exhibits a "slated" structure, which comes to the surface, so to speak, through the process of repetition.

However, the slates are not absolutely identical. And since the purpose of myth is to provide a logical model capable of overcoming a contradiction (an impossible achievement if, as it happens, the contradiction is real), a theoretically infinite number of slates will be generated, each one slightly different from the others. Thus, myth grows spiralwise until the intellectual impulse which has produced it is exhausted. Its *growth* is a continuous process, whereas its *structure* remains discontinuous. If this is the case, we should assume that it closely corresponds, in the realm of the spoken word, to a crystal in the realm of physical matter. This analogy may help us to better understand the relationship of myth to both *langue* on the one hand and *parole* on the other. Myth is an intermediary entity between a statistical aggregate of molecules and the molecular structure itself.

Prevalent attempts to explain alleged differences between the so-called primitive mind and scientific thought have resorted to qualitative differences between the working processes of the mind in both cases, while assuming that the entities which they were studying remained very much the same. If our interpretation is correct, we are led toward a completely different view — namely, that the kind of logic in mythical thought is as rigorous as that of modern science, and that the difference lies, not in the quality of the intellectual process, but in the nature of the things to which it is applied. This is well in agreement with the situation known to prevail in the field of technology: What makes a steel axe superior to a stone axe is not that the first one is better made than the second. They are equally well made, but steel is quite different from stone. In the same way we may be able to show that the same logical processes operate in myth as in science, and that man has always been thinking equally well; the improvement lies, not in an alleged progress of man's mind, but in the discovery of new areas to which it may apply its unchanged and unchanging powers.

Notes

[1] In Boas' Introduction to James Teit, 'Traditions of the Thompson River Indians of British Columbia', *Memoirs of the American Folklore Society*, VI *(1898)*, p. 18.
[2] See, for instance, Sir R. A. Paget, 'The Origin of Language', *Journal of World History*, I, No. 2 (UNESCO, 1953).
[3] See Emile Benveniste, 'Nature du signe linguistique', *Acta Linguistica*, I, No. 1, (1939).
[4] Jules Michelet, *Histoire de la Révolution française*, IV. i. I took this quotation from M. Merleau-Ponty, *Les Aventures de la dialectique* (Paris, 1955) p. 273.
[5] We are not trying to become involved with specialists in an argument; this would be presumptuous and even meaningless on our part. Since the Oedipus myth is taken here merely as an example treated in arbitrary fashion, the chthonian nature ascribed to the Sphinx might seem surprising; we shall refer to the testimony of Marie Delcourt: 'In the archaic legends, [she is] certainly born of the Earth itself' (*Oedipe ou la légende du conquérant*, (Liège, 1944) p. 108. No matter how remote from Delcourt's our method may be (and our conclusions would

be, no doubt, if we were competent to deal with the problem in depth) it seems to us that she has convincingly established the nature of the Sphinx in the archaic tradition, namely, that of the female monster who attacks and rapes young men; in other words, the personification of a female being with an inversion of the sign. This explains why, in the handsome iconography compiled by Delcourt at the end of her work, men and women are always found in an inverted 'sky/earth' relationship.

4.2 Introduction to the Structural Analysis of Narratives
Roland Barthes

The narratives of the world are numberless. Narrative is first and foremost a prodigious variety of genres, themselves distributed amongst different substances — as though any material were fit to receive man's stories. Able to be carried by articulated language, spoken or written, fixed or moving images, gestures, and the ordered mixture of all these substances; narrative is present in myth, legend, fable, tale, novella, epic, history, tragedy, drama, comedy, mime, painting (think of Carpaccio's *Saint Ursula*), stained glass windows, cinema, comics, news item, conversation. Moreover, under this almost infinite diversity of forms, narrative is present in every age, in every place, in every society; it begins with the very history of mankind and there nowhere is nor has been a people without narrative. All classes, all human groups, have their narratives, enjoyment of which is very often shared by men with different, even opposing,[1] cultural backgrounds. Caring nothing for the division between good and bad literature, narrative is international, transhistorical, transcultural: it is simply there, like life itself.

Must we conclude from this universality that narrative is insignificant? Is it so general that we can have nothing to say about it except for the modest description of a few highly individualized varieties, something literary history occasionally undertakes? But then how are we to master even these varieties, how are we to justify our right to differentiate and identify them? How is novel to be set against novella, tale against myth, drama against tragedy (as has been done a thousand times) without reference to a common model? Such a model is implied by every proposition relating to the most individual, the most historical, of narrative forms. It is thus legitimate that, far from the abandoning of any idea of dealing with narrative on the grounds of its universality, there should have been (from Aristotle on) a periodic interest in narrative form and it is normal that the newly developing structuralism should make this form one of its first concerns — is not structuralism's constant aim to master the infinity of utterances [*paroles*] by describing the 'language' [*'langue'*] of which they are the products and from which

'Introduction to the Structural Analysis of Narratives', in Heath, S. (trans. and ed.) (1977) *Image – Music – Text*, Fontana/Collins, pp. 79-124. Originally published in French in *Communications*, 8, 1966.

they can be generated. Faced with the infinity of narratives, the multiplicity of standpoints — historical, psychological, sociological, ethnological, aesthetic, etc. — from which they can be studied, the analyst finds himself in more or less the same situation as Saussure confronted by the heterogeneity of language [*langue*] and seeking to extract a principle of classification and a central focus for description from the apparent confusion of the individual messages. Keeping simply to modern times, the Russian Formalists, Propp and Lévi-Strauss have taught us to recognize the following dilemma: either a narrative is merely a rambling collection of events, in which case nothing can be said about it other than by referring back to the storyteller's (the author's) art, talent or genius — all mythical forms of chance[2] — or else it shares with other narratives a common structure which is open to analysis, no matter how much patience its formulation requires. There is a world of difference between the most complex randomness and the most elementary combinatory scheme, and it is impossible to combine (to produce) a narrative without reference to an implicit system of units and rules.

Where then are we to look for the structure of narrative? Doubtless, in narratives themselves. *Each and every* narrative? Many commentators who accept the idea of a narrative structure are nevertheless unable to resign themselves to dissociating literary analysis from the example of the experimental sciences; nothing daunted, they ask that a purely inductive method be applied to narrative and that one start by studying all the narratives within a genre, a period, a society. This commonsense view is utopian. Linguistics itself, with only some three thousand languages to embrace, cannot manage such a programme and has wisely turned deductive, a step which in fact marked its veritable constitution as a science and the beginning of its spectacular progress, it even succeeding in anticipating facts prior to their discovery.[3] So what of narrative analysis, faced as it is with millions of narratives? Of necessity, it is condemned to a deductive procedure, obliged first to devise a hypothetical model of description (what American linguists call a 'theory') and then gradually to work down from this model towards the different narrative species which at once conform to and depart from the model. It is only at the level of these conformities and departures that analysis will be able to come back to, but now equipped with a single descriptive tool, the plurality of narratives, to their historical, geographical and cultural diversity.[4]

Thus, in order to describe and classify the infinite number of narratives, a 'theory' (in this pragmatic sense) is needed and the immediate task is that of finding it, of starting to define it. Its development can be greatly facilitated if one begins from a model able to provide it with its initial terms and principles. In the current state of research, it seems reasonable[5] that the structural analysis of narrative be given linguistics itself as founding model.

I. The Language of Narrative

1. Beyond the sentence

As we know, linguistics stops at the sentence, the last unit which it considers to fall within its scope. If the sentence, being an order and not a series, cannot be reduced to the sum of the words which compose it and constitutes thereby a specific unit, a piece of discourse, on the contrary, is no more than the succession of the sentences composing it. From the point of view of linguistics, there is nothing in discourse that is not to be found in the sentence: 'The sentence,' writes Martinet, 'is the smallest segment that is perfectly and wholly representative of discourse.'[6] Hence there can be no question of linguistics setting itself an object superior to the sentence, since beyond the sentence are only more sentences — having described the flower, the botanist is not to get involved in describing the bouquet.

And yet it is evident that discourse itself (as a set of sentences) is organized and that, through this organization, it can be seen as the message of another language, one operating at a higher level than the language of the linguists.[7] Discourse has its units, its rules, its 'grammar': beyond the sentence, and though consisting solely of sentences, it must naturally form the object of a second linguistics. For a long time indeed, such a linguistics of discourse bore a glorious name, that of Rhetoric. As a result of a complex historical movement, however, in which Rhetoric went over to belles-lettres and the latter was divorced from the study of language, it has recently become necessary to take up the problem afresh. The new linguistics of discourse has still to be developed, but at least it is being postulated, and by the linguists themselves.[8] This last fact is not without significance, for, although constituting an autonomous object, discourse must be studied from the basis of linguistics. If a working hypothesis is needed for an analysis whose task is immense and whose materials infinite, then the most reasonable thing is to posit a homological relation between sentence and discourse insofar as it is likely that a similar formal organization orders all semiotic systems, whatever their substances and dimensions. A discourse is a long 'sentence' (the units of which are not necessarily sentences), just as a sentence, allowing for certain specifications, is a short 'discourse'. This hypothesis accords well with a number of propositions put forward in contemporary anthropology. Jakobson and Lévi-Strauss have pointed out that mankind can be defined by the ability to create secondary — 'self-multiplying' — systems (tools for the manufacture of other tools, double articulation of language, incest taboo permitting the fanning out of families) while the Soviet linguist Ivanov supposes that artificial languages can only have been acquired after natural language: what is important for men is to have the use of several systems of meaning and natural language helps in the elaboration of artificial languages. It is therefore legitimate to posit a 'secondary' relation between sentence and discourse – a relation which will be referred to as homological, in order to respect the purely formal nature of the correspondences.

The general language [*langue*] of narrative is one (and clearly only one) of the idioms apt for consideration by the linguistics of discourse[9] and it accordingly comes under the homological hypothesis. Structurally, narrative shares the characteristics of the sentence without ever being reducible to the simple sum of its sentences: a narrative is a long sentence, just as every constative sentence is in a way the rough outline of a short narrative. Although there provided with different signifiers (often extremely complex), one does find in narrative, expanded and transformed proportionately, the principal verbal categories: tenses, aspects, mood, persons. Moreover the 'subjects' themselves, as opposed to the verbal predicates, readily yield to the sentence model; the actantial typology proposed by A. J. Greimas[10] discovers in the multitude of narrative characters the elementary functions of grammatical analysis. Nor does the homology suggested here have merely a heuristic value: it implies an identity between language and literature (inasmuch as the latter can be seen as a sort of privileged vehicle of narrative). It is hardly possible any longer to conceive of literature as an art that abandons all further relation with language the moment it has used it as an instrument to express ideas, passion or beauty: language never ceases to accompany discourse, holding up to it the mirror of its own structure – does not literature, particularly today, make a language of the very conditions of language?[11]

2. Levels of meaning

From the outset, linguistics furnishes the structural analysis of narrative with a concept which is decisive in that, making explicit immediately what is essential in every system of meaning, namely its organization, it allows us both to show how a narrative is not a simple sum of propositions and to classify the enormous mass of elements which go to make up a narrative. This concept is that of *level of description*.[12]

A sentence can be described, linguistically, on several levels (phonetic, phonological, grammatical, contextual) and these levels are in a hierarchical relationship with one another, for, while all have their own units and correlations (whence the necessity for a separate description of each of them) no level on its own can produce meaning. A unit belonging to a particular level only takes on meaning if it can be integrated in a higher level; a phoneme, though perfectly describable, means nothing in itself: it participates in meaning only when integrated in a word, and the word itself must in turn be integrated in a sentence.[13] The theory of levels (as set out by Benveniste) gives two types of relations: distributional (if the relations are situated on the same level) and integrational (if they are grasped from one level to the next); consequently, distributional relations alone are not sufficient to account for meaning. In order to conduct a structural analysis, it is thus first of all necessary to distinguish several levels or instances of description and to place these instances within a hierarchical (integrationary) perspective.

The levels are operations.[14] It is therefore normal that, as it progresses, linguistics should tend to multiply them. Discourse analysis, however, is as yet only able to work on rudimentary levels. In its own way, rhetoric had assigned at least two planes of description to discourse: *dispositio* and *elocutio*.[15] Today, in his analysis of the structure of myth, Lévi-Strauss has already indicated that the constituent units of mythical discourse (mythemes) acquire meaning only because they are grouped in bundles and because these bundles themselves combine together.[16] As too, Tzvetan Todorov, reviving the distinction made by the Russian Formalists, proposes working on two major levels, themselves subdivided: *story* (the argument), comprising a logic of actions and a 'syntax' of characters, and *discourse*, comprising the tenses, aspects and modes of the narrative.[17] But however many levels are proposed and whatever definition they are given, there can be no doubt that narrative is a hierarchy of instances. To understand a narrative is not merely to follow the unfolding of the story, it is also to recognize its construction in 'storeys', to project the horizontal concatenations of the narrative 'thread' on to an implicitly vertical axis; to read (to listen to) a narrative is not merely to move from one word to the next, it is also to move from one level to the next. Perhaps I may be allowed to offer a kind of apologue in this connection. In *The Purloined Letter*, Poe gives an acute analysis of the failure of the chief commissioner of the Paris police, powerless to find the letter. His investigations, says Poe, were perfect 'within the sphere of his speciality',[18] he searched everywhere, saturated entirely the level of the 'police search', but in order to find the letter, protected by its conspicuousness, it was necessary to shift to another level, to substitute the concealer's principle of relevance for that of the policeman. Similarly, the 'search' carried out over a horizontal set of narrative relations may well be as thorough as possible but must still, to be effective, also operate 'vertically': meaning is not 'at the end' of the narrative, it runs across it; just as conspicuous as the purloined letter, meaning eludes all unilateral investigation.

A great deal of tentative effort is still required before it will be possible to ascertain precisely the levels of narrative. Those that are suggested in what follows constitute a provisional profile whose merit remains almost exclusively didactic; they enable us to locate and group together the different problems, and this without, I think, being at variance with the few analyses so far.[19] It is proposed to distinguish three levels of description in the narrative work: the level of 'functions' (in the sense this word has in Propp and Bremond), the level of 'actions' (in the sense this word has in Greimas when he talks of characters as actants) and the level of 'narration' (which is roughly the level of 'discourse' in Todorov). These three levels are bound together according to a mode of progressive integration: a function only has meaning insofar as it occupies a place in the general action of an actant, and this action in turn receives its final meaning from the fact that it is narrated, entrusted to a discourse which possesses its own code.

II. Functions

1. The determination of the units

Any system being the combination of units of known classes, the first task is to divide up narrative and determine the segments of narrative discourse that can be distributed into a limited number of classes. In a word, we have to define the smallest narrative units.

Given the integrational perspective described above, the analysis cannot rest satisfied with a purely distributional definition of the units. From the start, meaning must be the criterion of the unit: it is the functional nature of certain segments of the story that makes them units — hence the name 'functions' immediately attributed to these first units. Since the Russian Formalists,[20] a unit has been taken as any segment of the story which can be seen as the term of a correlation. The essence of a function is, so to speak, the seed that it sows in the narrative, planting an element that will come to fruition later — either on the same level or elsewhere, on another level. If in *Un Cœur Simple* Flaubert at one point tells the reader, seemingly without emphasis, that the daughters of the Sous-Préfet of Pont-l'Evêque owned a parrot, it is because this parrot is subsequently to have a great importance in Félicité's life: the statement of this detail (whatever its linguistic form) thus constitutes a function, or narrative unit.

Is everything in a narrative function? Does everything, down to the slightest detail, have a meaning? Can narrative be divided up entirely into functional units? We shall see in a moment that there are several kinds of functions, there being several kinds of correlations, but this does not alter the fact that a narrative is never made up of anything other than functions: in differing degrees, everything in it signifies. This is not a matter of art (on the part of the narrator), but of structure; in the realm of discourse, what is noted is by definition notable. Even were a detail to appear irretrievably insignificant, resistant to all functionality, it would nonetheless end up with precisely the meaning of absurdity or uselessness: everything has a meaning, or nothing has. To put it another way, one could say that art is without noise (as that term is employed in information theory):[21] art is a system which is pure, no unit ever goes wasted,[22] however long, however loose, however tenuous may be the thread connecting it to one of the levels of the story[23]

From the linguistic point of view, the function is clearly a unit of content: it is 'what it says' that makes of a statement a functional unit,[24] not the manner in which it is said. This constitutive signified may have a number of different signifiers, often very intricate. If I am told (in *Goldfinger*) that *Bond saw a man of about fifty*, the piece of information holds simultaneously two functions of unequal pressure: on the one hand, the character's age fits into a certain description of the man (the 'usefulness' of which for the rest of the story is not nil, but diffuse, delayed); while on the other, the immediate signified of the statement is that Bond is unacquainted with his future interlocutor, the unit thus implying a very strong correlation (initiation of a threat and the need to establish the man's identity). In order to determine the initial narrative units, it is therefore vital never to lose sight of the functional nature of the segments under consideration and to recognize in advance that they will not necessarily coincide with the forms into which we traditionally cast the various parts of narrative discourse (actions, scenes, paragraphs, dialogues, interior monologues, etc.) still less with 'psychological' divisions (modes of behaviour, feelings, intentions, motivations, rationalizations of characters).

In the same way, since the 'language' [*'langue'*] of narrative is not the language [*langue*] of articulated language [*langue articulée*] — though very often vehicled by it — narrative units will be substantially independent of linguistic units; they may indeed coincide with the latter, but occasionally, not systematically. Functions will be represented sometimes by units higher than the sentence (groups of sentences of varying lengths, up to the work in its entirety) and sometimes by lower ones (syntagm, word and even, within the word, certain literary elements only[25]). When we are told that — the telephone ringing during night duty at Secret Service headquarters — *Bond picked up one of the four receivers,* the moneme *four* in itself constitutes a functional unit, referring as it does to a concept necessary to the story (that of a highly developed bureaucratic technology). In fact, the narrative unit in this case is not the linguistic unit (the word) but only its connoted value (linguistically, the word /four/ never means 'four'); which explains how certain functional units can be shorter than the sentence without ceasing to belong to the order of discourse: such units then extend not beyond the sentence, than which they remain materially shorter, but beyond the level of denotation, which, like the sentence, is the province of linguistics properly speaking.

2. Classes of units

The functional units must be distributed into a small number of classes. If these classes are to be determined without recourse to the substance of content (psychological substance for example), it is again necessary to consider the different levels of meaning: some units have as correlates units on the same level, while the saturation of others requires a change of levels; hence, straightaway, two major classes of functions, distributional and integrational. The former correspond to what Propp and subsequently Bremond (in particular) take as functions but they will be treated here in a much more detailed way than is the case in their work. The term *'functions'* will be reserved for these units (though the other units are also functional), the model of description for which has become classic since Tomachevski's analysis: the purchase of a revolver has for correlate the moment when it will be used (and if not used, the notation is reversed into a sign of indecision, etc.); picking up the telephone has for correlate the moment when it will be put down; the intrusion of the parrot into Félicité's home has for correlate the episode of the stuffing, the worshipping of the parrot, etc. As for the latter, the integrational units, these comprise all the *'indices'* (in the very broad sense of the word[26]), the unit now referring not to a complementary and consequential act but to a more or less diffuse concept which is nevertheless necessary to the meaning of the story: psychological indices concerning the characters, data regarding their identity, notations of 'atmosphere', and so on. The relation between the unit and its correlate is now no longer distributional (often several indices refer to the same signified and the order of their occurrence in the discourse is not necessarily pertinent) but integrational. In order to understand what an indicial notation 'is for', one must move to a higher level (characters' actions or narration), for only there is the indice clarified: the power of the administrative machine behind Bond, indexed by the number of telephones, has no bearing on the sequence of actions in which Bond is involved by answering the call; it finds its meaning only on the level of a general typology of the actants (Bond is on the side of order). Indices, because of the, in some sort, vertical nature of their relations, are truly semantic units: unlike 'functions' (in the strict sense), they refer to a signified, not to an 'operation'. The ratification of indices is 'higher up', sometimes even remaining virtual, outside any explicit syntagm (the 'character' of a narrative agent may very well never be explicitly named while yet being constantly indexed), is a paradigmatic ratification. That of functions, by contrast, is always 'further on', is a syntagmatic ratification.[27] *Functions* and *indices* thus overlay another classic distinction: functions involve metonymic relata, indices metaphoric relata; the former correspond to a functionality of doing, the latter to a functionality of being.[28]

These two main classes of units, functions and indices, should already allow a certain classification of narratives. Some narratives are heavily functional (such as folktales), while others on the contrary are heavily indicial (such as 'psychological' novels); between these two poles lies a whole series of intermediary forms, dependent on history, society, genre. But we can go further. Within each of the two main classes it is immediately possible to determine two sub-classes of narrative units. Returning to the class of functions, its units are not all of the same 'importance': some constitute real hinge-points of the narrative (or of a fragment of the narrative); others merely 'fill in' the narrative space separating the hinge functions. Let us call the former *cardinal functions* (or *nuclei*) and the latter, having regard to their complementary nature, *catalysers*. For a function to be cardinal, it is enough that the action to which it refers open (or continue, or close) an alternative that is of direct consequence for the subsequent development of the story, in short that it inaugurate or conclude an uncertainty. If, in a fragment of narrative, *the telephone rings*, it is equally possible to answer or not answer: two acts which will unfailingly carry the narrative along different paths. Between two cardinal functions however, it is always possible to set out subsidiary notations which cluster around one or other nucleus without modifying its alternative nature: the space separating *the telephone rang* from *Bond answered* can be saturated with a host of trivial incidents or descriptions — *Bond moved towards the desk, picked up one of the receivers, put down his cigarette*, etc. These catalysers are still functional, insofar as they enter into correlation with a nucleus, but their functionality is attenuated, unilateral, parasitic; it is a question of a purely chronological functionality (what is described is what separates two moments of the story), whereas the tie between two cardinal functions is invested with a double functionality, at once chronological and logical. Catalysers are only consecutive units, cardinal functions are both consecutive and consequential. Everything suggests, indeed, that the mainspring of narrative is precisely the confusion of consecution and consequence, what comes *after* being read in narrative as what is *caused by*: in which case narrative would be a systematic application of the logical fallacy denounced by Scholasticism in the formula *post hoc, ergo propter hoc* — a good motto for Destiny, of which narrative all things considered is no more than the 'language'.

It is the structural framework of cardinal functions which accomplishes this 'telescoping' of logic and temporality. At first sight, such functions may appear extremely insignificant; what defines them is not their spectacularity (importance, volume, unusualness or force of the narrated action) but, so to speak, the risk they entail: cardinal functions are the risky moments of a narrative. Between these points of alternative, these 'dispatchers', the catalysers lay out areas of safety, rests, luxuries. Luxuries which are not, however, useless: it must be stressed again that from the point of view of the story a catalyser's functionality may be weak but not nil. Were a catalyser purely redundant (in relation to its nucleus), it would nonetheless participate in the economy of the message; in fact, an apparently merely expletive notation always has a discursive function: it accelerates, delays, gives fresh impetus to the discourse, it summarizes, anticipates and sometimes even leads astray.[29] Since what is noted always appears as being notable, the catalyser ceaselessly revives the semantic tension of the discourse, says ceaselessly that there has been, that there is going to be, meaning. Thus, in the final analysis, the catalyser has a constant function which is, to use Jakobson's term, a phatic one: [30] it maintains the contact between narrator and addressee. A nucleus cannot be deleted without altering the story, but neither can a catalyst without altering the discourse.

As for the other main class of units, the indices, an integrational class, its units have in common that they can only be saturated (completed) on the level of characters or on the level of narration. They are thus part of a *parametrical* relation[31] whose second — implicit — term is continuous, extended over an episode, a character or the whole work. A distinction can be made, however, between *indices* proper, referring to the character of a narrative agent, a feeling, an atmosphere (for example suspicion) or a philosophy, and *informants*, serving to identify, to locate in time and space. To say that through the window of the office where Bond is on duty the moon can be seen half-hidden by thick billowing clouds, is to index a stormy summer night, this deduction in turn forming an index of atmosphere with reference to the heavy, anguish-laden climate of an action as yet unknown to the reader. Indices always have implicit signifieds. Informants, however, do not, at least on the level of the story: they are pure data with immediate signification. Indices involve an activity of deciphering, the reader is to learn to know a character or an atmosphere; informants bring ready-made knowledge, their functionality, like that of catalysers, is thus weak without being nil. Whatever its 'flatness' in relation to the rest of the story, the informant (for example, the exact age of a character) always serves to authenticate the reality of the referent, to embed fiction in the real world. Informants are realist operators and as such possess an undeniable functionality not on the level of the story but on that of the discourse.[32]

Nuclei and catalysers, indices and informants (again, the names are of little importance), these, it seems, are the initial classes into which the functional level units can be divided. This classification must be completed by two remarks. Firstly, a unit can at the same time belong to two different classes: to drink a whisky (in an airport lounge) is an action which can act as a catalyser to the (cardinal) notation of *waiting* but it is also, and simultaneously, the indice of a certain atmosphere (modernity, relaxation, reminiscence, etc.). In other words, certain units can be mixed, giving a play of possibilities in the narrative economy. In the novel *Goldfinger*, Bond, having to search his adversary's bedroom, is given a master-key by his associate: the notation is a pure (cardinal) function. In the film, this detail is altered and Bond laughingly takes a set of keys from a willing chamber-maid: the notation is no longer simply functional but also indicial, referring to Bond's character (his easy charm and success with women). Secondly, it should be noted (this will be taken up again later) that the four classes just described can be distributed in a different way which is moreover closer to the linguistic model. Catalysers, indices and informants have a common characteristic: in relation to nuclei, they are *expansions*. Nuclei (as will be seen in a moment) form finite sets grouping a small number of terms, are governed by a logic, are at once necessary and sufficient. Once the framework they provide is given, the other units fill it out according to a mode of proliferation in principle infinite. As we know, this is what happens in the case of the sentence, which is made up of simple proportions endlessly complicated with duplications, paddings, embeddings and so on. So great an importance did Mallarmé attach to this type of structure that from it he constructed *Jamais un coup de dés,* a poem which with its 'nodes' and 'loops', its 'nucleus-words' and its 'lace-words', can well be regarded as the emblem of every narrative — of every language.

3. Functional syntax

How, according to what 'grammar', are the different units strung together along the narrative syntagm? What are the rules of the functional combinatory system? Informants and indices can combine freely together: as for example in the portrait which readily juxtaposes data concerning civil status and traits of character. Catalysers and nuclei are linked by a simple relation of implication: a catalyser necessarily implies the existence of a cardinal function to which it can connect, but not vice-versa. As for cardinal functions, they are bound together by a relation of solidarity: a function of this type calls for another function of the same type and reciprocally. It is this last relation which needs to be considered further for a moment — first, because it defines the very framework of the narrative (expansions can be deleted, nuclei cannot); second, because it is the main concern of those trying to work towards a structure of narrative.

It has already been pointed out that structurally narrative institutes a confusion between consecution and consequence, temporality and logic. This ambiguity forms the central problem of narrative syntax. Is there an atemporal logic lying behind the temporality of narrative? Researchers were still quite recently divided on this point. Propp, whose analytic study of the folktale paved the way for the work going on today, is totally committed to the idea of the irreducibility of the chronological order: he sees time as reality and for this reason is convinced of the necessity for rooting the tale in temporality. Yet Aristotle himself, in his contrast between tragedy (defined by the unity of action) and historical narrative (defined by the plurality of actions and the unity of time), was already giving primacy to the logical over the chronological.[33] As do all contemporary researchers (Lévi-Strauss, Greimas, Bremond, Todorov), all of whom (while differing on other points) could subscribe to Lévi-Strauss's proposition that 'the order of chronological succession is absorbed in an atemporal matrix structure'.[34] Analysis today tends to 'dechronologize' the narrative continuum and to 'relogicize' it, to make it dependent on what Mallarmé called with regard to the French language '*the primitive thunderbolts of logic*',[35] or rather, more exactly (such at least is our wish), the task is to succeed in giving a structural description of the chronological illusion — it is for narrative logic to account for narrative time. To put it another way, one could say that temporality is only a structural category of narrative (of discourse), just as in language [*langue*] temporality only exists in the form of a system; from the point of view of narrative, what we call time does not exist, or at least only exists functionally, as an element of a semiotic system. Time belongs not to discourse strictly speaking but to the referent; both narrative and language know only a semiotic time, 'true' time being a 'realist', referential illusion, as Propp's commentary shows. It is as such that structural analysis must deal with it.[36]

What then is the logic which regulates the principal narrative functions? It is this that current work is actively trying to establish and that has so far been the major focus of debate. Three main directions of research can be seen. The first (Bremond) is more properly logical in approach: it aims to reconstitute the syntax of human behaviour utilized in narrative, to retrace the course of the 'choices' which inevi-ably face[37] the individual character at every point in the story and so to bring out what could be called an energetic logic,[38] since it grasps the characters at the moment when they choose to act. The second (Lévi-Strauss, Jakobson) is linguistic: its essential concern is to demonstrate paradigmatic oppositions in the functions, oppositions which, in accordance with the Jakobsonian definition of the 'poetic',[39] are 'extended' along the line of the narrative (new developments in Greimas's work correct or complete the conception of the paradigmatic nature of functions).[40] The third (Todorov) is somewhat different in that it sets the analysis at the level of the 'actions' (that is to say, of the character), attempting to determine the rules by which narrative combines, varies and transforms a certain number of basic predicates.

There is no question of choosing between these working hypotheses; they are not competitive but concurrent, and at present moreover are in the throes of elaboration. The only complement we will attempt to give them here concerns the dimensions of the analysis. Even leaving aside the indices, informants and catalysers, there still remains in a narrative (especially if it is a novel and no longer a tale) a very large number of cardinal functions and many of these cannot be mastered by the analyses just mentioned, which until now have worked on the major articulations of narrative. Provision needs to be made, however, for a description sufficiently close as to account for *all* the narrative units, for the smallest narrative segments. We must remember that cardinal functions cannot be determined by their 'importance', only by the (doubly implicative) nature of their relations. A 'telephone call', no matter how futile it may seem, on the one hand itself comprises some few cardinal functions (telephone ringing, picking up the receiver, speaking, putting down the receiver), while on the other, taken as a whole, it must be linkable — at the very least proceeding step by step — to the major articulations of the anecdote. The functional covering of the narrative necessitates an organization of relays the basic unit of which can only be a small group of functions, hereafter referred to (following Bremond) as a *sequence*.

A sequence is a logical succession of nuclei bound together by a relation of solidarity:[41] the sequence opens when one of its terms has no solidary antecedent and closes when another of its terms has no consequent. To take a deliberately trivial example, the different functions order a drink, obtain it, drink it, pay for it, constitute an obviously closed sequence, it being impossible to put anything before the order or after the payment without moving out of the homogeneous group *'Having a drink'*. The sequence indeed is always nameable. Determining the major functions of the folktale, Propp and subsequently Bremond have been led to name them (*Fraud, Betrayal, Struggle, Contract, Seduction*, etc.); the naming operation is equally inevitable in the case of trivial sequences, the 'micro-sequences' which often form the finest grain of the narrative tissue. Are these namings solely the province of the analyst? In other words, are they purely metalinguistic? No doubt they are, dealing as they do with the code of narrative. Yet at the same time they can be imagined as forming part of an inner metalanguage in the reader (or listener) him who grasps every logical succession of actions as a nominal whole: to read is to name; to listen is not only to perceive a language, it is also to construct it. Sequence titles are similar enough to the *cover-words* of translation machines which acceptably cover a wide variety of meanings and shades of meaning. The narrative language [*la langue du récit*] within us comprises from the start these essential headings: the closing logic which structures a sequence is inextricably linked to its name; any function which initiates a *seduction* prescribes from the moment it appears, in the name to which it gives rise, the entire process of seduction such as we have learned it from all the narratives which have fashioned in us the language of narrative.

However minimal its importance, a sequence, since it is made up of a small number of nuclei (that is to say, in fact, of 'dispatchers'), always involves moments of risk and it is this which justifies analysing it. It might seem futile to constitute into a sequence the logical succession of trifling acts which go to make up the offer of a cigarette (*offering, accepting, lighting, smoking*), but precisely, at every one of these points, an alternative — and hence a freedom of meaning — is possible. Du Pont, Bond's future partner, offers him a light from his lighter but Bond refuses; the meaning of this bifurcation is that Bond instinctively fears a booby-trapped gadget.[42] A sequence is thus, one can say, a *threatened logical unit,* this being its justification *a minimo.* It is also founded *a maximo*: enclosed on its function, subsumed under a name, the sequence itself constitutes a new unit, ready to function as a simple term in another, more extensive sequence. Here, for example, is a micro-sequence: *hand held out, hand shaken, hand released.* This *Greeting* then becomes a simple function: on the one hand, it assumes the role of an indice (flabbiness of Du Pont, Bond's distaste); on the other, it forms globally a term in a larger sequence, with the name *Meeting,* whose other terms (*approach, halt, interpellation, sitting down*) can themselves be micro-sequences. A whole network of subrogations structures the narrative in this way, from the smallest matrices to the largest functions. What is in question here, of course, is a hierarchy that remains within the functional level: it is only when it has been possible to widen the narrative out step by step, from Du Pont's cigarette to Bond's battle against Goldfinger, that functional analysis is over – the pyramid of functions then touches the next level (that of the Actions). There is both a syntax within the sequences and a (subrogating) syntax between the sequences together. The first episode of *Goldfinger* thus takes on a 'stemmatic' aspect:

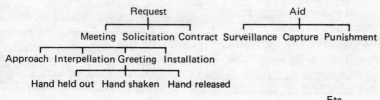

Obviously this representation is analytical; the reader perceives a linear succession of terms. What needs to be noted, however, is that the terms from several sequences can easily be imbricated in one another: a sequence is not yet completed when already, cutting in, the first term of a new sequence may appear. Sequences move in counterpoint;[43] functionally, the structure of narrative is fugued; thus it is that narrative at once 'holds' and 'pulls on'. Within the single work, the imbrication of sequences can indeed only be allowed to come to a halt with a radical break if the sealed-off blocks which then compose it are in some sort recuperated at the higher level of the Actions (of the characters). *Goldfinger* is composed of three functionally independent episodes, their functional stemmas twice ceasing to intercommunicate: there is no sequential relation between the swimming-pool episode and the Fort Knox episode; but there remains an actantial relation, for the characters (and consequently the structure of their relations) are the same. One can recognize here the epic pattern (a 'whole made of multiple fables'): the epic is a narrative broken at the functional level but unitary at the actantial level (something which can be verified in the *Odyssey* or in Brecht's plays). The level of functions (which provides the major part of the narrative syntagm) must thus be capped by a higher level from which, step by step, the first level units draw their meaning, the level of actions.

III. Actions

1. Towards a structural status of characters

In Aristotelian poetics, the notion of character is secondary, entirely subsidiary to the notion of action: there may be actions without 'characters', says Aristotle, but not characters without an action; a view taken over by classical theoreticians (Vossius). Later the character, who until then had been only a name, the agent of an action,[44] acquired a psychological consistency, became an individual, a 'person', in short a fully constituted 'being', even should he do nothing and of course even before acting.[45] Characters stopped being subordinate to the action, embodied immediately psychological essences; which essences could be drawn up into lists, as can be seen in its purest form in the list of 'character parts' in bourgeois theatre (the coquette, the noble father, etc.). From its very outset, structural analysis has shown the utmost reluctance to treat the character as an essence, even merely for purposes of classification. Tomachevski went so far as to deny the character any narrative importance, a point of view he subsequently modified. Without leaving characters out of the analysis altogether, Propp reduced them to a simple typology based not on psychology but on the unity of the actions assigned them by the narrative (*Donor of a magical agent, Helper, Villain*, etc.).

Since Propp, the character has constantly set the structural analysis of narrative the same problem. On the one hand, the characters (whatever one calls them – *dramatis personae* or *actants*) form a necessary plane of description, outside of which the slightest reported 'actions' cease to be intelligible; so that it can be said that there is not a single narrative in the world without 'characters',[46] or at least without agents. Yet on the other hand, these – extremely numerous – 'agents' can be neither described nor classified in terms of 'persons' – whether the 'person' be considered as a purely historical form, limited to certain genres (those most familiar to us it is true), in which case it is necessary to leave out of account the very large number of narratives (popular tales, modern texts) comprising agents but not persons, or whether the 'person' is declared to be no more than a critical rationalization foisted by our age on pure narrative agents. Structural analysis, much concerned not to define characters in terms of psychological essences, has so far striven, using various hypotheses, to define a character not as a 'being' but as a 'participant'. For Bremond, every character (even secondary) can be the agent of sequences of actions which belong to him (*Fraud, Seduction*); when a single sequence involves two characters (as is usual), it comprises two perspectives, two names (what is *Fraud* for the one is *Gullibility* for the other); in short, every character (even secondary) is the hero of his own sequence. Todorov, analysing a 'psychological' novel (*Les Liaisons Dangereuses*), starts not from the character-persons but from the three major relationships in which they can engage and which he calls base predicates (love, communication, help). The analysis brings these relationships under two sorts of rules: rules of *derivation*, when it is a question of accounting for other relationships, and rules of *action*, when it is a question of describing the transformation of the major relationships in the course of the story. There are many characters in *Les Liaisons Dangereuses* but 'what is said of them' (their predicates) can be classified. Finally, Greimas has proposed to describe and classify the characters of narrative not according to what they are but according to what they do (whence the name *actants*), inasmuch as they participate in three main semantic axes (also to be found in the sentence: subject, object, indirect object, adjunct) which are communication, desire (or quest) and ordeal.[47] Since this participation is ordered in couples, the infinite world of characters is, it too, bound by a paradigmatic structure (*Subject/Object, Donor/Receiver, Helper/Opponent*) which is projected along the narrative; and since an actant defines a class, it can be filled by different actors, mobilized according to rules of multiplication, substitution or replacement.

These three conceptions have many points in common. The most important, it must be stressed again, is the definition of the character according to participation in a sphere of actions, these spheres being few in number, typical and classifiable; which is why the second level of description, despite its being that of the characters, has here been called the level of Actions: the word *actions* is not to be understood in the sense of the trifling acts which form the tissue of the first level but in that of the major articulations of *praxis* (desire, communication, struggle).

2. The problem of the subject

The problems raised by a classification of the characters of narrative are not as yet satisfactorily resolved. Certainly there is ready agreement on the fact that the innumerable characters of narrative can be brought under rules of substitution and that, even within the one work, a single figure can absorb different characters.[48] Again, the actantial model proposed by Greimas (and adopted by Todorov in another perspective) seems to stand the test of a large number of narratives. Like any structural model, its value lies less in its canonic form (a matrix of six actants) than in the regulated transformations (replacements, confusions, duplications, substitutions) to which it lends itself, thus holding out the hope of an actantial typology of narratives.[49] A difficulty, however, is that when the matrix has a high classificational power (as is the case with Greimas's actants) it fails adequately to account for the multiplicity of participations as soon as these are analysed in terms of perspectives and that when these perspectives are respected (as in Bremond's description) the system of characters remains too fragmented. The reduction proposed by Todorov avoids both pitfalls but has so far only been applied to one narrative. All this, it seems, can be quickly and harmoniously resolved. The real difficulty posed by the classification of characters is the place (and hence the existence) of the *subject* in any actantial matrix, whatever its formulation. *Who* is the subject (the hero) of a narrative? Is there — or not — a privileged class of actors? The novel has accustomed us to emphasize in one way or another — sometimes in a devious (negative) way — one character in particular. But such privileging is far from extending over the whole of narrative literature. Many narratives, for example, set two adversaries in conflict over some stake; the subject is then truly double, not reducible further by substitution. Indeed, this is even perhaps a common archaic form, as though narrative, after the fashion of certain languages, had also known a *dual* of persons. This dual is all the more interesting in that it relates narrative to the structures of certain (very modern) games in which two equal opponents try to gain possession of an object put into circulation by a referee; a schema which recalls the actantial matrix proposed by Greimas, and there is nothing surprising in this if one is willing to allow that a game, being a language, depends on the same symbolic structure as is to be found in language and narrative: a game too is a sentence.[50] If therefore a privileged class of actors is retained (the subject of the quest, of the desire, of the action), it needs at least to be made more flexible by bringing that actant under the very categories of the grammatical (and not psychological) person. Once again, it will be necessary to look towards linguistics for the possibility of describing and classifying the personal (*je/tu,* first person/second person) or apersonal (*il,* third person), singular, dual or plural, instance of the action. It will — perhaps — be the grammatical categories of the person (accessible in our pronouns) which will provide the key to the actional level; but since these categories can only be defined in relation to the instance of discourse, not to that of reality,[51] characters, as units of the actional level, find their meaning (their intelligibility) only if integrated in the third level of description, here called the level of Narration (as opposed to Functions and Actions).

IV. Narration

1. *Narrative communication*
Just as there is within narrative a major function of exchange (set out

between a donor and a beneficiary), so, homologically, narrative as object is the point of a communication: there is a donor of the narrative and a receiver of the narrative. In linguistic communication, *je* and *tu* (*I* and *you*) are absolutely presupposed by one another; similarly, there can be no narrative without a narrator and a listener (or reader). Banal perhaps, but still little developed. Certainly the role of the sender has been abundantly enlarged upon (much study of the 'author' of a novel, though without any consideration of whether he really is the 'narrator'); when it comes to the reader, however, literary theory is much more modest. In fact, the problem is not to introspect the motives of the narrator or the effects the narration produces on the reader, it is to describe the code by which narrator and reader are signified throughout the narrative itself. At first sight, the signs of the narrator appear more evident and more numerous than those of the reader (a narrative more frequently says *I* than *you*); in actual fact, the latter are simply more oblique than the former. Thus, each time the narrator stops 'representing' and reports details which he knows perfectly well but which are unknown to the reader, there occurs, by signifying failure, a sign of reading, for there would be no sense in the narrator giving himself a piece of information. *Leo was the owner of the joint,*[52] we are told in a first-person novel: a sign of the reader, close to what Jakobson calls the conative function of communication. Lacking an inventory however, we shall leave aside for the moment these signs of reception (though they are of equal importance) and say a few words concerning the signs of narration.[53]

Who is the donor of the narrative? So far, three conceptions seem to have been formulated. The first holds that a narrative emanates from a person (in the fully psychological sense of the term). The person has a name, the author, in whom there is an endless exchange between the 'personality' and the 'art' of a perfectly identified individual who periodically takes up his pen to write a story: the narrative (notably the novel) then being simply the expression of an *I* external to it. The second conception regards the narrator as a sort of omniscient, apparently impersonal, consciousness that tells the story from a superior point of view, that of God:[54] the narrator is at once inside his characters (since he knows everything that goes on in them) and outside them (since he never identifies with any one more than another). The third and most recent conception (Henry James, Sartre) decrees that the narrator must limit his narrative to what the characters can observe or know, everything proceeding as if each of the characters in turn were the sender of the narrative. All three conceptions are equally difficult in that they seem to consider narrator and characters as real — 'living' — people (the unfailing power of this literary myth is well known), as though a narrative were originally determined at its referential level (it is a matter of equally 'realist' conceptions). Narrator and characters, however, at least from our perspective, are essentially 'paper beings';

the (material) author of a narrative is in no way to be confused with the narrator of that narrative.[55] The signs of the narrator are immanent to the narrative and hence readily accessible to a semiological analysis; but in order to conclude that the author himself (whether declared, hidden or withdrawn) has 'signs' at his disposal which he sprinkles through his work, it is necessary to assume the existence between this 'person' and his language of a straight descriptive relation which makes the author a full subject and the narrative the instrumental expression of that fullness. Structural analysis is unwilling to accept such an assumption: *who speaks* (in the narrative) is not *who writes* (in real life) and *who writes* is not *who is.*[56]

In fact, narration strictly speaking (the code of the narrator), like language, knows only two systems of signs: personal and apersonal. These two narrational systems do not necessarily present the linguistic marks attached to person (*I*) and non-person (*he*): there are narratives or at least narrative episodes, for example, which though written in the third person nevertheless have as their true instance the first person. How can we tell? It suffices to rewrite the narrative (or the passage) from *he* to *I*: so long as the rewriting entails no alteration of the discourse other than this change of the grammatical pronouns, we can be sure that we are dealing with a personal system. The whole of the beginning of *Goldfinger*, though written in the third person, is in fact 'spoken' by James Bond. For the instance to change, rewriting must become impossible; thus the sentence 'he saw a man in his fifties, still young-looking . . .' is perfectly personal despite the *he* ('I, James Bond, saw . . .'), but the narrative statement 'the tinkling of the ice against the glass appeared to give Bond a sudden inspiration' cannot be personal on account of the verb 'appeared', it (and not the *he*) becoming a sign of the apersonal. There is no doubt that the apersonal is the traditional mode of narrative, language having developed a whole tense system peculiar to narrative (based on the aorist[57]), designed to wipe out the present of the speaker. As Benveniste puts it: 'In narrative, no one speaks.' The personal instance (under more or less disguised forms) has, however, gradually invaded narrative, the narration being referred to the *hic et nunc* of the locutionary act (which is the definition of the personal system). Thus it is that today many narratives are to be found (and of the most common kinds) which mix together in extremely rapid succession, often within the limits of a single sentence, the personal and the apersonal; as for instance this sentence from *Goldfinger*:

His eyes,	*personal*
grey-blue,	*apersonal*
looked into those of Mr Du Pont who did not know what face to put on	*personal*
for this look held in a mixture of candour, irony and self-deprecation,	*apersonal*

The mixing of the systems is clearly felt as a facility and this facility can go as far as trick effects. A detective novel by Agatha Christie (*The Sittaford Mystery*) only keeps the enigma going by cheating on the person of the narration: a character is described from within when he is already the murderer[58] as if in a single person there were the consciousness of a witness, immanent to the discourse, and the consciousness of a murderer, immanent to the referent, with the dishonest tourniquet of the two systems alone producing the enigma. Hence it is understandable that at the other pole of literature the choice of a rigorous system should have been made a necessary condition of a work — without it always being easy fully to meet that condition.

Rigour of this kind — the aim of certain contemporary writers — is not necessarily an aesthetic imperative. What is called the psychological novel usually shows a mixture of the two systems, successively mobilizing the signs of non-person and those of person; 'psychology', that is, paradoxically, cannot accommodate itself to a pure system, for by bringing the whole narrative down to the sole instance of the discourse — or, if one prefers, to the locutionary act — it is the very content of the person which is threatened: the psychological person (of referential order) bears no relation to the linguistic person, the latter never defined by states of mind, intentions or traits of character but only by its (coded) place in discourse. It is this formal person that writers today are attempting to speak and such an attempt represents an important subversion (the public moreover has the impression that 'novels' are no longer being written) for it aims to transpose narrative from the purely constative plane, which it has occupied until now, to the performative plane, whereby the meaning of an utterance is the very act by which it is uttered:[59] today, writing is not 'telling' but saying that one is telling and assigning all the referent ('what one says') to this act of locution; which is why part of contemporary literature is no longer descriptive, but transitive, striving to accomplish so pure a present in its language that the whole of the discourse is identified with the act of its delivery, the whole *logos* being brought down — or extended — to a *lexis*.[60]

2. Narrative situation

The narrational level is thus occupied by the signs of narrativity, the set of operators which reintegrate functions and actions in the narrative communication articulated on its donor and its addressee. Some of these signs have already received study; we are familiar in oral literatures with certain codes of recitation (metrical formulae, conventional presentation protocols) and we know that here the 'author' is not the person who invents the finest stories but the person who best masters the code which is practised equally by his listeners: in such literatures the narrational level is so clearly defined, its rules so binding, that it is difficult to conceive of a 'tale' devoid of the coded signs of narrative ('*once upon a time*', etc.). In our written literatures, the 'forms of discourse' (which are in fact signs of narrativity) were early identified: classification of the modes of authorial intervention (outlined by Plato and developed by Diomedes[61]), coding of the beginnings and endings of narratives, definition of the different styles of representation (*oratio directa, oratio indirecta* with its *inquit, oratio tecta*),[62] study of 'points of view' and so on. All these elements form part of the narrational level, to which must obviously be added the writing as a whole, its role being not to 'transmit' the narrative but to display it.

It is indeed precisely in a display of the narrative that the units of the lower levels find integration: the ultimate form of the narrative, as narrative, transcends its contents and its strictly narrative forms (functions and actions). This explains why the narrational code should be the final level attainable by our analysis, other than by going outside of the narrative-object, other, that is, than by transgressing the rule of immanence on which the analysis is based. Narration can only receive its meaning from the world which makes use of it: beyond the narrational level begins the world, other systems (social, economic, ideological) whose terms are no longer simply narratives but elements of a different substance (historical facts, determinations, behaviours, etc.). Just as linguistics stops at the sentence, so narrative analysis stops at discourse — from there it is necessary to shift to another semiotics. Linguistics is acquainted with such boundaries which it has already postulated — if not explored — under the name of *situations*. Halliday defines the 'situation' (in relation to a sentence) as 'the associated non-linguistic factors',[63] Prieto as 'the set of facts known by the receiver at the moment of the semic act and independently of this act'.[64] In the same way, one can say that every narrative is dependent on a 'narrative situation', the set of protocols according to which the narrative is 'consumed'. In so-called 'archaic' societies, the narrative situation is heavily coded;[65] nowadays, avant-garde literature alone still dreams of reading protocols — spectacular in the case of Mallarmé who wanted the book to be recited in public according to a precise combinatory scheme, typographical in that of Butor who tries to provide the book with its own specific signs. Generally, however, our society takes the greatest pains to conjure away the coding of the narrative situation: there is no counting the number of narrational devices which seek to naturalize the subsequent narrative by feigning to make it the outcome of some natural circumstance and thus, as it were, 'disinaugurating' it: epistolary novels, supposedly rediscovered manuscripts, author who met the narrator, films which begin the story before the credits. The reluctance to declare its codes characterizes bourgeois society and the mass culture issuing from it: both demand signs which do not look like signs. Yet this is only, so to speak, a structural epiphenomenon: however familiar, however casual may today be the act of opening a novel or a newspaper or of turning on the television, nothing can prevent that humble act from installing in us, all at once and in its entirety, the narrative code we are going to need. Hence the narrational level has an ambiguous role: contiguous to the narrative situation (and sometimes even including it), it gives on to the world in which the narrative is undone (consumed), while at the same time, capping the preceding levels, it closes the narrative, constitutes it definitively as utterance of a language [*langue*] which provides for and bears along its own metalanguage.

V. *The System of Narrative*

Language [*langue*] proper can be defined by the concurrence of two fundamental processes: articulation, or segmentation, which produces units (this being what Benveniste calls *form*), and integration, which gathers these units into units of a higher rank (this being *meaning*). This dual process can be found in the language of narrative [*la langue du récit*] which also has an articulation and an integration, a form and a meaning.

1. Distortion and expansion

The form of narrative is essentially characterized by two powers: that of distending its signs over the length of the story and that of inserting unforeseeable expansions into these distortions. The two powers appear to be points of freedom but the nature of narrative is precisely to include these 'deviations' within its language.[66]

The distortion of signs exists in linguistic language [*langue*] and was studied by Bally with reference to French and German.[67] Dystaxia occurs when the signs (of a message) are no longer simply juxtaposed, when the (logical) linearity is disturbed (predicate before subject for example). A notable form of dystaxia is found when the parts of one sign are separated by other signs along the chain of the message (for instance, the negative *ne jamais* and the verb *a pardonné* in *elle ne nous a jamais pardonné*): the sign split into fractional parts, its signified is shared out amongst several signifiers, distant from one another and not comprehensible on their own. This, as was seen in connection with the functional level, is exactly what happens in narrative: the units of a sequence, although forming a whole at the level of that very sequence, may be separated from one another by the insertion of units from other sequences — as was said, the structure of the functional level is fugued.[68] According to Bally's terminology, which opposes synthetic languages where dystaxia is predominant (such as German) and analytic languages with a greater respect for logical linearity and monosemy (such as French), narrative would be a highly synthetic language, essentially founded on a syntax of embedding and enveloping: each part of the narrative radiates in several directions at once. When Bond orders a whisky while waiting for his plane, the whisky as indice has a polysemic value, is a kind of symbolic node grouping several signifieds (modernity, wealth, leisure); as a functional unit, however, the ordering of the whisky has to run step by step through numerous relays (consumption, waiting, departure, etc.) in order to find its final meaning: the unit is 'taken' by the whole narrative at the same time that the narrative only 'holds' by the distortion and irradiation of its units.

This generalized distortion is what gives the language of narrative its special character. A purely logical phenomenon, since founded on an often distant relation and mobilizing a sort of confidence in intellective memory, it ceaselessly substitutes meaning for the straightforward copy of the events recounted. On meeting in 'life', it is most unlikely that the invitation to take a seat would not immediately be followed by the act of sitting down; in narrative these two units, contiguous from a mimetic point of view, may be separated by a long series of insertions belonging to quite different functional spheres. Thus is established a kind of *logical time* which has very little connection with real time, the apparent pulverization of units always being firmly held in place by the logic that binds together the nuclei of the sequence. 'Suspense' is clearly only a privileged — or 'exacerbated' — form of distortion: on the one hand, by keeping a sequence open (through emphatic procedures of delay and renewal), it reinforces the contact with the reader (the listener), has a manifestly phatic function; while on the other, it offers the threat of an uncompleted sequence, of an open paradigm (if, as we believe, every sequence has two poles), that is to say, of a logical disturbance, it being this disturbance which is consumed with anxiety and pleasure (all the more so because it is always made right in the end). 'Suspense', therefore, is a game with structure, designed to endanger and glorify it, constituting a veritable 'thrilling' of intelligibility: by representing order (and no longer series) in its fragility, 'suspense' accomplishes the very idea of language: what seems the most pathetic is also the most intellectual — 'suspense' grips you in the 'mind', not in the 'guts'.[69]

What can be separated can also be filled. Distended, the functional nuclei furnish intercalating spaces which can be packed out almost infinitely; the interstices can be filled in with a very large number of catalysers. Here, however, a new typology comes in, for the freedom to catalyse can be regulated according both to the content of the functions (certain functions are more apt than others for catalysing — as for example *Waiting*[70]) and to the substance of the narrative (writing contains possibilities of diaresis — and so of catalysing — far superior to those of film: a gesture related linguistically can be 'cut up' much more easily than the same gesture visualized[71]). The catalystic power of narrative has for corollary its elliptic power. Firstly, a function (*he had a good meal*) can economize on all the potential catalysers it covers over (the details of the meal)[72]; secondly, it is possible to reduce a sequence to its nuclei and a hierarchy of sequences to its higher terms without altering the meaning of the story: a narrative can be identified even if its total syntagm be reduced to its actants and its main functions as these result from the progressive upwards integration of its functional units.[73] In other words, narrative lends itself to *summary* (what used to be called the *argument*). At first sight this is true of any discourse, but each discourse has its own kind of summary. A lyric poem, for example, is simply the vast metaphor of a single signified[74] and to summarize it is thus to give this signified, an operation so drastic that it eliminates the poem's identity (summarized, lyric poems come down to the signifieds *Love* and *Death*) — hence the conviction that poems cannot be summarized. By contrast, the summary of a narrative (if conducted according to structural criteria) preserves the individuality of the message; narrative, in other words, is *translatable* without fundamental damage. What is untranslatable is determined only at the last, narrational, level. The signifiers of narrativity, for instance, are not readily transferable from novel to film, the latter utilizing the personal mode of treatment only very exceptionally;[75] while the last layer of the narrational level, namely the writing, resists transference from one language to another (or transfers very badly). The translatability of narrative is a result of the structure of its language, so that it would be possible, proceeding in reverse, to determine this structure by identifying and classifying the (varyingly) translatable and untranslatable elements of a narrative. The existence (now) of different and concurrent semiotics (literature, cinema, comics, radio-television) would greatly facilitate this kind of analysis.

2. Mimesis and meaning

The second important process in the language of narrative is integration: what has been disjoined at a certain level (a sequence for example) is most often joined again at a higher level (a hierarchically important sequence, the global signified of a number of scattered indices, the action of a class of characters). The complexity of a narrative can be compared to that of an organization profile chart, capable of integrating backwards and forwards movements; or, more accurately, it is integration in various forms which compensates for the seemingly unmasterable complexity of units on a particular level. Integration guides the understanding of the discontinuous elements, simultaneously contiguous and heterogeneous (it is thus that they appear in the syntagm which knows only one dimension — that of succession). If, with Greimas, we call *isotopy* the unity of meaning (that, for instance, which impregnates a sign and its context), then we can say that integration is a factor of isotopy: each (integrational) level gives its isotopy to the units of the level below, prevents the meaning from 'dangling' — inevitable if the staggering of levels were not perceived. Narrative integration, however, does not present itself in a serenely regular manner like some fine architectural style leading by symmetrical chicaneries from an infinite variety of simple elements to a few complex masses. Very often a single unit will have two correlates, one on one level (function of a sequence), the other on another (indice with reference to an actant). Narrative thus appears as a succession of tightly interlocking mediate and immediate elements; dystaxia determines a 'horizontal' reading, while integration superimposes a 'vertical' reading: there is a sort of structural 'limping', an incessant play of potentials whose varying falls give the narrative its dynamism or energy: each unit is perceived at once in its surfacing and in its depth and it is thus that the narrative 'works'; through the concourse of these two movements the structure ramifies, proliferates, uncovers itself — and recovers itself, pulls itself together: the new never fails in its regularity. There is, of course, a freedom of narrative (just as there is a freedom for every speaker with regard to his or her language), but this freedom is limited, literally *hemmed in*: between the powerful code of language [*langue*] and the powerful code of narrative a hollow is set up — the sentence. If one attempts to embrace the whole of a written narrative, one finds that it starts from the most highly coded (the phonematic, or even the merismatic, level), gradually relaxes until it reaches the sentence, the farthest point of combinatorial freedom, and then begins to tighten up again, moving progressively from small groups of sentences (micro-sequences), which are still very free, until it comes to the main actions, which form a strong and restricted code. The creativity of narrative (at least under its mythical appearance of 'life') is thus situated *between two codes*, the linguistic and the translinguistic. That is why it can be said paradoxically that *art* (in the Romantic sense of the term) is a matter of statements of detail, whereas *imagination* is mastery of the code: 'It will be found in fact,' wrote Poe, 'that the ingenious are always fanciful, and the *truly* imaginative never otherwise than analytic . . .'[76]

Claims concerning the 'realism' of narrative are therefore to be discounted. When a telephone call comes through in the office where he is on duty, Bond, so the author tells us, reflects that 'Communications with Hong-Kong are as bad as they always were and just as difficult to obtain'. Neither Bond's 'reflection' nor the poor quality of the telephone call is the real piece of information; this contingency perhaps gives things more 'life' but the true information, which will come to fruition later, is the localization of the telephone call, Hong-Kong. In all narrative imitation remains contingent.[77] The function of narrative is not to 'represent', it is to constitute a spectacle still very enigmatic for us but in any case not of a mimetic order. The 'reality' of a sequence lies not in the 'natural' succession of the actions composing it but in the logic there exposed, risked and satisfied. Putting it another way, one could say that the origin of a sequence is not the observation of reality, but the need to vary and transcend the first *form* given man, namely repetition: a sequence is essentially a whole within which nothing is repeated. Logic has here an emancipatory value — and with it the entire narrative. It may be that men ceaselessly re-inject into narrative what they have known, what they have experienced; but if they do, at least it is in a form which has vanquished repetition and instituted the model of a process of becoming. Narrative does not show, does not imitate; the passion which may excite us in reading a novel is not that of a 'vision' (in actual fact, we do not 'see' anything). Rather it is that of meaning, that of a higher order of relation which also has its emotions, its hopes, its dangers, its triumphs. 'What takes place' in a narrative is from the referential (reality) point of view literally *nothing*;[78] 'what happens' is language alone, the adventure of language, the unceasing celebration of its coming. Although we know scarcely more about the origins of narrative than we do about the origins of language, it can reasonably be suggested that narrative is contemporaneous with monologue, a creation seemingly posterior to that of dialogue. At all events, without wanting to strain the phylogenetic hypothesis, it may be significant that it is at the same moment (around the age of three) that the little human 'invents' at once sentence, narrative, and the Oedipus.

Notes

[1] It must be remembered that this is not the case with either poetry or the essay, both of which are dependent on the cultural level of their consumers.

[2] There does, of course, exist an 'art' of the storyteller, which is the ability to generate narratives (messages) from the structure (the code). This art corresponds to the notion of *performance* in Chomsky and is far removed from the 'genius' of the author, romantically conceived as some barely explicable personal secret.

[3] See the history of the Hittite *a*, postulated by Saussure and actually discovered fifty years later, as given in Emile Benveniste, *Problèmes de Linguistique générale*, Paris 1966, p. 35 [*Problems of General Linguistics*, Coral Gables, Florida 1971, p. 32].

[4] Let us bear in mind the present conditions of linguistic description: '. . . linguistic "structure" is always relative not just to the data or corpus but also to the grammatical theory describing the data', E. Bach, *An Introduction to Transformational Grammars*, New York 1964, p. 29; 'it has been recognized that language must be described as a formal structure, but that the description first of all necessitates specification of adequate procedures and criteria and that, finally, the reality of the object is inseparable from the method given for its description', Benveniste, op. cit., p. 119 [trans. p. 101].

[5] But not imperative: see Claude Bremond, 'La logique des possibles narratifs', *Communications* 8, 1966, which is more logical than linguistic. [Bremond's various studies in this field have now been collected in a volume entitled, precisely, *Logique du récit*, Paris 1973; his work consists in the analysis of narrative according to the pattern of possible alternatives, each narrative moment — or function — giving rise to a set of different possible resolutions, the actualization of any one of which in turn produces a new set of alternatives.]

[6] André Martinet, 'Réflexions sur la phrase', in *Language and Society* (Studies presented to Jansen), Copenhagen 1961, p. 113.

[7] It goes without saying, as Jakobson has noted, that between the sentence and

what lies beyond the sentence there are transitions; co-ordination, for instance, can work over the limit of the sentence.

[8] See especially: Benveniste, op. cit., Chapter 10; Z. S. Harris, 'Discourse Analysis', *Language* 28, 1952, pp. 18-23 & 474-94; N. Ruwet, 'Analyse structurale d'un poème français', *Linguistics* 3, 1964, pp. 62-83.

[9] One of the tasks of such a linguistics would be precisely that of establishing a typology of forms and discourse. Three broad types can be recognized provisionally: metonymic (narrative), metaphoric (lyric poetry, sapiential discourse), enthymematic (intellectual discourse).

[10] See below III.1.

[11] Remember Mallarmé's insight at the time when he was contemplating a work of linguistics: 'Language appeared to him the instrument of fiction: he will follow the method of language (determine it). Language self-reflecting. So fiction seems to him the very process of the human mind — it is this that sets in play all method, and man is reduced to will (*Œuvres complètes,* Bibliothèque de la Pléiade, Paris 1961, p. 851). It will be recalled that for Mallarmé 'Fiction' and 'Poetry' are taken synonymously (cf. ibid., p. 335).

[12] 'Linguistic descriptions are not, so to speak, monovalent. A description is not simply "right" or "wrong" in itself . . . it is better thought of as more useful or less', M. A. K. Halliday, 'General linguistics and its application to language teaching', *Patterns of Language,* London 1966, p. 8.

[13] The levels of integration were postulated by the Prague School (vid. J. Vachek, *A Prague School Reader in Linguistics,* Bloomington 1964, p. 468) and have been adopted since by many linguists. It is Benveniste who, in my opinion, has given the most illuminating analysis in this respect; op cit., Chapter 10.

[14] 'In somewhat vague terms, a level may be considered as a system of symbols, rules, and so on, to be used for representing utterances', Bach, op. cit., p. 57.

[15] The third part of rhetoric, *inventio,* did not concern language — it had to do with *res,* not with *verba.*

[16] Claude Lévi-Strauss, *Anthropologie structurale,* Paris 1958, p. 233 [*Structural Anthropology,* New York and London 1963, p. 211]. [*Editor's note*: see also this volume, pp. 232–43.]

[17] See T. Todorov, 'Les catégories du récit littéraire', *Communications* 8, 1966 [Todorov's work on narrative is now most easily accessible in two books, *Littérature et Signification,* Paris 1967; *Poétique de la prose,* Paris 1972. For a short account in English, see 'Structural analysis of narrative', *Novel* I, 3, 1969, pp. 70-6].

[18] [This in accordance with the Baudelaire version of the Poe story from which Barthes quotes; Poe's original reads: 'so far as his labours extended'.]

[19] I have been concerned in this introduction to impede research in progress as little as possible.

[20] See especially B. Tomachevski, 'Thématique' (1925), in *Théorie de la littérature* ed. T. Todorov, Paris 1965, pp. 263-307. A little later, Propp defined the function as 'an act of a character, defined from the point of view of its significance for the course of the action' *Morphology of the Folktale,* Austin and London 1968, p.21.

[21] This is what separates art from 'life', the latter knowing only 'fuzzy' or 'blurred' communications. 'Fuzziness' (that beyond which it is impossible to see) can exist in art, but it does so as a coded element (in Watteau for example). Even then, such 'fuzziness' is unknown to the written code: writing is inescapably distinct.

[22] At least in literature, where the freedom of notation (in consequence of the abstract nature of articulated language) leads to a much greater responsibility than in the 'analogical' arts such as cinema.

[23] The functionality of a narrative unit is more or less immediate (and hence apparent) according to the level on which it operates: when the units are situated on the same level (as for instance in the case of suspense), the functionality is very clear; it is much less so when the function is saturated on the narrational

level – a modern text, weakly signifying on the plane of the anecdote, only finds a full force of meaning on the plane of the writing.

[24] 'Syntactical units beyond the sentence are in fact units of content' A. J. Greimas, *Cours de sémantique structurale* (roneoed), 1964, VI, 5 [cf. *Sémantique structurale*, pp. 116f.]. The exploration of the functional level is thus part of general semantics.

[25] 'The word must not be treated as an indivisible element of literary art, like a brick in building. It can be broken down into much finer "verbal elements"', J. Tynianov, quoted by T. Todorov in *Langages* 6, 1971, p. 18.

[26] These designations, like those that follow, may all be provisional.

[27] Which does not mean that the syntagmatic setting out of functions may not *finally* hold paradigmatic relations between separate functions, as is recognized since Lévi-Strauss and Greimas.

[28] Functions cannot be reduced to actions (verbs), nor indices to qualities (adjectives), for there are actions that are indicial, being 'signs' of a character, an atmosphere, etc.

[29] Valery spoke of 'dilatory signs'. The detective novel makes abundant use of such 'confusing' units.

[30] [For the scheme of the six factors of verbal communication and their corresponding linguistic functions – emotive, conative, referential, phatic, metalinguistic and poetic – see R. Jakobson, 'Linguistics and Poetics' in *Style in Language*, ed. T. A. Sebeok, New York 1960, pp. 350-77.]

[31] N. Ruwet calls 'parametrical' an element which remains constant for the whole duration of a piece of music (for instance, the tempo in a Bach allegro or the monodic character of a solo).

[32] In 'Frontières du récit', *Communications* 8, 1966 [reprinted in Figures II, Paris 1969], Gérard Genette distinguishes two types of description: ornamental and significant. The second clearly relates to the level of the story; the first to that of the discourse, which explains why for a long time it formed a perfectly coded rhetorical 'piece': *descriptio* or *ekphrasis,* a very highly valued exercise in neo-rhetoric.

[33] *Poetics,* 1459a.

[34] Quoted by Claude Bremond, 'Le message narratif', *Communications* 4, 1964 [Claude Lévi-Strauss, 'La structure et la forme', *Cahiers de l'Institut de Science Economique Appliquée* 99, March 1960 (Série M. No. 7), p. 29; article reprinted in *Anthropologie structurale II*, Paris 1974].

[35] *Œuvres complètes*, p. 386.

[36] In his own way – as always perspicacious but left undeveloped – Valéry well expressed the status of narrative time: 'The belief in time as agent and guiding thread is based on *the mechanism of memory and on that of combinatory discourse'*, Tel Quel, *Œuvres* Vol. II, Bibliothèque de la Pléiade, Paris 1957, p. 348 (my italics); the illusion is precisely produced by the discourse itself.

[37] This idea recalls Aristotle: *proairesis,* the rational choice of actions to be undertaken, is the foundation of *praxis,* the practical science which, contrary to *poiesis,* produces no object-work distinct from its agent. Using these terms, one can say that the analyst tries to reconstitute the praxis inherent in narrative.

[38] Such a logic, based on alternatives (*doing this or that*), has the merit of accounting for the process of dramatization for which narrative is usually the occasion.

[39] ['The poetic function projects the principle of equivalence of the axis of selection on to the axis of combination.' Jakobson, 'Linguistics and Poetics', p. 3.]

[40] See A. J. Greimas, 'Eléments pour une théorie de l'interprétation du récit mythique', *Communications* 8, 1966 [article reprinted in *Du Sens,* Paris 1970].

[41] In the Hjelmslevian sense of double implication: two terms presuppose one another.

[42] It is quite possible to identify even at this infinitesimal level an opposition of paradigmatic type, if not between two terms, at least between two poles of the sequence: the sequence *Offer of a cigarette* spreads out, by suspending it, the paradigm *Danger/Safety* (demonstrated by Cheglov in his analysis of the Sherlock Holmes cycle), *Suspicion/Protection, Aggressiveness/Friendliness.*

[43] This counterpoint was recognized by the Russian Formalists who outlined its typology; it is not without recalling the principal 'intricate' structures of the sentence (see below V.I.).

[44] It must not be forgotten that classical tragedy as yet knows only 'actors', not 'characters'.

[45] The 'character-person' reigns in the bourgeois novel; in *War and Peace,* Nikolay Rostov is from the start a good fellow, loyal, courageous and passionate, Prince Andrey a disillusioned individual of noble birth, etc. What happens illustrates them, it does not form them.

[46] If one section of contemporary literature has attacked the 'character', it is not in order to destroy it (which is impossible) but to depersonalize it, which is quite different. A novel seemingly devoid of characters, such as *Drame* by Philippe Sollers, gets rid of the person to the benefit of language but nonetheless retains a fundamental play of actants confronting the very action of discourse. There is still a 'subject' in this literature, but that 'subject' is henceforth that of language.

[47] *Sémantique structurale* pp. 129f.

[48] Psychoanalysis has widely accredited these operations of condensation. Mallarmé was saying already, writing of *Hamlet*: 'Supernumeraries, necessarily! for in the ideal painting of the stage, everything moves according to a symbolic reciprocity of types amongst themselves or relatively to a single figure.' *Crayonné au théâtre, Œuvres complètes,* p. 301.

[49] For example: narratives where object and subject are confounded in a single character, that is narratives of the search for oneself, for one's own identity (*The Golden Ass); narratives* where the subject pursues successive objects *(Madame Bovary),* etc.

[50] Umberto Eco's analysis of the James Bond cycle ('James Bond: une combinatoire narrative', *Communications* 8, 1966) refers more to game than to language.

[51] See the analyses of person given by Benveniste in *Problèmes de linguistique générale.*

[52] *Double Bang à Bangkok* [secret agent thriller by Jean Bruce, Paris 1959). The sentence functions as a 'wink' to the reader as if he was being turned towards. By contrast, the statement 'So Leo had just left' is a sign of the narrator, part of a process of reasoning conducted by a 'person'.

[53] In 'Les catégories du récit littéraire' Todorov deals with the images of narrator and reader.

[54] When will someone write from the point of view of a *superior joke, that* is as God sees things from above?' Flaubert, *Préface à la vie d'écrivain,* ed. G. Bollème, Paris 1965, p. 91.

[55] A distinction all the more necessary, given the scale at which we are working, in that historically a large mass of narratives are without authors (oral narratives, folktales, epics entrusted to bards, reciters, etc.).

[56] J. Lacan: 'Is the subject I speak of when I speak the same as the subject who speaks?'

[57] E. Benveniste, op. cit. [especially Chapter XIX].

[58] Personal mode: It even seemed to Burnaby that nothing looked changed . . .' 'The device is still more blatant in *The Murder of Roger Ackroyd,* since there the murderer actually says *I*.

[59] On the performative, see Todorov's 'Les catégories du récit littéraire'. The classic example of a performative is the statement *I declare war* which neither 'constates' nor 'describes' anything but exhausts its meaning in the act of its utterance (by contrast to the statement *the king declared war,* which constates,

describes).

[60]For the opposition logos/lexis, see Genette, 'Frontières du récit'.

[61]*Genus activum vel imitativum* (no intervention of the narrator in the discourse: as for example theatre); *genus ennarativum* (the poet alone speaks: sententiae, didactic poems); *genus commune* (mixture of the two kinds: epic poems).

[62]H. Sorensen in *Language and Society* (Studies presented to Jansen), p.150.

[63]M. A. K. Halliday, op. cit., p. 4.

[64]L. H. Prieto, *Principes de noologie,* Paris and The Hague 1964, p. 36.

[65]A tale, as Lucien Sebag stressed, can be told anywhere anytime, but not a mythical narrative.

[66]Valéry: 'Formally the novel is close to the dream; both can be defined by consideration of this curious property: *all their deviations form part of them.'*

[67]Charles Bally, *Linguistique générale et linguistique française,* Paris 1932.

[68]Cf. Lévi-Strauss: 'Relations pertaining to the same bundle may appear diachronically at remote intervals' *Anthropologie structurale,* p. 234 [trans. p.211 *Editor's note:* see also this volume, pp.232–43]. A. J. Greimas has emphasized the spacing out of functions.

[69]J. P. Faye, writing of Klossowski's *Baphomet*: 'Rarely has fiction (or narrative) so clearly revealed what it always is, necessarily: an experimentation of "thought" on "life".' *Tel Quel 22*, p. 88.

[70]Logically *Waiting* has only two nuclei: 1. the wait established 2. the wait rewarded or disappointed; the first, however, can be extensively catalysed, occasionally even indefinitely (*Waiting for Godot*): yet another game – this time extreme – with structure.

[71]Valéry: 'Proust divides up – and gives us the feelings of being able to divide up indefinitely – what other writers are in the habit of passing over'.

[72]Here again, there are qualifications according to substance: literature has an unrivalled elliptic power – which cinema lacks.

[73]This reduction does not necessarily correspond to the division of the book into chapters: on the contrary, it seems that increasingly chapters have the role of introducing breaks, points of suspense (serial technique).

[74]N. Ruwet: 'A poem can be understood as the outcome of a series of transformations applied to the proposition "I love you".' 'Analyse structurale d'un poème français', *Linguistics* 3, 1964, p. 82. Ruwet here refers precisely to the analysis of paranoiac delirium given by Freud in connection with President Schreber ('Psychoanalytic Notes on an Autobiographical Account of a Case of Paranoia', *Standard Edition* Vol. 12).

[75]Once again, there is no relation between the grammatical 'person' of the narrator and the 'personality' (or subjectivity) that a film director puts into his way of presenting a story: the *camera-I* (continuously identified with the vision of a particular character) is exceptional in the history of cinema.

[76]*The Murders in the Rue Morgue.*

[77]G. Genette rightly reduces *Mimesis* to passages of directly reported dialogue (cf. 'Frontières du récit'); yet even dialogue always contains a function of intelligibility, not of mimesis.

[78]Mallarmé: 'A dramatic work displays the succession of exteriors of the act without any moment retaining reality and, in the end, anything happening.' *Crayonné au théâtre, Œuvres complètes,* p. 296.

4.3   Introduction to the Problems of a Sociology of the Novel
Lucien Goldmann

Two years ago, in January 1961, the Institute of Sociology in the Free University of Brussels asked me to lead a research group into the sociology of literature, beginning with the novels of André Malraux. With a good deal of apprehension, I accepted. My work on seventeenth-century philosophy and tragedy in no way prejudiced me against the possibility of a similar study of the novel, even of a body of fiction so nearly contemporary as Malraux's. In fact, we spent the first year on a preliminary study of the problems of the novel as a literary form, taking as our starting-point Georg Lukács's already almost classic work — though still little known in France — *The Theory of the Novel*[1] and René Girard's recently published *Mensonge romantique et vérité romanesque,*[2] in which Girard — unknown to himself, as he later told me — discovered the Lukácsian analyses, while modifying them on several particular points.

Our study of *The Theory of the Novel* and Girard's book led me to formulate a number of sociological hypotheses that seem to me to be particularly interesting, and on the basis of which my later work on Malraux's novels was developed.

These hypotheses concern, on the one hand, the homology between the structure of the classical novel and the structure of exchange in the liberal economy and, on the other hand, certain parallels in their later evolutions.

Let us begin by tracking the outlines of the structure described by Lukács. This structure may not, as he believed, characterize the novel form in general, but it does characterize at least its most important aspects (and probably, from the genetic point of view, its primordial aspect). The novel form studied by Lukács is that characterized by a hero that he very felicitously calls the *problematic hero*.[3]

The novel is the story of a *degraded* (what Lukács calls 'demoniacal') search, a search for authentic values in a world itself degraded, but at an otherwise advanced level according to a different mode.

By authentic values, I mean, of course, not the values that the critic or the reader regards as authentic, but those which, without being manifestly present in the novel, organize in accordance with an *implicit*

Towards a Sociology of the Novel, Tavistock, 1975, Chapter 1, pp. 1-17. Originally published by Gallimard (1964). This translation by Alan Sheridan.

mode its world as a whole. It goes without saying that these values are specific to each novel and different from one novel to another.

Since the novel is an epic genre characterized, unlike the folk tale or the epic poem itself, by the insurmountable rupture between the hero and the world, there is in Lukács an analysis of the nature of two degradations (that of the hero and that of the world) that must engender both a *constitutive opposition*, the foundation of this insurmountable rupture, and an *adequate community* to make possible the existence of an epic form.

The radical rupture alone would, in effect, have led to tragedy or to lyric poetry; the absence of rupture or the existence of a merely accidental rupture would have led to the epic poem or the folk tale.

Situated between the two, the novel has a dialectical nature in so far as it derives specifically, on the one hand, from the fundamental community of the hero and of the world presupposed by all epic forms and, on the other hand, from their insurmountable rupture; the community of the hero and of the world resulting from the fact that they are both degraded in relation to authentic values, the opposition resulting from the difference of nature between each of these two degradations.

The *demoniacal* hero of the novel is a madman or a criminal, in any case, as I have said, a *problematic* character whose degraded, and therefore inauthentic, search for authentic values in a world of conformity and convention constitute the content of this new literary genre known as the 'novel' that writers created in an individualistic society.

On the basis of this analysis, Lukács develops a typology of the novel. Setting out from the relation between the hero and the world, he distinguishes three schematic types of the Western novel in the nineteenth century, to which is added a fourth that already constitutes a transformation from the novel form towards new modalities that would require a different type of analysis. In 1920, this fourth possibility seemed to him to be expressed pre-eminently in the novels of Tolstoy, which strive towards the epic. The three types of novel on which his analysis bears are as follows:

a) the novel of 'abstract idealism'; characterized by the activity of the hero and by his over-narrow consciousness in relation to the complexity of the world (*Don Quixote, Le Rouge et le Noir*);
b) the psychological novel; concerned above all with the analysis of the inner life, and characterized by the passivity of the hero and a consciousness too broad to be satisfied by what the world of convention can offer him (*Oblomov* and *L'Education Sentimentale*);
c) the *Bildungsroman*, which ends with a *self-imposed limitation;* although the hero gives up the problematic search, he does not accept the world of convention or abandon the implicit scale of values – a

self-imposed limitation that must be characterized by the term 'virile maturity' (Goethe's *Wilhelm Meister* or Gottfried Keller's *Der grüne Heinrich*).

At a distance of forty years, René Girard's analyses are often very close to those of Lukács. For Girard, too, the novel is the story of a degraded search (which he calls 'idolatrous') for authentic values, by a problematic hero, in a degraded world. The terminology he uses is Heideggerian in origin, but he often gives it a content that is somewhat different from that of Heidegger himself. Without going into detail, we might say that Girard replaces Heidegger's duality of the ontological and the ontic by the obviously related duality of the ontological and the metaphysical, with correspond for him to the authentic and the inauthentic; but whereas, for Heidegger, any idea of progress and retreat is to be eliminated, Girard confers on his terminology of the ontological and the metaphysical a content much closer to the positions of Lukács than to those of Heidegger, by introducing between the two terms a relation governed by the categories of progress and regression.[4]

Girard's typology of the novel is based on the idea that the degradation of the fictional world is the result of a more or less advanced ontological sickness (this 'more or less' is strictly contrary to Heidegger's thinking) to which corresponds, within the fictional world, an increase of metaphysical desire, that is to say, of degraded desire.

It is based therefore on the idea of degradation, and it is here that Girard introduces into the Lukácsian analysis a precision that seems to me particularly important. For him, indeed, the degradation of the fictional world, the progress of the ontological sickness, and the increase of metaphysical desire are expressed in a greater or lesser *mediatization* that progressively increases the distance between metaphysical desire and authentic search, the search for 'vertical transcendence'.

There are a great many examples of mediation in Girard's work, from the novels of chivalry that stand between *Don Quixote* and the search for chivalric values to the lover that stands between the husband and his desire for his wife, in Dostoievsky's *The Eternal Husband*. Incidentally, it does not seem to me that his examples are always as well chosen. Moreover, I am not at all sure that mediatization is as universal a category in the fictional world as Girard thinks. The term 'degradation' seems to me broader and more appropriate, on condition of course that the nature of this degradation is specified in each particular analysis.

Nevertheless, by introducing the category of mediation, and even by exaggerating its importance, Girard has elucidated the analysis of a structure that involved not only the most important form of degradation in the fictional world but also the form that is, from a genetic point of view, probably the first, that which gave birth to the literary genre of the novel, the novel itself having emerged as the result of other derived forms of degradation.

From this point on, Girard's typology is based first of all on the existence of two forms of mediation, external and internal, the first characterized by the fact that the mediating agent is external to the world in which the hero's search takes place (for example, the novels of chivalry in *Don Quixote*), the second by the fact that the mediating agent belongs to this world (the lover in *The Eternal Husband*).

Within these two qualitatively different groups, there is the idea of a progressive degradation that is expressed by the increasing proximity between the fictional character and the mediating agent, and the increasing distance between this character and *vertical transcendence*.

Let us now try to elucidate an essential point on which Lukács and Girard are in fundamental disagreement. As the story of a degraded search for authentic values in an inauthentic world, the novel is necessarily both a biography and a social chronicle. A particularly important fact is that the situation of the writer in relation to the world he has created is, in the novel, different from the situation in relation to the world of any other literary form. This particular situation, Girard calls *humour*; Lukács calls it *irony*. Both agree that the novelist must supersede the consciousness of his heroes and that his supersession (humour or irony) is aesthetically constitutive of fictional creation. But they diverge as to the nature of this supersession and, on this point, it is the position of Lukács that seems to me to be acceptable and not that of Girard.

For Girard, the novelist has left the world of degradation and rediscovered authenticity, vertical transcendence, at the moment he writes his work. This is why he thinks that most great novels end with a conversion of the hero to this vertical transcendence and that the abstract character of certain endings (*Don Quixote, Le Rouge et le Noir,* one might also add *La Princesse de Clèves*) is either an illusion on the part of the reader, or the result of survivals from the past in the consciousness of the writer.

Such a notion is strictly contrary to Lukács aesthetic, for which any *literary form* (and any great artistic form in general) is born out of the need to express an *essential* content. If the fictional degradation were really superseded by the writer, even through the ultimate conversion of a number of heroes, the story of this degradation would be no more than a mere incident and its expression would have at most the character of a more or less entertaining narrative.

And yet the writer's irony, his autonomy in relation to his characters, the ultimate conversion of the fictional heroes are undoubted realities.

However, Lukács thinks that precisely to the extent that the novel is the imaginary creation of a world governed by *universal* degradation, this supersession cannot itself be other than degraded, *abstract, conceptual*, and not experienced as a concrete reality.

According to Lukács the novelist's irony is directed not only on to the hero, whose demoniacal character he is well aware of, but also on the abstract, and therefore inadequate and degraded, character of his own consciousness. That is why the story of the degraded search, whether demoniacal or idolatrous, always remains the sole way of expressing essential realities.

The ultimate conversion of Don Quixote or Julien Sorel* is not, as Girard believes, a discovery of authenticity, vertical transcendence, but simply an awareness of this vanity, the degraded character not only of the earlier search, but also of any hope, of any possible search. That is why it is an end and not a beginning and it is the existence of this irony (which is always a self-irony, as well) than enables Lukács to make two related definitions that seem to me particularly appropriate to this form of the novel: *the Way is begun, the journey is ended*, and *the novel is the form of virile maturity,* the second formula defining more specifically, as we have seen, the *Bildungsroman* of the *Wilhelm Meister* type, which ends with a self-imposed limitation (the hero gives up the problematic search, without accepting the world of convention or abandoning the explicit scale of values).

Thus the novel, in the sense given it by Lukacs and Girard, appears as a literary genre in which authentic values, which are always involved, cannot be present in the work in the form of conscious characters or concrete realities. These values exist only in an abstract, conceptual form in the consciousness of the novelist in which they take on an *ethical* character. But abstract ideas have no place in a literary work where they would form a heterogeneous element.

The problem of the novel, therefore, is to make what in the novelist's consciousness is *abstract* and *ethical* the essential element of a work in which reality can exist only in the mode of a non-thematized (Girard would say mediatized) absence or, which is equivalent, a degraded presence. As Lukács says, the novel is the only literary genre in which *the novelist's ethic becomes an aesthetic problem of the work.*

The problem of a sociology of the novel has always preoccupied sociologists of literature, though, as yet, no decisive step towards its elucidation has so far been attempted. Basically, the novel, for the first part of its history, was a biography and a social chronicle and so it has always been possible to show that the social chronicle reflected to a greater or lesser degree the society of the period — and one does not have to be a sociologist to see that.

On the other hand, a connection has also been made between the transformation of the novel since Kafka and the Marxist analysis of reification. Here, too, it has to be said that serious sociologists should have seen this as a problem rather than as an explanation. Although it is obvious that the absurd worlds of Kafka or Camus's *L'Etranger*

Editor's note: The hero of the novel *Le Rouge et Le Noir* mentioned above.

or Robbe-Grillet's world composed of relatively autonomous objects, correspond to the analysis of reification as developed by Marx and later Marxists, the problem arises as to why, when this analysis was elaborated in the second half of the nineteenth century and concerned a phenomenon that appeared in a still earlier period, this same phenomenon was expressed in the novel only at the end of World War I.

In short, all these analyses concern the relation between certain elements of the *content* of fictional literature and the existence of a social reality that they reflect almost without transposition or by means of a more or less transparent transposition.

But the first problem that a sociology of the novel should have confronted is that of the relation between the *novel form* itself and the *structure* of the social environment in which it developed, that is to say, between the novel as a literary genre and individualistic modern society.

It seems to me today that a combination of the analyses of Lukács and Girard, even though they were both developed without specifically sociological preoccupations, makes it possible, if not to elucidate this problem entirely, at least to make a decisive step towards its elucidation.

I have just said that the novel can be characterized as the story of a search for authentic values in a degraded mode, in a degraded society, and that this degradation, in so far as it concerns the hero, is expressed principally through the mediatization, the reduction of authentic values to the implicit level and their disappearance as manifest realities. This is obviously a particularly complex structure and it would be difficult to imagine that it could one day emerge simply from individual invention without any basis in the social life of the group.

What, however, would be quite inconceivable, is that a literary form of such dialectical complexity should be rediscovered, over a period of centuries, among the most different writers in the most varied countries, that it should have become the form *par excellence* in which was expressed, on the literary plane, the content of a whole period, without there being either a homology or a significant relation between this form and the most important aspects of social life.

This hypothesis seems to me particularly simple and above all productive and credible, though it has taken me years to find it.

The novel form seems to me, in effect, to be *the transposition on the literary plane of everyday life in the individualistic society created by market production*. There is a *rigorous homology* between the literary form of the novel, as I have defined it with the help of Lukács and Girard, and the everyday relation between man and commodities in general, and by extension between men and other men, in a market society.

The natural, healthy relation between men and commodities is that in which production is consciously governed by future consumption, by the concrete qualities of objects, by their *use value*.

Now what characterizes market production is, on the contrary, the elimination of this relation with men's consciousness, its reduction to the implicit through the mediation of the new economic reality created by this form of production: *exchange value*.

In other forms of society, when a man needed an article of clothing, or a house, he had to produce them himself or obtain them from someone capable of producing them and who was under an obligation to provide him with them, either in accordance with certain traditional rules, or for reasons of authority, friendship, etc., or as part of some reciprocal arrangement.[5]

If one wishes to obtain an article of clothing or a house today, one has to find the money needed to buy them. The producer of clothes or houses is indifferent to the use values of the objects he produces. For him, these objects are no more than a necessary evil to obtain what alone interests him, an exchange value sufficient to ensure the viability of his enterprise. In the economic life, which constitutes the most important part of modern social life, every authentic relation with the qualitative aspect of objects and persons tends to disappear — interhuman relations as well as those between men and things — and be replaced by a mediatized and degraded relation: the relation with purely quantitative exchange values.

Of course, use values continue to exist and even to govern, in the last resort, the whole of the economic life; but their action assumes an *implicit character, exactly like that of authentic values in the fictional world*.

On the conscious, manifest plane, *the economic life* is composed of people orientated exclusively towards exchange values, degraded values, to which are added in production a number of individuals — the creators in every sphere — who remain essentially orientated towards use values and who by virtue of that fact are situated on the fringes of society and become *problematic individuals*; and, of course, even these individuals unless they accept the romantic illusion (Girard would say lie) of the *total* rupture between essence and appearance, between the inner life and the social life, cannot be deluded as to the degradations that their creative activity undergoes in a market society, when this activity is manifested externally, when it becomes a book, a painting, teaching, a musical composition, etc., enjoying a certain prestige, and having therefore a certain price. It should be added that as the ultimate consumer, opposed in the very act of exchange to the producers, any individual in a market society finds himself at certain moments of the day aiming at qualitative use values that he can obtain only through the mediation of exchange values.

In view of this, there is nothing surprising about the creation of the novel as a literary genre. Its apparently extremely complex form is the one in which men live every day, when they are obliged to seek all quality, all use value in a mode degraded by the mediation of quantity of exchange value — and this in a society in which any effort to orientate oneself *directly* towards use value can only produce individuals who are themselves degraded, but in a different mode, that of *the problematic individual*.

Thus the two structures, that of an important fictional genre and that of exchange proved to be strictly homologous, to the point at which one might speak of one and the same structure manifesting itself on two different planes. Furthermore, as we shall see later, the *evolution* of the fictional form that corresponds to the world of reification can be understood only in so far as it is related to a *homologous history* of the structure of reification.

However, before making a few remarks about this homology between the two evolutions we must examine the problem, particularly important for the sociologist, of the process by which the literary form was able to emerge out of the economic reality, and of the modifications that the study of this process forces us to introduce into the traditional representation of the sociological conditioning of literary creation.

One fact is striking at the outset; the traditional scheme of literary sociology, whether Marxist or not, cannot be applied in the case of the structural homology just referred to. Most work in the sociology of literature established as a relation between the most important literary works and the collective *consciousness* of the particular social group from which they emerged. On this point, the traditional Marxist position does not differ essentially from non-Marxist sociological work as a whole, in relation to which it introduces only four new ideas, namely:

a) The literary work is not the mere reflection of a real, given collective consciousness, but the culmination at a very advanced level of coherence of tendencies peculiar to the consciousness of a particular group, a consciousness that must be conceived as a dynamic reality, orientated towards a certain state of equilibrium. What really separates, in this as in all other spheres, Marxist sociology from positivistic, relativist, or eclectic sociological tendencies is the fact that it sees the key concept not in the *real* collective consciousness, but in the constructed concept (*zugerechnet*) of *possible consciousness* which, alone, makes an understanding of the first possible.

b) The relation between collective ideology and great individual literary, philosophical, theological etc. creations resides not in an identity of content, but in a more advanced coherence and in a homology of structures, which can be expressed in imaginary contents very different from the real content of the collective consciousness.

c) The work corresponding to the mental structure of the particular social group may be elaborated in certain exceptional cases by an individual with very few relations with this group. The *social* character of the work resides above all in the fact that an individual can never establish by himself a coherent mental structure corresponding to what is called a 'world view'. Such a structure can be elaborated only by a group, the individual being capable only of carrying it to a very high degree of coherence and transposing it on the level of imaginary creation, conceptual thought, etc.

d) The collective consciousness is neither a primary reality, nor an autonomous reality; it is elaborated implicitly in the over-all behaviour of individuals participating in the economic, social, political life, etc.

These are evidently extremely important theses, sufficient to establish a very great difference between Marxist thinking and other conceptions of the sociology of literature. Nevertheless, despite these differences, Marxist theoreticians, like positivistic or relativistic sociologists of literature, have always thought that the social life can be expressed on the literary, artistic, or philosophical plane only through the inteimediary link of the collective consciousness.

In the case we have just studied, however, what strikes one first is the fact that although we find a strict homology between the structures of economic life and a certain particularly important manifestation, one can detect no analogous structure at the level of the *collective consciousness* that seemed hitherto to be the indispensable intermediary link to realize either the homology or an intelligible, significant relation between the different aspects of social existence.

The novel analysed by Lukács and Girard no longer seems to be the imaginary transposition of the *conscious structures* of a particular group, but seems to express on the contrary (and this may be the case of a very large part of modern art in general) a search for values that no social group defines effectively and that the economic life tends to make implicit in all members of the society.

The old Marxist thesis whereby the proletariat was seen as the only social group capable of constituting the basis of a new culture, by virtue of the fact that it was not integrated into the reified society, set out from the traditional sociological representation that presupposed that all authentic, important cultural creation could emerge only from a fundamental harmony between the mental structure of the creator and that of a partial group of relative size, but universal ambition. In reality, for Western society at least, the Marxist analysis has proved inadequate; the Western proletariat, far from remaining alien to the reified society and opposing it as a revolutionary force, has on the contrary become integrated into it to a large degree, and its trade union and political action, far from overthrowing this society and replacing it by a socialist world, has enabled it to gain a relatively better place in it than Marx's analysis foresaw.

Furthermore, cultural creation, although increasingly threatened by the reified society, has continued to flourish. Fictional literature, as perhaps modern poetic creation and contemporary painting, are authentic forms of cultural creation even though they cannot be attached to the consciousness — even a potential one — of a particular social group.

Before embarking on a study of the processes that made possible and produced this *direct* transposition of the economic life into the literary life, we should perhaps remark that although such a process seems contrary to the whole tradition of Marxist studies of cultural creation, it confirms nevertheless, in a quite unexpected way, one of the most important Marxist analyses of bourgeois thought, namely the theory of the fetishization of merchandise and reification. This analysis, which Marx regarded as one of his most important discoveries, affirms in effect that in market societies (that is to say, in types of society in which economic activity predominates), the collective consciousness gradually loses all active reality and tends to become a mere reflection[6] of the economic life and, ultimately, to disappear.

There was obviously, therefore, between this *particular* analysis of Marx and the general theory of literary and philosophical creation of later Marxists, who presupposed an active role of the collective consciousness, not a contradiction but an incoherence. The latter theory never envisaged the consequences for the sociology of literature of Marx's belief that there survives in market societies a radical modification of the status of the individual and collective consciousness and, implicitly, relations between the infrastructure and the superstructure. The analysis of reification elaborated first by Marx on the level of everyday life, then developed by Lukács in the field of philosophical scientific, and political thought, finally taken up by a number of theoreticians in various specific domains, and about which I have myself published a study, would appear therefore, for the moment at least, to be confirmed by the facts in the sociological analysis of a certain fictional form.

Having said this, the question arises as to how the link between the economic structures and literary manifestations is made in a society in which this link occurs *outside the collective consciousness*.

With regard to this I have formulated the hypothesis of the convergent action of four different factors, namely:

a) The birth in the thinking of members of bourgeois society, on the basis of economic behaviour and the existence of exchange value, of the *category of mediation* as a fundamental and increasingly developed form of thought, with an implicit tendency to replace this thought by a total false consciousness in which the mediating value becomes an absolute value and in which the mediated value disappears entirely or, to put it more clearly, with the tendency to conceive of the access to all values from the point of view of mediation, together with a propensity to make of money and social prestige absolute values and not merely mediations that provide access to other values of a qualitative character.

b) The survival in this society of a number of individuals who are essentially *problematic* in so far as their thinking and behaviour remain dominated by qualitative values, even though they are unable to extract themselves entirely from the existence of the degrading mediation whose action permeates the whole of the social structure.

These individuals include, above all, the creators, writers, artists, philosophers, theologians, men of action, etc., whose thought and behaviour are governed above all by the quality of their work even though they cannot escape entirely from the action of the market and from the welcome extended them by the reified society.

c) Since no important work can be the expression of a purely individual experience, it is likely that the novel genre could emerge and be developed only in so far as a *non-conceptualized*, affective discontent, an affective aspiration towards qualitative values, was developed either in society as a whole, or perhaps solely among the middle strata from which most novelists have come.[7]

d) Lastly, in the liberal market societies, there was a set of values, which, though not trans-individual, nevertheless, had a universal aim and, within these societies, a general validity. These were the values of liberal individualism that were bound up with the very existence of the competitive market (in France, liberty, equality, and property, in Germany, *Bildungsideal*, with their derivatives, tolerance, the rights of man, development of the personality, etc.). On the basis of these values, there developed the category of *individual* biography that became the constitutive element of the novel. Here, however, it assumed the form of the *problematic* individual, on the basis of the following:

1. the personal experience of the problematic individuals mentioned above under *b*);
2. the internal contradiction between individualism as a universal value produced by bourgeois society and the important and painful limitations that this society itself brought to the possibilities of the development of the individual.

This hypothetical schema seems to me to be confirmed among other things by the fact that, when one of these four elements, individualism, has gradually been eliminated by the transformation of the economic life and the replacement of the economy of free competition by an economy of cartels and monopolies (a transformation that began at the end of the nineteenth century, but whose qualitative turning-point most economists would place between 1900 and 1910), we witness a parallel transformation of the novel form that culminates in the gradual dissolution and disappearance of the individual character, of the hero; a transformation that seems to me to be characterized in an extremely schematic way by the existence of two periods:

a) The first, transitional period, during which the disappearance of the importance of the individual brings with it attempts to replace biography as the content of the work of fiction with values produced by different ideologies. For although, in Western societies, these values have proved to be too weak to produce their own literary forms, they might well give a new lease of life to an already existing form that was losing its former content. First and foremost, on this level, are the ideas of community and collective reality (institutions, family, social group, revolution, etc.) that had been introduced and developed in Western thinking by the socialist ideology.

b) The second period, which begins more or less with Kafka and continues to the contemporary *nouveau roman*, and which has not yet come to an end, is characterized by an abandonment of any attempt to replace the problematic hero and individual biography by another reality and by the effort to write the novel of the absence of the subject, of the non-existence of any ongoing search.[8]

It goes without saying that this attempt to safeguard the novel form by giving it a content, related no doubt to the content of the traditional novel (it had always been the literary form of the problematic search and the absence of positive values), but nevertheless essentially different (it now involves the elimination of two essential elements of the specific content of the novel: the psychology of the problematic hero and the story of his demoniacal search), was to produce at the same time parallel orientations towards different forms of expression. There may be here elements for a sociology of the theatre of absence (Beckett, Ionesco, Adamov during a certain period) and also of certain aspects of non-figurative painting.

Lastly, we should mention a problem that might and ought to be the subject of later research. The novel form that we have just studied is essentially critical and oppositional. It is a form of resistance to developing bourgeois society. An individual resistance that can fall back, within a group, only on *affective* and *non-conceptualized* psychical processes precisely because conscious resistances that might have elaborated literary forms implying the possibility of a positive hero (in the first place, a proletarian oppositional consciousness such as Marx had hoped for and predicted) had not become sufficiently developed in Western societies. The novel with a problematic hero thus proves, contrary to traditional opinion, to be a literary form bound up certainly with history and the development of a bourgeoisie, but not the expression of the real or possible consciousness of that class.

But the problem remains as to whether, parallel with this literary form, there did not develop other forms that might correspond to the conscious values and effective aspirations of the bourgeoisie; and, on this point, I should like to mention, merely as a general and hypothetical suggestion, the possibility that the work of Balzac — whose structure ought, indeed, to be analysed from this point of view — might constitute the only great literary expression of the world as structured by the conscious values of the bourgeoisie: individualism, the thirst for power, money, and eroticism, which triumph over the ancient feudal values of altruism, charity, and love.

Sociologically, this hypothesis, if it proves to be correct, might be related to the fact that the work of Balzac is situated precisely at a period in which individualism, ahistorical in itself, structured the consciousness of a bourgeoisie that was in the process of constructing a new society and found itself at the highest and most intense level of its real historical efficacity.

We should also ask ourselves why, with the exception of this single case, this form of fictional literature had only a secondary importance in the history of Western culture, why the real consciousness and aspirations of the bourgeoisie never succeeded again, in the course of the nineteenth and twentieth centuries, in creating a literary form of its own that might be situated on the same level as the other forms that constitute the Western literary tradition.

On this point, I would like to make a few general hypotheses. The analysis that I have just developed extends to one of the most important novel forms a statement that now seems to me to be valid for almost all forms of *authentic cultural creation*. In relation to this statement the only expression that I could see for the moment was constituted precisely by the work of Balzac[9], who was able to create a great literary universe structured by purely individualistic values, at a historical moment when, concurrently, men animated by ahistorical values were accomplishing a considerable historical upheaval (an upheaval that was not really completed in France until the end of the bourgeois revolution in 1848). With this single exception (but perhaps one should add a few other possible exceptions that may have escaped my attention), it seems to me that there is valid literary and artistic creation only when there is an aspiration to transcendence on the part of the individual and a search for qualitative trans-individual values. 'Man passes beyond man,' I have written, slightly altering Pascal. This means that man can be authentic only in so far as he conceives himself or feels himself as part of a developing whole and situates himself in a historical or transcendent trans-individual dimension. But bourgeois ideology, bound up like bourgeois society itself with the existence of economic activity, is precisely the first ideology in history that is both radically profane and ahistorical; the first ideology whose tendency is to deny anything sacred, whether the otherworldly sacredness of the transcendent religions or the immanent sacredness of the historical future. It is, it seems to me, the fundamental reason why bourgeois society created the first radically nonaesthetic form of consciousness. The essential character of bourgeois ideology, rationalism, ignores in its extreme expressions the very existence of art. There is no Cartesian or Spinozian aesthetics, or even an aesthetics for Baumgarten — art is merely an inferior form of knowledge.

It is no accident therefore if, with the exception of a few particular situations, we do not find any great literary manifestations of the bourgeois consciousness itself. In a society bound up with the market, the artist is, as I have already said, a problematic individual, and this means a critical individual, opposed to society.

Nevertheless reified bourgeois ideology had its thematic values, values that were sometimes authentic, such as those of individualism, sometimes purely conventional, which Lukács called false consciousness and, in their extreme forms, bad faith, and Heidegger's 'chatter'. These stereotypes, whether authentic or conventional, thematized in the collective consciousness, were later able to produce, side by side with the authentic novel form, a parallel literature that also recounted an individual history and, naturally enough, since conceptualized values were involved, could depict a positive hero.

It would be interesting to follow the meanderings of the secondary novel forms that might be based, quite naturally, on the collective consciousness. One would end up perhaps — I have not yet made such a study — with a very varied spectrum, from the lowest forms of the Delly type to the highest forms to be found perhaps in such writers as Alexandre Dumas or Eugène Sue. It is also perhaps on this plane that we should situate, parallel with the *nouveau roman*, certain best-sellers that are bound up with the new forms of collective consciousness.

However, the extremely schematic sketch that I have just traced seems to me to provide a framework for a sociological study of the novel form. Such a study would be all the more important in that, apart from its own object, it would constitute a not inconsiderable contribution to the study of the psychical structures of certain social groups, the middle strata in particular.

Notes and References

[1]Georg Lukács, *The Theory of the Novel* (1971) (trans., A. Bostock) London, Merlin Press.

[2]René Girard, *Mensonge romantique et vérité romanesque* (1961) Paris, Grasset.

[3]I should say however that, in my opinion, the field of validity of this hypothesis must be contracted, for, although the hypothesis may be applied to such important works in the history of literature as Cervantes' *Don Quixote,* Stendhal's *Le Rouge et le Noir,* and Flaubert's *Madame Bovary* and *L'Education Sentimentale,* it can be applied only very partially to *La Chartreuse de Parme* and not at all to the works of Balzac, which occupy a considerable place in the history of the Western novel. As such, however, Lukács's analyses enable us, it seems to me, to undertake a serious sociological study of the novel form.

[4]In Heidegger's thinking, as indeed in that of Lukács, there is a radical break between Being (For Lukács, Totality) and whatever may be spoken of in the indicative (a judgement of fact), or in the imperative (a judgement of value).

It is this difference that Heidegger designates as that of the ontological and the ontic. And, from this point of view, metaphysics, which is one of the highest and most general forms of thought in the indicative, remains in the final resort in the domain of the ontic.

While agreeing on the necessary distinction between the ontological and the ontic, totality and the theoretical, the moral and the metaphysical, the positions of Heidegger and Lukács are essentially different in the way these relations are conceived.

As a philosophy of history, Lukács's thought implies the idea of a coming-into-being (*devenir*) of knowledge, of a hope in progress, and a risk of regression. Now, for him, progress is the bringing together of positive thought and the category of totality; regression, the distancing of these two, ultimately inseparable, elements. The task of philosophy is precisely to introduce the category of totality as the basis of all partial research and of all reflection on positive data.

Heidegger, on the other hand, establishes a radical separation (and, by the very fact, an abstract and conceptual one) between Being and the datum, between the ontological and the ontic, between philosophy and positive science, thus eliminating any idea of progress and regression. He, too, arrives in the end at a philosophy of history, but it is an abstract philosophy with two dimensions, the authentic and the inauthentic, openness to Being and oblivion of Being.

So, although Girard's terminology is Heideggerian in origin, the introduction of the categories of progress and regression brings him closer to Lukács.
[5] While every exchange remains sporadic *because* it bears solely on surpluses or because it has the character of an exchange of use values that individuals or groups cannot produce within an essentially natural economy, the mental structure of mediation does not appear or remains secondary. The fundamental transformation in the development of reification results from the advent of *market production.*
[6] I speak of a 'consciousness-reflection' when the content of this consciousness and the set of relations between the different elements of the content (what I call its structure) undergo the action of certain other domains of the social life, without acting in turn on them. In practice, this situation has probably never been reached in capitalist society. This society creates, however, a tendency to the rapid and gradual diminution of the action of consciousness on the economic life and, conversely, to a continual increase of the action of the economic sector of the social life on the content and structure of consciousness.
[7] There arises a problem here that is difficult to solve at the moment, but which might one day be solved by concrete sociological research. I mean the problem of the collective, affective, non-conceptualized 'sound-box' that made possible the development of the novel form.

Initially, I thought that reification, while tending to dissolve and to integrate in the over-all society different partial groups, and, therefore, to deprive them to a certain extent of their specificity, had a character so contrary to both the biological and psychological reality of the individual human being that it could not fail to engender in *all* individual human beings, to a greater or lesser degree, reactions of opposition (or, if this reification becomes degraded in a qualitatively more advanced way, to reactions of evasion), thus creating a diffuse resistance to the reified world, a resistance that would constitute the background of fictional creation.

Later, however, it seemed to me that this hypothesis contained an unproved *a priori* supposition: that of the existence of a biological nature whose external manifestations could not be entirely denatured by social reality.

In fact, it is just as likely that resistances, even affective ones, to reification are circumscribed within certain particular social strata, which positive research ought to delimit.
[8] Lukács characterized the time of the traditional novel by the proposition 'We have started on our way, our journey is over.' One might characterize the new novel by the suppression of the first half of this statement. Its time might be characterized by the statement: 'The aspiration is there, but the journey is over' (Kafka, Nathalie Sarraute), or simply by the observation that 'the journey is

already over, though we never started on our way' (Robbe-Grillet's first three novels).

[9]A year ago, when dealing with the same problems and mentioning the existence of the novel with a problematic hero and of a fictional sub-literature with a positive hero, I wrote, 'Last, I shall conclude this article with a great question mark, that of the sociological study of the works of Balzac. These works, it seems to me, constitute a novel form of their own, one that integrates important elements belonging to the two types of novels that I have mentioned and probably represents the most important form of fictional expression in history.'

The remarks formulated in these pages are an attempt to develop in greater detail the hypothesis hinted at in these lines.

4.4 Literature as an Ideological Form: Some Marxist Propositions
Pierre Macherey and **Etienne Balibar**

Is there a Marxist theory of literature? In what could it consist? This is a classic question, and often purely academic. We intend to reformulate it in two stages and suggest new propositions.[1]

1. Marxist Theses on Literature and the Category of 'Reflection'

1.1 Can there be a 'Marxist aesthetic'?
It is not our intention to give an account of the attempts which have been made to substantiate this idea nor the controversies which have surrounded it. We will merely point out that to constitute an aesthetic (and particularly a literary aesthetic) has always presented Marxism with two kinds of problem, which can be combined or held separate:

(i) How to explain the specific ideological mode for 'art' and the 'aesthetic' effect

(ii) How to analyse and explain the class position (or the class *positions*, which may be contradictory in themselves) of the author and more materially the 'literary text', within the ideological class struggle.

The first problem is obviously brought in, *imposed* on Marxism by the dominant ideology so as to force the Marxist critic to *produce his own aesthetic* and to 'settle accounts' with art, the work of art, the aesthetic effect, just like Lessing, or Hegel, or Tain, or Valéry, et al. Since the problem is imposed on Marxism from outside, it offers two alternatives: to reject the problem and so be 'proved' unable to explain not so much a 'reality' as an absolute 'value' of our time, which is now supreme since it has replaced religious value; or to recognise the problem and therefore be forced to acknowledge aesthetic 'values', i.e., to submit to them. This is an even better result for the dominant ideology since it thereby makes Marxism concede to the 'values' of the dominant classes *within its own problematic* — a result which has great political significance in a period when Marxism becomes the ideology of the working class.

The second problem meanwhile is induced from within the theory and practice of Marxism, *on its own terrain,* but in such a way that it can remain a formal and mechanical presentation. In this case the necessary criterion is that of practice, in the first place of scientific practice. The question for Marxism should be, does the act of confronting literary texts with their class positions result in the *opening* of new fields of knowledge and in the first place simply in the siting of new *problems*? The proof of the right formulation would be whether it makes objectively clear within historical materialism itself whole sets of unsolved and sometimes as yet unrecognized problems.

The second test is of political practice itself, insomuch as it is operative within literature. The least one should therefore ask a Marxist theory is that it should bring about real transformation, new practice, whether in the production of texts and 'works of art' or in their *social* 'consumption'. But is this a real transformation, even if at times it does have an immediate political effect − the simple fact of instilling the practitioners of art (writers and artists, but also teachers and students) − with a Marxist ideology of the form and *social* function of art (even if this operation may sometimes have a certain immediate political interest)? Is it enough simply to give Marxism and its adherents their turn to taste and consume works of art in their own way? In effect experience proves that it is perfectly possible to substitute new 'Marxist' themes, i.e. formulated in the language of Marxism, for the ideological notions dominant in 'cultural life', notions that are bourgeois or petit-bourgeois in origin, and yet not alter at all the place of art and literature within social practice, nor therefore the practical *relationship* of individuals and classes to the works of art they produce and consume. The category of art in general dominates production and consumption, which are conceived and practised within this mode − whether 'committed', 'socialist', 'proletarian', or whatever.

Yet in the Marxist classics there were elements which can open a path [*frayer la voie*] − not an 'aesthetic', nor a 'theory of literature', any more than a 'theory of knowledge'. Yet through their mode of practising literature and the implications of a theoretical position based ultimately on revolutionary class practice, they pose certain theses about [*thèses sur*] literary effects, which, worked within historical materialism, make theses for [*thèses pour*] a scientific and therefore historical analysis of literary effects.[2]

These very general premises are enough to show at once that the two types of problems between which Marxist attempts are divided, are really *one and the same*. To be able to analyse the nature and expression of class positions *in* literature and its output (the 'texts', 'works' perceived as literature) is simultaneously to be able to define and know the ideological mode of literature. But this means that the problem must be posed in terms of a theory of the *history* of literary effects, clearly showing the primary elements of their relation to their material base, their progressions (for they are not eternal) and their tendential transformations (for they are not immutable).

1.2 The materialist category of reflection

Let us be clear. The classic Marxist theses on literature and art set out from the essential philosophical category of the *reflection*. To understand this category fully is therefore the key to the Marxist conception of literature.

In the Marxist texts on the materialist concept, Marx and Engels on Balzac, Lenin on Tolstoy, it is qua material reflection, reflection of objective reality, that literature is conceived as an *historic* reality – in its very form, which scientific analysis seeks to grasp.

In the *Talks at the Yenan Forum on Literature and Art,*[3] Mao Tse-Tung writes, 'Works of literature and art, as ideological forms are products of the reflection in the human brain of the life of a given society.' So the first implication of the category of reflection for Marxist theoreticians is to provide an *index of reality* of literature. It does not 'fall from the heavens', the product of a mysterious 'creation', but is the product of social practice (rather a *particular* social practice); neither is it an 'imaginary' activity, albeit it produces imaginary effects, but inescapably part of a material process, 'the product of the reflection. . . of the life of a given society'.

The Marxist conception thus inscribes literature in its place in the unevenly determined system of real social practices: one of several ideological forms within the *ideological superstructure,* corresponding to a base of social relations of production which are historically determined and transformed, and historically linked to other ideological forms. Be sure that in using the term ideological *forms* no reference to *formalism* is intended – the historical materialist concept does not refer to 'form' in opposition to 'content', but to the objective coherence of an ideological formation – we shall come back to this point. Let us note too that this first, very general but absolutely essential premise, has no truck with queries about what *ideological form* is taken by literature within the ideological instance. There is no 'reduction' of literature to morality, religion, politics, etc.

The Marxist concept of reflection has suffered from so many misinterpretations and distortions that we must stop here for a moment. The conclusions reached by Dominique Lecourt[4] through an attentive reading of Lenin's *Materialism and Empiriocriticism* will be useful to us.

Dominique Lecourt shows that the Marxist and Leninist category of reflection contains two propositions which are combined within a constitutive *order* – or better, *two articulated successive problems.* (Thus according to Lecourt there is not one simple thesis, but a double thesis of the reflection of things in thought.)

The first problem, which materialism always re-establishes in its priority, is the problem of the *objectivity* of the reflection. It poses the question 'Is there an *existent material reality* reflected in the mind which *determines* thought?' And consequently it has the rider, 'Is thought itself a materially determined reality?' Dialectical materialism asserts the objectivity of the reflection and the objectivity of thought as reflection, i.e., the determinance of the existent reality which precedes thought and is irreducible to it, and the material reality of thought itself.

The second problem, which can only be posed correctly on the basis of the first, concerns the scientific knowledge of the exactitude of the reflection. It poses the question, '*If* thought reflects an existent reality how accurate is its reflection?' or better, 'Under what conditions (i.e. historical conditions whereby the dialectic between 'absolute truth' and 'relative truth' intervenes) can it provide an accurate reflection?' The answer lies in the analysis of the relatively autonomous *process* of the history of science. In the context, it is clear that this second problem poses the question, '*What form does the reflection take?*' But it only has a materialist implication *once* the first question has been posed and the objectivity of the reflection affirmed.

The result of this analysis, which we have only given in outline, is to show that the Marxist category of the 'reflection' is quite separate from the empiricist and sensualist concept of the *image*, reflection as 'mirroring'. The reflection, in dialectical materialism, is a 'reflection without a mirror'; in the history of philosophy this is the only effective destruction of the empiricist ideology which calls the relation of thought to the real a speculary (and therefore reversible) reflection. This is thanks to the *complexity* of the Marxist theory of 'reflection': it poses the *separate nature* of two propositions and their articulation in an irreversible order within which the materialist account is realised.

These observations are central to the problem of the 'theory of literature'. A rigorous use of this complex structure eliminates the *seeming* opposition of two contrary descriptions: that between formalism and the 'critical' or 'normative' use of the notion of 'realism'. That is, on one side an intention to study the reflection 'for itself', independent of its relationship to the material world; on the other, a confusion of both aspects and an assertion of the primacy of thought, a reversal of the materialist order.

Hence the advantage of a rigorous definition like Lenin's, for it is then possible to articulate, in theory as in fact, two aspects which must be both kept separate and in a constitutive order: literature as an ideological form (amongst others), and the specific process of literary production.

1.3 Literature as an ideological form

It is important to 'locate' the production of literary effects historically as part of the ensemble of social practices. For this to be seen dialectically rather than mechanically, it is important to understand that the relationship of 'history' to 'literature' is not like the relation-ship or 'correspondence' of *two 'branches'*, but concerns the developing forms of an internal *contradiction*. Literature and history are not each set up externally to each other (not even as the history *of* literature, social and political history), but are in an intricate and connected relationship, the historical conditions of existence of anything like a literature. Very generally, this internal relationship is what constitutes the definition of literature as an ideological form.

But this definition is significant only in so far as its implications are then developed. Ideological forms, to be sure, are not straightforward systems of 'ideas' and 'discourses', but are manifested through the workings and history of determinate *practices* in determinate social relations, what Althusser calls the *Ideological State Apparatus* (I.S.A.). The objectivity of literary production therefore is inseparable from given social practices in a given I.S.A. More precisely, we shall see that it is inseparable from a given *linguistic practice* (there is a 'French' literature because there is a linguistic practice 'French', i.e., a contrad-ictory ensemble making a national tongue), in itself inseparable from an *academic or schooling practice* which defines both the conditions for the consumption of literature and the very conditions of its production also. By connecting the objective existence of literature to this ensemble of practices, one can define the material anchoring points which *make* literature an historic and social reality.

First, then, literature is historically constituted *in the bourgeois epoch* as an ensemble of language − or rather of specific linguistic practices − inserted in a general schooling process so as to provide appropriate fictional effects, thereby reproducing bourgeois ideology as the dominant ideology. Literature submits to a threefold determina-tion: 'linguistic', 'pedagogic', and 'fictive' [*imaginaire*] (we must return to this point, for it involves the question of a recourse to psycho-analysis for an explanation of literary effects). There is a linguistic determinance because the work of literary production depends on the existence of a common language codifying linguistic exchange, both for its material and for its aims − insomuch as literature contributes directly to the maintenance of a 'common language'. That it has this starting point is proved by the fact that divergences from the common language are not arbitrary but determined. In our introduction to the work of R. Balibar and D. Laporte[5], we sketched out an explanation of the historical process by which this 'common language' is set up. Following their thought, we stressed that the common language, i.e. the *national language,* is bound to be the political form of 'bourgeois democracy' and is the historical outcome of particular class struggles. Like bourgeois *right,* its parallel, the common national language is needed to unify a new class domination, thereby universalising it and providing it with progressive forms throughout its epoch. It refers therefore to a social *contradiction* perpetually reproduced via the process which surmounts it. What is the basis of this contradiction?

It is the effect of the historic conditions under which the bourgeois class established its political, economic and ideological dominance. To achieve hegemony, it had not only to transform the base, the relations of production, but also radically to transform the superstructure, the ideological formations. This transformation could be called the bourgeois 'cultural revolution' since it involves not only the formation of a new ideology, but its realization as the dominant ideology, through new I.S.A.'s and the remoulding of the relationships between the different I.S.A.'s. This revolutionary transformation, which took more than a century but which was preparing itself for far longer, is characterised by making the school apparatus the means of forcing submission to the dominant ideology — individual submission, but also, and more importantly, the submission of the very ideology of the dominated classes. Therefore in the last analysis, all the ideological contradictions rest on the contradictions of the school apparatus, and become contradictions subordinated to the form of schooling, within the form of schooling itself.

We are beginning to work out the form taken by social contradictions in the schooling apparatus. It can only establish itself through the formal unity of a unique and unifying educational system, the product of this same unity, which is itself formed from the co-existence of two systems of contradictory networks: those which, by following the institutional division of 'levels of teaching' which in France has long served to materialise this contradiction, we could call the apparatus of 'basic education' [*primaire-professionnel*] and that of 'advanced education' [*secondaire-supérieur*].[6]

This division in schooling, which reproduces the social division of a society based on the sale and purchase of individual labour-power, while assuring the dominance of bourgeois ideology through asserting a specifically national unity, is primarily and throughout based on a *linguistic division*. Let us be clear: there as well, the unifying form is the essential means of the division and of the contradiction. The linguistic division inherent in schooling is not like the division between different 'languages' observable in certain pre-capitalist social formations — those languages being a 'language of the common people' (dialect, patois or argot), and a 'language of the bourgeoisie'; on the contrary — the division pre-supposes a *common* language, and is the contradiction between *different practices of the same language*. Specifically, it is in and through the educational system that the contradiction is instituted — through the contradiction between the basic language [*français élémentaire*], as taught at primary school, and the literary language [*français littéraire*] reserved for the advanced level of teaching. This is the basis of the contradiction in schooling techniques, particularly between the basic exercises of '*rédaction-narration*', a mere training in 'correct' usage and the reporting of 'reality', and the advanced exercise of comprehension, the *'dissertation-explication de textes'*, so-called 'creative' work which presupposes the incorporation and imitation of literary material. Hence the contradictions in schooling practice, and in ideological practice and in social practice. What thus appears as the basis of literary production is an *unequal and contradictory relation* to the *same ideology*, the dominant one. But this contradiction would not exist if the dominant ideology did not have to struggle all the time for its priority.

From this analysis, given in mere outline, there is an essential point to be grasped: the objectivity of literature, i.e. its relation to objective reality by which it is historically determined, is not a relation to an 'object' which it represents, is not *representative*. Nor is it purely and simply the instrument for using and transforming its immediate material, the linguistic practices determined within the practice of teaching. Precisely because of their contradictions, they cannot be used as a simple primary material: thus all use is an intervention, made from a standpoint, a declaration (in a general sense) from within the contradiction and hence a further development of it. *So, the objectivity of literature is its necessary place within the determinate processes and reproduction of the contradictory linguistic practices of the common tongue, in which the effectivity of the ideology of bourgeois education is realised.*

This siting of the problem abolishes the old idealist question, 'What is literature?', which is not a question about its objective determinance, but a question about its universal essence, human and artistic. It abolishes it because it shows us directly the material function of literature, inserted within a process which literature cannot determine even though it is indispensible to it. If literary production has for its material and specific base the contradictions of linguistic practices in schooling taken up and internalised (through an indefinitely repeated labour of fiction), it is because literature itself is one of the terms of the contradiction whose other term is determinately bound to literature. Dialectically, literature is simultaneously product and material condition of the linguistic division in education, term and effect of its own contradictions.

Not surprising therefore that the ideology of literature, itself a part of literature, should work ceaselessly to *deny* this objective base: to represent literature supremely as 'style', as individual genius, conscious or natural, as creativity, etc., as something outside (and above) the process of education, which is merely able to disseminate literature, and to comment on it exhaustively, though with no possibility of finally capturing it. The root of this constitutive repression is the objective status of literature as an historic ideological form, its relation to the class struggle. And the first and last commandment in its ideology is: 'Thou shalt describe *all* forms of class struggle, *save* that which determines thine own self.'

By the same token, the question of the relation of literature to the dominant ideology is posed afresh — escaping a confrontation of universal essences, in which many Marxist discussions have been trapped. To see literature as ideologically determined is not — cannot be — to 'reduce' it to moral ideologies or to political, religious, even aesthetic ideologies which are definable outside literature. Nor is it to make ideology the *content* to which literature brings *form* — even when there are themes and ideological statements which are more or less perfectly separable. Such a pairing is thoroughly mechanical, and, moreover, serves to corroborate the way in which the ideology of literature by displacement misconstrues its historic determinance. It merely prolongs the endless false dialectic of 'form' and 'content' whereby the artificially imposed terms alternate so that literature is sometimes perceived as content (ideology), sometimes as form ('real' literature). To define literature as a particular ideological form is to pose quite another problem: the *specificity of ideological effects* produced by literature and the means (techniques) of production. This returns us to the *second question* involved in the dialectical materialist concept of reflection.

2. The Process of Production of Aesthetic Effects in Literature

By now, thanks to the proper use of the Marxist concept of reflection, we are able to avoid the false dilemma of the literary critic (should he analyse literature *on its own ground* — search out its essence — or *from an external standpoint* — find out its function?). Once we know better than to *reduce* literature either to something other than itself or to itself, but instead analyse its ideological specificity[7], helped by the conclusions of R. Balibar, we can attempt to trace the material concepts which appear in this analysis. Of course such a sketch has only a *provisional* value — but it helps us to see the consistency of the material concept of literature and its conceptual place within historical materialism.

As we see it, these concepts have three moments. They refer simultaneously to (i) the contradictions which ideological literary formations (texts) realise and develop; (ii) the mode of ideological *identification* produced by the action of *fiction*; and (iii) the place of *literary aesthetic effects* in the reproduction of the dominant ideology. Let us deal with each one schematically.

2.1 The specific complexity of literary formations — ideological contradictions and linguistic conflicts

The first principle of a materialist analysis would be: literary productions must not be studied from the standpoint of their *unity* which is illusory and false, but from their material *disparity*. One must not look for unifying effects but for signs of the contradictions (historically determined) which produced them and which appear as unevenly resolved conflicts in the text.

So, in searching out the determinant contradictions, the materialist analysis of literature rejects on principle the notion of 'the work' — i.e., the illusory presentation of the unity of a text, its totality, self-sufficiency and perfection (in both senses of the word: success and completion). More precisely, it recognises the notion of 'the work' (and its correlative, 'the author') only in order to identify both as necessary illusions written into *the ideology of literature*, the accompaniment of all literary production. The text is produced under conditions which represent it as a finished work, providing a requisite order, expressing either a subjective theme or the spirit of the age, according to whether the reading is a naive or a sophisticated one. Yet in itself the text is none of these things: on the contrary, it is materially incomplete, disparate and diffuse from being the outcome of the conflicting contradictory effect of superimposing real processes which cannot be abolished in it except in an imaginary way.[8]

To be more explicit: literature is produced finally through the effect of one or more ideological contradictions precisely because these contradictions cannot be solved within the ideology, i.e., in the last analysis through the effect of contradictory class positions within the ideology, as such irreconcilable. Obviously these contradictory ideological positions are not in themselves 'literary' — that would lead us back into the closed circle of 'literature'. They are ideological positions within theory and practice, covering the whole field of the ideological class struggle, i.e. religious, judicial, and political, and they correspond to the conjunctures of the class struggle itself. But it would be pointless to look in the texts for the 'original' bare discourse of these ideological positions, as they were 'before' their 'literary' realisation, *for these ideological positions can only be formed in the materiality of the literary text*. That is, they can only appear in a form which provides their *imaginary solution*, or better still, which displaces them by substituting imaginary contradictions soluble within the ideological practice of religion, politics, morality, aesthetics and psychology.

Let us approach this phenomenon more closely. We shall say that literature 'begins' with the imaginary solution of implacable ideological contradictions, with the representation of that solution: not in the sense of representing i.e. 'figuring' (by images, allegories, symbols or arguments) a solution which is really there (to repeat, literature is produced because such a solution is impossible) but in that sense of providing a 'mise en scène', a *presentation as solution* of the very terms of an insurmountable contradiction, by means of various displacements and substitutions. For there to be a literature, it must be the very terms of the contradiction (and hence of the contradictory ideological elements) that are enunciated in a special language, a language of 'compromise', realising in advance the fiction of a forthcoming conciliation. Or better still it finds a language of 'compromise' which presents the conciliation as 'natural' and so both necessary and inevitable.

In *Pour une Théorie de la Production Littéraire,*[9] with reference to Lenin's work on Tolstoy, and Verne and Balzac, the attempt was made to use materialist principles to show the complex contradictions which produce the literary text: in each case, specifically, what can be identified as the ideological project of the author, the expression of *one* determinate class position, is only *one* of the terms of the contradiction of whose oppositions the text makes an imaginary synthesis despite the real oppositions which it cannot abolish. Hence the idea that the literary text is not so much the expression of ideology (its 'putting into words' [*sa mise en mots*]) as its *staging* [*mise en scène*], its display, an operation which has an inbuilt disadvantage since it cannot be done without showing its limits thereby revealing its inability to subsume a hostile ideology.

But what remained unclear in *Pour une Théorie* is the process of literary production, the textual devices which present the contradictions of an ideological discourse *at the same time as* the fiction of its unity and its reconciliation, conditionally upon this same fiction. What still evades us, in other words, is the specific mechanism of the literary 'compromise', insomuch as the materialist account is still too general. The work of R. Balibar makes it possible to surmount this difficulty and so not only complete the account but also to correct and transform it.

What does R. Balibar show us? That the discourse, literature's own special 'language', in which the contradictions are set out, is not *outside* ideological struggles as if veiling them in a neutral, neutralising way. Its relation to these struggles is not secondary but constitutive; it is always already implicated in producing them. *Literary language is itself formed by the effects of a class contradiction.* This is fundamental, bringing us back to the material base of all literature. Literary language is produced in its specificity (and in all permitted individual variants) at the level of *linguistic conflicts*, historically determined in the bourgeois epoch by the development of a 'common language' and of an educational system which imposes it on all, whether cultured or not.

This, schematically put, is the principle of the complex nature of literary formations, the production of which shares the material conditions necessary to the bourgeois social formation and transforms itself accordingly. It is the imaginary solution of ideological contradictions insomuch as they are formulated in a special language which is both *different* from the common language and *within it* (the common language itself being the product of an internal conflict), and which realises and masks in a series of compromises the conflict which constitutes it. It is this displacement of contradictions which R. Balibar calls 'literary style' and whose dialectic she has begun to analyse. It is a remarkable dialectic, for it succeeds *in producing the effect and the illusion of an imaginary reconciliation of irreconcilable terms* by displacing the ensemble of ideological contradictions on to a single one, or a single aspect, the linguistic conflict itself. So the imaginary solution has no other 'secret' than the development, the redoubling of the contradiction: this is surely if one knows how to analyse it and work it out, the proof of its irreconcilable nature.

We are now ready to outline the principal aspects of the aesthetic effect of literature as an ideological device.

2.2 Fiction and realism: the mechanism of identification in literature

Here we must pause, even if over-schematically, to consider a characteristic literary effect which has already been briefly mentioned: the identification effect. Brecht was the first marxist theoretician to focus on this by showing how the ideological effects of literature (and of the theatre, with the specific transformations that implies) materialise via an identification process between the reader or the audience and the hero or anti-hero, the simultaneous mutual constitution of the fictive 'consciousness' of the character with the ideological 'consciousness' of the reader.

But it is obvious that any process of identification is dependent on the constitution and recognition of the individual as 'subject' – to use a very common ideological notion lifted by philosophy from the juridical and turning up under various forms in all other levels of bourgeois ideology. Now, all ideology, as Althusser shows in his essay 'Ideology and Ideological State Apparatuses',[10] must in a practical way 'hail or interpellate individuals as subjects': so that they perceive themselves as such, with rights and duties, the obligatory accompaniments. Each ideology has its specific mode: each gives to the 'subject' – and therefore to other real or imaginary subjects to confront the individual and present him with his ideological identification in a personal form – one or more appropriate names. In the ideology of literature, the nomenclature is: Authors (i.e. signatures), Works (i.e. titles), Readers, and Characters (with their social background, real or imaginary). But in literature, the process of constituting subjects and setting up their relationships of mutual recognition necessarily takes a detour via the fictional world and its values, because that process (i.e. of constitution and setting-up) embraces within its circle the 'concrete' or 'abstract' 'persons' which the text stages. We now reach a classic general problem: what is specifically 'fictional' about literature? We shall preface our solution with a parenthesis.

Mostly when one speaks of fiction in literature it means the singling out of certain 'genres' privileged as fiction: the novel, tale, short story. More generally, it indicates something which, whatever its traditional genre, can be appealed to as novelistic, it 'tells a story', whether about the teller himself or about other characters, about an individual or an idea. In this sense, the idea of fiction becomes allegorically the definition of literature *in general*, since all literary texts involve a *story* or a plot, realistic or symbolic, and arrange in a 'time', actual or not, chronological or quasi-chronological, an unrolling of events which do or do not make sense (in formalist texts, order can be reduced to a verbal structure only). All description of literature in general, as of fiction, seems to involve a primary element: the dependence on a story which is analogous to 'life'.

But this characteristic involves another, more crucial still: the *idea of confronting a model*. All 'fiction', it seems, has a reference point, whether to 'reality' or to 'truth', and takes its meaning from that. To define literature as fiction means taking an old philosophical position, which since Plato has been linked with the establishing of a theory of knowledge, and confronting the fictional discourse with a reality, whether in nature or history, so that the text is a transposition, a reproduction, adequate or not, and valued accordingly and in relation to standards of verisimilitude and artistic licence.

No need to go further into details: it is enough to recognise the consistency which links the definition of literature as fiction with a particular appropriation of the category *realism*.

As everyone knows, realism is the key-word of a school: that in favour of a realist 'literature' in place of 'pure fiction', i.e. bad fiction. This too implies a definition of literature in general: all literature must be realist, in one way or another, a representation of reality, even and especially when it gives reality an image outside immediate perception and daily life and common experience. The 'shores' of reality can stretch to infinity.

And yet the idea of realism is not the opposite of fiction: it scarcely differs from it. It too has the idea of a model and of its reproduction, however complex that may be — a model *outside* the representation, at least for the fleeting instant of evaluation — and of a norm, even if it is nameless.

After this digression we can get back to the problem we had set ourselves. Marxist propositions, provisory and immature as they may be, are nevertheless bound to carry out a profound critical transformation of the classic idealist problematic. Let us have no doubt, for instance, that the classics of Marxism, no more than Brecht and Gramsci who can be our guides here, never dealt with literature in terms of 'realism'. The category of reflection, central to the Marxist problematic as we have shown, *is not concerned with realism but with materialism*, which is profoundly different. Marxism cannot define literature in general as fiction in the classic sense.

Literature is not fiction, a fictive image of the real, because it cannot define itself simply as a figuration, an appearance of reality. By a complex process, literature is the production of a certain reality, not indeed (one cannot over-emphasise this) an autonomous reality, but a material reality, and of a certain social effect (we shall conclude with this). Literature is not therefore fiction, but *the production of fiction*: or better still, the production of fiction-effects (and in the first place the provider of the material means for the production of fiction-effects).

Similarly, as the 'reflection of the life of a given society', historically given (Mao), literature is still not providing a 'realist' reproduction of it, even and least of all when it proclaims itself to be such, because even then it cannot be reduced to a straight mirroring. But it is true that the text does produce *a reality-effect*. More precisely it produces simultaneously a reality-effect and a fiction-effect, emphasizing first one and then the other, interpreting each by each in turn but always *on the basis of their dualism*.

So, it comes to this once more: fiction and realism are not *the concepts for* the production of literature but on the contrary the notions produced by literature. But this leads to remarkable consequences for it means that the *model*, the real referent 'outside' the discourse which both fiction and realism presuppose, has no function here as a non-literary non-discursive anchoring point predating the text. (We know by now that this anchorage, the primacy of the real, is different from and more complex than a 'representation'.) But it does function as an effect of the discourse. *So, the literary discourse itself institutes and projects the presence of the 'real' in the manner of an hallucination.*

How is this materially possible? How can the text so control what it says, what it describes, what it sets up (or 'those' it sets up) with its sign of hallucinatory reality, or contrastingly, its fictive sign, diverging, infinitesimally perhaps, from the 'real'? On this point too, in parts of their deep analysis, the works we have used supply the material for an answer. Once more they refer us to the effects and forms of the fundamental linguistic conflict.

In a study of 'modern' French literary texts, carefully dated in each case according to their place in the history of the common language and of the educational system, R. Balibar refers to the production of 'imaginary French' [*français fictif*]. What does this mean? Clearly not pseudo-French, elements of a pseudo-language, seeing that these literary instances do also appear in certain contexts chosen by particular individuals, e.g. by compilers of dictionaries who illustrate their rubrics only with literary quotations. Nor is it simply a case of the language being produced *in* fiction (with its own usages, syntax and vocabulary), i.e. that of characters in a narrative making an imaginary discourse in an imaginary language. Instead, it is a case of expressions which *always* diverge in one or more salient details from those used in practice outside the literary discourse, even when both are grammatically 'correct'. These are linguistic 'compromise formations', compromising between usages which are socially contradictory in practice and hence mutually exclude each other. In these compromise formations there is an essential place, more or less disguised but *recognisable*, for the reproduction of 'simple' language, 'ordinary' language, French 'just like that', i.e. the language which is taught in elementary school as the 'pure and simple' expression of 'reality'. In R. Balibar's book there are numerous examples which 'speak' to everyone, re-awakening or reviving memories which are usually repressed (it is their presence, their reproduction – the reason for a character or his words and for what the 'author' makes himself responsible for without naming himself – which produces the effect of 'naturalness' and 'reality', even if it is only by a single phrase uttered as if in passing). In comparison, all other expressions seem 'arguable,' 'reflected' in a subjectivity. It is necessary that first of all there should be expressions which seem *objective*: these are the ones which *in* the text itself produce the imaginary referent of an elusive 'reality'.

Finally, to go back to our starting point: the ideological effect of identification produced by literature or rather by literary texts, which Brecht, thanks to his position as a revolutionary and materialist dramatist, was the first to theorise. But there is only ever identification *of one subject with another* (potentially with 'oneself': 'Madame Bovary, c'est moi', familiar example, signed Gustave Flaubert). And there are only ever subjects through the interpellation of the individual into a subject *by* a Subject who names him, as Althusser shows: 'tu es Un tel, et c'est à toi que Je m'adresse': 'Hypocrite lecteur, mon semblable, mon frère', another familiar example, signed Charles Baudelaire. Through the endless functioning of its texts, literature unceasingly 'produces' *subjects*, on display for everyone. So paradoxically using the same schema we can say: literature endlessly transforms (concrete) individuals into subjects and endows them with a quasi-real hallucinatory individuality. According to the fundamental mechanism of the whole of bourgeois ideology, to produce subjects ('persons' and 'characters') *one must oppose them to objects*, i.e. to *things*, by placing them *in* and *against* a world of 'real' things, outside it but always *in relation* to it. The realistic effect is the basis of this interpellation which makes characters or merely discourse 'live' and which makes readers take up an attitude towards imaginary struggles as they would towards real ones, though undangerously. They flourish here, the subjects we have already named: the Author and his Readers, but also the Author and his Characters, and the Reader and his Characters via the mediator, the Author – the Author identified with his Characters, or 'on the contrary' with one of their Judges, and likewise for the Reader. And from there, the Author, the Reader, the Characters opposite their universal abstract subjects: God, History, the People, Art. The list is neither final nor finishable: the work of literature is by definition to prolong and expand it indefinitely.

2.3 The aesthetic effect of literature as ideological domination-effect

The analysis of literature (its theory, criticism, science etc.) has always had as its given object either — from a spiritualist perspective — the essence of Works and Authors, or better of the Work (or Art) and of Writing, above history, even and especially when seeming its privileged expression; or — from an empiricist (but still idealist) perspective — the ensemble of literary 'facts', the supposedly objective and documentary givens which lend biographical and stylistic support to 'general facts,' the 'laws' of genres, styles and periods. From a materialist point of view, one would analyse *literary effects* (more precisely, aesthetic literary effects) as effects which cannot be reduced to ideology 'in general' because they are particular ideological effects, *in the midst of others* (religious, juridical, political) to which they are *linked* but from which they are separate.

This effect must finally be described at a threefold level, relating to the three aspects of one social process and its successive historical forms:

1) its production under determinate social conditions,
2) its moment in the reproduction of the dominant ideology,
3) and consequently as in itself an ideological domination-effect.

To demonstrate this:

The literary effect is socially *produced* in a determined material process. This is the process of constitution, i.e. the making and composing of texts, the 'work' of literature. Now, the writer is neither supreme creator, founder of the very conditions to which he submits (in particular, as we have seen, certain objective contradictions within ideology), nor its opposite — expendable medium, *through* whom is revealed the nameless power of inspiration, or history, or period, or even class (which comes to the same thing). But he is a material agent, an intermediary inserted in a particular place, under conditions he has not created, in submission to contradictions which by definition he cannot control, through a particular social division of labour, characteristic of the ideological superstructure of bourgeois society, which individuates him.

The literary effect is produced as a complex effect, not only, as shown, because its determinant is the imaginary resolution of one contradiction within another, but because the effect produced is simultaneously and inseparably the materiality of the text (the arrangement of sentences), and its status as a 'literary' text, its 'aesthetic' status. That is, it is both a material outcome and a particular ideological effect, or rather the production of a material outcome *stamped* with a particular ideological effect which marks it ineradicably. It is the status of the text in its characteristics — no matter what the terms, which are only variants: its 'charm', 'beauty', 'truth', 'significance', 'worth', 'profundity', 'style', 'writing', 'art', etc. Finally, it is the status of the text per se, quite simply, for in our society only the text is valid in itself, revealer of its true form; equally, all texts once 'written' are valid as 'literary'. This status extends as well to all the historic dissimilar modes of reading texts: the 'free' reading, reading for the pure 'pleasure' of letters, the critical reading giving a more or less theorized, more or less 'scientific' commentary on form and content, meaning, 'style', 'textuality' (revealing neologism!) — and behind all readings, the explication of texts by academics which conditions all the rest.

Therefore, the literary effect is not just produced by a determinate process, but actively inserts itself within the *reproduction* of other ideological effects; it is not only itself the effect of material causes but is also an effect on socially determined individuals, constraining them materially to treat literary texts in a certain way. So, ideologically, the literary effect is not just in the domain of 'feeling', 'taste', 'judgment', and hence of aesthetic and literary ideas; it sets up a process itself: the ritual of literary consumption and 'cultural' practice.

That is why it is possible (and necessary) when analysing the literary effect as produced qua text and by means of the text, to treat as equivalents the 'reader' and the 'author'. Equivalent too are the 'intentions' of the author — what he expresses whether in the text itself (integrated within the 'surface' narrative) or alongside the text (in his declarations or even in his 'unconscious' motives as sought out by literary psychoanalysis) — and the interpretations, criticisms and commentaries evoked from readers, whether sophisticated or not.

It is not important to know whether the interpretation 'really' identifies the author's intention (since the latter is not the cause of literary effects but is one of the effects). Interpretations and commentaries reveal the (literary) aesthetic effect, precisely, in full view. Literariness is what is recognised as such, and it is recognised as such precisely in the time and to the extent that it activates the interpretations, the criticisms and the 'readings'. This is why a text can very easily *stop* being literary or *become* so under new conditions.

Freud was the first to follow this procedure in his account of the dream-work and more generally in his method of analysing the compromise formations of the unconscious; he defined what must be understood by the 'text' of the dream. He gave no importance to restoring the manifest content of the dream — to a careful isolated reconstruction of the 'real' dream. Or at least he accedes to it only through the intermediary of the 'dream narrative', which is *already* a transposition through which via condensation, displacement, and dream symbolism, repressed material makes its play. And he posited that the text of the dream was both the object of analysis and explanation simultaneously, through its own contradictions, the means of its own explanation: it is not just the manifest text, the narrative of the dream, but also all the 'free' associations (i.e., as one well knows, the forced associations, imposed by the psychic conflicts of the unconscious), the 'latent thoughts' for which the dream (or symptom) can serve as a pretext and which it arouses.

In the same way, criticism, the discourse of literary ideology, an endless commentary on the 'beauty' and 'truth' of literary texts, is a train of 'free' associations (in actuality forced and predetermined) which develops and realises the ideological effects of a literary text. In a materialist account of the text one must take them not as located *above* the text, as the beginnings of its explication, but as belonging *to the same* level as the text, or more precisely to the same level as the 'surface' narrative whether that is figurative, allegorically treating with certain general ideas (as in the novel or autobiography) or straightforwardly 'abstract', non-figurative (as in the moral or political essay). They are the tendential prolongation of this facade. Free from all question of the *individuality* of the 'writer', the 'reader' or the 'critic', these are the same ideological conflicts, resulting in the last instance from the same historical contradictions, or from their transformations, that produce the form of the text and of its commentaries.

Here is the index of the structure of the process of reproduction in which the literary effect is inserted. What is in fact 'the primary material' of the literary text? (But a raw material which always seems to have been already transformed by it). It is the ideological contradictions which are *not* specifically literary but political, religious, etc.; in the last analysis, contradictory ideological realisations of determinate class positions in the class struggle. And what is the 'effect' of the literary text? (*at least* on those readers who recognise it as such, those of the *dominant* cultured class). Its effect is to provoke other ideological discourses which can sometimes be recognised as literary ones but which are usually merely aesthetic, moral, political, religious discourses in which the dominant ideology is realised.

We can now say that the literary text is the *agent* for the *reproduction* of ideology in its ensemble. In other words, it induces by the literary effect the production of 'new' discourses which always reproduce (under constantly varied forms) the *same* ideology (with its contradictions). It enables individuals to *appropriate* ideology and make themselves its 'free' *bearers* and even its 'free' *creators*. The literary text is a privileged operator in the concrete relations between the individual and ideology in bourgeois society and ensures its reproduction. To the extent that it induces the ideological discourse to leave its subject matter which has always already been invested as the aesthetic effect, in the form of the work of art, it does not seem a mechanical imposition, forced, revealed like a religious dogma, on individuals who must repeat it faithfully. Instead it appears as if offered for interpretations, a free choice, for the subjective private use of individuals. It is the privileged agent of ideological subjection, in the democratic and 'critical' form of 'freedom of thought'.[11]

Under these conditions, the aesthetic effect is also inevitably an effect of *domination*: the subjection of individuals to the dominant ideology, the dominance of the ideology of the ruling class.

It is inevitably therefore an *uneven* effect which does not operate uniformly on individuals and particularly does not operate in the same way on different and antagonistic social classes. 'Subjection' must be felt by the dominant class as by the dominated but in two different ways. Formally, literature as an ideological formation realised in the common language, is provided and destined for all and makes no distinctions between readers but for their own differing tastes and sensibilities, natural or acquired. But concretely, subjection means one thing for the members of the educated dominant class: 'freedom' to think within ideology, a submission which is experienced and practised as if it were a mastery, another for those who belong to the exploited classes: manual workers or even skilled workers, employees, those who according to official statistics never 'read' or rarely. These find in reading nothing but the confirmation of their inferiority: subjection means domination and repression by the literary discourse of a discourse deemed 'inarticulate' and 'faulty' and inadequate for the expression of complex ideas and feelings.

This point is vital to an analysis. It shows that the difference is not set up *after the event* as a straightforward inequality of reading power and assimilation, conditioned by other social inequalities. It is implicit in the very production of the literary effect and materially inscribed in the constitution of the text.

But one might say, how is it clear that what is implicit in the structure of the text is not just the discourse of those who practise literature but also, *most significantly*, the discourse of those who do not know the text and whom it does not know; i.e. the discourse of those who 'write' (books) and 'read' them, and the discourse of those who do not know how to do it although quite simply they 'know how to read and write' — a play of words and a profoundly revealing double usage. One can understand this only by reconstituting and analysing the linguistic conflict in its determinant place as that which produces the literary text and which opposes two antagonistic usages, equal but inseparable, of the common language: on one side, 'literary' French which is studied in higher education (l'enseignement secondaire et supérieur) and on the other 'basic', 'ordinary' French which, far from being natural, is also taught at the other level (à l'école primaire). It is 'basic' only by reason of its *unequal relation* to the other, which is 'literary' by the same reason. This is proved by a comparative and historical analysis of their lexical and syntactical forms — which R. Balibar is one of the first to undertake systematically.

So, if in the way things are, literature can and must be used in secondary education both to fabricate and simultaneously dominate, isolate and repress the 'basic' language' of the dominated classes, it is only on condition that that same basic language should be present in literature, as one of the terms of its constitutive contradiction — disguised and masked, but also necessarily given away and exhibited in the fictive reconstructions. And ultimately this is because literary French embodied in literary texts is both tendentially *distinguished from* (and opposed to) the common language and *placed within* its constitution and historic development so long as this process characterises general education because of its material importance to the development of bourgeois society. That is why it is possible to assert that the use of literature in schools and its place in education is only the converse of the *place of education in literature* and that therefore the basis of the production of literary effects is the very structure and historical role of the currently dominant ideological state apparatus. And that too is why it is possible to denounce as a denial of their own real practice the claims of the writer and his cultured readers to rise above simple classroom exercises, and evade them.

The effect of domination realised by literary production presupposes the presence of the dominated ideology within the dominant ideology itself. It implies the constant 'activation' of the contradiction and its attendent ideological risk — it thrives on this very risk which is the source of its power. That is why, dialectically, in bourgeois democratic society, the agent of the reproduction of ideology moves tendentially via the effects of literary 'style' and linguistic forms of compromise. Class struggle is not abolished in the literary text and the literary effects which it produces. They bring about the reproduction, as dominant, of the ideology of the dominant class.

Notes

[1] See Renée Balibar, Geneviève Merlin, and Gilles Tret, *Les Français fictifs; le rapport des styles littéraires au français national*, Paris, Hachette, 1974, in the series *Analyses* edited by Althusser.

[2] Lenin shows this clearly in his articles on Tolstoy.

[3] *Selected Readings from the Works of Mao Tse-Tung (A)*, Peking, Foreign Languages Press, 1971, p.250ff.

[4] Dominique Lecourt, *Une Crise et son enjeu* (Essai sur la position de Lénine en philosophie). Collection *Théorie*, Paris, Maspero, 1973.

[5] R. Balibar and D. Laporte, *Le Français National: constitution de la langue nationale commune à l'epoque de la révolution démocratique bourgeoise*, introduction by E. Balibar and P. Macherey, Editions Hachette 1974, in *Analyses*.

[6] Readers are referred to the first two chapters of *L'Ecole capitaliste en France*, Baudelot and Establet, Maspero, 1972.

[7] See P. Macherey, *Pour une Théorie de la Production Littéraire*, Collection *Théorie*, Paris, Maspero, 1966.

[8] Rejecting the mythical unity and completeness of a work of art does not mean adopting a reverse position, i.e. the work of art as anti-nature, a violation of order (cf. *Tel Quel*). Such reversals are characteristic of conservative ideology: 'For oft a fine disorder stems from art' (Boileau)!

[9] Cf.supra, note 6.

[10] In *La Pensée* no. 151, June 1970; *Lenin and Philosophy,* trans. B. Brewster, NLB, 1971.

[11] One could say that there is no proper *religious literature*; at least that there was not before the bourgeois epoch, by which time religion had been instituted as a form (subordinant and contradictory) of the bourgeois ideology itself. Rather, literature itself and the aesthetic ideology played a decisive part in the struggle against religion, the ideology of the dominant feudal class.

SECTION 5

Talk and Text

Introduction

The papers in this section are all concerned with the description of structure 'beyond the sentence', both in the sense that they deal with longer stretches of talk or text, and in the sense that they look beyond the grammatical structure of the sentence for meaning, to an inter-action between readers and texts, and speakers and listeners.

Speech Act Theory is a theory of how, in Austin's words, we 'do things with words'. How do we assert or warn; order or request; promise or apologise? Such acts, Searle suggests in the first reading, are the 'minimal units of linguistic communication'. Searle investigates the nature of an illocutionary act. He shows for example, that successful promises depend less on the use of the words 'I promise' than on knowledge of context, intentions and conventions.

Speech Act Theory has informed many of the more successful analyses of talk. Two such approaches are represented here. Sinclair and Coulthard belong to a tradition which has been called 'discourse analysis'. They describe, in the extract from their book, how they arrived at a classification system for classroom dialogue. Such teacher-pupil dialogue seems to display an orderly structure which is less apparent in casual conversation, but even here, some scholars — particularly a group of sociologists who have become known as 'conversation analysts' — have tried to show how all talk is orderly.

Turner, in the third reading, argues that one can usefully start an analysis by applying one's intuitive recognition that 'something is going on' in a conversation. Such intuitions, it is argued, are available to all members of the speech community and they can be explained by a careful examination of both the conversation and its context. Conversation analysts thus place an emphasis on the way certain interactional problems and events are managed and how conversations rely on the joint efforts of participants for their execution.

The remaining papers in the section are concerned with texts and readers than conversationalists, but some of the same issues are evident. How can text structure be described? Can it be isolated and defined in the abstract, or do we have to take into account readers and the knowledge and expectations with which they approach a text?

The article by Stokes examines the reliability of readability formulae, with seven readability measures applied to samples from eleven books used in schools. He considers the extent to which formulae agree with each other as well as how consistent they are when applied to several samples from one text. Although he found quite high intercorrelations between formulae there was little agreement with regard to the grade levels any two formulae gave for texts and no two formulae consistently shared agreement. Stokes cautions care in the application of formulae and in interpretation of their results. He also advises fuller consideration than hitherto of their assumptions.

Readability formulae seek to deal with texts mathematically in order to produce parsimonious (if partial) descriptions of them. No direct account is taken of the reader and it was this weakness which gave rise to the widespread use of cloze procedure. The article by Neville and Pugh is concerned with the use of context by children aged 9 and 10 in reading and listening tasks. Comparisons of the type of error made by children in a later study suggested that poorer readers were reading using strategies more suited to listening whereas better readers used a fuller range of context when, as in reading, it was available.

The article in the present collection may be taken to suggest that, however texts are constructed, recipients will use them differently. In this case the different strategies were related to mode of presentation though in the later study (Neville and Pugh 1976) there was evidence that they were related to developmental stages.

Bower is concerned with the re-emerging tradition in the psychology of memory which considers the study of memory for text (and other things) in realistic settings to be more important than the work on artificial tasks, which has characterized much research into memory. Bower includes a review of some approaches to describing the structure of stories, including story grammars, but he also takes account of the reader, and his inferences, for example. In addition be briefly reports several studies relevant to 'how people process and understand text'. This field he sees as revealing 'the operation of the most sophisticated cognitive machinery which men have assembled'.

Reference

Neville, Mary H. and Pugh, A. K. (1976) 'Content in reading and listening: Variations in approach to cloze tasks', *Reading Research Quarterly*, 12 (1) pp. 13-31

D. Graddol

5.1 What is a Speech Act?
John Searle

I. Introduction

In a typical speech situation involving a speaker, a hearer, and an utterance by the speaker, there are many kinds of acts associated with the speaker's utterance. The speaker will characteristically have moved his jaw and tongue and made noises. In addition, he will characteristically have performed some acts within the class which includes informing or irritating or boring his hearers; he will further characteristically have performed acts within the class which includes referring to Kennedy or Khrushchev or the North Pole; and he will also have performed acts within the class which includes making statements, asking questions, issuing commands, giving reports, greeting, and warning. The members of this last class are what Austin[1] called illocutionary acts and it is with this class that I shall be concerned in this paper, so the paper might have been called 'What is an Illocutionary Act?' I do not attempt to define the expression 'illocutionary act', although if my analysis of a particular illocutionary act succeeds it may provide the basis for a definition. Some of the English verbs and verb phrases associated with illocutionary acts are: state, assert, describe, warn, remark, comment, command, order, request, criticize, apologize, censure, approve, welcome, promise, express approval, and express regret. Austin claimed that there were over a thousand such expressions in English.

By way of introduction, perhaps I can say why I think it is of interest and importance in the philosophy of language to study speech acts, or, as they are sometimes called, language acts or linguistic acts. I think it is essential to any specimen of linguistic communication that it involve a linguistic act. It is not, as has generally been supposed, the symbol or word or sentence, or even the token of the symbol or word or sentence, which is the unit of linguistic communication, but rather it is the *production* of the token in the performance of the speech act that constitutes the basic unit of linguistic communication. To put this point more precisely, the production of the sentence token under certain conditions is the illocutionary act, and the illocutionary act is the minimal unit of linguistic communcation.

Philosophy in America, M. Black (ed.), Allen and Unwin, Cornell, 1965, Chapter 11.

I do not know how to *prove* that linguistic communication essentially involves acts but I can think of arguments with which one might attempt to convince someone who was sceptical. One argument would be to call the sceptic's attention to the fact that when he takes a noise or a mark on paper to be an instance of linguistic communication, as a message, one of the things that is involved in his so taking that noise or mark is that he should regard it as having been produced by a being with certain intentions. He cannot just regard it as a natural phenomenon, like a stone, a waterfall, or a tree. In order to regard it as an instance of linguistic communication one must suppose that its production is what I am calling a speech act. It is a logical presupposition, for example, of current attempts to decipher the Mayan hieroglyphs that we at least hypothesize that the marks we see on the stones were produced by beings more or less like ourselves and produced with certain kinds of intentions. If we were certain the marks were a consequence of, say, water erosion, then the question of deciphering them or even calling them hieroglyphs could not arise. To construe them under the category of linguistic communication necessarily involves construing their production as speech acts.

To perform illocutionary acts is to engage in a rule-governed form of behaviour. I shall argue that such things as asking questions or making statements are rule-governed in ways quite similar to those in which getting a base hit in baseball or moving a knight in chess are rule-governed forms of acts. I intend therefore to explicate the notion of an illocutionary act by stating a set of necessary and sufficient conditions for the performance of a particular kind of illocutionary act, and extracting from it a set of semantical rules for the use of the expression (or syntactic device) which marks the utterance as an illocutionary act of that kind. If I am successful in stating the conditions and the corresponding rules for even one kind of illocutionary act, that will provide us with a pattern for analysing other kinds of acts and consequently for explicating the notion in general. But in order to set the stage for actually stating conditions and extracting rules for performing an illocutionary act I have to discuss three other preliminary notions: *rules, propositions,* and *meaning.* I shall confine my discussion of these notions to those aspects which are essential to my main purposes in this paper, but, even so, what I wish to say concerning each of these notions, if it were to be at all complete, would require a paper for each; however, sometimes it may be worth sacrificing thoroughness for the sake of scope and I shall therefore be very brief.

II. Rules

In recent years there has been in the philosophy of language considerable discussion involving the notion of rules for the use of expressions. Some philosophers have even said that knowing the meaning of a word is simply a matter of knowing the rules for its use or employment. One disquieting feature of such discussions is that no philosopher, to my knowledge at least, has ever given anything like an adequate formulation of the rules for the use of even one expression. If meaning is a matter of rules of use, surely we ought to be able to state the rules for the use of expressions in a way which would explicate the meaning of those expressions. Certain other philosophers, dismayed perhaps by the failure of their colleagues to produce any rules, have denied the fashionable view that meaning is a matter of rules and have asserted that there are no semantical rules of the proposed kind at all. I am inclined to think that this scepticism is premature and stems from a failure to distinguish different sorts of rules, in a way which I shall now attempt to explain.

I distinguish between two sorts of rules: Some regulate antecedently existing forms of behaviour; for example, the rules of etiquette regulate interpersonal relationships, but these relationships exist independently of the rules of etiquette. Some rules on the other hand do not merely regulate but create or define new forms of behaviour. The rules of football, for example, do not merely regulate the game of football but as it were create the possibility of or define that activity. The activity of playing football is constituted by acting in accordance with these rules; football has no existence apart from these rules. I call the latter kind of rules constitutive rules and the former kind regulative rules. Regulative rules regulate a pre-existing activity, an activity whose existence is logically independent of the existence of the rules. Constitutive rules constitute (and also regulate) an activity the existence of which is logically dependent on the rules.[2]

Regulative rules characteristically take the form of or can be paraphrased as imperatives, e.g. 'When cutting food hold the knife in the right hand', or 'Officers are to wear ties at dinner'. Some constitutive rules take quite a different form, e.g. a checkmate is made if the king is attacked in such a way that no move will leave it unattacked; a touchdown is scored when a player crosses the opponents' goal line in possession of the ball while play is in progress. If our paradigms of rules are imperative regulative rules, such non-imperative constitutive rules are likely to strike us as extremely curious and hardly even as rules at all. Notice that they are almost tautological in character, for what the 'rule' seems to offer is a partial definition of 'checkmate' or 'touchdown'. But, of course, this quasi-tautological character is a necessary consequence of their being constitutive rules: the rules concerning touchdowns must define the notion of 'touchdown' in the same way that the rules concerning football define 'football'. That, for example, a touchdown can be scored in such and such ways and counts six points can appear sometimes as a rule, sometimes as an analytic truth; and that it can be construed as a tautology is a clue to the fact that the rule in question is a constitutive one. Regulative rules generally have the form 'Do X' or 'If Y do X'. Some members of the set of constitutive rules have this form but some also have the form 'X counts as Y'.[3]

The failure to perceive this is of some importance in philosophy. Thus, e.g., some philosophers ask 'How can a promise create an obligation?' A similar question would be 'How can a touchdown create six points?' And as they stand both questions can only be answered by stating a rule of the form 'X counts as Y'.

I am inclined to think that both the failure of some philosophers to state rules for the use of expressions and the scepticism of other philosophers concerning the existence of any such rules stem at least in part from a failure to recognize the distinctions between constitutive and regulative rules. The model or paradigm of a rule which most philosophers have is that of a regulative rule, and if one looks in semantics for purely regulative rules one is not likely to find anything interesting from the point of view of logical analysis. There are no doubt social rules of the form 'One ought not to utter obscenities at formal gatherings', but that hardly seems a rule of the sort that is crucial in explicating the semantics of a language. The hypothesis that lies behind the present paper is that the semantics of a language can be regarded as a series of systems of constitutive rules and that illocutionary acts are acts performed in accordance with these sets of constitutive rules. One of the aims of this paper is to formulate a set of constitutive rules for a certain kind of speech act. And if what I have said concerning constitutive rules is correct, we should not be surprised if not all these rules take the form of imperative rules. Indeed we shall see that the rules fall into several different categories, none of which is quite like the rules of etiquette. The effort to state the rules for an illocutionary act can also be regarded as a kind of test of the hypothesis that there are constitutive rules underlying speech acts. If we are unable to give any satisfactory rule formulations, our failure could be construed as partially disconfirming evidence against the hypothesis.

III. Propositions

Different illocutionary acts often have features in common with each other. Consider utterances of the following sentences:

(1)   Will John leave the room?
(2)   John will leave the room.
(3)   John, leave the room!
(4)   Would that John left the room.
(5)   If John will leave the room, I will leave also.

Utterances of each of these on a given occasion would characteristically be performances of different illocutionary acts. The first would, characteristically, be a question, the second an assertion about the future, that is, a prediction, the third a request or order, the fourth an expression of a wish, and the fifth a hypothetical expression of intention. Yet in the performance of each the speaker would character-istically perform some subsidiary acts which are common to all five illocutionary acts. In the utterance of each the speaker *refers* to a particular person John and *predicates* the act of leaving the room of that person. In no case is that all he does, but in every case it is a part of what he does. I shall say, therefore, that in each of these cases, although the illocutionary acts are different, at least some of the non-illocutionary acts of reference and predication are the same.

The reference to some person John and predication of the same thing of him in each of these illocutionary acts inclines me to say that there is a common *content* in each of them. Something expressible by the clause 'that John will leave the room' seems to be a common feature of all. We could, with not too much distortion, write each of these sentences in a way which would isolate this common feature: 'I assert that John will leave the room', 'I ask whether John will leave the room', etc.

For lack of a better word I propose to call this common content a proposition, and I shall describe this feature of these illocutionary acts by saying that in the utterance of each of (1)–(5) the speaker expresses the proposition that John will leave the room. Notice that I do not say that the sentence expresses the proposition; I do not know how sentences could perform acts of that kind. But I shall say that in the utterance of the sentence the speaker expresses a proposition. Notice also that I am distinguishing between a proposition and an assertion or statement of that proposition. The proposition that John will leave the room is expressed in the utterance of all of (1)–(5) but only in (2) is that proposition asserted. An assertion is an illocutionary act, but a proposition is not an act at all, although the act of expressing a proposition is a part of performing certain illocutionary acts.

I might summarise this by saying that I am distinguishing between the illocutionary act and the propositional content of an illocutionary act. Of course, not all illocutionary acts have a propositional content, for example, an utterance of 'Hurrah!' or 'Ouch!' does not. In one version or another this distinction is an old one and has been marked in different ways by authors as diverse as Frege, Sheffer, Lewis, Reichenbach and Hare, to mention only a few.

From a semantical point of view we can distinguish between the propositional indicator in the sentence and the indicator of illocution-ary force. That is, for a large class of sentences used to perform illocutionary acts, we can say for the purpose of our analysis that the sentence has two (not necessarily separate) parts, the proposition indicating element and the function indicating device.[4] The function indicating device shows how the proposition is to be taken, or, to put it in another way, what illocutionary force the utterance is to have, that is, what illocutionary act the speaker is performing in the utterance of the sentence. Function indicating devices in English include word order, stress, intonation contour, punctuation, the mood of the verb, and finally a set of so-called performative verbs: I may indicate the kind of illocutionary act I am performing by beginning the sentence with 'I apologize', 'I warn', 'I state', etc. Often in actual speech situations the context will make it clear what the illocutionary force of the utterance is, without its being necessary to invoke the appropriate function indicating device.

If this semantical distinction is of any real importance, it seems likely that it should have some syntactical analogue, and certain recent developments in transformational grammar tend to support the view that it does. In the underlying phrase marker of a sentence there is a distinction between those elements which correspond to the function indicating device and those which correspond to the propositional content.

The distinction between the function indicating device and the proposition indicating device will prove very useful to us in giving an analysis of an illocutionary act. Since the same proposition can be common to all sorts of illocutionary acts, we can separate our analysis of the proposition from our analysis of kinds of illocutionary acts. I think there are rules for expressing propositions, rules for such things as reference and predication, but those rules can be discussed independently of the rules for function indicating. In this paper I shall not attempt to discuss propositional rules but shall concentrate on rules for using certain kinds of function indicating devices.

IV. Meaning

Speech acts are characteristically performed in the utterance of sounds or the making of marks. What is the difference between *just* uttering sounds or making marks and performing a speech act? One difference is that the sounds or marks one makes in the performance of a speech act are characteristically said to *have meaning,* and a second related difference is that one is characteristically said to *mean something* by those sounds or marks. Characteristically when one speaks one means something by what one says, and what one says, the string of morphemes that one emits, is characteristically said to have a meaning. Here, incidentally, is another point at which our analogy between performing speech acts and playing games breaks down. The pieces in a game like chess are not characteristically said to have a meaning, and furthermore when one makes a move one is not characteristically said to mean anything by that move.

But what is it for one to mean something by what one says, and what is it for something to have a meaning? To answer the first of these questions I propose to borrow and revise some ideas of Paul Grice. In an article entitled 'Meaning',[5] Grice gives the following analysis of one sense of the notion of 'meaning'. To say that A meant something by x is to say that 'A intended the utterance of x to produce some effect in an audience by means of the recognition of this intention'. This seems to me a useful start on an analysis of meaning, first because it shows the close relationship between the notion of meaning and the notion of intention, and secondly because it captures something which is, I think, essential to speaking a language: in speaking a language I attempt to communicate things to my hearer by means of getting him to recognize my intention to communicate just those things. For example, character-istically, when I make an assertion, I attempt to communicate to and convince my hearer of the truth of a certain proposition; and the means I employ to do this are to utter certain sounds, which utterance I intend to produce in him the desired effect by means of his recognition of my intention to produce just that effect. I shall illustrate this with an example. I might on the one hand attempt to get you to believe that I am French by speaking French all the time, dressing in the French manner, showing wild enthusiasm for de Gaulle, and cultivating French acquaintances. But I might on the other hand attempt to get you to believe that I am French by simply telling you that I am French. Now, what is the difference between these two ways of my attempting to get you to believe that I am French? One crucial difference is that in the second case I attempt to get you to believe that I am French by getting you to recognize that it is my purported intention to get you to believe just that. That is one of the things involved in telling you that I am French. But of course if I try to get you to believe that I am French by putting on the act I described, then your recognition of my intention to produce in you the belief that I am French is not the means I am employing. Indeed in this case you would, I think, become rather suspicious if you recognized my intention.

However valuable this analysis of meaning is, it seems to me to be in certain respects defective. First of all, it fails to distinguish the different kinds of effects — perlocutionary versus illocutionary — that one may intend to produce in one's hearers, and it further fails to show the way in which these different kinds of effects are related to the notion of meaning. A second defect is that it fails to account for the extent to which meaning is a matter of rules or conventions. That is, this account of meaning does not show the connection between one's meaning something by what one says and what that which one says actually means in the language. In order to illustrate this point I now wish to present a counter-example to this analysis of meaning. The point of the counter-example will be to illustrate the connection between what a speaker means and what the words he utters mean.

Suppose that I am an American soldier in the Second World War and that I am captured by Italian troops. And suppose also that I wish to get these troops to believe that I am a German officer in order to get them to release me. What I would like to do is to tell them in German or Italian that I am a German officer. But let us suppose I don't know enough German or Italian to do that. So I, as it were, attempt to put on a show of telling them that I am a German officer by reciting those few bits of German that I know, trusting that they don't know enough German to see through my plan. Let us suppose I know only one line of German, which I remember from a poem I had to memorize in a high school German course. Therefore I, a captured American, address my Italian captors with the following sentence: 'Kennst du das Land, wo Zitronen blühen?' Now, let us describe the situation in Gricean terms. I intend to produce a certain effect in them, namely, the effect of believing that I am a German officer; and I intend to produce this effect by means of their recognition of my intention. I intend that they should think that I am trying to tell them that I am a German officer. But does it follow from this account that when I say 'Kennst du das Land . . .' etc., what I mean is, 'I am a German officer'? Not only does it not follow, but in this case it seems plainly false that when I utter the German sentence what I mean is 'I am a German officer', or even 'Ich bin ein deutscher Offizier', because what the words mean is, 'Knowest thou the land where the lemon trees bloom?' Of course, I want my captors to be deceived into thinking that what I mean is 'I am a German officer', but part of what is involved in the deception is getting them to think that that is what the words which I utter mean in German. At one point in the *Philosophical Investigations* Wittgenstein says 'Say "it's cold here" and mean "it's warm here" '.[6] The reason we are unable to do this is that what we can mean is a function of what we are saying. Meaning is more than a matter of intention, it is also a matter of convention.

Grice's account can be amended to deal with counter-examples of this kind. We have here a case where I am trying to produce a certain effect by means of recognition of my intention to produce that effect, but the device I use to produce this effect is one which is conventionally, by the rules governing the use of that device, used as a means of producing quite different illocutionary effects. We must therefore reformulate the Gricean account of meaning in such a way as to make it clear that one's meaning something when one says something is more than just contingently related to what the sentence means in the language one is speaking. In our analysis of illocutionary acts, we must capture both the intentional and the conventional aspects and especially the relationship between them. In the performance of an illocutionary act the speaker intends to produce a certain effect by means of getting the hearer to recognize his intention to produce that effect, and furthermore, if he is using words literally, he intends this recognition to be achieved in virtue of the fact that the rules for using the expressions he utters associate the expressions with the production of that effect. It is this *combination* of elements which we shall need to express in our analysis of the illocutionary act.

V. How to Promise

I shall now attempt to give an analysis of the illocutionary act of promising. In order to do this I shall ask what conditions are necessary and sufficient for the act of promising to have been performed in the utterance of a given sentence. I shall attempt to answer this question by stating these conditions as a set of propositions such that the conjunction of the members of the set entails the proposition that a speaker made a promise, and the proposition that the speaker made a promise entails this conjunction. Thus each condition will be a necessary condition for the performance of the act of promising, and taken collectively the set of conditions will be a sufficient condition for the act to have been performed.

If we get such a set of conditions we can extract from them a set of rules for the use of the function indicating device. The method here is analogous to discovering the rules of chess by asking oneself what are the necessary and sufficient conditions under which one can be said to have correctly moved a knight or castled or checkmated a player, etc. We are in the position of someone who has learned to play chess without ever having the rules formulated and who wants such a formulation. We learned how to play the game of illocutionary acts, but in general it was done without an explicit formulation of the rules, and the first step in getting such a formulation is to set out the conditions for the performance of a particular illocutionary act. Our enquiry will therefore serve a double philosophical purpose. By stating a set of conditions for the performance of a particular illocutionary act we shall have offered a partial explication of that notion and shall also have paved the way for the second step, the formulation of the rules.

I find the statement of the conditions very difficult to do, and I am not entirely satisfied with the list I am about to present. One reason for the difficulty is that the notion of a promise, like most notions in ordinary language, does not have absolutely strict rules. There are all sorts of odd, deviant, and borderline promises; and counter-examples, more or less bizarre, can be produced against my analysis. I am inclined to think we shall not be able to get a set of knock down necessary and sufficient conditions that will exactly mirror the ordinary use of the word 'promise'. I am confining my discussion, therefore, to the centre of the concept of promising and ignoring the fringe, borderline, and partially defective cases. I also confine my discussion to full-blown explicit promises and ignore promises made by elliptical turns of phrase, hints, metaphors, etc.

Another difficulty arises from my desire to state the conditions without certain forms of circularity. I want to give a list of conditions for the performance of a certain illocutionary act, which do not themselves mention the performance of any illocutionary acts. I need to satisfy this condition in order to offer an explication of the notion of an illocutionary act in general, otherwise I should simply be showing the relation between different illocutionary acts. However, although there will be no reference to illocutionary *acts*, certain illocutionary *concepts* will appear in the analysans as well as in the analysandum; and I think this form of circularity is unavoidable because of the nature of constitutive rules.

In the presentation of the conditions I shall first consider the case of a sincere promise and then show how to modify the conditions to allow for insincere promises. As our inquiry is semantical rather than syntactical, I shall simply assume the existence of grammatically well-formed sentences.

Given that a speaker S utters a sentence T in the presence of a hearer H, then, in the utterance of T, S sincerely (and non-defectively) promises that p to H if and only if:

(1) Normal Input and Output Conditions obtain.

I use the terms 'input' and 'output' to cover the large and indefinite range of conditions under which any kind of serious linguistic communication is possible. 'Output' covers the conditions for intelligible speaking and 'input' covers the conditions for understanding. Together they include such things as that the speaker and hearer both know how to speak the language; both are conscious of what they are doing; the speaker is not acting under duress or threats; they have no physical impediments to communication, such as deafness, aphasia, or laryngitis; they are not acting in a play or telling jokes, etc.

(2) S expresses that p in the utterance of T.

This condition isolates the propositional content from the rest of the speech act and enables us to concentrate on the peculiarities of promising in the rest of the analysis.

(3) In expressing that p, S predicates a future act A of S.

In the case of promising the function indicating device is an expression whose scope includes certain features of the proposition. In a promise an act must be predicated of the speaker and it cannot be a past act. I cannot promise to have done something, and I cannot promise that someone else will do something. (Although I can promise to see that he will do it.) The notion of an act, as I am construing it for present purposes, includes refraining from acts, performing series of acts, and may also include states and conditions: I may promise not to do something, I may promise to do something repeatedly, and I may promise to be or remain in a certain state or condition. I call conditions (2) and (3) the *propositional content conditions*.

(4) H would prefer S's doing A to his not doing A, and S believes H would prefer his doing A to his not doing A.

One crucial distinction between promises on the one hand and threats on the other is that a promise is a pledge to do something for you, not to you, but a threat is a pledge to do something to you, not for you. A promise is defective if the thing promised is something the promisee does not want done; and it is further defective if the promisor does not believe the promisee wants it done, since a non-defective promise must be intended as a promise and not as a threat or warning. I think both halves of this double condition are necessary in order to avoid fairly obvious counter-examples.

One can, however, think of apparent counter-examples to this condition as stated. Suppose I say to a lazy student 'If you don't hand in your paper on time I promise you I will give you a failing grade in the course'. Is this utterance a promise? I am inclined to think not; we would more naturally describe it as a warning or possibly even a threat. But why then is it possible to use the locution 'I promise' in such a case? I think we use it here because 'I promise' and 'I hereby promise' are among the strongest function indicating devices for *commitment* provided by the English language. For that reason we often use these expressions in the performance of speech acts which are not strictly speaking promises but in which we wish to emphasize our commitment. To illustrate this, consider another apparent counter-example to the analysis along different lines. Sometimes, more commonly I think in the United States than in England, one hears people say 'I promise' when making an emphatic assertion. Suppose, for example, I accuse you of having stolen the money. I say, 'You stole that money, didn't you?' You reply 'No, I didn't, I promise you I didn't'. Did you make a promise in this case? I find it very unnatural to describe your utterance as a promise. This utterance would be more aptly described as an emphatic denial, and we can explain the occurrence of the function indicating device 'I promise' as derivative from genuine promises and serving here as an expression adding emphasis to your denial.

In general the point stated in condition (4) is that if a purported promise is to be non-defective the thing promised must be something the hearer wants done, or considers to be in his interest, or would prefer being done to not being done, etc.; and the speaker must be aware of or believe or know, etc. that this is the case. I think a more elegant and exact formulation of this condition would require the introduction of technical terminology.

(5) It is not obvious to both S and H that S will do A in the normal course of events.

This condition is an instance of a general condition on many different kinds of illocutionary acts to the effect that the act must have a point.

For example, if I make a request to someone to do something which it is obvious that he is already doing or is about to do, then my request is pointless and to that extent defective. In an actual speech situation, listeners, knowing the rules for performing illocutionary acts, will assume that this condition is satisfied. Suppose, for example, that in the course of a public speech I say to a member of my audience 'Look here, Smith, pay attention to what I am saying'. In order to make sense of this utterance the audience will have to assume that Smith has not been paying attention or at any rate that it is not obvious that he has been paying attention, that the question of his paying attention has arisen in some way; because a condition for making a request is that it is not obvious that the hearer is doing or about to do the thing requested.

Similarly with promises. It is out of order for me to promise to do something that it is obvious I am going to do anyhow. If I do seem to be making such a promise, the only way my audience can make sense of my utterance is to assume that I believe that it is not obvious that I am going to do the thing promised. A happily married man who promises his wife he will not desert her in the next week is likely to provide more anxiety than comfort.

Parenthetically I think this condition is an instance of the sort of phenomenon stated in Zipf's law. I think there is operating in our language, as in most forms of human behaviour, a principle of least effort, in this case a principle of maximum illocutionary ends with minimum phonetic effort; and I think condition (5) is an instance of it.

I call conditions such as (4) and (5) *preparatory conditions.* They are *sine quibus non* of happy promising, but they do not yet state the essential feature.

(6) *S intends to do A.*

The most important distinction between sincere and insincere promises is that in the case of the sincere promise the speaker intends to do the act promised, in the case of the insincere promise he does not intend to do the act. Also in sincere promises the speaker believes it is possible for him to do the act (or to refrain from doing it), but I think the proposition that he intends to do it entails that he thinks it possible to do (or refrain from doing) it, so I am not stating that as an extra condition. I call this condition the *sincerity condition.*

(7) *S intends that the utterance of T will place him under an obligation to do A.*

The essential feature of a promise is that it is the undertaking of an obligation to perform a certain act. I think that this condition distinguishes promises (and other members of the same family such as vows) from other kinds of speech acts. Notice that in the statement of the condition we only specify the speaker's intention; further conditions will make clear how that intention is realized. It is clear, however, that having this intention is a necessary condition of making a promise; for if a speaker can demonstrate that he did not have this intention in a given utterance, he can prove that the utterance was not a promise We know, for example, that Mr Pickwick did not promise to marry the woman because we know he did not have the appropriate intention.

I call this the *essential condition.*

(8) S intends that the utterance of T will produce in H a belief that conditions (6) and (7) obtain by means of the recognition of the intention to produce that belief, and he intends this recognition to be achieved by means of the recognition of the sentence as one conventionally used to produce such beliefs.

This captures our amended Gricean analysis of what it is for the speaker to mean to make a promise. The speaker intends to produce a certain illocutionary effect by means of getting the hearer to recognize his intention to produce that effect, and he also intends this recognition to be achieved in virtue of the fact that the lexical and syntactical character of the item he utters conventionally associates it with producing that effect.

Strictly speaking this condition could be formulated as part of condition (1), but it is of enough philosophical interest to be worth stating separately. I find it troublesome for the following reason. If my original objection to Grice is really valid, then surely, one might say, all these iterated intentions are superfluous; all that is necessary is that the speaker should seriously utter a sentence. The production of all these effects is simply a consequence of the hearer's knowledge of what the sentence means, which in turn is a consequence of his knowledge of the language, which is assumed by the speaker at the outset. I think the correct reply to this objection is that condition (8) explicates what it is for the speaker to 'seriously' utter the sentence, i.e. to utter it and mean it, but I am not completely confident about either the force of the objection or of the reply.

(9) The semantical rules of the dialect spoken by S and H are such that T is correctly and sincerely uttered if and only if conditions (1)–(8) obtain.

This condition is intended to make clear that the sentence uttered is one which by the semantical rules of the language is used to make a promise. Taken together with condition (8), it eliminates counter-examples like the captured soldier example considered earlier. Exactly what the formulation of the rules is, we shall soon see.

So far we have considered only the case of a sincere promise. But insincere promises are promises nonetheless, and we now need to show how to modify the conditions to allow for them. In making an insincere promise the speaker does not have all the intentions and beliefs he has when making a sincere promise. However, he purports to have them.

Indeed it is because he purports to have intentions and beliefs which he does not have that we describe his act as insincere. So to allow for insincere promises we need only to revise our conditions to state that the speaker takes responsibility for having the beliefs and intentions rather than stating that he actually has them. A clue that the speaker does take such responsibility is the fact that he could not say without absurdity, e.g. 'I promise to do A but I do not intend to do A'. To say 'I promise to do A' is to take responsibility for intending to do A, and this condition holds whether the utterance was sincere or insincere. To allow for the possibility of an insincere promise then we have only to revise condition (6) so that it states not that the speaker intends to do A, but that he takes responsibility for intending to do A, and to avoid the charge of circularity I shall phrase this as follows:

(6*) *S intends that the utterance of T will make him responsible for intending to do A.*

Thus amended (and with 'sincerely' dropped from our analysandum and from condition (9)), our analysis is neutral on the question whether the promise was sincere or insincere.

VI. Rules for the Use of the Function Indicating Device

Our next task is to extract from our set of conditions a set of rules for the use of the function indicating device. Obviously not all of our conditions are equally relevant to this task. Condition (1) and conditions of the forms (8) and (9) apply generally to all kinds of normal illocutionary acts and are not peculiar to promising. Rules for the function indicating device for promising are to be found corresponding to conditions (2)–(7).

The semantical rules for the use of any function indicating device P for promising are:

Rule 1. P is to be uttered only in the context of a sentence (or larger stretch of discourse) the utterance of which predicates some future act A of the speaker S.

I call this the *propositional content rule*. It is derived from the propositional content conditions (2) and (3).

Rule 2. P is to be uttered only if the hearer H would prefer S's doing A to his not doing A, and S believes H would prefer S's doing A to his not doing A.

Rule 3. P is to be uttered only if it is not obvious to both S and H that S will do A in the normal course of events.

I call rules (2) and (3) *preparatory rules*. They are derived from the preparatory conditions (4) and (5).

Rule 4. *P* is to be uttered only if *S* intends to do *A*.

I call this the *sincerity rule*. It is derived from the sincerity condition (6).

Rule 5. The utterance of *P* counts as the undertaking of an obligation to do *A*.

I call this the *essential rule*.

These rules are ordered: Rules 2–5 apply only if Rule 1 is satisfied, and Rule 5 applies only if Rules 2 and 3 are satisfied as well.

Notice that whereas Rules 1–4 take the form of quasi-imperatives, i.e. they are of the form: utter *P* only if *x*, Rule 5 is of the form: the utterance of *P* counts as *Y*. Thus Rule 5 is of the kind peculiar to systems of constitutive rules which I discussed in section II.

Notice also that the rather tiresome analogy with games is holding up remarkably well. If we ask ourselves under what conditions a player could be said to move a knight correctly, we would find preparatory conditions, such as that it must be his turn to move, as well as the essential condition stating the actual positions the knight can move to. I think that there is even a sincerity rule for competitive games, the rule that each side tries to win. I suggest that the team which 'throws' the game is behaving in a way closely analogous to the speaker who lies or makes false promises. Of course, there usually are no propositional content rules for games, because games do not, by and large, represent states of affairs.

If this analysis is of any general interest beyond the case of promising then it would seem that these distinctions should carry over into other types of speech act, and I think a little reflection will show that they do. Consider, e.g., giving an order. The preparatory conditions include that the speaker should be in a position of authority over the hearer, the sincerity condition is that the speaker wants the ordered act done. and the essential condition has to do with the fact that the utterance is an attempt to get the hearer to do it. For assertions, the preparatory conditions include the fact that the hearer must have some basis for supposing the asserted proposition is true, the sincerity condition is that he must believe it to be true, and the essential condition has to do with the fact that the utterance is an attempt to inform the hearer and convince him of its truth. Greetings are a much simpler kind of speech act, but even here some of the distinctions apply. In the utterance of 'Hello' there is no propositional content and no sincerity condition. The preparatory condition is that the speaker must have just encountered the hearer, and the essential rule is that the utterance indicates courteous recognition of the hearer.

A proposal for further research then is to carry out a similar analysis of other types of speech acts. Not only would this give us an analysis of concepts interesting in themselves, but the comparison of different analyses would deepen our understanding of the whole subject and incidentally provide a basis for a more serious taxonomy than any of the usual facile categories such as evaluative versus descriptive, or cognitive versus emotive.

Notes

[1] J. L. Austin, *How To Do Things With Words,* Oxford 1962.

[2] This distinction occurs in J. Rawls, 'Two Concepts of Rules', *Philosophical Review*, 1955, and J. R. Searle, 'How to Derive "Ought" from "is"', *Philosophical Review*, 1964.

[3] The formulation '*X* counts as *Y*' was originally suggested to me by Max Black.

[4] In the sentence 'I promise that I will come' the function indicating device and the propositional element are separate. In the sentence 'I promise to come', which means the same as the first and is derived from it by certain transformations, the two elements are not separate.

[5] *Philosophical Review*, 1957.

[6] *Philosophical Investigations*, Oxford 1953, para. 510.

5.2 Towards an Analysis of Classroom Discourse
J. McH. Sinclair and R. M. Coulthard

The Development of the System

[. . .] We had no preconceptions about the organization or extent of linguistic patterning in long texts. Obviously lessons are highly structured but our problem was to discover how much of this structure was pedagogical and how much linguistic. It seemed possible that the presence of a linguistic introduction was a clue to the boundary of a linguistic unit, but we quickly realized that this is not a useful criterion. On the first morning of the session a headmaster may greet the new intake, 'Good morning children. Welcome to Waseley. This is an important day for you . . .', introducing them to several years of schooling. When the children go to their form-master he also welcomes them and explains their timetables. They go to their first subject lesson. Here the teacher perhaps introduces his subject and goes on to delimit part of it. 'This year we are going to study world geography, starting with the continent of Africa. Let's start with the map. Now, let's see if we can find the main rivers and learn their names − can *you* tell us the name of one river, any one.'

Everything the headmaster and teachers have said so far could be considered as introductions to a series of hierarchically-ordered *units*: the whole of the child's secondary education; a year's work; one subject; a section of that subject; a period or so's work; a part of that period; and a small interactive episode with one pupil. [. . .]

However, while the language of introduction to each unit is potentially distinctive, despite overlap, we would not want to suggest that for instance 'a year's work' has any linguistic structure. The majority of the units we recognized above are pedagogic ones. To avoid the danger of confusing pedagogic with linguistic structure we determined to work upwards from the smallest linguistic unit. The research problem with contiguous utterances is primarily a descriptive one; major theoretical problems arise when more extensive units are postulated.

Towards an Analysis of Discourse, O.U.P. (1975), pp. 19−27. This article consists of extracts from Chapter 3, 'The System of Analysis'.

We decided to use a rank scale for our descriptive model because of its flexibility. The major advantage of describing new data with a rank scale is that no rank has any more importance than any other and thus if, as we did, one discovers new patterning it is a fairly simple process to create a new rank to handle it. There is, of course, the ever-present temptation of creating new ranks to cope with every little problem. [. . .]

The basic assumption of a rank scale is that a unit at a given rank, for example, *word*, is made up of one or more units of the rank below, *morphemes*, and combines with other units at the same rank to make one unit at the rank above, *group* (Halliday 1961). The unit at the lowest rank has no structure. For example, in grammar 'morpheme' is the smallest unit, and cannot be subdivided into smaller grammatical units. However, if one moves from the *level* of grammar to the level of phonology, morphemes can be shown to be composed of a series of phonemes. Similarly, the smallest unit at the level of discourse will have no structure, although it is composed of words, groups or clauses at the level of grammar.

Each rank above the lowest has a structure which can be expressed in terms of the units next below. Thus, the structure of a clause can be expressed in terms of nominal, verbal, adverbial, and prepositional groups. The unit at the highest rank is one which has a structure that can be expressed in terms of lower units, but does not itself form part of the structure of any higher unit. It is for this reason that 'sentence' is regarded as the highest unit of grammar. Paragraphs have no grammatical structure; they consist of a series of sentences of any type in any order. Where there are no grammatical constraints on what an individual can do, variations are often dubbed 'stylistic'.

We assumed that when, from a linguistic point of view, classroom discourse became an unconstrained string of units, the organization would have become fundamentally pedagogic. While we could then make observations on teacher style, further analysis of structure would require a change of level not rank.

We then looked at adjacent utterances, trying to discover what constituted an appropriate reply to a teacher's question, and how the teacher signalled whether the reply was appropriate or inappropriate.

Initially we felt the need for only two ranks, *utterance* and *exchange*; utterance was defined as everything said by one speaker before another began to speak, exchange as two or more utterances. The following example has three utterances, but how many exchanges?

Teacher	Can you tell me why do you eat all that food?
	Yes.
Pupil	To keep you strong.
Teacher	To keep you strong. Yes. To keep you strong.
	Why do you want to be strong? (Text G)

The obvious boundary occurs in the middle of the teacher's second utterance, which suggests that there is a unit smaller than utterance. Following Bellack *et al* (1966) we called this a *move*, and wondered for a while whether moves combined to form utterances which in turn combined to form exchanges. However, the example above is not an isolated one; the vast majority of exchanges have their boundaries within utterances. Thus, although utterances had many points to recommend it as a unit of discourse, not least ease of definition, we reluctantly abandoned it. We now express the structure of exchanges in terms of moves. A typical exchange in the classroom consists of an *initiation* by the teacher, followed by a *response* from the pupil, followed by *feedback*, to the pupil's response from the teacher, as in the above example. These categories correspond very closely with Bellack's moves, soliciting, responding, and reacting.

While we were looking at exchanges we noticed that a small set of words – 'right', 'well', 'good'. 'O.K.', 'now', recurred frequently in the speech of all teachers. We realized that these words functioned to indicate boundaries in the lesson, the end of one stage and the beginning of the next. Silverman (1972) notes their occurrence in job interviews and Pearce (1973) in broadcast interviews where the function is exactly the same. We labelled them *frame*. Teachers vary in the particular word they favour but a frame occurs invariably at the beginning of a lesson, marking off the settling-down time.

Now,
I want to tell you about a King who lived a long time ago in Ancient Egypt. (Text B)

Well,
today, erm, I thought we'd do three quizzes. (Text D)

An example of a frame within a lesson is:

> Energy. Yes.
> When you put petrol in the car you're putting another kind of energy in the car from the petrol. So we get energy from petrol and we get energy from food. Two kinds of energy.

Frame   *Now then*
> I want you to take your pen and rub it as hard as you can on something woollen. (Text G)

We then observed that frames, especially those at the beginning of a lesson, are frequently followed by a special kind of statement, the function of which is to tell the class what is going to happen (see the examples from Texts B and D above). These items are not strictly part of the discourse, but rather metastatements about the discourse – we call them *focus*, and these correspond very closely with Bellack's structuring moves. The boundary elements, frame and focus, were the first positive evidence of the existence of a unit above exchange, which we later labelled *transaction*.

We have isolated a large number of exchange types with unique structures; exchanges combine to form transactions and it seems probable that there will also be a number of transaction types — concerned mainly with giving information, or directing pupil activity, or question-and-answer routines — but we cannot isolate them yet. The unanswered question is whether we will be able to provide structures for transactions or whether the way exchanges are combined to form transactions will prove to be purely a feature of teacher style.

The highest unit of classroom discourse, consisting of one or more transactions, we call *lesson*. This unit may frequently be co-extensive with the pedagogical unit *period*, but need not be.

For several months we continued using these four ranks — move, exchange, transaction, lesson — but found that we were experiencing difficulty coding at the lowest rank. For example, to code the following as simply an initiation seemed inadequate.

Now I'm going to show you a word and I want you — anyone who can — to tell me if they can tell me what the word says. Now it's a bit difficult. It's upside down for some of you isn't it? Anyone think they know what it says?

(Hands raised)

Two people. Three people. Let's see what you think, Martin, what do you think it says?

We then realized that moves were structured and so we needed another rank with which we could describe their structure. This we called *act*.

Acts and moves in discourse are very similar to morphemes and words in grammar. By definition, move is the smallest free unit although it has a structure in terms of acts. Just as there are bound morphemes which cannot alone realize words, so there are bound acts which cannot alone realize moves.

We need to distinguish discourse acts from grammatical structures, or there would be no point in proposing a new level of language description — we would simply be analysing the higher ranks of grammar. Of course if acts did turn out to be arrangements of clauses in a consistent and hierarchical fashion, then they would replace (in speech) our confusing notions of 'sentence' and the higher ranks of what we now call discourse would arrange themselves on top.

The evidence is not conclusive and we need comparative data from other types of discourse. We would argue, however, for a separate level of discourse because, as we show in detail later, grammatical structure is not sufficient to determine which discourse act a particular grammatical unit realizes — one needs to take account of both relevant situational information and position in the discourse.

The lowest rank of the discourse scale overlaps with the top of the grammar scale (see figure 1). Discourse acts are typically one free clause, plus any subordinate clauses, but there are certain closed classes where we can specify almost all the possible realizations which consist of single words or groups.

Figure 1 Levels and ranks

Non-Linguistic Organization	DISCOURSE	Grammar
course period topic	LESSON TRANSACTION EXCHANGE MOVE ACT	sentence clause group word morpheme

There is a similar overlap at the top of the discourse scale. We have been constantly aware of the danger of creating a rank for which there is only pedagogical evidence. We have deliberately chosen *lesson*, a word specific to the particular language situation we are investigating, as the label for the top rank. We feel fairly certain that the four lower ranks will be present in other discourse; the fifth may also be, in which case, once we have studied comparative data, we will use a more general label.

We see the level of discourse as lying between the level of *grammar* and *non-linguistic organization*. There is no need to suppose a one-to-one correspondence of units between levels; the levels of phonology and grammar overlap considerably, but have only broad general correspondence. We see the top of our discourse scale, lesson, corresponding roughly to the rank *period* in the non-linguistic level, and the bottom of our scale, *act*, corresponding roughly to the clause complex in grammar.

Summary of the System of Analysis

This research has been very much text-based. We began with very few preconceptions and the descriptive system has grown and been modified to cope with problems thrown up by the data. The system we have produced is hierarchical and our method of presentation is closely modelled on Halliday's *Categories of a Theory of Grammar*. All the terms used — structure, system, rank, level, delicacy, realization, marked, unmarked — are Halliday's. To permit readers to gain an over-

all impression, the whole system is now presented at primary delicacy.
[...]

Working downwards, each rank is first named. Then the elements
of structure are named, and the structure is stated in a general way,
using shortened forms of the names of elements. Brackets indicate
options.

The link between one rank and the next below is through *classes*.
A class realizes an element of structure, and in this summary classes
are both numbered and named.

Let us look at one of the tables as an example:

RANK II: Transaction

Elements of Structure	Structures	Classes of Exchange
Preliminary (P) Medial Terminal (T)	$PM (M^2 \ldots M^n) (T)$	P. T: Boundary (II.1) M: Teaching (II.2)

This table identifies the rank as second from the top of the scale, i.e.
transaction. It states that there are three elements of structure, called
Preliminary (short symbol P), *Medial* (M), and *Terminal* (T). In the next
column is given a composite statement of the possible structures of this
transaction – $PM (M^2 \ldots M^n) (T)$. Anything within brackets is optional,
so this formula states:

a) there must be a preliminary move in each transaction,
b) there must be one medial move, but there may be any number of
   them,
c) there can be a terminal move, but not necessarily.

In the third column the elements of transaction structure are associated
with the classes of the rank next below (exchange), because each element is realized by a class of exchange. Preliminary and terminal
exchange, it is claimed, are selected from the same class of move called
Boundary moves, and this is numbered for ease of reference. The
element medial is realized by a class of exchange called *Teaching*.
Later tables develop the structure of these exchanges at rank III.

RANK I: Lesson

Elements of Structure	Structures	Classes
	an unordered series of transactions	

RANK III: Exchange (Boundary)

Elements of Structure	Structure	Classes of Move
Frame (Fr) Focus (Fo)	(Fr) (Fo)	Fr: Framing (III.1) Fo: Focusing (III.2)

RANK III: Exchange (Teaching)

Elements of Structure	Structures	Classes of Move
Initiation (I) Response (R) Feedback (F)	I(R)(F)	I: Opening (III.3) R: Answering (III.4) F: Follow-up (III.5)

RANK IV: Move (Opening)

Elements of Structure	Structures	Classes of Act
signal(s) pre-head (pre-h) head (h) post-head (post-h) select (sel)	(s) (pre-h) h (post-h) (sel) (sel) (pre-h) h	s: marker (IV.1) pre-h: starter (IV.2) h: system operating at h; choice of elicitation, directive, informative, check (IV.3) post-h: system operating at post-h; choice from prompt and clue (IV.4) sel: ((cue) bid) nomination (IV.5)

RANK IV: Move (Answering)

Elements of Structure	Structures	Classes of Act
pre-head (pre-h) head (h) post-head (post-h)	(pre-h) h (post-h)	pre-h; acknowledge (IV.6) h: system operating at h; choice of reply, react, acknowledge (IV.7) post-h: comment (IV.8)

RANK IV: Move (Follow-up)

Elements of Structure	Structures	Classes of Act
pre-head (pre-h) head (h) post-head (post-h)	(pre-h) (h) (post-h)	pre-h: accept (IV.9) h: evaluate (IV.10) post-h: comment (IV.8)

RANK IV: Move (Framing)

Elements of Structure	Structures	Classes of Act
head (h) qualifier (q)	hq	h: marker (IV.1) Q: silent stress (IV.11)

RANK IV; Move (Focusing)

Elements of Structure	Structures	Classes of Act

signal (s)
 pre-head (pre-h)
 head (h)
 post-head (post-h)
	(s) (pre-h) h(post-h)	s: marker (IV.1)
		 pre-h: starter (IV.2)
		 h: system at h: choice
		     from metastatement or
		     conclusion (IV.12)
		 post-h: comment (IV.8)

References

Bellack, A. A., Kleibard, H. M., Hyman, R. T., and Smith, F. L. *The Language of the Classroom*, New York, Teachers College Press, 1966.

Halliday, M. A. K. 'Categories of the Theory of Grammar', *Word* 17, 1961, pp. 241-92.

Pearce, R. D. *The Structure of Discourse in Broadcast Interviews*, M.A. thesis, University of Birmingham, 1973.

5.3 Recognizing Complaints
Roy Turner

Here is a piece of talk pulled out of a transcript made from a tape-recorded occasion. I shall deliberately withhold any description of the occasion or the setting for the moment, since issues concerning their relevance are part of what we have to discuss.

BERT	Yea, Yeah, that's correct, I uh uh really did know im and uh he was with me in the Alexander Psychiatric Institute in in Alexander, Western Province. I I don't remember his name but we uh we always buddied around together when uh we were at the hospital and we always (( )) French. And uh I saw him out at Western City about three weeks ago, and I said to 'm, 'Hello, howarya doing?' He said 'I don't know you − who are you?' 'well, lookit', I said, 'You *must* know me.' He says, 'No, I don't know you. 'Now he was with another fellow there too − waal he didn't want to admit that he was in a mental hospital uh in a hospital − he didn't want to admit it to the other fellow that was with him. So he just walked off and that was it. He wouldn't say hello to me. He wouldn't say nothin!
ROB	What was you view there? Do you have your own views on that? A touchy point.
BERT	Uh.
?	(( ))
JAKE	Perhaps he didn't like the idea of being in that place. Maybe he didn't want/
BERT	Well no he had to say it − there was another fellow with him you see/
JAKE	Well he didn't want to admit/
BERT	Who hadn't been in a mental hospital probable, and he *was* in the hospital. He didn't want *him* to know.
ART	You mean he
?:	This other guy
COUNS	But he
BERT	Oh, oh never been in a hospital
BERT	He didn't want to know his friends.[1]

Roy Turner (1970), 'Words, Utterances and Activities' in Jack Douglas (ed.) *Understanding Everyday Life*, Aldine, 1970, pp. 165–87. This reading is an extract from the original article.

Now, given such materials as these, the practical issue is: how might they be analysed in a sociologically relevant way — that is to say, as a demonstration of their orderliness? An initial problem seems to be that as societal members we find that such materials are often terribly obvious, if not trite (and I imagine that the reader was able to find sense in the talk on the basis of a very rapid reading, despite the fact that he has no personal knowledge of Bert and the other speakers); while as sociologists, confronted with the task of obtaining some leverage in providing an analytical description, the very same set of utterances become forbiddingly opaque. It becomes opaque, I believe, under the condition that as sociologists we suppose that we must locate instances (or indicators) of concepts posited by an explicit theory; and yet we obviously have no such theory to guide us in analysing talk in any detail. Thus an elementary problem might be formulated as: what are we to attend to as units — words, sentences, utterances?

Let us assume that we are agreed for the moment that we want to locate and look at instances of activities. The problem still remains. I take it that Austin did not doubt that we can *recognize* activities; indeed, his method of operation seems to require, first, the collection of a number of performative utterances, treated as non-problematic in itself, after it has been explained what shall count as a performative utterance, and, then, the search for formal criteria that distinguish the class of performatives from other classes of utterances. Of course, if we isolated the formal criteria, we should then have no problem in scanning further candidates of performatives to decide their membership status; but that scarcely solves the problem of how we assemble our first collection of utterances on the basis of which the formal criteria are to be derived.

As a solution to the vexed problem of the relation between the shared cultural knowledge (members' knowledge) that the sociologist possesses and the analytical apparatus that it is his responsibility to produce, I propose the following:

1. *The sociologist inevitably trades on his members' knowledge* in recognizing the activities that participants to interaction are engaged in; for example, it is by virtue of my status as a competent member that I can recurrently locate in my transcripts instances of 'the same' activity. This is not to claim that members are infallible or that there is perfect agreement in recognizing any and every instance; it is only to claim that no resolution of problematic cases can be effected by resorting to procedures that are supposedly uncontaminated by members' knowledge. (Arbitrary resolutions, made for the sake of easing the problems of 'coding', are of course no resolution at all for the present enterprise.)

2. The sociologist, having made his first-level decision on the basis of members' knowledge, must then *pose as problematic* how utterances

come off as recognizable unit activities. This requires the sociologist to *explicate the resources* he shares with the participants in making sense of utterances in a stretch of talk. At every step of the way, inevitably, the sociologist will continue to employ his socialized competence, while continuing to make explicit *what* these resources are and *how* he employs them. I see no alternative to these procedures, except to pay no explicit attention to one's socialized knowledge while continuing to use it as an indispensable aid. In short, sociological discoveries are ineluctably discoveries *from within the society.*

Now leaving the programmatics aside, let me cite Austin's admonition (Austin (1965) page 147) that 'the total speech act in the total speech situation is the *only actual* phenomenon which, in the last resort, we are engaged in elucidating'. Supposing we decide to take this seriously, how do we bring it to bear on the data presented above? What, for example, is 'the total speech situation' of the talk recorded and transcribed?

Consider the possibility that more than one technically correct description of the occasion of the talk might be provided. Thus I could propose that a tape recording was made of Bert and a few acquaintances sitting around having an evening's chat. Another possible description of the occasion is as follows: a number of former mental patients voluntarily attended an evening group discussion sponsored by a mental health association; the discussion was in the charge of a counsellor whose instructions were to help members of the group discuss their problems. As between these two possible descriptions I offer the latter as the more useful, employing the following criterion: the latter description characterizes the occasion as that occasion was organized, announced, and made available to the participants; an act of self-identification as a 'former mental patient' was any member's entitlement to attend, and his entitlement to see that his fellow participants (apart from the 'counsellor') were likewise 'former mental patients.'

Why does this matter? It matters, I argue, in that it provides participants with an orientation and a set of criteria for contributing and recognizing activities. Whatever one says during the course of the evening may be treated as 'something said by a former mental patient', not on the 'technical' grounds that after all one *is* such a person but on the grounds that that identification is occasioned and thereby warranted as relevant.

Presumably this does not end a characterization of the 'total speech situation' of any unit of speech smaller than the whole conversation. Thus consider Bert's remark 'So he just walked off and that was it.' I assume that in order to see the sense of this remark it is necessary to notice its ties to at least the earlier parts of the utterance from which it is extracted. Notice, for instance, that given its position in the utterance, the 'he' in the remark 'So he just walked off and that was it' can be given a determinate reading by hearers (and now readers). Put crudely, then, one task of an analysis such as this is to make explicit just what features of the occasion and the talk are appealed to as providing for the force of an utterance or the character of an activity.

I hear Bert's remarks in this portion of the talk as constituting a 'complaint', or 'doing complaining'. In so identifying it, I am unable to locate any obvious syntactic properties that might be seen as structural correlates of complaints, nor do I have any operational means for identifying its boundaries. I take it that Bert may have begun his complaint in an utterance previous to the first utterance given here; and I further assume that Bert's last utterance given here (but not the end of the talk), 'He didn't want to know his friends', is in some sense 'part of' the complaint. I know of no *a priori* reason an activity should be expected to require so many words or so many utterances; in any piece of data being considered it will be an issue to note the boundedness of an activity.

I now want to look at the production of a recognizable complaint in some detail, to look at the resources and components of Bert's complaint. I use the term resources carefully, since I take it that there is an issue of bringing off an activity in such a way that one's hearers can bring to the talk the necessary equipment and materials to make out its intended character.

Commonsensically there is no difficulty in saying that the basis of Bert's complaints is a 'snub'. More specifically, I take it that Bert's account is of 'a former mental patient being snubbed', and thus is produced as an instance of 'the kind of thing that can happen to a former mental patient'.

Let us assume for the moment that a snub or slight, in the form of a refusal of recognition, can happen to 'anyone'. For the person to whom it has happened, such an event can presumably constitute a puzzle — that is to say, it is an event requiring an explanation. If I walk down the corridor and meet a colleague I encounter in such circumstances daily, and if we exchange greetings, then an interactional routine will have been achieved that — *for members* — is nonproblematic. Thus, if you are accompanying me at the time and you ask 'Why did that guy smile at you?' I assume that an answer such as 'He's a colleague of mine', will be sufficient, that is, that it would be 'odd' for you to persist, 'I know that, but why did he smile at you?' A snub becomes a puzzle, presumably, just because such a nonproblematic routine is breached.

Now if after being snubbed one makes that event the basis of an anecdote for others, one thing they may do, it seems, is to offer possible 'explanations' or queries directed to uncovering 'what happened'. One readily available explanation has the consequence of inviting you to reconsider the event, to see that it wasn't a snub after all, perhaps that 'there was some mistake' — that it wasn't who you thought it was. He looked remarkably like an old friend, but you caught only a glimpse, and it was probably a stranger. I mention this routine treatment because if we look carefully at Bert's first utterance we can see that Bert orients to the possibility of this being forthcoming from his hearers, and forestalls it: 'I uh uh really did know im.' The reader should notice here the interplay between common-sense knowledge offered as how I make out what is going on, and sociological concern, in that I take it as an analytical responsibility to account for the remark 'I uh uh really did know im', while having recourse to members' knowledge in providing the substance of my account.

Now if we look at Bert's first utterance as a unit, it seems that it (a) recounts the occurrence of the snub, and (b) provides an explanation for it. Nevertheless, at the same time it is via the character of the explanation that I see that Bert is constructing a complaint. In effect, this leads us to consider the 'mechanics' of doing an activity. If Bert is to bring off a successful instance of a complaint, he must build it out of components that will provide for its recognition by hearers who are presumed to be − like Bert, and like readers − 'experts' in constructing and recognizing a repertoire of activities. In looking at the talk in detail, then, we are discovering how the materials at hand are made to serve the requirements of certain invariant properties of activities. The following considerations lead me to argue that the explanation provides for Bert to be seen as 'complaining'.

1. Recall Austin's requirement for the successful achievement of a performative utterance, that 'the particular persons and circumstances in a given case must be appropriate for the invocation of the particular procedure involved'. How is that relevant to the present issue? In the first place, since we are not analysing as data the talk that took place between Bert and his acquaintance upon the occasion of the snub, we are hardly in a position to characterize that 'total speech situation' in a way that a transcript of the occasion might permit. What we have, rather, is Bert's characterization of the occasion, developed as a resource for constructing a complaint. In effect, then, we are dealing with the societal member's concern with providing for the 'appropriateness' of the 'particular persons and circumstances' as features that will properly orient hearers to the sense of the occasion − that is, orient them to a sense of the occasion that will enable them to recognize what Bert is *now* doing. This permits us to ask: *how* does Bert provide such an orientation?

Notice first, then, that Bert does not simply tell his listeners that he was snubbed by 'an acquaintance', 'an old friend' or 'a guy I knew', although presumably any of these would have been a sufficient and proper identification of the party to allow for what happened to be seen as a snub. Bert identified the snubber as a man who 'was with me

in the Alexander Psychiatric Institute'. Now I take it that this identification is not warranted simply by its literal correctness, since a range
of possible 'correct' identifications is always available (in this case, for
example, 'a fellow I used to know in Western Province') and it is not a
matter of indifference which item of a set of possible items is selected.
One thing we can note about the identification selected, then, is a
relevance provided by the occasion, by the presence of this collection
of hearers, in that the party mentioned is mentioned now as 'one of
us'. Beyond that, the identification of the snubber as 'he was with me
in the Alexander Psychiatric Institute' provides that Bert himself could
be seen by the other party as a 'released mental patient'.

2. Bert tells his listeners that on recognizing the other party he said to
him, 'Hello, howarya doing?' Now given that he has already indicated
that (and *how*) they were acquainted, a greeting is seen to be in order
and to require a greeting in return, since an exchange of greetings is a
procedure permitted among acquainted persons; and upon one party's
offering a greeting the other is taken to be under obligation to return
it. In short, I take it that Bert is invoking what I have just stated in the
form of a 'norm', and that it is by reference to such a procedure that it
becomes 'obvious' to his listeners that 'something was wrong' when
instead of the greeting the greeted party returned with 'I don't know
you – who are you?' That this is the case is further provided for by
Bert's remark 'He wouldn't say hello to me. He wouldn't say nothin!'
As I understand Bert's remark, assumption of shared knowledge that a
greeting acquaintance has an *obligation* to respond with a greeting is
both a requirement and a resource for seeing how Bert is entitled to say
'He *wouldn't* say hello to me', in that he is thus enabling his listeners to
find the 'absence of a greeting' as a motivated act.[2]

So far, then, all we have seen is an account of a breached norm, the
norm that requires acquainted persons to acknowledge one another
upon meeting face-to-face. This component of the account constitutes
the occurrence of a 'trouble', in this case, a snub.

3. If we look further at the utterance we find that Bert claims to see
why he was offered a slight by an aquaintance who owed him at least
the return of a greeting. Thus, Bert remarks: 'Now he was with another
fellow there too – waal he didn't want to admit that he was in a mental
hospital uh in a hospital – he didn't want to admit to the other fellow
that was with him. So he just walked off and that was it.'

Now the interesting question to ask is: *How does this come off as an
explanation?* To set it up with heuristic naïvité, what could Bert be
talking about in saying of the other party 'He didn't want to admit . . .
that he was in a mental hospital?' How does the question of making an
admission arise? To put the question in somewhat different form, we
may ask: are there any resources that Bert's listeners (as well as

ourselves) might bring to bear on this remark to see in it the sense it is presumably intended to have (as grounds for the refusal to return a greeting)? How might it be seen that a returned greeting would be, or would lead to, an 'admission to the other fellow' that he had been in a mental hospital? To put it differently, and in common-sense terms, it might be argued that it would have been entirely inconsequential for Bert's former fellow-patient to have responded, for example, 'Pretty good, thanks. How's yourself?'

I take it that Bert is able to trade upon an 'obvious' feature of 'chance encounters', namely, their informational value. The paradigm case is suggested by the following hypothetical conversation.

A Who was that guy who waved from across the street?
B Oh, just a fellow I knew in the Marines.
A Really? I didn't know you were in the Marines! When was that?

Bert's friend, then, could be depicted as motivated to refuse an acknowledgement of the acquaintance on the grounds that it might have opened him up to 'explaining' to his companion 'who' Bert was — where the relevant sense of 'who' would require a reference to the basis of their being acquainted. But beyond that, there are other norms relating to the situation of renewing acquaintance that are possibly being invoked here.

An issue in the orderly conduct of conversation may be termed 'the distribution of speaker's rights' (see Garfinkel and Sacks, 1970: Speier 1968). Thus Sacks has pointed out with respect to questions and answers as paired units that a potentially infinite chain of utterances may be produced under the auspices of the following rule: *the questioner has a right to talk again when an answer is returned,* that is, when the answerer finishes his turn at talking the right to speak passes back to the questioner, *and the questioner has a right to ask another question* (thus providing for another answer and a further question; and so the cycle may be repeated, as court transcripts nicely indicate). Similarly, Schegloff (1968) has indicated that within the structure of a telephone call the caller may select the first topic for talk. With respect to face-to-face social contacts among the acquainted it appears to be the case that a simple exchange of greetings — 'hello', 'hello' — may constitute an adequate 'conversation', and the parties may separate without breach of the relationship. However, it further appears to be the case that the initial greeter has the right to talk again when a greeting is returned, and that he thus becomes a 'first speaker' with respect to rights of topic selection. If this is the case, then (as I take it Bert and his listeners could see), to acknowledge a greeting by returning a greeting is to open oneself up to the initial greeter's developing a conversation and to his initiating a topic. In the cited incident, Bert would have had the right to so talk, providing that his acquaintance did not attach the opening of topical talk to the utterance returning a greeting.

If we shift our attention for the moment from the initiation of talk to the issue of the *management of relationships,* conversations can be seen as having sequential properties; that is, when related parties meet, the conversational possibilities may be constrained by 'what happened last time' or by events that have intervened. Thus, persons employ opening slots in conversations to 'bring one another up-to-date', or — when the passage of time has been considerable, or 'circumstances' have changed — to talk over 'when we last saw each other', or, as in reunions, to 'talk over old times'. Notice again that I am suggesting this not as an analysis independent of members' knowledge and members' concerns but as integral to them, and I take it that it is a commonplace experience to 'look forward to' or 'avoid' persons with whom such conversations are to be expected.

In this connection it is relevant to note that Bert's development of the situation permits his hearers to see that indeed 'bringing up-to-date' might have been in order, in that this was apparently a first meeting since the hospital days, and in a city more than a thousand miles from the hospital. In short, the locational and temporal features of the occasion are not simply descriptive but are *explanatory*: a 'reunion' would have 'normally' been in order, and a reunion could be seen as precisely what a former mental patient who is 'passing' could anticipate as a threat.[3] Returning a greeting, then, is not without cost.[4] For Bert's acquaintance, the return of a greeting, carrying with it an acknowledgement of their relationship, would have entitled Bert to develop talk about what each had done 'since the hospital', etc. Thus potential conversational partners may avoid eye contacts, give signs of 'being in a hurry', or balk at the first interchange, where the 'danger' is seen to be located at some later (and unspecifiable) spot in the conversation that mutual acknowledgement may generate.

4. To recapitulate, I have suggested that the visible breach of a norm requiring acquainted persons to acknowledge one another, or at least return a proffered greeting, has constituted a trouble for Bert — he has been snubbed. Bert saw and made available to his hearers an explanation of the snub; it was by no means a case of mistaken identity but rather a matter of 'deliberate' (motivated) refusal to 'know a friend' on the part of one who might find that the cost of an acknowledgement would be disclosure to a companion that he had been a 'mental patient'.

But — and this I suppose to be crucial — it isn't the mere fact that the snubber had been a 'mental patient' that constitutes *Bert's* embarrassment or chagrin: for Bert the complaint-worthy item is presumably *that he sees that he himself had been identified as a 'former mental patient';* the snubber's own problems stemmed from *Bert's* former-patient status.

This I take to be the feature of the account that constitutes it as a complaint, where the complaint could be formulated, for example, as 'He wouldn't talk to me because I've been a mental patient.' The complaint, then, is directed to the recurrent kinds of 'troubles' that persons can find themselves inheriting along with an unwanted categorial identification — in this case the identification that constitutes the tie between participants to the group talk and that is taken by them to generate the occasion in the first place. The complaint thus becomes a *category-generated activity*, providing for any members of the category (such as Bert's hearers) to see that 'what happened to him' could happen to 'us'.

[. . .]

Notes

[1] This transcript was supplied to me by Anthony Crowle.

[2] On the notion of 'relevant absences', see Sacks, unpublished lectures and research notebooks. Compare Schegloff's discussion of 'conditional relevance' in Schegloff (1968).

[3] Stan Persky pointed out to me the importance, for the account, of the encounter being seen as 'the first since the hospital'. An instance of the fulfillment of such a threat is contained in the following account given me by a former mental patient, in response to my asking if he would greet 'fellow former patients' he might meet on the street:

Al: Yes I do. I stop and say hello to them and one case I came across was . . . we used to buy our groceries from the New Market Store and he was the manager — of the New Market Store. Well, he went out to State Hospital. I met him out there and I said hello to him out there and talked to him for a while. A year later I met him downtown in Western City. He was with his wife and I said, 'Oh, hello, Mr Robbins. Remember me out at State Hospital?' And his wife looked at me and said, 'He's never been out in State Hospital.' But there was no mistaking it. It was him. (laughs) I thought that was quite funny.

[4] Compare the anecdote cited by Schegloff to make the point 'that conversational oaks may out of conversational acorns grow', in Schegloff (1968, p. 1094).

References

Austin, J. L. (1965) *How to Do Things with Words*, J. O. Urmson (ed.) Oxford University Press, Inc.

Garfinkel, H. (1967), *Studies in Ethnomethodology*, Prentice-Hall.

Garfinkel, H., and Sacks, H. (1970), 'On formal structures of practical actions' in J. C. McKinney and E. A. Tiryakian (eds), *Theoretical Sociology: Perspectives and Development*, Appleton-Century-Crofts.

Schegloff, E. A. (1968), 'Sequencing in conversational openings', *American Anthropologist*, vol. 70.

Speier, M. (1968), 'Some conversational problems for interactional analysis', in D. Sudnow (ed.) *Studies in Social Interaction*, Free Press.

Wittgenstein, L. (1968), *The Blue and the Brown Books*, Harper & Row

5.4 The Reliability of Readability Formulae
Alan Stokes

Abstract

Increasing use of readability formulae necessitates careful examination of their reliability and validity. This study was mainly concerned with testing the hypothesis that there is no significant difference in mean grade levels predicted by seven readability measures applied to 100 word systematic samples in eleven books used in schools. A computer program was developed for this task. It was found that the mean levels predicted by the formulae were significantly different overall ($p < .01$ to $p < .001$ according to the book used). Also it was found that no formula consistently predicted a similar grade level to any other formula. An examination of intercorrelations between formulae scores revealed differences in degree and type of relationship. As this work is part of a larger study, findings are not given in full, but it is suggested that readability formulae must be used with caution and that it is unsatisfactory to attempt to validate formulae by means of correlation with other formulae.

Introduction

Readability formulae aim to predict and quantify the comprehensibility of a text for its intended readership. No account is normally taken, however, of extra-linguistic factors such as graphic design. The methods used for quantification of readability are much the same for most formulae. A series of graded passages, notably those of McCall and Crabbs (1926 with later revisions), is taken and used to identify variables such as average word length, number of polysyllabic words per N sentences, or monosyllables per 100 words. Since there is no obvious limit to the number of variables which can be used, those which are found to correlate best with the grade level of the passages are often combined using a multiple regression formula. The readability formula thus devised may be applied to a text and an index of comprehensibility (often a grade level or a reading age) is obtained for the text.

A considerable number of readability formulae are now available, especially in the United States. Their use has been steadily increasing

Journal of Research in Reading, 1 (1) (1978) pp. 21-34.

in the United Kingdom and may well continue to do so as a result of interest generated by the Schools Council *Effective Use of Reading* Project (Lunzer and Gardner 1977). With the proliferation of formulae, has come an extensive literature on their development and application as well as on their advantages and shortcomings. Nevertheless, the teacher or librarian cannot be expected to have made a specialist study of this field, so that choice of formula may frequently be rather arbitrary, and dependent upon what the user has chanced upon[1]. This would not matter if it could be assumed that all of the formulae will give more or less the same result when applied to a particular text – at least in the long run, though of course some random error may be expected to cause differentiation in short passages. The present study examines first whether this is true of seven methods of assessing the difficulty level of texts. These are:

1) *The Flesch Reading Ease Formula* (Flesch 1948)
2) The *FOG* Formula (Gunning 1952)
3) The *SMOG* Formula (McLaughlin 1969)
4) The recalculation by Powers, Sumner, Kearl (Powers, Sumner and Kearl 1958) of the formula by Flesch.
5) The *Farr, Jenkins, Paterson Formula* (Farr, Jenkins and Paterson 1961).
6) An estimated *Dale Index*[2] (Dale and Chall 1948) based on the *Flesch Formula.*
7) The simple counting of 'hard' words (defined here as words of three or more syllables). Though not really a formula, it will be convenient to refer to it as such here.

These measures were chosen because they are among the most widely used formulae as is evidenced by the fact that they were used in the Schools Council project already mentioned. The technique of counting polysyllabic words was included rather as a tracer variable, in this case to act as a yardstick against which to assess the performance of the more sophisticated 'true' formulae.

The majority of studies investigating the validity and reliability of readability formulae have been less concerned with the grade placement of text than with the rank-ordering of texts, and thus the grades given by a formula are frequently accepted uncritically. Nevertheless, there have been some studies concerned with how well formulae predict grade levels. Usually these have compared the levels obtained by applying a number of formulae.

Larrick (1954) compared the grade placements indicated by five formulae, for two children's books – one a work of fiction and one a work of non-fiction. Considerable variation between the formulae became evident. The grades given by each formula for each book were as follows:—

AUTHOR OF FORMULA	FICTION	NON-FICTION
Dale and Chall (1948)	9-10	5-6
Lorge (1944)	6.17	5.04
Washburne and Norphett (1938)	9.05	6.21
Yoakam (1948)	12.0	5.1
Flesch (1948)	7.0	7.0

A study by Taylor (1962) is unusual in that it used British books and teachers. It showed that age-placements by (American) formulae were higher than those by pooled teachers' ratings. However, the results also suggest that caution must be exercised in interpreting cross-correlational evidence used to validate formulae. Taylor found intercorrelations of between .8 and .9 for the three formulae used (Lorge 1944; Dale and Chall 1948; and Devereux unpublished), despite the fact that the Devereux formula's correlation with polled teacher ratings was only .5, whereas the Lorge formula's correlation with this 'external' criterion was .7 — as high, that is, as the inter-correlations of the teachers' judgements themselves.

W. Pauk (1969) reports findings from a group of students under his supervision who compared the grade levels of twenty articles according to three formula — Dale-Chall, Fry (1968) and McLaughlin's *SMOG*. In nine out of twenty cases, Dale-Chall and Fry gave similar grade scores. *SMOG* and Fry did so in three of the twenty cases. *SMOG* and Dale-Chall only gave similar grade scores once.

Daines and Mason (1972) set out 'to compare the grade level ratings assigned to test-item selections of several reading tests with the plotted grade level ratings of these same test-item selections using Fry's *Readability Graph (Extended through Pre-Primer Level)* as an instrument to determine grade level', (p. 598). These tests included the *Gray Oral Reading Test,* the *Gilmore Oral Reading Test* and the *Durrell Analysis of Reading Difficulty*, though there were eight tests in all. Two conclusions were reached. The first was that the *Fry Extended Readability Graph* did not produce grade level designations that consistently agreed with the assigned grade levels of test item selections. The second was that Spearman Rank Correlation was an inappropriate statistic to determine agreement of two sets of grade-level designations. This could, of course, have been decided a priori from the nature of the correlational procedure itself, but shows how easily inappropriate correlational procedures find their way into studies of this sort. The use of these procedures has continually blurred the distinction between the rank-ordering of texts by formulae, where agreement between formulae may be very great, and grade-placement of texts by formulae, where agreement may be very poor.

A secondary purpose of the present study arises from the high intercorrelations reported between the scores deriving from different formulae for the same texts (see e.g. Lunzer and Gardner 1977). This suggests that the formulae are all measuring much the same thing, even if the scores produced differ from formula to formula. If they are measuring the same thing, then the production of arithmetical rules for converting one formula score into another using simple regression, should be readily accomplished. Formulae predictions could be interconverted or "standardized", and any problems concerning choice of formulae would disappear. This study will also investigate the soundness and practicability of attempting to convert scores.

Comparisons of Grade Levels

(i) Method

For the investigation of the extent to which formulae agreed in predicting grade level, nineteen to thirty-six passages of about 100 words were taken from each of eleven books[3]. The number of passages varied with the length of the books. Ten of the books were school history texts, covering a broad range of topics. One book was a popular work of children's fiction. Systematic sampling was used, such that each passage was deemed to begin at the start of the first complete sentence at the top of every Nth page, N being determined by the decision to take approximately twenty to thirty passages from each book. Altogether 350 passages were selected.

The seven formulae were applied to each passage in turn using a computer program developed by the author and called *ASTRA 3*. The *Flesch Formula* like the *Farr, Jenkins, Paterson Formula* provides a score in terms of an index figure between 100 and 0. It is American practice to give more meaning to this scale by dividing it into bands variously labelled as 'high school' or 'college graduate' level. In this study these indices are turned directly into grade levels using an algorithm originating in the General Motors *STAR* program mentioned earlier, which was also used to provide the Flesch Grade in the School Council *Effective Use of Reading Project* (Lunzer and Gardner 1977). The American school grade levels predicted by the seven assessment methods were tabulated separately for each book, means and standard deviations being calculated for each series of values.

(ii) Formal hypothesis

Let μ be the population mean[4] (over all possible passages) for the formulae. Then formally the null hypothesis is:

$$\mu_1 = \mu_2 = \mu_3 = \mu_4 = \mu_5 = \mu_6 = \mu_7$$

A test of a null hypothesis of this form is presented by Anderson (1968, Section 5, 3.5). This involves Hotellings T-square from which an F-test can be derived. The method of testing is appropriate since it allows for the fact that grade-levels predicted by the formulae are correlated, in that they are obtained from the same text.

(iii) Results

Table 1 gives for one book the grade levels predicted by each of the seven formula for each sample passage and also shows the mean and standard deviation over all the passages.

Applying the test of significance to the data in Table 1 revealed:— $T^2 = 3834.61$, $F(7,12) = 365,201$ ($p < .001$). Results for the other books are not presented here, but in every case F far exceeded the 0.1% significance level.

The fact that overall the seven formulae yield different means, even in the long run, does not of course necessarily imply that all pairs of formulae which can be formed from these seven would yield different means. The significance of the difference between any pair were tested using the correlated t-test. (The problem of multiple t-tests on the same data is discussed in Hays, 1963, Section 14.8). Results for two of the books are given in Table 2 where differences between mean grade levels predicted by the formula pairs were tabulated together with the significance levels attached to those differences by the t-test.

Over all eleven books there was no formula pair which consistently failed to produce significantly different mean grade levels. There is then no evidence here to suggest that there is a particular formula pair which could, in the long run, be relied upon to supply more or less the same mean grade level.

(iv) Comment

A rather surprising fact to emerge from the examination of the mean grade levels predicted by the seven formulae for the eleven books is that the simple count of multisyllabic words gives mean scores which, if interpreted as grade levels, are of much the same order of magnitude as those resulting from the application of far more complicated formulae. The standard deviation of the simple count tends however to be higher than those typical of other formulae, and insomuch as this indicates the unreliability of the method it detracts from what appears at first sight to be an attractively convenient form of quantitative text assessment.

Whatever method of assessment is chosen, it may critically affect judgements regarding the appropriate use of a text. Though it may not matter which of two formulae are chosen for use on one particular text, it may on another text, and, of course, it is difficult to tell beforehand which will be the case. It is clear that the hypothesis that all seven formulae will, at least in the long term give similar results cannot then be supported by the results of this study.

Table 1: Grade scores, means and standard deviations predicted by seven formulae applied to ninteen samples from *Man Looks Outwards* (Pitcher and Harris, 1972)

Passage No.	Flesch	Dale	PSK	FOG	SMOG	FJP	Simple Count
1	13.6	8.92	6.89	15.61	12	14.7	13
2	8.5	7.94	5.75	10.80	9	9.6	8
3	7.8	7.70	5.50	10.40	9	8.7	6
4	7.8	7.73	5.40	9.75	9	8.7	10
5	8.2	7.77	5.66	12.19	11	8.9	13
6	6.9	7.22	4.88	7.93	7	7.7	6
7	8.9	8.06	5.81	11.94	11	9.2	15
8	9.1	8.12	5.78	10.25	9	10.7	13
9	8.0	7.81	5.58	11.43	10	9.5	11
10	10.0	8.36	6.17	12.83	11	12.2	12
11	8.5	7.95	5.65	10.27	9	10.4	11
12	7.5	7.54	5.25	8.66	8	9.4	6
13	6.7	7.12	4.75	7.19	7	7.6	5
14	6.9	7.25	4.86	7.46	7	7.7	7
15	7.7	7.69	5.50	10.57	9	8.9	6
16	7.4	7.49	5.10	8.18	8	8.2	8
17	7.3	7.46	5.22	10.01	8	7.8	7
18	8.1	7.85	5.62	11.43	10	9.2	11
19	8.4	7.94	5.65	9.67	9	11.6	6
MEAN	8.28	7.79	5.53	10.35	9.11	9.46	9.16
S.D.	1.49	0.41	0.48	2.56	1.41	1.77	3.20

Correlations Between Formulae

(i) Results

Despite the fact that the formulae were found to give widely differing grade levels when applied to a text high correlations were nevertheless found to exist between the formulae. Table 3 gives findings from one book; correlations for the other books were similarly high. Such correlations suggest that inter-convertibility might be possible, but to do this would require these high correlations to be highly reliable and consistent. It must be asked to what extent these high correlations persist from one difficulty level to another and from one text to another.

Table 2: Differences in mean grades produced by all possible combinations of seven formulae applied to two books

FLESCH / DALE	FLESCH / PSK	FLESCH / FOG	FLESCH / SMOG	FLESCH / FJP	FLESCH / SIMPLE COUNT	DALE / PSK
0.49 (N/S)	2.75 (p <.001)	2.65 (p <.001)	0.83 (p. <.001)	1.18 (p <.001)	0.88 (N/S)	2.26 (p <.001)
DALE / FOG	DALE / SMOG	DALE / FJP	DALE / SIMPLE COUNT	PSK / FOG	PSK / SMOG	PSK / FJP
2.56 (p <.001)	1.32 (p <.001)	1.67 (p <.001)	1.37 (N/S)	4.82 (p <.001)	3.58 (p <.001)	3.99 (p <.001)
PSK / SIMPLE COUNT	FOG / SMOG	FOG / FJP	FOG / SIMPLE COUNT	SMOG / FJP	SMOG / SIMPLE COUNT	FJP / SIMPLE COUNT
3.63 (p <.001)	1.24 (p <.001)	0.89 (p <.05)	1.19 (p <.05)	0.35 (N/S)	0.05 (N/S)	0.3 (N/S)

Nineteen passages from *Man Looks Outwards* (Pitcher and Harris 1972)

FLESCH / DALE	FLESCH / PSK	FLESCH / FOG	FLESCH / SMOG	FLESCH / FJP	FLESCH / SIMPLE COUNT	DALE / PSK
2.41 (p <.001)	4.77 (p <.001)	− 0.62 (p <.01)	0.63 (p <.01)	− 1.38 (p <.001)	4.37 (p <.001)	2.36 (p <.001)
DALE / FOG	DALE / SMOG	DALE / FJP	DALE / SIMPLE COUNT	PSK / FOG	PSK / SMOG	PSK / FJP
− 3.03 (p <.001)	− 1.78 (p <.001)	− 3.79 (p <.001)	6.81 (p <.001)	5.39 (p <.001)	4.14 (p <.001)	− 6.15 (p <.001)
PSK / SIMPLE COUNT	FOG / SMOG	FOG / FJP	FOG / SIMPLE COUNT	SMOG / FJP	SMOG / SIMPLE COUNT	FJP / SIMPLE COUNT
9.14 (p <.001)	1.25 (p <.001)	− 0.76 (p <.05)	3.75 (p <.001)	− 2.01 (p <.001)	5.00 (p <.001)	2.99 (p <.01)

Thirty-three passages from *Modern World* (Snellgrove 1968)

**Table 3: Product movement correlation coefficients using the seven
formulae on nineteen samples from *Man Looks Outwards*
(Pitcher and Harris 1972)**

	Flesch	Dale	PSK	FOG	SMOG	FJP	Simple Count
Flesch	1.00	.95	.95	.86	.79	.91	.62
Dale		1.00	.99	.91	.89	.90	.72
P.S.K.			1.00	.95	.90	.89	.68
FOG				1.00	.96	.72	.72
SMOG-H					1.00	.66	.80
F.J.P.						1.00	.45
Simple Count							1.00

Figure 1 is a scattergram based on data from all the eleven books, with
grade levels predicted by the *Flesch Reading Ease Formula* plotted
against those predicted by the *Farr, Jenkins, Patterson Formula.* The
correlation between the two is 0.88. The conversion rule based on this
scattergram is:—

Flesch Grade = 1.34741 + 0.73664 x F.J.P.

The standard error of the conversion is overall about one school year
either way.

The scattergram suggests that high correlation coefficients may serve
to conceal the fact that the relationship between the formulae weakens
markedly with increasing grade levels. Scattergrams were plotted using
the other formulae pairs, and although the correlation coeffcients
overall were almost always very high, a variety of more or less complex
relationships was displayed between the formulae. Some scattergrams
suggest non-linear relationships between formulae, e.g. *FOG* and *F.J.P.*,
Flesh and *P.S.K.*

It is apparent from analyses of the kind given in Table 3, that not
only do correlations differ from formulae pair to formulae pair, but
they differ within a particular pair from text to text. The correlation
between *F.J.P.* and *SMOG,* is 0.35 in the book *Towards a New Man,*
0.44 in *Elidor,* 0.54 in *Modern World,* 0.72 in *Roosevelt and Kennedy,*
and 0.82 in *Britain's Heritage.* The picture is similar for most of the
other possible combinations. The correlation between the *Flesch
Reading Grade* and the *FOG* grade, for example, varies from 0.66 to
0.93, and for *FOG* and *F.J.P.* from 0.40 to 0.68. These differences are
not in this case the result of the variation of mean grade level from

Figure 1: Scattergram showing intercorrelations between two formulae on all passages in the eleven books

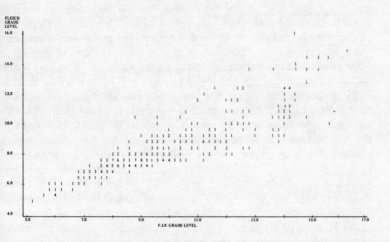

book to book, for there is no systematic increase or decrease in the mean grade levels of the books mentioned above.

The only formulae that intercorrelated consistently well at all grade levels and on all the texts were *Flesch, Dale Estimate,* and *P.S.K.* Since the *Dale Estimate* is derived from *Flesch,* the only useful conversion would be between *Flesch* and *P.S.K.* This gives the rule.

$$Flesch \text{ grade} = 7.18837 + 2.83736 \times P.S.K.$$
The Standard error of estimate = 0.65

(ii) Comment

It is evidently not possible to rely on the correlation coefficient between one formula and another remaining constant under varying conditions. The production of a set of conversion rules for standard-izing formulae would increase the hazards of using formulae, for the accuracy of the conversation would vary. The extra statistical work involved in determining the accuracy of the conversion is not likely to be undertaken by many formula users, who already pay scant attention both to the standard error of the formulae themselves and to the possibility of considerable sampling error. Thus, conversion rules would increase the likelihood of error still further.

Conclusions and Discussion

Many of those using readability formulae will be doing so in order to collect more information to assist them in determining whether or not a text is appropriate for a particular readership. Teachers in particular will be interested in knowing the age range with which a text may be used. It is in this respect that readability formulae are at their least useful — indeed they may be positively misleading. The formulae do not give appreciably similar results even in the long run, and cannot, despite their overall high intercorrelations, be standardized by conversion factors. To assert that the formulae are nevertheless very good at rank-ordering passages is in this context largely irrelevant. "For reliable classroom use . . . exact grading rather than ranking is the important criterion". (Lunzer and Gardner 1977, Chapter 3, p. 28).

Most commentators on the merits of readability formulae have nevertheless exhibited less interest in the grade level prediction than in the rank-ordering powers of formulae. Indeed there is a tendency for the use of formulae to be defended with evidence from correlational studies, which of course can say nothing about the accuracy of any particular formula's grade predictions, yet at the same time the formulae are widely used with grade level prediction in mind. Cloze Procedure similarly gives results in terms of ranked difficulty and does not provide performance norms to establish the validity of formulae.

As Manzo (1970) puts it, "readability can only rank-order materials, that is, compare them on the same linguistic variables. If there is any validity to this process it is only to the extent to which there is agreement with existing standards (as when early formulae compared their rankings with those derived from basal readers as a means of designating appropriateness for given grade levels). This is incestuous . . . (and) makes readability research a construct without a point of reference". (Manzo 1970, p. 962).

It may be suggested that a way of circumventing this problem would be to identify the formula whose scores correlate most highly with teachers assessments, and recommend it for general use. A move towards this has been made by Harrison (1977). However, the fact that one formula correlates highly with another does not mean that the grade predicted by a formula will approximate to that predicted by the other. Furthermore, as Harrison points out, the evidence from the Schools Council *Effective Use of Reading* Project indicates that overall there is no systematic grading of texts used in the schools observed in the study and that many texts in daily use are likely to be too demanding for their readers. This may perhaps suggest that teachers' perceptions (individually or collectively) of what is the appropriate difficulty level of texts for certain readers are not very accurate. If so, there would be little value in validating grade levels predicted by formulae against their judgements.

Though there is a considerable range of difficulty levels in the test passages used in this study, the variety of texts is nevertheless limited. It may well be the case that the differences between readability formulae are even more pronounced when the texts are of a more diverse nature. These differences between the formulae can only be explained by reference to the details of their development. The formulae are built on different criteria of "adequate comprehension". They often use different variables, or give different weightings to those variables they have in common. In order to use a formula intelligently it is necessary to understand the assumptions behind it and the factors that it does not take into account. Dunlap (1954) counted 56 formulae, and Klare (1975) identifies another 23 devised since 1960, not including those developed for use with foreign languages. The task of investigating and evaluating even a few of the many extant formulae is considerable, especially when criteria for evaluation are unclear.

In 1944, well before the period when the number of newly devised formulae began to increase very rapidly, Leifeste (1944) argued that the training required of the person who is to use these formulae varies with the techniques. She considered several techniques to be so complicated that their utility is beyond the classroom teacher, and the time required to check books is almost prohibitive for anyone unless it is for research purposes. Time taken up in the assessment, choice and application of a formula is, furthermore, time spent on the evaluation of only one of the factors affecting whether a book is suitable for a particular purpose. One of the advantages of the human brain as a readability assessing device is that, rather than analysing one or two factors contributing to readability, it can syntheize judgments of these many contributing factors into an overall assessment of a text. The unreliability of such judgements (DuVall 1966; Jorgenson 1975; Jongsma 1972; and Sprague 1967) suggests however that formulae may have a useful role as training devices, inasmuch as experience in their use certainly increases sensitivity to the syntactic and lexical difficulty of text.

Though readability formulae may be regarded as worthwhile research tools, they are for the casual user "so varied, and are used for such diverse purposes, that recommendations are likely to be either too simple to be accurate or too complex to be convenient" (Klare, 1975, p. 96). Findings given here support this view and suggest that it is essential that users of readability formulae make themselves fully aware of the assumptions and characteristics of any formula to be used, and that they exercise more caution, both in the choice of formula and in the interpretation of results, than has hitherto been usual.

Notes

[1]The FOG formula (Gunning 1952), for example, was introduced to many teachers because it happened to be the one chosen as an example in the Open University Reading Development Course (Davis 1973).
[2]Based on an arithmetic rule appearing in the computer program "STAR" devised for the General Motors Corporation (undated).
[3]Full references to all eleven books are given below.

⁴The writer recognizes that in all research concerning sampling from the popu lation of texts there is difficulty in deciding what properly constitutes such population and what methods could be employed to ensure an unbiased sample

References

Anderson, T. W. (1958) *An Introduction to Multivariate Statistica Analysis*, New York, Wiley.

Dale, E., Chall, J. S. (1948) 'A formula for predicting readability *Educational Research Bulletin, 27*, 11-20.

Daines, D. and Mason, L. G. (1972) 'A comparison of placement test and readability graphs', *Journal of Reading, 15*, 597-603.

Davis, A. (1973) *Printed Media and the Reader* (Reader Developmen Course PE261, Units 8 and 9) Milton Keynes, Open University Pres:

Dunlap, C. C. (1948) *Readability Measurement: A Review an Comparison,* University of Maryland, unpublished doctoral disserta tion, (Library of Congress no. 55-59460).

DuVall, C. R. (1966) *Agreement of Judgements of Elementar Teachers and Measured Reliability Level of Selected Free an Inexpensive Social Studies Material,* Ohio University, unpublishe dissertation, (Dissertation Abstracts no. 67-1217).

Farr, J. N., Jenkins, J. J., and Paterson, D. G. (1951) 'Simplication o the Flesch Reading Ease Formula,' *Journal of Applied Psychology 35*, 333-337.

Flesch, R. (1948) 'A new readability yardstick,' *Journal of Applie Psychology, 32*, 221-233.

Fry, E. (1968) 'A readability formula that saves time: Readabilit Graph,' *Journal of Reading, 11*, 513-516.

Gunning, R. (1952) *The Technique of Clear Writing,* New York McGraw-Hill.

Harrison, C. (1977) 'Assessing the readability of school texts,' in Gilliland (ed) *Reading: Research and Classroom Practice,* Londor Ward Lock Educational, 65-80.

Hays, W. L. (1963) *Statistics,* New York, Holt, Rinehart and Winstor

Jongsma, E. A. (1972) 'The difficulty of children's books: librarians judgements versus formula estimates,' *Elementary English, 49* 20-26.

Jorgenson, G. W. (1975) 'An analysis of teachers' judgements of readin level,' *American Educational Research Journal, 12*, (1), 65-75.

Klare, G. R. (1975) 'Assessing readability,' *Reading Research Quarterly 10*, (1), 62-102.

Larrick, N. (1954) 'Try it on for fit,' *Library Journal, 79*, (April) 729-733.

Leifeste, B. V. (1944) 'An investigation of the reliability of th sampling of reading material,' *Journal of Educational Research, 37* 442.

Lorge, I. (1944) 'Predicting readability,' *Teachers College Record 4: 404-419.

Lunzer, E. A. and Gardner, W. K. (eds.) (1977) *The Effective Use o Reading,* (Schools Council Project, Draft Report), Nottingham University of Nottingham School of Education.

Manzo, A. (1970) 'Readability: a postscript', *Elementary English, 47,* (7), 962.

McCall, W. A. and Crabbs, L. M. (1926) *Standard Test Lessons in Reading*, New York, Columbia University Teachers College Press. (Further editions 1950 and 1961).

McLaughlin, G. H. (1969) 'Smog-grading – a new readability formula', *Journal of Reading, 12*, 639-646.

Pauk, W. (1969) 'A practical note on readability formulas', *Journal of Reading, 13*, 207-210.

Powers, R. D., Sumner, W. A., and Kearl, B. E. (1958) 'A recalculation of four readability formulas', *Journal of Educational Psychology, 49*, 99-105.

Sprague, C. W. (1967) 'Textbook Readability: Measurements of Objective Formulas Compared to Judgements of Experienced Teachers', University of North Carolina, unpublished doctoral dissertation (Dissertation Abstracts no. 69-1682.)

Taylor, M. (1962) 'An Evaluation of Readability Formulae in Assessing Age-Placement in Text Books', University of Aberdeen, unpublished Ed.B. thesis.

Washburne, C. and Morphett, M. V. (1938) 'Grade placement of childrens' books', *Elementary School Journal, 38*, 355-364.

Yoakam, G. A. (1948) 'Revised Directions for using the Yoakam Readability Formula,' University of Pittsburg, unpublished study, (cited in Larrick, 1954).

Text References

Bareham, J. D. *et al* (1972) *Changing History (Book 1)*, Edinburgh, Holmes McDougall.

Garner, A. (1965) *Elidor*, London, Collins.

Larkin, P. J. (1959) *Britain's Heritage (Book 2)*, London, Hulton Educational.

Pitcher, R. and Harris, A. (1969) *Man Makes his Way*, London, Longman.

Pitcher, R. and Harris, A. (1972) *Towards a New Man*, London, Longman.

Pitcher, R. and Harris, A. (1972) *Man Looks Outwards*, London, Longman.

Snellgrove, L. E. (1968) *Modern World*, London, Longman.

Ray, J. (1970a) *Hitler and Mussolini*, London, Heinemann Educational.

Ray, J. (1970b) *Lloyd George and Churchill*, London, Heinemann Educational.

Ray, J. (1970c) *Roosevelt and Kennedy*, London, Heinemann Educational.

Worsnop, R. (1974) *Living History: North of England*, Edinburgh, Holmes McDougall.

5.5   Context in Reading and Listening: A Comparison of Children's Errors in Cloze Tests

Mary H. Neville and A. K. Pugh

Summary

Sixty-six children aged 9–10 years were tested in two groups with two parallel cloze tests of reading comprehension. The same tests were then given as cloze tests of listening comprehension. Each group received different parallel forms in each of the language modes. The scores for the listening tests for both groups were significantly lower than the reading scores.

Significantly fewer responses were made in the listening mode. Analysis of errors made in both modes revealed that 44 per cent of errors in the reading tests and 37 per cent of errors in the listening tests were syntactically appropriate responses.

Introduction

Errors made in reading have been the subject of study for a considerable time. In the early tachistoscopic experiments reviewed by Huey (1908) errors. The literature is summarized by Weber (1968) and it is only necessary here to draw attention to some recent issues and emphases. what he saw. Since then attempts have been made, in a number of ways, to infer from errors made in oral reading, the causes of those errors. The literature is summarised by Weber (1968) and it is only necessary here to draw attention to some recent issues and emphases.

Although certain writers still consider that research activity should be directed at the word level (Shankweiler and Liberman 1972) the general tendency has been to look beyond the word to its context for cues which cause misreadings. Studies of the errors made by children reading continuous prose have drawn attention to the grammatical constraint operating within sentences; it has usually been found that preceding linguistic structure affects the kind of error made (Goodman 1967; Biemiller 1970; Weber 1970). There is some doubt, however, that all children can use contextual restraints in reading; Francis (1972) found that lack of ability to span several words, and a functional rather than a formal use of language structures, militated against the use of context in initial reading.

British Journal of Educational Psychology, 44, (1974) pp. 224-232.

Rather little attention has been paid to constraints working across sentences, although a study by Ramanauskas (1972) strongly suggests that such constraints do operate. There is some debate as to how far removed constrainst may be in order to affect responses. MacGinitie (1961), for instance, found that cues more than five words away are rarely used, yet other writers (Carroll, Carton and Wilds 1959) found that remote constraints can affect responses.

Studies have also been made of the effect of different sentence structures on reading, and it would seem (Gibson 1972) that it is possible to identify types of sentence structure which give rise to varying degrees of difficulty in reading. Yet, as Gibson stresses, how precisely the reader develops his knowledge of structures so that it becomes incorporated in his reading habits remains a mystery.

Since it is generally agreed that grammatical constraints do affect reading performance, attempts have been made to teach the use of knowledge of structure. Gibson (1972) argues that the use of structural information cannot be taught, on the grounds that perceptual learning is involved and reinforcement must be internal and self-regulated. Nevertheless, it is accepted that children should be encouraged to use context as an aid to word recognition in initial reading (Clay 1972) as well as in the development of what have been called the 'intermediate skills' (Merritt 1970). Justifications for such a view include the child's able use of context in listening before he begins to read (Langman 1960) and the similarities which are assumed to exist between use of context in listening and reading (Gates 1962).

A positive relationship is generally found between the receptive language skills of reading and listening (Reddin 1969) and it has often been suggested that reading skills can be developed by improving listening skills (Bracken 1972).

Kennedy and Weener (1973) investigated a means of improving performance in these two language modes with third-grade children. They found that subjects improved in both reading and listening and that there was transfer of the improvement from reading to listening; however, transfer in the reverse direction was not so well established.

This investigation is particularly relevant to the present study, since cloze procedures were used for the skill training. Cloze technique involves the deletion of those words occurring at certain predetermined intervals in a message. Most commonly every fifth, seventh or tenth word is deleted. The text or message is then administered to readers or listeners who attempt to supply the deleted words and make the message complete again (Taylor 1953). Although deletions are usually linguistically random, another approach is to select certain predetermined linguistic items for deletion (Goodacre 1971).

The results of Kennedy and Weener give rise to some questions about the similarity of reading and listening and, in particular, the use of context by the reader and the listener when using the cloze procedure.

An assumption commonly made concerning the use of context is that a person often anticipates in reading just as he does in listening (Goodman 1967). Guesses at an unknown word or blank in a text then tend to be regarded as highly influenced by predictions already made from preceding textual information (Merritt 1970). But Burns (1967) referring to Weaver, suggests that the words following a strange word may be better aids in guessing from context.

It seems likely that cues which a child uses in cloze procedure will depend upon at least three interrelated factors: his mode of reading (i.e., whether he is reading orally or silently); his proficiency in silent reading; and the set he adopts (i.e., whether he feels it permissible to look ahead). It has been argued (Pugh 1974; Morris 1963) that true silent reading involves non-sequential processes which differentiate it from reading modelled on oral reading. In contrast, in listening information is received sequentially and the listener usually has no control of the message for forward and backward scanning. This difference in the two language modes may affect the cues available to the child. Possibly, then, the information and strategies which are available to the child when he uses context to help him provide words omitted in a cloze test, will not be the same when reading silently and when listening.

This problem was investigated in the present study, where the purpose was to compare children's performance on similar cloze tests of reading and listening with regard to incidence and type of errors.

Subjects

The sample comprised all children (N = 66) aged between 8 years 10 months and 10 years 9 months attending a Roman Catholic primary school in Yorkshire. Most of the children were from working class or lower middle class homes. The sample consisted of 40 girls and 26 boys.

Subjects were allocated randomly to two groups so that, in each group, the numbers from each school class were equivalent. Group X contained 32 subjects and group Y, 34 subjects.

Procedure

Materials

The GAP test of silent reading comprehension (McLeod and Unwin 1970) was administered. This is a cloze type test in which approximately every tenth word (linguistically random) is deleted. Two parallel forms (R and B) are available. Although of Australian origin, it has been standardized in the United Kingdom and is of known reliability and validity.

The test was modified so that it could also be used as a test of listening. For this purpose both forms of the test were recorded by a female adult reader. Initially, the recording was done with the gaps filled in by the reader, the intention being to mechanically delete the inserted word. By this means the intonation patterns would have remained normal but it was found impossible to satisfactorily delete certain words owing to their elision with other words in the text. Finally, it was decided to read the passages in such a way that a hiatus of minimal length occurred whenever a 'gap' occurred in the test. The passages were then re-recorded so that the length of the hiatus was increased to a constant 10 seconds.

For each of the parallel forms (R and B) of the GAP test an answer paper was prepared with numbered lines relating to the 'gaps' in the recorded cloze test passage.

Testing

The two groups were tested simultaneously by two experienced experimenters, each with an assistant. Group X was first tested with the Form R of the GAP reading test, while group Y was tested with the Form B. The test manual instructions were followed.

After a short rest group X received the Form B of the GAP test, but now used as a test of listening. Group Y accordingly heard Form R.

Practice examples were given for both reading and listening, but these were given twice for the listening test owing to its novelty. Subjects then heard a tape recording of the appropriate form of the test and whenever a 'gap' occurred they wrote their response on their answer sheet. As with the reading test it was stressed that subjects should try their best to respond but that they could, of course, leave a blank on their answer sheet.

Scoring

The test papers were scored according to the manual which follows the procedure laid down by Taylor (1953) in not allowing synonyms. Consideration was given to the possibility of allowing points for words in the correct semantic field but this was rejected because of the subjectivity involved.

Errors were classed in three categories. Firstly there were omissions, secondly there were responses which were wholly inappropriate, and thirdly there were responses which were incorrect according to the manual but, in their context, were to some extent linguistically appropriate.

These partly appropriate responses were judged in two respects, the syntactic and the semantic. A syntactically appropriate word was a part of speech acceptable for the gap in the test passage. A semantically appropriate word had the identical stem to the correct word. Words could be both semantically and syntactically appropriate yet still be classed as errors where the form was not appropriate morphologically, that is with respect to tense, person, case, or number. Those responses which were syntactically appropriate could also be appropriate morphologically.

Other data available
One month before the investigation the whole sample had been tested in school with NFER Reading Test AD (Watts 1970). Formerly described as Sentence Reading Test 1, this test is of the multiple-choice sentence completion type, the word required always being at the end of the sentence. The results of this test were available to the experimenters.

Results

The means and standard deviations for both the GAP Reading and the GAP Listening tests for the groups X and Y and for the scores of these groups combined (total sample) are given in Table 1. Since each subject had taken both reading and listening tests, the two means for the total sample were compared by a t test for related samples ($t = 5.93$, $P < .001$).

The lower listening mean of the whole sample is equivalent to a reading age of 8 years 9 months on the GAP test norms; the higher reading mean for the whole sample gives a reading age of 10 years 7 months, compared to the mean chronological age of 9 years 8 months.

Table 1

Means and Standard Deviations of GAP Tests for Total Sample and for Groups

GAP Tests	Group X	Group Y	Total
Reading	(Form R)	(Form B)	
Mean	25.38	23.88	24.60
SD	4.99	5.26	5.22
Listening	(Form B)	(Form R)	
Mean	17.81	10.18	13.87
SD	4.39	3.53	5.53
N	32	34	66

In order to discover whether the randomly chosen groups X and Y were in fact similar, the means of the two groups were compared for the NFER Reading Test AD and the Reading and Listening GAP Tests by t tests for independent samples. These tests gave only one significant result; for the Listening GAP Test, $t = 7.74$ (P<.001). There were thus no significant differences between the groups in their performance on either of the standardized reading tests. However, for the listening test, Group Y, which listened to Form R, obtained a significantly lower mean than group X, which listened to Form B (see Table 1).

To determine the relationship between scores on the three tests for the whole sample, Pearson product-moment correlation coefficients were calculated. These are given in Table 2.

Table 2

Relationships Between Test Scores for the Whole Sample

Tests	r	P
Reading Test A D–GAP Reading	0.80	<.01
Reading Test A D–GAP Listening . . .	0.50	<.01
GAP Reading–GAP Listening	0.48	<.01

The correlation between the two reading tests is high, while a significant relationship is found to exist between the reading tests and the test of listening.

The method of analysing errors on the GAP tests has already been described. The frequencies and percentages of the various errors on forms B and R in both reading and listening modes are given in Table 3. Chi squares were calculated to permit the comparison of the incidence of different types of error made in the two forms, B and R, of the GAP test in both the listening and reading modes. For this purpose omissions were ignored. When the B and R forms of the reading test were compared there were no significant differences between observed and expected frequencies of types of error ($X^2 = 1.99$, df = 4). The incidence of types of error in responses to the two reading tests was similar (as were the means of correct responses, see Table 1).

However, when the errors made in the two listening tests (B and R) were considered, a significant difference between error pattern was discovered ($\chi^2 = 24.43$, df = 4, P < .001). Examination of the cell frequencies showed that for Form B the observed frequencies of errors which were wholly inappropriate and those which were appropriate syntactically only were lower than the expected frequencies.

A comparison of the B forms of the test showed no significant difference between types of error made when the rest was used in the reading mode compared to the listening mode ($\chi^2 = 6.64$). Thus Form B could be regarded as acting similarly whether used in the reading or the listening mode, with regard to type of error, though not, of course, with regard to mean score of correct responses (see Table 1).

A significant difference was, however, found in the comparison of types of error in the R form of the tests when used in the listening and reading modes. A X^2 of 9.62 (P < .05) was calculated and, on examination, the frequency of the observed syntactically appropriate errors was lower than their expected frequency for the reading mode.

Thus, the frequency of some types of error in the R form of the listening test was significantly higher than expected when compared either with Form B of the listening test or with the same Form R used for reading.

The very high frequency of omissions in both forms of the listening test, relative to the reading test, will be noted from Table 3. The frequencies of omission errors and total remaining errors were thus compared by a 2 x 2 table for the two forms of the test in both the reading and listening mode. A significant difference in number of omissions between the two modes of Form R was discovered (X^2 = 57.31, P < .001) and also between Form B in the two modes (X^2 = 60.4, P < .001). It was found also that when the two Forms B and R of the reading test were compared there was again a highly significant difference between the tests with regard to omissions and total remaining errors (X^2 = 15.9, P < .001). Similarly, when the two forms used in the listening tests were compared, a significant difference between the forms was found in respect of omissions and remaining errors (X^2 = 26.27, P < .001). In each comparison of the two forms, in either reading or listening mode. Form B is seen to have higher frequencies of omissions than Form R.

Discussion

It is clear that when the children listened they found more difficulty than when they read, in successfully completing the cloze test. In particular, when a test blank occurred near the beginning of a sentence they could not anticipate the word and this is reflected in the large numbers of omissions or errors totally inappropriate to the text. However, generally when children had sufficient preceding information in listening and in reading, they did try to choose words for the blanks which were syntactically, and to a lesser extent, semantically appropriate.

The fact that, when they could, the children used contextual cues in their choice of word in both listening and reading tests is shown by the error analyses in Form B of the reading and listening tests. Here, if omissions were ignored, the incidence of type of error was very similar. This was not so for Form R, and here the fact that there were many more blanks right at the beginning of sentences in this text, compared to Form B, must be noted. It appears that because certain cloze tests are equivalent measures of reading comprehension, they are not necessarily equivalent tests of listening comprehension.

Table 3

Frequencies of Types of Error in Forms B and R of the GAP Tests
(Percentages in parenthesis)

Test and Form	Omissions	Wholly inappropriate	Incorrect but appropriate				Total
			Syntactically	Syntactically and morphologically	Semantically	Syntactically and Semantically	
Reading: R	21 (4)	270 (51)	34 (6)	169 (32)	—	34 (7)	528
Reading: B	58 (9)	259 (43)	34 (6)	195 (32)	32 (5)	32 (5)	610
Listening: R ...	186 (17)	514 (47)	72 (7)	280 (26)	—	31 (3)	1083
Listening: B ...	204 (27)	249 (33)	43 (6)	214 (28)	20 (3)	22 (3)	752

In the present investigation, the reason for this seems to be that in the reading test the children were able, not only to anticipate, but also to adopt a non-sequential approach and use subsequent reading information to help them fill an earlier blank. In the listening test, without this opportunity, the child was entirely dependent on the preceding information.

The high relationship between the two reading tests is interesting because the NFER test consists of a number of sentence completion tasks. Here full information is available before the appropriate word is to be chosen; moreover, the five words from which the child must choose are usually all the same part of speech and with morphology appropriate to the sentence. A comparison of such a test in reading and listening modes might thus show fewer differences than the present comparison using cloze tests. Here the different nature of the reading and listening tasks is reflected in the quite moderate relationship shown between the listening tests and each of the reading tests.

Two general points arise from the present investigation. First, the beginner in reading may, as Francis (1972) suggests, have some difficulty in using context when he reads a new text, particularly when unknown words come at, or near, the beginning of a sentence. If the child has written the text himself, or if it has been discussed or read aloud to him (Clay 1972; Morris 1972; Neville 1968), the situation is closer to that of the moderately fluent reader who is able to scan ahead. A beginner cannot do this (although the teacher 'hearing' him read will certainly have done so) and is normally helped only by what he has already deciphered, some modest phonic knowledge and, possibly, by a picture.

Second, because of these difficulties there is probably a minimum reading age below which cloze reading tasks with random deletion cease to be useful. At the same time, the protracted use of cloze procedures for training in comprehension in either listening or reading should, perhaps, be examined further. The need to scan ahead and then regress to fill in blanks could possibly inhibit the efforts of the child visually and mentally to organize the text as he reads. In listening, also, the blanks destroy the organization of the message provided by the intonation of the speaker. In his review of the cloze procedure as a teaching technique, Jongsma (1971) concludes that, on the research evidence available, there is some doubt as to the effectiveness of the cloze procedure as a teaching technique.

The present study was only exploratory. Further work is required in more closely comparable reading and listening test situations. We hope also to provide more detailed analyses of the types of errors in the listening and reading tests which may help to clarify further how children, as they listen and read, 'use the context.'

References

Biemiller, A. (1970) 'The development of the use of graphic and contextual information as children learn to read', *Reading Research Quarterly*, 6, 75-96.

Bracken, D. K. (1972) 'Research and practice in improving listening', in Southgate, V. (ed.), *Literacy at All Levels* London, Ward Lock.

Burns, P. (1967) 'Vocabulary growth through the use of context in elementary grades', in Figurel, J. A. (ed.), *Forging Ahead in Reading*, Newark, Delaware, International Reading Association.

Carroll, J. B., Carton, A. S., and Wilds, C. P. (1959) *An Investigation of Cloze Items in the Measurement of Achievement in Foreign Languages*, Cambridge, Mass., Laboratory for Research and Instruction, Harvard University Graduate School of Education.

Clay, M. M. (1972) *Reading: The Patterning of Complex Behaviour*, London, Heinemann Educational.

Francis, H. (1972) 'Sentence structure and learning to read', *British Journal of Educational Psychology*, 42, 113-119.

Gates, A. I. (1962) *The Improvement of Reading*, New York, Macmillan.

Gibson, E. J. (1972) 'Reading for some purpose', in Kavanagh, J. F., and Mattingly, I. G. (eds.), *Language by Ear and by Eye*, Cambridge, Mass., MIT Press.

Goodacre, E. J. (1971) *Children and Learning to Read*, London, Routledge and Kegan Paul.

Goodman, K. S. (1967) 'Reading: a psycholinguistic guessing game' *Journal of the Reading Specialist*, 6, 126-135.

Huey, E. P. (1908) *The Psychology and Pedagogy of Reading*, New York, Macmillan.

Jongsma, E. (1971) *The Cloze Procedure as a Teaching Technique*, Newark, Delaware, International Reading Association.

Kennedy, D. K., and Weener, P. (1973) 'Visual and auditory training with the cloze procedure to improve reading and listening comprehension, *Reading Research Quarterly*, 8, 524-543.

Langman, M. P. (1960) 'The reading process: a descriptive, interdisplinary approach', *Genetic Psychology Monographs*, 62, 3-40.

MacGinitie, W. H. (1961) 'Contextual constraint in English prose passages', *Journal of Psychology*, 51, 121-130.

McLeod, J., and Unwin, D. (1970) *GAP Reading Comprehension Test*, London, Heinemann Educational.

Merritt, J. (1970) 'The intermediate skills', in Gardner, K. (ed.), *Reading Skills*, London, Ward Lock.

Morris, R. (1963) *Success and Failure in Learning to Read*, London, Oldbourne.

Morris, R. (1972) 'The language experience approach today: reappraisal and development' in Southgate, V. (ed.), *Literacy at All Levels*, London, Ward Lock.

Neville, M. H. (1968) 'Effects of oral and echoic responses in beginning reading', *Journal of Educational Psychology*, 59, 362-369.

Pugh, A. K. (1974) 'The development of silent reading', in Latham, W. (ed.), *The Road to Effective Reading*, London, Ward Lock.

Ramanauskas, S. (1972) 'The responsiveness of cloze readability measures to linguistic variables operating over segments of text longer than a sentence', *Reading Research Quarterly*, 8, 72-91.

Reddin, E. (1969) 'Informal listening instruction and reading improvement', *Reading Teacher,* 22, 742-745.

Shankweiler, D., and Liberman, I. Y. (1972) 'Misreading: a search for causes', in Kavanagh, J. F., and Mattingly, I. G. (eds.), *Language by Ear and by Eye*, Cambridge, Mass., MIT Press.

Taylor, W. L. (1953) 'Cloze procedure: a new tool for measuring readability', *Journalism Quarterly*, 30, 415-433.

Watts, A. F. (1970) *Reading Test A D*, Slough, NFER.

Weaver, W. W. and Kingston, A. J. (1972) 'Modelling the effects of oral language upon reading language', *Reading Research Quarterly*, 7, 613-627.

Weber, R. M. (1968) 'The study of oral reading errors: a survey of the literature', *Reading Research Quarterly*, 4, 96-119.

Weber, R. M. (1970) 'A linguistic analysis of first-grade reading errors', *Reading Research Quarterly*, 5, 427-451.

5.6 Experiments on Story Understanding and Recall*

Gordon H. Bower

It is a special honour for me to deliver the Sir Frederick Bartlett Lecture. He was one of the outstanding intellects of psychology, his work was classic, and it established an important tradition, Since publication of his book *Remembering*, psychologists engaged in laboratory studies of human memory have had his example and challenge before them. That challenge was to break away from the constraints of experiments involving learning of artificial material such as nonsense-syllable lists, and to move on to studying memory in more realistic settings, such as the way people remember or reconstruct text, stories or real-world episodes. Bartlett was concerned with the way readers impose a conceptual schemata onto the information they receive, and how the scheme guides later reconstruction of the story. His idea in this respect have proven seminal but frustratingly difficult to tie down. Those of us who work on people's ability to recall text have built upon the basic intuitions which Bartlett expressed about reconstructive memory. This paper — which is about how people understand and remember simple stories — is a further attempt to analyse and clarify a few of Bartlett's ideas of schema-application and reconstructive memory.

Let us begin with the familiar observation that texts we read differ a tremendous amount in their comprehensibility and in their memorability. In fact, some are so difficult that the only memorable thing about them is how incomprehensible they were. I recall taking a literature course in college where we read James Joyce's *Finnigan's Wake*; although I enjoyed the flow of words and images, I could not remember enough about what I had read in order to discuss it when I went to class the next day. The same is true today if I read experimental-fiction writers such as John Hawkes. The language and imagery is often stunning and beautiful, but I barely remember enough to know where to pick up by reading again in case I lose my bookmark. One might attribute all this to my poor memory. But on the other hand, I find I have very good memory for adventure stories and folktales, for stories like those in *Canterbury Tales, The Decameron*, for detective thrillers or simple Western-cowboy stories. Most readers or movie-goers have

*Text of the Fifth Sir Frederick Bartlett Lecture given at a meeting of the Experimental Psychology Society in Durham, 8 April 1976.

Quarterly Journal of Experimental Psychology, 28, (1976) pp. 511-534.

similar experiences. It is such observations that cause psychologists to become interested in how people understand and remember simple stories.

A number of very bright people have become interested in this topic in the past few years — linguists, psychologists and computer scientists. My largest intellectual debts on this topic are owed to David Rumelhart (1975), Walter Kintsch (1974), Tuen van Dijk (1975), Roger Schank (1975a; Schank et al. 1975), Bob Abelson (1975), and to colleagues at Stanford University. This paper relates some of our current thoughts regarding story understanding and memory. I will also describe some experiments on story recall done by my research group, particularly those planned in collaboration with my student, Perry Thorndyke, and these comprised his Ph.D. dissertation (Thorndyke 1975; 1976a, b).

Story understanding and recall is interesting for several reasons. First, the procedures people use to understand and recall stories seem to be very general; they are much like those they use to understand the various happenings around them. And psychologists should be centrally concerned with the way people understand and construct models of the world around them so as to guide their actions and decisions. Thus, stories may provide a small microcosm in which general features of human understanding can be studied. Second, reading stories has strong face-validity as a task humans frequently perform with the goal of remembering. It is not the least bit 'artificial'. There is the remote hope that one's findings may be of practical significance, either in better designing stories for young children, in teaching elements of story-telling, or in mechanically summarizing tests for a large information-revival system — such as a file of all news stories from the *Times* for the past five years.

Stories have a Constituent Structure

My first point is that simple stories have a very definite 'structure'; that is, they have a constant set of abstract constituents such as a setting, characters, a plot, episodes, a resolution, and so on, all of which are put together in a principled way so as to make a coherent whole. The claim here for simple stories is analogous to linguists' claim that, say, sentences have a definite constituent structure described by grammatical rules which tell us the difference between grammatical and ungrammatical sentences. Indeed, for a class of what are called 'problem-solving' folktales, there may even be a grammar describing the structure of well-formed stories (see Rumelhart 1975). By using the grammar, one can generate the possible allowable plot-structures. The hypothesis would say further that texts that radically violate the rules of such a grammar would be incoherent or incomprehensible as stories.

The claim that simple stories have a quite definite structure is hardly controversial: historians of folktales have for the past century conducted research on the premise that a common structure or set of rules underlies thousands of folktales and fables found throughout the world (see Colby 1973; Propp 1968). Many folktales had to have a simple structure because they were part of an oral tradition, and were passed from parent to child across many generations. One could think of the process of forgetting as a natural selective pressure which operates across successive re-tellings of a story, forcing the folktale into a simple, memorable structure. Illogical and incomprehensible elements simply would not survive natural selection as the folktale filtered through the fallible memories of successive generations.

Frames or Schemas for Understanding

I think we can use the notion of a schema or a framework to represent our abstract knowledge of simple stories (see Minksy 1975). I suppose that people in our culture as a result of hearing hundreds of such simple stories have abstracted a common framework or set of inter-related schemata depicting the prototypic story and variations on it. This is concept formation of a rather high-level, and I have no idea how it occurs in detail.

This abstract framework serves two important functions: first, we use it to interpret new stories we hear; second, we use it to guide our construction of a new story or our re-telling of a series of real-life episodes which we believe comprise a story. You can notice your own frameworks in operation if you are asked to compose a perfectly boring little Western-cowboy script. or to compose a script for a standard police or detective programme on TV. You would start with a setting, introduce a case of characters — in particular, the hero — and create some sort of problem. The story then consists of a series of attempts by the hero to solve this problem or subproblems it generates. The exact content would vary across authors but the abstract structure of the stories would be very similar. Very young children, who do not yet know this framework, will, of course, tell fractured stories with various elements missing, unexplained, or out of order.

I think these general frameworks are what adults use when they listen to and understand a story. You can think of the story framework as an abstract concept which you fit onto incoming data, by instantiating certain variables with particular exemplars (see Minsky 1975). The framework is a set of related categories or slots which are to be filled by particular objects and events in the story. To clarify this notion, consider your framework of a soccer game. You have lots of organized knowledge about the various players, their roles, relations and goals. When you go out to watch an actual game, I suppose that you call up this soccer framework from memory and proceed to instantiate its elements with the actual characters and events you see before you. That framework is the background allowing you to understand the significance of particular events — for example, to understand the differing significances of a player kicking the ball into the goal net from in front of it and in bounds vs. from behind it and out of bounds. The framework helps us distinguish major from minor events in terms of the goals of the players. The framework which helps us to understand the events also helps us remember what has happened. Suppose, on the other hand, you had no 'soccer-frame', no script for interpreting events (e.g., we take an Australian bushman to a professional soccer match); then a game would appear as an incomprehensible jumble. Similarly, if I were to stage a crazy soccer game in which all the standard forms and rules were repeatedly violated in multiple ways, you would not be able to understand what is going on.

Now the general script for a soccer game is known in fair detail by most of us. It is also claimed that we know the general script for folktales. People who work on story grammars think they can write down the rules that characterize a subset of simple problem-solving stories. You can think of these rules as good guesses about the categories or slots in our story framework, and guesses about the relations among these abstract elements in the story framework. Table I shows a set of rewrite rules proposed by Perry Thorndyke (1975), following upon earlier work by David Rumelhart (1975). These rules are tentative and they probably apply unambiguously only to a small set of stories. The exact details of the story grammar are not important as these will surely be modified as it is extended to describe a greater range of stories. However, the general form of the structural analysis is important and likely to survive.

Table I Grammar rules for simple stories

Rule number		
(1)	Story	→ setting + theme + plot + resolution
(2)	Setting	→ characters + location + time
(3)	Theme	→ (event)* + goal
(4)	Plot	→ episode*
(5)	Episode	→ subgoal + attempt* + outcome
(6)	Attempt	→ $\begin{cases} \text{event*} \\ \text{episode} \end{cases}$
(7)	Outcome	→ $\begin{cases} \text{event} \\ \text{state} \end{cases}$
(8)	Resolution	→ $\begin{cases} \text{event} \\ \text{state} \end{cases}$
(9)	Subgoal Goal	$\Big\}$ → desired state
(10)	Characters Location Time	$\Big\}$ → statives

Examining the grammar, we note that the first rule defines a story frame to consist of slots to be filled by a setting, a theme, a plot, and a resolution, these elements usually occurring in that order in the story. In Rule 2 the setting frame consists of slots to be filled by the characters, and, optionally, the location and the time of the story. Rule 10 says these are simple stative (i.e., existence) propositions, as in the classic 'Once upon a time in the land of Nod there lived an old king with three lovely daughters'. Rule 3 says that the theme of a story is typically just a goal of the main character. For example, the goal may be to rescue the beautiful damsel from the dragon, or to change a frog back into a prince, or to find the murderer. Often, a story begins with some events that create the goal (see Rule 3) — for example, we witness the damsel-kidnapping or the bank robbery that creates the goal for our hero.

The plot in Rule 3 is the action-line itself, a series of episodes. Rule 5 says that each episode has a subgoal, one or more attempts, and an outcome. The subgoal is something that is instrumental to achieving the main goal — for example, our hero wants to find a horse to ride to the dragons's cave, or our detective wants to find witnesses to the crime. The attempt itself (in Rule 6) is the action or event — the hero asks the king for a horse, or the detective interviews a witness. The outcome in Rule 7 is often the achivement of some new state — for example, the hero comes in possession of a horse or the detective acquires a clue provided by an eye-witness. After a series of such episodes, an outcome occurs which matches the goal of the main character, ending the plot and ushering in the final resolution. The resolution in Rule 8 may either be an event — for instance, after the hero rescues the damsel from the dragon, he returns her to her father, the king, who marries them and they live happily ever after — or the resolution may be an evaluation or 'moral' to the fable. Events are not defined in the grammar but they are action-based scenarios with the basic case-frame slots of actors, recipients, instruments, source, or goal (see, e.g., Schank 1975b).

This framework allows for embedding subgoals within goals since Rule 5 writes an episode as an attempt while Rule 6 may rewrite an attempt as another episode. Thus the hero may want to carry out some action but he can't do that until he has set up certain conditions by doing other things — the hero can't slay the dragon until he transports himself to the cave, so he sets up a subgoal to get there, which sets up the subgoal of finding a horse, and so on. Rules 5 and 6 allow hierarchical embedding of subgoals. The relation between goals and outcomes in his hierarchy is usually that of enablement: the action at one level has an outcome which enables the action at the next higher level to achieve its goal. For instance, transporting the hero to the dragon's cave enables his action of slaying the dragon. For those familiar with computer simulation models, this is very reminiscent of the subgoal hierarchy generated by the General Problem Solver model of Newell and Simon (1972) when that program is attempting to solve a problem.

A story having this multiply embedded character is the 'Old Farmer and his Stubborn Animals'. We have adapted it from Rumelhart (1975)

Old Farmer normal story

(1) There was once an old farmer (2) who owned a very stubborn donkey. (3) One evening the farmer was trying to put his donkey into its shed. (4) First, the farmer pulled the donkey, (5) but the donkey wouldn't move. (6) Then the farmer pushed the donkey, (7) but still the donkey wouldn't move. (8) Finally, the farmer asked his dog (9) to bark loudly at the donkey (10) and thereby frighten him into the shed. (11) But the dog refused. (12) So then, the farmer asked his cat (13) to scratch the dog (14) so the dog would bark loudly (15) and thereby frighten the donkey into the shed. (16) But the cat replied, 'I would gladly scratch the dog (17) if only you would get me some milk'. (18) So the farmer went to his cow (19) and asked for some milk (20) to give to the cat. (21) But the cow replied, (22) 'I would gladly give you some milk (23) if only you would give me some hay'. (24) Thus, the farmer went to the haystack and got some hay. (26) As soon as he gave the hay to the cow, (27) the cow gave the farmer some milk. (28) Then the farmer went to the cat (29) and gave the milk to the cat. (30) As soon as the cat got the milk, (31), it began to scratch the dog. (32) As soon as the cat scratched the dog, (33) the dog began to bark loudly. (34) The barking so frightened the donkey (35) that it jumped immediately into its shed.

Reading this, you notice how a series of subgoals are being recursively generated and stacked up on one another, to a level of about four deep; and then the main character just knocks them over like dominoes in order to achieve his final goal. The Farmer story has what we call a very tightly-knit goal structure.

Experimental on Violating Goal-structure Rules

One of the first experiments that we planned and Thorndyke ran was to delete certain critical components of the goal-structure in the Farmer story. If we remove the over-riding goal and re-order the events so that the subject cannot detect the implicity goal hierarchy of the original story, we get the text entitled 'narrative-no theme'.

Old Farmer narrative-no theme

There was once an old farmer who owned some very stubborn animals. One evening the farmer was taking a walk, when he saw his donkey. The farmer pulled the donkey, but the donkey didn't move. Then he pushed the donkey, but still the donkey didn't move. Then the farmer went to his cow and asked for some milk.

But the cow replied, 'I would rather have you give me some hay to eat'. Then the farmer saw his dog, and he asked him to bark loudly. But the dog refused. Then the farmer went to the haystack and got some hay. When he gave the hay to the cow, the cow gave the farmer some milk. Then the farmer asked his cat to scratch the dog. But the cat replied, 'I am thirsty and would be happy if you would get me some milk'. So the farmer gave his milk to the cat. As soon as the cat got the milk, it began to scratch the dog. As soon as the cat scratched the dog, the dog began to bark loudly. The barking so frightened the donkey that it jumped immediately into its shed, which the farmer had built at the time he had purchased the donkey.

The propositions here correspond rather closely to those of the original story — they even preserve many local causal and temporal relations — yet the text as a whole seems like a series of unrelated episodes involving the main character but without any over-riding goal tying the episodes together. The expectation, of course, is that subjects would be poorer at understanding and recalling this second passage.

Two other text conditions were included in the experiment: one is just like the narrative text above except the overall goal of the farmer was inserted as a statement at the end of the passage — that is, replace the final clause with the clause 'which is what the farmer had been trying to get the donkey to do from the beginning'. The question is whether providing such a goal at the end of the text will enable the subject to go back over and partially reorganize and make sense of the unrelated events he has just read. Finally, a fourth group read a totally random arrangement of the original story. This random control provides a baseline measure of how memorable specific sentences are considered as unrelated statements.

So four different groups of eight college students read these four passages at their natural pace, instructed only to rate their text for its comprehensibility on a 10-point scale. They had no idea they would have to recall it later. All read it within 90s. They then engaged in another, unrelated learning task for 40 min, they were unexpectedly asked to recall the Farmer passage. Recall was scored according to the gist of propositions that appeared in some form in recall. These clauses are marked in the first Farmer text shown above.

The results of this initial experiment are shown in Figure 1. This shows recall and comprehensibility ratings for the four types of texts. The texts are ordered along the horizontal axis according to the amount of goal structure they provide. As anticipated, the more tightly knit the goal structure of the text, the more coherent and comprehensible it was judged to be, and the better it was recalled later.

Let us consider why a coherent story is remembered better than the narration of a series of unrelated events. Several factors probably

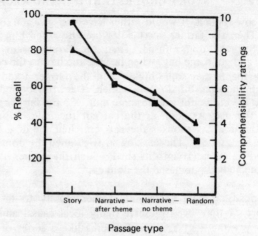

Figure 1 Recall (▲) and comprehensibility (■) ratings related to amount of plot structure in the text.

contribute to the difference.

First, the coherent story is more easily comprehended during learning because it fits the story frame so well that the reader's predictions about events are being consistently confirmed. That is, ease of understanding an event depends upon its predictability given the context.

Second, the abstract story framework provides a restrictive set of retrieval cues which the person can generate to prompt his recall of the several components and episodes. You can think of this advantage as much like that produced by providing a free-recall subject with the names of the categories represented on the word list he is recalling. Subjects who studied the unrelated episodes of the narrative tend to show all-or-none forgetting of entire episodes much like a free-recall subject may fail to retrieve a whole category of words from his study list. In contrast, the story-frame provides a set of cues that prevent this complete loss from occurring for subjects who read the coherent story.

A third factor promoting better recall of the coherent story is that the redundancy or interconnectedness of the text components is much greater for the coherent story than for the narration of unrelated events. A given episode in the goal hierarchy of the coherent story becomes connected in memory to the superordinate actions and goals which it enables and to the subordinate actions and outcomes upon which it depends. The events in the normal Farmer story tend also to be logically related in pairs, so that a subgoal-plus-attempt that is frustrated becomes logically paired off to a later outcome which enables that attempt to achieve its desired subgoal; for instance, the cat's refusal to scratch the dog is later reversed by giving the cat some milk to do this. Of course, over-riding this local causation is the higher-order goal which ties all the events together, namely, the intention of the farmer to get the donkey in the shed. We can expect that any event inserted into the story which is not on the main-line, goal-directed action chain will be forgotten, discarded as inessential and irrelevant. In contrast to this strong causal chain linking events in coherent stories, the narrative-no theme text appears to be a series of disjointed, arbitrary events related only by their temporal order of mention.

Looking at the structural diagrams of the tightly-knit, coherent story versus the rambling narrative (see Figure 2 later for an example), the salient difference is that the poor narrative has a shallow but broad structure (i.e., a temporal conjunction of episodes at the same level), whereas the coherent story has a narrow but 'deep' subgoal hierarchy with action-enablement or causal links from one level to the next.

Notice in Figure 1 that recall of the narrative version was improved if a statement about the farmer's goal was inserted at the end. We suppose this is because these subjects partially reorganized and rearranged the events of the narrative in memory so as to now interpret them as the farmer's attempts to get his donkey into the shed. (We know it was not because subjects re-read the text after the final goal-statement; the same effect occurred in an experiment where they simply listened to the narrative.) This reorganization of the text in memory was reflected in the way these subjects recalled. About 75% of them moved the goal statement from the end of the text to near the initial position during their recall — that is, to the beginning place where the theme of a story typically occurs. This order-error occurred despite their being asked for exact reproduction of the text. In contrast to this 75% intrusion, none of the subjects in the "narrative-no theme" condition intruded an overall theme or goal anywhere in their recall protocols. So, this is strong evidence that people reorganize a narrative according to a theme given to them, and that their telling of the reorganized narrative moves the top goal into its normal initial position. We shall see evidence of this reorganization again, in the data depicted later in Figure 3.

Hierarchical Ordering of Propositions within a Story

Let us consider another interesting aspect of story recall data. A story grammar like that in Table I assigns a hierarchical description to the propositions of a story. We suppose that the higher up in the hierarchy a given proposition is, the more salient it is, the easier it is to identify, the more central or important it is to the story, the more attention the person will pay to it and the more likely it is to be remembered.

As an example, consider the Circle Island story as rewritten by Thorndyke (1975).

Circle Island

(1) Circle Island is located in the middle of the Atlantic Ocean, (2) north of Ronald Island. (3) The main occupations on the island are farming and ranching. (4) Circle Island has good soil, (5) but few rivers and (6) hence a shortage of water. (7) The island is run democratically. (8) All issues are decided by a majority vote of the islanders. (9) The governing body is a senate, (10) whose job is to carry out the will of the majority. (11) Recently, an island scientist discovered a cheap method (12) of converting salt water into fresh water. (13) As a result, the island farmers wanted (14) to build a canal across the island, (15) so that they could use water from the canal (16) to cultivate the island's cultural region. (17) Therefore, the farmers formed a pro-canal association (18) and persuaded a few senators (19) to join. (20) The pro-canal association brought the construction idea to a vote. (21) All the islanders voted. (22) The majority voted in favour of construction. (23) The senate, however, decided that (24) the farmers' proposed canal was ecologically unsound. (25) The senators agreed (26) to build a smaller canal (27) that was 2 feet wide and 1 foot deep. (28) After starting construction on the smaller canal, (29) the islanders discovered that (30) no water would flow into it. (31) Thus the project was abandoned. (32) The farmers were angry (33) because of the failure of the canal project. (34) Civil War appeared inevitable.

Propositions one through 10 supply setting information; propositions 13-16 give the theme or goal of the farmers, and lines 17 through 27 relate a series of action episodes. Proposition 31 describes the frustration of the top goal, and 32 through 34 give the resolution of the plot.

That's the surface structure of the story. Figure 2 shows the hierarchical description assigned to the Circle Island story by the text grammar. Numbers in this figure refer to numbered propositions in the Circle Island story above.

The text propositions occur in this story at four different levels. So the centrality hypothesis predicts that a proposition like no. 34 ('Civil War appeared inevitable'), which is high in the hierarchy, will be much more salient and much better recalled than a proposition like no. 21 ('All the islanders voted on the construction issue'), which is at a lower level.

To gather data on this issue, Thorndyke ran another experiment using the same four text conditions as before (story, narrative-no theme, narrative-after theme, and random) along with a fifth text condition, the descriptive text. This was a list of 'existence' propositions stating the content of the text as one might describe a static painting, without causal or even temporal connections between the actions. These five variants were written for both the Farmer text and the Circle Island text, and each subject studied both texts. Learning was

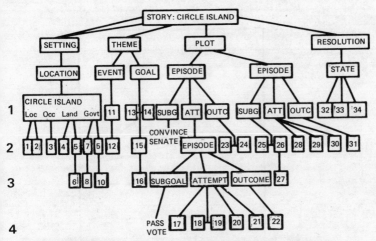

**Figure 2 Hierarchical structure assigned by the grammar to
propositions in the Circle Island story. Numbers in boxes
refer to propositions of the text.**

by the intentional method and a verbatim recall was requested within a
minute after each story was read.

The results on recall and comprehensibility ratings fully confirmed
those of the earlier study, with the descriptive passage falling between
the narrative-no theme and random variants of the text. Of greater
interest is the way recall of a proposition varied according to its level in
the hierarchy of the normal, coherent story.

The results for the Circle Island story are shown in Figure 3; results
for the Farmer story were similar. The first important result is that for
the coherent story version, recall is best for propositions at higher-levels
of the hierarchy ('lower numbers' in depth) and it declines across
lower levels. That is, propositions corresponding to the top-level
constituents of the story as analysed by the grammar are better
recalled. On the other hand, the flatness of the controls – the random,
no-theme and description curves – indicates that in the absence of a
plot the propositions at levels 1-4 of the story do not differ in their
inherent memorability. The difference is induced onto them by the
insertion of a plot structure in the goal-directed story.

It is interesting to note in Figure 3 that the narrative-after theme
text, which gives subjects just a last second's glance at the top-level
goal, produces a sloping recall function, with events that are
structurally salient in the diguised story being selected for recall from
the disjointed narrative.

So, to summarize briefly here, the story grammar identified those
propositions which are structurally significant to the plot insofar as
they tend to be recalled well, whereas structurally insignificant

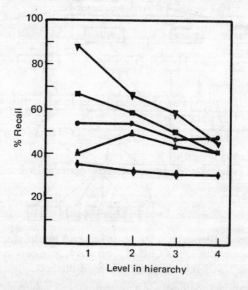

Figure 3. Percentage recall of propositions according to their hierarchical level in the normal story, for the separate kinds of texts. Story (▼); after-theme (■); no-theme (●); description (▲) random passages (♦).

elements at the bottom of the hierarchy are poorly recalled.

Another way to validate the story grammar's ability to pick out the salient parts of a text is to ask a group of students to read the story and have them rate each proposition for its 'importance' to the overall plot. Two of my students, Justine Owens and John Black, recently collected such 'importance ratings' for propositions from the Farmer and Circle Island stories. Subjects used essentially a 'magnitude estimation' response scale, so medians were taken. Table II shows the average of the median importance ratings assigned to propositions at the several levels of the story hierarchy. Lower levels of the Farmer story are grouped to keep reasonable sample sizes. The trend is unmistakable; propositions that the grammar assigns to the top level of the hierarchy are rated as more structurally important or central to the gist of the story.

A third possible index of the structural salience of a proposition may be provided by asking people to write out a summary of the story as they can remember it. Summaries should pick up only the most important highlights of a story, deleting, collapsing and compressing others. As you might imagine, a summary generally includes many fewer details than does a verbatim recall. People use a number of rules to summarize information at lower levels of the story hierarchy

Table II Importance ratings for propositions at various levels of the hierarchy for two stories (0-10 scale)

Level	Farmer story	Level	Circle Island
1	7.8	1	7.1
2	7.0	2	6.6
3-7	6.9	3	6.9
8-12	5.9	4	5.9
13-16	5.0		

Rumelhart 1975; van Dijk 1975). One rule, for example, is to delete unsuccessful attempts and report only the final attempt which succeeds. Another prominent rule people apply to summarize a nested series of embedded subgoals is to collapse all the specific actions into an 'ultimate outcome achievement' sentence. Thus, people will summarize the long action sequence in the Farmer story by saying 'The old farmer did some things which finally got his dog to frighten the donkey into its shed'. These summarization rules are interesting objects to study in their own right, but they are not our concern at the moment. Rather, we are more concerned here with whether propositions high in the structural hierarchy are likely to appear in summaries.

After his subjects had studied then recalled the Farmer and Circle Island stories, Thorndyke asked them to write from memory a summary for each story. To control for memory differences between propositions at the various levels at the time the summary was requested, Thorndyke calculated the probability that a proposition was mentioned in the summary conditional upon its having been recalled earlier. Figure 4 shows how this summarization measure varies according to the level in the hierarchy of the propositions. The more salient the proposition, according to the grammar, the more likely it was to be mentioned in the person's summary. This same result was obtained for the Old Farmer story as well. Kintsch and van Dijk (1976) have recently reported a similar finding. Thus, we tentatively conclude that story summaries tend to include information which is high in the structural hierarchy assigned to that story by the grammar. These higher elements are also better recalled in a free recall situation, possibly because they are more closely connected to the implicit retrieval cues provided by the abstract framework for stories and possibly because of subjects' bias to retell a story in terms of these basic constituents, leaving out inessential details. [. . .]

Role of Inferences in Text Understand and Memory

My final topic concerns the role of inferences in understanding text. Basically, the idea, promoted particularly by Roger Schank (1975), is

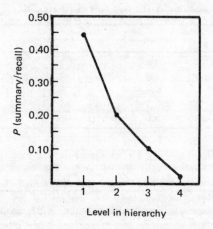

Figure 4. Conditional probability that a statement was in the summary given that it was recalled plotted against its level in the hierarchy.

that as a person hears a story, he is connecting up each sentence he i
hearing to earlier sentences in the story. He is constantly asking himself
'Does this statement "fit", given what I already know? Have the pre
conditions for this action been set up? If not, can they be inferred by
bridging back to some earlier statement in the text? Is there a plausible
causal chain I can infer from earlier statements to help me understand
the reason for the current statement?' Thus, if I read in a newspaper
story that U.S. President Ford fired Defence Secretary Schlesinger, I
can relate that back to earlier statements in the text (or in my memory)
about disagreements between Ford and Schlesinger regarding the
United States' military posture during our period of detente. The claim
is that we draw such backwards inferences automatically as we read
text.

Figure 5 (from Thorndyke 1975) schematizes this process of
inferencing. As each event-statement comes in, we first check whether
it fits into the active context or framework — if so, fine, we just plug
the event into the frame, and continue on. For example, if the
currently active frame is about a mechanic repairing a car engine, we
can easily understand a sentence about his checking over the
carburator. However, I would momentarily boggle and have to do some
extra cognitive work if the next sentence is 'Suddenly, he went to the
telephone and called Mrs Jones'. I could understand that only by
getting outside the 'car-repair frame', remembering that the car
belongs to Mrs Jones, and that she had asked to be called to okay any
expensive repairs. So, I would infer that the mechanic has located an

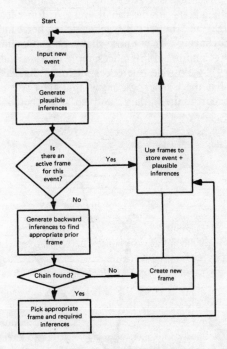

Figure 5 Flow chart of the inference-drawing process.

expensive malfunction and is probably calling to inform her of this. Moreover, I will store in memory the telephoning event plus the inferential chain needed to connect up the two statements. For example, I would store the inference that the mechanic discovered that the car repair would be very expensive.

If we come across a sentence we cannot connect up to earlier events, either we assume some completely new episode has started or else we leave in memory some sort of 'peculiarity' tag on the proposition — a 'what's that again?' tag. For instance, if after establishing that the main character is blind, I tell you that he likes to attend art shows, the statement should receive some kind of peculiarity marking because it violates expectations.

Such anecdotes illustrate that we often monitor for whether a given statement fits into the prevailing context. If there is no direct fit, then we try to link up the statement by a causal chain to an earlier event or frame of the story. The particular implication that we tested in an experiment by Thorndyke (1976*b*) is that a person's memory of a story contains these bridging inferences.

Figure 6 schematizes the inference process as well as the experiment done to test this process. A story line is going along when a statement occurs describing some event, call it event A. For example, the event statement might be 'The school teacher swung her hand at little Mary who was misbehaving'. We suppose that such statements give rise to a potentially large number of inferences, more or less simultaneously (see, e.g., Reiger 1975). Possible inferences might be that the teacher swung and missed, that the teacher was angry, that Mary was a problem child, that the teacher injured Mary, and so on. There are many such

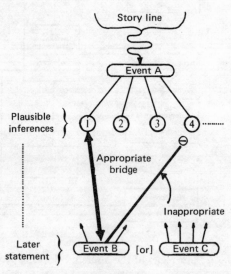

Fig 6 Schematic of backwards inferencing process for the neutral (event C) vs. the loaded (event B) texts. Inferences 1, 2, 3, 4 are implicitly activated when event A occurs.

inferences one could draw, and one or more may be relevant to what might occur later. Thorndyke made up two stories that were identical except for a later statement inserted a few lines later in the text. Let us call these statements describing events B or C. Event C is neutral and irrelevant to the plausibility of the several inferences from event A. For example, even C might be the later statement 'Mary heard some birds singing outside the classroom window'; this would not alter the plausibility of any of the former inferences from A. The other text however, contains statement B which describes a loaded event such as 'Mary noticed that her lip was bleeding'. This event can be understood by bridging back to event A via the inference (marked (1) in Figure 6) that the teacher actually hit Mary and injured her. So, by the bridging hypothesis, we expect a proposition corresponding to inference (1) to become more plausible and to be incorporated into the memory

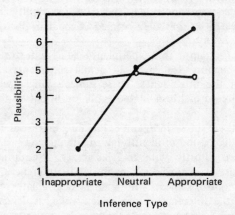

Figure 7 Plausibility ratings for appropriate (1), neutral (2 and 3), and inappropriate (4) inferences, for the control (AC) (○) passage and the experimental (AB) (●) passage.

representation of the story because it has served to bind together causally two events in the story. Therefore, on a later recognition memory test, subjects who read the 'bloody lip' statement should false alarm a lot to inference (1), saying that the teacher injured Mary. For the same reason, the 'bloody lip' event B lowers the plausibility of other potential inferences from event A, in particular that labelled (4) here – for example, the inference that 'The teacher's hand missed Mary' has been lowered in plausibility. Note that these inferences are not logically required, only strongly implied – the teacher could have missed and Mary could have bit her lip, causing it to bleed. Finally, there are some inferences from event A which do not have their plausibilities altered according to whether events B or C occur – these inferences, labelled (2) and (3) in Figure 6, comprise neutral inferences like 'The teacher was angry at Mary', 'The teacher believes Mary is a problem-child', and so on.

From this outline, the design of the experiment should be reasonably obvious. Subjects studied four different passages of 20 sentences. Each passage contained two such critical 'event A' sentences. Different subjects read stories that were identical except for the loaded B statement or the neutral C statement. Two different groups were tested; one rated the plausibility of various inferences whereas the other performed a recognition memory test. After reading each story, the raters judged on a seven-point scale the plausibility or likely truth-value of various inferences, such as inferences 1, 2, 3 and 4 in Figure 6. The average plausibility ratings are shown in Figure 7, and they simply validate the construction of the stories in that appropriate inferences used in chaining from the loaded event are viewed as very plausible in the Experimental (AB) stories whereas other inferences incompatible with the loaded event are seen as having low plausibility. The inferences were pre-selected so that they seemed of medium plausibility for the control ('AC') story.

The second group in this experiment read all four stories, then had a recognition memory test over 24 actual statements along with 24 inferences of the three types. These subjects judged whether or not each test sentence had been stated explicitly in one of the four stories they had read.

The results are shown in Figure 8, revealing that for the experimental passages the likelihood of identifying an inference as having been in the text increased directly with its plausibility. Appropriate inferences drew 58% false alarms, whereas inappropriate inferences drew 6% false alarms. The control subjects who read the neutral later sentence (event C) treat all the inferences more or less alike, as deserving of about 25% false alarms. Test statements that were verbatim true were checked as seen 85% of the time.

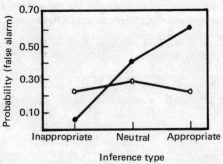

Figure 8 Probability of a false-positive recognition decision for inferences of the three types for the experimental (●) and control (○) passages.

As always, the subject confused in memory what was said explicitly with what inferences were plausible based on what was said. The results suggest that the memory representation of a story does not include all possible inferences potentially derivable from each event; rather, nonessential inferences naturally fade away and our memory keeps only those central inferences used in bridging between salient events of the text. The appropriate inferences are strengthened in memory, I suppose, because they are activated twice, once at input of event A and once upon reactivating this inference while finding the causal bridge to event B.

This account supposes the effect of the loaded-event story is to increase the activation or strength of a bridging inference in memory at the time the text is read. An alternative and equally plausible account currently being tested is that the effect is not due to strength in memory of the bridging inference but rather is due to a subject's willingness ('response bias') during testing to accept any statement that he does not remember but which has high plausibility based on the propositions (like A and B) that he can remember. Differentiating these two explanations involves some theory-bound complications I will not go into here.

Summary and Ending

Let me summarize my main points.

First, simple stories or folktales have a definite abstract structure, which is so regular in fact that some people are tempted to write a set of rules for generating the general class of episodes in problem-solving stories.

Second, from experiencing hundreds of such stories over their lifetime people acquire this abstract framework about simple stories. They then apply this tacit framework to sort out and understand any new story they hear: they instantiate concepts such as setting, protagonist, goals, and then problem-solving actions in terms of the concrete particulars of the given story. They also use this framework to reconstruct a story they have heard.

Third, if a text violates some of the critical rules — for example, by leaving out the theme or main goal of the central character — then the text seems less coherent, is harder to learn, and is forgotten more readily.

Fourth, the story grammar we considered assigns a hierarchical description to the propositions of the few stories considered. Elements at higher levels in this hierarchy proved to be the more important components of the story; they are most likely to be remembered and to be included in summaries; since details are forgotten, over time and recall of a story tends increasingly to look like a summary of it. [. . .]

Further, understanding some sentences in a story requires the listener to build a backwards bridge of inferences to information provided by an earlier statement in the text. Often the bridge comprises a plausible causal chain from a selected earlier event to the present event. It is claimed that this bridging inference thereby gains in plausibility and is likely to enter the person's memory representation of the story. This special status of a bridging inference from the earlier statement is in contrast to the many other potential inferences which are never needed for connecting up to later events in the text. This account of how inferences are activated and lodged in memory was supported by high false alarm rates to such bridging inferences.

In closing, let me note that these are only beginning steps in analysing what is surely a very complex phenomena, namely, how people process and understand text. Nonetheless, I think the topic is too central to cognitive psychology for us to continue postponing investigating it until we first figure out how lists of nonsense syllables are learned. I think there is every indication that studies of story understanding and recall provide an experimental microcosm in which are revealed the operation of the most sophisticated cognitive machinery that men have assembled. I believe such studies have a really exciting future.

References

Abelson, R. P. (1975) 'Concepts for representing mundane reality in plans' in Bobrow, D. G. and Collins, A. (eds.), *Representation and Understanding,* pp. 273-309, New York, Academic Press.

Colby, B. N. (1973) 'A partial grammar of Eskimo folktales', *American Anthropologist,* 75, 645-62.

Kintsch, W. (1974) *The representation of meaning in memory,* Hillsdale, New Jersey, L. Erlbaum Associates.

Kintsch, W. and Van Dijk, T. (1976) 'Recalling and summarizing stories', *Language,* in press, (in French).

Minsky, M. (1975) 'A framework for representing knowledge', in Winston, P. (ed.), *The Psychology of Computer Vision,* pp. 211-277, New York, McGraw-Hill.

Newell, A. and Simon, H. A. (1972) *Human Problem-Solving,* Englewood Cliffs, New Jersey, Prentice Hall.

Propp, V. (1968) *Morphology of the Folktale,* Austin, University of Texas Press.

Rieger, C. J. (1975) 'Conceptual Memory and Inference' in Schank, R. C., *Conceptual Information Processing,* Chapter 5, Amsterdam, North-Holland Publishing Co.

Rumelhart, D. E. (1975) 'Notes on a schema for stories', in Bobrow, D. G. and Collins, A. (eds.), *Representation and Understanding,* pp. 211-236, New York, Academic Press.

Schank, R. C. (1975a) 'The structure of episodes in memory', in Bobrow, D. G. and Collins, A. (eds.), *Representation and Understanding,* pp. 237-272, New York, Academic Press.

Schank, R. C. (1975b) *Conceptual information processing,* Amsterdam, North Holland Publishing Co.

Schank, R. C. et al. (1975) *SAM – A Story Understander,* Department of Computer Research Science Research Report No. 43, Yale University, New Haven, Conn.

Thorndyke, P. W. (1975) *Cognitive Structures in Human Story Comprehension and Memory,* Ph.D. Thesis, Department of Psychology, Stanford University, Stanford, Calif. Also *Technical Report* P-5513, The Rand Corporation, Santa Monica, Calif.

Thorndyke, P. W. (1976a) 'Cognitive structures in comprehension and memory of narrative discourse', *Cognitive Psychology,* in press.

Thorndyke, P. W. (1976b) 'The role of inferences in discourse comprehension', *Journal of Verbal Learning and Verbal Behaviour,* in press.

Van Dijk, T. A. (1975) *Recalling and summarizing complex discourse,* University of Amsterdam mimeo, Department of General Literacy Studies.

Index